B629/BZX629 Managing 2: Marketing and finance

The Open University
Business School

Module Activities

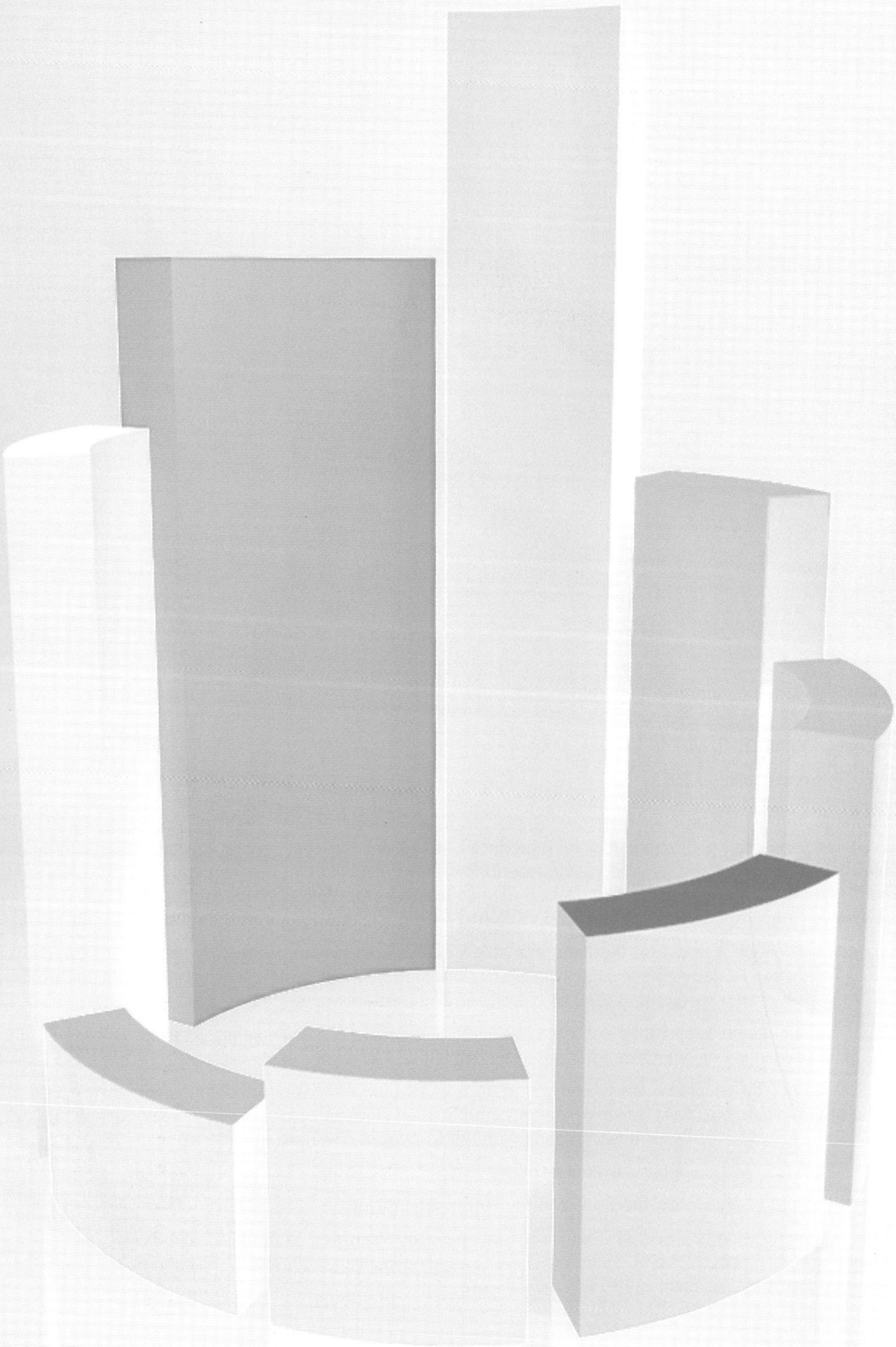

This publication forms part of the Open University module B629/BZX629 *Managing 2: Marketing and finance*. Details of this and other Open University modules can be obtained from the Student Registration and Enquiry Service, The Open University, PO Box 197, Milton Keynes MK7 6BJ, United Kingdom (tel. +44 (0)845 300 60 90; email general-enquiries@open.ac.uk).

Alternatively, you may visit the Open University website at www.open.ac.uk where you can learn more about the wide range of modules and packs offered at all levels by The Open University.

To purchase a selection of Open University module materials visit www.ouw.co.uk, or contact Open University Worldwide, Walton Hall, Milton Keynes MK7 6AA, United Kingdom for a brochure (tel. +44 (0)1908 858793; fax +44 (0)1908 858787; email ouw-customer-services@open.ac.uk).

The Open University, Walton Hall, Milton Keynes, MK7 6AA

First published 2010. Second edition 2011.

Edited, designed and typeset by The Open University.

Printed in the United Kingdom by Hobbs the Printers Ltd, Totton, Hampshire.

The paper used in this publication is procured from forests independently certified to the level of Forest Stewardship Council® (FSC®) principles and criteria Chain of custody certification allows the tracing of this paper back to specific forest-management units (see www.fsc.org).

FSC www.fsc.org MIX Paper from responsible sources FSC® C020438

ISBN 978 1 8487 3654 2

3.1

Contents

Week 1 What is marketing?

Introduction

Welcome to Week 1 of *Managing 2: Marketing and finance* (B629/BZX629). You will have read in the Module Guide that marketing is the first of the two areas to be studied. We begin our coverage of it by examining what marketing is. In doing so, we hope to demonstrate that marketing activities can be undertaken in a range of different types of organisation and by people working in very different roles. You don't have to be a marketer to make good use of marketing ideas!

This week's activities encourage you to think about the application of marketing to your own situation regardless of the sector or your position. Although people commonly associate terms such as 'customers', 'selling' and 'advertising' with marketing, what we will see is that marketing can be undertaken even where none of these is relevant. In fact the only condition that needs to be fulfilled is that an exchange takes place, that is, someone gives something to someone else in return for something else.

As this is the start of the module, it is useful for you to get to know the fellow students in your tutor group. You can learn a great deal from sharing your ideas and experiences with them and with your tutor. Take advantage of the opportunity to see how different people, organisations and sectors work. Very often we limit our approaches to problem-solving and decision-making to what we think are acceptable to the organisation we work for. Sharing ideas and experiences will help you to see new ways of doing things and to challenge the ways in which you think.

Week 1 activities

- Activity 1 Introduce yourself to your fellow students and provide your personal view of marketing. (Allow 30 minutes for this activity.)
- Activity 2 Devise a definition of marketing for your work context, share this with other students and make comparisons. (Allow 60 minutes for this activity.)
- Activity 3 Identify your customers, consumers and/or clients. (Allow 45 minutes for this activity.)
- Activity 4 Compare satisfactory and unsatisfactory marketing exchanges. (Allow 60 minutes for this activity.)
- Activity 5 Suggest how the unsatisfactory exchange identified in Activity 4 could be resolved. (Allow 60 minutes for this activity.)

Readings

- Reading 1 What is marketing?
- Reading 2 Marketing in different contexts
- Reading 3 Customers, consumers and clients
- Reading 4 Exchange, fairness and satisfaction

Activity 1

Allow 30 minutes for this activity.

One of the benefits of studying with other managers is that you can compare what happens in the organisation you work for, or your part of it, with theirs. You can compare activities and practices which will provide you with valuable learning and insights that few textbooks can provide. Thus, your first task in the module is to introduce yourself to the fellow students in your tutor group. The purpose of this activity is to 'meet' those you will be working with and get to know them a little.

It is quite usual to be a little nervous about this (and perhaps about beginning a course of study), but be reassured that other students will be feeling just as nervous!

Post a message in the tutor group forum (TGF). Include your name (or the name by which you prefer to be called), what your job is, the sector you work in and a little bit about your job; add your personal view of marketing – that is, what you think it is, or what you think of it. You don't have to give the name of your organisation if you prefer not to, but most students choose to say which organisation they work for. Read the messages from your fellow students and respond to at least one of them. Then return here to Module Activities Part 1.

Activity 1 outputs

- *A contribution to the TGF introducing yourself.*
- *A response to at least one other student.*

Readings 1 and 2

Your next task is to do some reading. Reading 1, *What is marketing?* in Chapter 1, introduces a commonly used definition of marketing and applies it to different contexts: for-profit, not-for-profit and when applied to other external and internal stakeholders. The reading points out that, while most marketing concepts have been developed in a for-profit context, many of the ideas behind them are just as relevant to other work contexts. The reading also introduces the idea that marketing is about much more than selling or advertising. It is good practice to take notes or make diagrams as you read and to think about how the ideas you are reading about apply to your work and the organisation you work for, or your part of it. This will help you to process what you read and give it meaning – this is known as 'deep' learning which you may have read about already in *The Manager's Good Study Guide*. An added benefit is that it will also help you with the activities you are required to do! As you read this first text, consider which of the contexts of marketing listed best fits your work situation.

Reading 2, *Marketing in different contexts* in Chapter 1, considers in more detail the different contexts in which marketing is applicable. Examples are given of how marketing can be applied in a public sector context, in a fundraising context where marketers are not addressing customers or consumers, and in two different internal marketing contexts. Some of the differences between marketing in a for-profit and a not-for-profit context are considered. As you read, think about your own work and how marketing does or could apply to it. If you thought marketing had little to do with your job, reading this text might change your mind. It might also change the view of marketing that you posted in the TGF earlier. Don't be concerned: changing your views in the light of new and sound evidence is effective learning!

Activity 2

Allow 60 minutes for this activity.

This activity asks you to define what marketing means for your own work context and then to share this with your fellow students in your activity forum. What marketing means and which marketing concepts are most useful for you will depend on your work context. If you work directly with external customers you will be able to apply most marketing concepts quite straightforwardly to your own work. If you do not work directly with external customers or your customers are not paying, for example, you may still be able to use many marketing concepts successfully to help you think through and solve problems at work. But you may have to think about marketing in slightly different ways. This activity is designed to help you start thinking about what marketing means for your work context. If you do not currently work, you could think about a previous work context, a context where you did some voluntary work, or you can think about the work context of a friend or family member; alternatively, you could try to put yourself into the shoes of someone working in a shop or other business organisation that you are familiar with (perhaps as a customer).

Although this is not a particularly long activity, you can spread it over several sessions. It is set out in steps.

Step 1: Think about your work context and what marketing might mean in this context. Take into account whose needs and expectations you must consider, the activities you carry out to satisfy these needs and expectations, and what benefit you receive in return (which may be direct or indirect).

You will find templates for all the tables mentioned in Module Activities on the B629 website.

Write a short definition of marketing for your work context, focusing on a single stakeholder and a single activity. As an example, your definition might read: 'In my work context, marketing means anticipating the needs and expectations of [...] and satisfying them by doing [...] so that I/my work unit receive(s) the benefit of [...]'. Use Table 1.1 to do this.

Then write short notes, again using Table 1.1, explaining in a little more detail:

- who the stakeholder is
- what their needs and expectations are (to the best of your knowledge)
- how you try to satisfy these needs and expectations
- the benefits you receive in return.

Notes of about 100 words will be sufficient.

Table 1.1 Marketing in my own work context

Definition of marketing in my work context
Who the stakeholder is
The stakeholder's needs and expectations
How I try to satisfy these needs and expectations
The benefits I receive in return

Step 2: Post your definition and explanatory notes from Step 1 in the forum. You can copy and paste your completed version of Table 1.1 into the message, or attach a copy of it.

Step 3: Read the postings of your fellow students. Select at least one and make notes on the similarities and differences between marketing in their and in your work context. Summarise these notes into three key similarities and/or differences that you found particularly interesting. No template is provided for this. Write your key points in a Word document and save it in the eportfolio that you can access from the module website, or save it to your computer. You will need it (along with your completed version of Table 1.1) for your TMA 01.

If you have not thought much about marketing in relation to your work context before you may not have found this activity particularly easy. This is likely to be the case if your work context does not involve dealing with customers. However, as the examples in Readings 1 and 2 show, the basic idea of anticipating and satisfying stakeholder needs, with some resulting benefit – direct or indirect – to your own work or work unit, can be applied to almost any work context. This activity will have shown you that some form of marketing thinking can be applied to your work even if you don't deal directly with external customers.

Activity 2 outputs

- *A completed version of Table 1.1 Marketing in my own work context.*
- *A contribution to the Activity Forum containing Table 1.1.*
- *A Word document containing three key points from a comparison of your completed version of Table 1.1 with that of at least one other student.*

Reading 3

Reading 3, *Customers, consumers and clients* in Chapter 1, looks in more detail at what we mean by 'customers' and how they are different from 'consumers' and 'clients'. This reading considers all external and internal stakeholders as customers, consumers or clients of a marketing activity. So, an internal stakeholder might be the consumer of a service performed by another department in the same organisation. This is the case when staff of an organisation are consumers of the stationery and other equipment purchased by the purchasing department. The key differences discussed in this reading are between those stakeholders who buy a product or service (the customers) and those who use it (the consumers). Customers and consumers may be the same or different people. Note what distinguishes a customer from a *client* and the different kind of relationship each has with a service provider. In your own work context, when are *you* a consumer, a customer and a client? Who are *your* consumers, customers and clients?

Activity 3

Allow 45 minutes for this activity.

In this activity you are asked to think further about what marketing means in your work context, focusing particularly on who your customers, consumers and/or clients are. The use of the words 'customer', 'consumer' and 'client' is not restricted to those external stakeholders who buy goods or services from for-profit organisations. Rather, any stakeholders whose needs and expectations you need to satisfy in your work can be regarded as customers, consumers or clients.

Step 1: Identify all stakeholders whose needs and expectations you and your work team or unit need to anticipate and satisfy, and list them in the first column of Table 1.2. Add more rows to Table 1.2 as necessary.

Step 2: For each of these stakeholders, consider whether you would classify them as customers, consumers and/or clients and briefly say why. Use the explanations and examples given in Reading 3 to help you make that classification. Note that in many cases customers and consumers may be the same. Enter this information in the second column of Table 1.2.

Step 3: Think about the needs and expectations of each of these customers, consumers or clients and enter this information in the third column of Table 1.2.

Step 4: Consider how much influence each of those customers, consumers and clients has over the service or products you deliver to them. Can they normally get what they want from you? Is the extent to which they can influence what they get related to their status as either customer, consumer or client? Enter these considerations in the last column of Table 1.2.

Table 1.2 Customers, consumers and clients in my work context

	Who are the stakeholders?	Are they customers, consumers or clients? Why?	What are their needs and expectations?	How much influence do they have over the service or product they get?
1				
2				
3				
...				

Having defined marketing for your work context in Activity 2, Activity 3 may have been a little easier to do. Depending on your work context, it may still seem rather unfamiliar to think of the people who use the outputs of your work as customers, consumers or clients. Thinking of them in this way does not, of course, mean that they cease to be your line manager, colleagues, patients, funders or however you normally think of them. But consideration of them as customers, consumers or clients can give you a new, additional perspective on their needs and expectations and how what you do can fulfil their needs and expectations, and thus improve working relationships with them.

Activity 3 output

- *A completed version of Table 1.2 Customers, consumers and clients in my work context.*

Reading 4

Reading 4, *Exchange, fairness and satisfaction* in Chapter 1, introduces the idea that a central concept in marketing is that of mutually satisfactory exchange between an organisation and its stakeholders. The reading, which is rather longer than the first three, does not discuss the concept of customer satisfaction in detail – this will be covered later in the module – but the extent to which an exchange is considered satisfactory for both parties is related to its perceived fairness. Exchanges that are considered fair tend to be seen as satisfactory. When an exchange is initially unsatisfactory, perceptions of fairness then often depend on how any complaint is handled. Whether or not both sides can get a fair and satisfactory exchange depends to some extent on their relative power in the marketing relationship. As you read, consider these issues from your own perspective as a provider and recipient of products and services. When have exchanges been unfair and unsatisfactory, and why? The text then discusses the role of ethics in marketing. Three common ethical theories are introduced. You might like to consider how each theory could be applied to an unsatisfactory exchange you experienced and what the 'solution' might have been, using each theory in turn. This will help you to understand how different perspectives can arise. Does the organisation you work for adopt a particular ethical perspective? Do you?

Activity 4

Allow 60 minutes for this activity.

This activity will help you think about the exchanges that you and your work team are involved in and what makes them satisfactory or unsatisfactory. You are asked to identify, in your role as a manager, two separate exchanges that you have undertaken with internal or external stakeholders. One of these exchanges should be one where you and the other party were happy with the result; the other should be one where either you or the other party (or both of you) were unhappy with the exchange. Try to identify exchanges over which you have control or influence, for example, where you had some discretion over how you dealt with an external customer, or where you did some work for someone else in your organisation in a non-standardised way.

Use Table 1.3 to record one example of a satisfactory and one example of an unsatisfactory exchange with a stakeholder. You need to describe who the exchange was with, and what was being exchanged. You then need to explain what made the exchange satisfactory or unsatisfactory from both your own and the exchange partner's perspective. In the case of the unsatisfactory exchange you should identify the underlying cause of the dissatisfaction.

Table 1.3 A satisfactory and an unsatisfactory exchange

The exchange	Who I exchanged with	What was exchanged (from me to the other person)	What was exchanged (what they gave me in return)	Why the exchange was satisfactory/ unsatisfactory (my perspective)	Why the exchange was satisfactory/ unsatisfactory (the other party's perspective)	What caused the exchange to be unsatisfactory
Satisfactory exchange						
Unsatisfactory exchange						

You may have found some aspects of this activity more demanding than the previous activities. In particular, it can sometimes be difficult to gain an understanding of what others think about a situation. For this reason, you may have found it challenging to identify the reasons why the other party found an exchange either satisfactory or unsatisfactory (unless they have told you, of course). Equally, identifying the underlying problem causing an unsatisfactory exchange is often not that easy. One of the underlying issues you may have identified is an unequal power relationship, where one party to the exchange can find it easier or more difficult to get what they require out of the exchange. Trying to work out these things allows us to think of improvements we can make to ensure future exchanges are more satisfactory.

Activity 4 output

- *A competed version of Table 1.3 A satisfactory and an unsatisfactory exchange.*

Activity 5

Allow 60 minutes for this activity.

This activity is designed to help you to resolve the problem you identified in Activity 4, in which you identified the cause of an unsatisfactory exchange. Now, you are required to explore what you could do differently to make the exchange satisfactory, should you have to repeat the exchange.

In Table 1.4, note down again the problem you identified as causing the unsatisfactory exchange you described in Activity 4. Then think about two actions that you could take to resolve or at least reduce this problem. Ideally, the actions should be practical, realistic ones that you have the authority to take. You may not be able to resolve the problem entirely but it should be possible to suggest actions that would have made the exchange *more* satisfactory than it was. If you discovered in Activity 4 that the cause of the problem was outside your influence or control, identify what actions would need to be taken, by whom, and what steps you would need to take to recommend these actions (for example, a memo to or discussion with your line manager or head of department).

Table 1.4 Actions to resolve problem leading to an unsatisfactory exchange

Nature of the problem
Proposed action 1
Proposed action 2

Depending on the problem you identified, thinking of actions to resolve it may have been more or less difficult. This will depend on partly the extent of your influence or control over the situation, and the actions you can take to resolve the problem. If the cause of the problem resides in your work group you will be in a better situation to address the problem than if it stems from higher up in your department or from a different part of the organisation or from your exchange partner. Although the focus of this activity was on what *you* can do, you may have had to consider actions that others in the organisation would have to implement.

Activity 5 output

- *A completed version of Table 1.4 Actions to resolve problem leading to unsatisfactory exchange.*

Week 1 activity outputs

1 A contribution to the TGF introducing yourself.
2 A response to at least one other student.
3 A completed version of Table 1.1 Marketing in my own work context.
4 A contribution to your activity forum containing Table 1.1.
5 A Word document containing three key points from a comparison of your completed version of Table 1.1 and that of at least one other student.
6 A completed version of Table 1.2 Customers, consumers and clients in my work context.
7 A competed version of Table 1.3 A satisfactory and an unsatisfactory exchange.
8 A completed version of Table 1.4 Actions to resolve problem leading to unsatisfactory exchange.

Learning outcomes

After completing this set of activities and readings you should be able to:

- understand what marketing is and how it applies to different contexts, including your own
- understand and identify customers, consumers and clients and their needs and expectations
- understand the concepts of exchange, satisfaction and fairness (marketing ethics)
- be able to apply these concepts to exchanges with stakeholders in your own workplace
- be able to suggest how to resolve a problem underlying an unsatisfactory exchange.

Week 2 Customer satisfaction

Introduction

Last week we introduced you to the way in which exchange underpins all marketing activities and encouraged you to explore the causes for an unsatisfactory exchange. A key problem in marketing is often where one party to an exchange is left dissatisfied after it has been completed. This is an important issue because it may mean that either they are not interested in taking part in future exchanges, or their frustration could manifest itself in other ways, such as, for example, complaining about their experiences to other people. This week we explore exchange and customer satisfaction in more detail. If an exchange has been unsatisfactory, what can we do about it?

Effective action often relies on problem-solving – identifying what caused a particular situation to arise and developing solutions that address those causes. Problem-solving is a core management skill. As a manager, you need to solve problems and think flexibly in order to make effective decisions, to put things right when something goes wrong, to improve a situation, to make the most of an opportunity or to make changes to keep up with changing conditions, expectations, regulations and so forth. Rather than viewing problem-solving as solely dealing with problems, you should view it as a means of investigating a situation, working out what the best options are, and identifying the most appropriate solution for your situation. This means also meeting the objectives of your organisation, or your part of it or those of your work group. Problem-solving allows organisations and individual managers to improve how they operate and maximise their efficiency and use of available resources.

Some organisations – for example, those that are committed to continuous improvement – often want managers to 'find' problems. That is, they want managers to look actively for ways of doing things better as part of an organisation-wide 'quality culture'. If you work in such an organisation, problem-finding and -solving – and making improvements – may be a routine part of your work.

If you have studied B628/BZX628 *Managing 1: Organisations and people* before starting this module, you will be quite familiar with the problem-solving approach. If you have not studied B628/BZX628, the problem-solving approach may be new to you. This week's activities are designed to introduce you to identifying and addressing marketing problems in your own work context. You will be working with many more marketing, and accounting and finance problems throughout this module.

Week 2 activities

- Activity 1 Understanding customer satisfaction. (Allow 30 minutes for this activity.)
- Activity 2 Identifying marketing problems at work. (Allow 30 minutes for this activity.)
- Activity 3 Solving a customer satisfaction problem. (Allow up to 3 hours for this activity.)

Readings

- Reading 1 Ways of thinking about problems – in *Tools and Techniques*
- Reading 2 Problem-solving – a framework – in *Tools and Techniques*
- Reading 3 Making decisions: comparing options and making choices – in *Tools and Techniques*
- Reading 4 Customer satisfaction
- Reading 5 Customer satisfaction and quality

Activity 1

Allow 30 minutes for this activity.

What is meant by customer satisfaction and how can managers influence it? The purpose of this activity is to help you begin to understand what makes for customer satisfaction or the lack of it. You will do this by looking at two instances where you have been a customer yourself: one where you were satisfied and another where you weren't satisfied.

Step 1: Think of two instances where you have been a customer yourself. One of these should be an example where you were satisfied with the service or product you bought and the experience of buying it, and the other should be an example where you were dissatisfied with your purchase. You should use examples about which you can remember a fair bit of detail. Describe these two instances briefly in column 2 of Table 2.1.

Step 2: Now think about the reasons why you were satisfied or dissatisfied with these two purchases. Did the product/service live up to your expectations? Why (not)? What was it about the product or service or the process of purchasing it that left you satisfied or dissatisfied? Enter this information into column 3 of Table 2.1.

Step 3: Think about the unsatisfactory exchange. Did you complain? Did the people selling you the product/service do something in order to rectify the situation? If so, what? What (else) could they have done to address your dissatisfaction? Enter this information in column 4 of Table 2.1.

Table 2.1 Two examples of my own customer satisfaction and dissatisfaction

	Description of example	What caused satisfaction or dissatisfaction	How did sellers address my dissatisfaction/how could they have addressed it?
Example where I was a satisfied customer			[no need to complete this field]
Example where I was a dissatisfied customer			

Most people can think quite readily of their own experiences as a customer and most of us regularly have both satisfactory and unsatisfactory customer experiences. You may have found it a little more difficult to identify exactly the reasons why you were satisfied or dissatisfied, perhaps particularly the reasons for being satisfied (we tend to think more about unsatisfactory experiences). But understanding what makes customers satisfied or dissatisfied is an important part of a manager's job and is a crucial step in addressing problems of customer dissatisfaction. The third step, i.e. thinking about what the sellers did or could have done to address your dissatisfaction is, from the manager's point of view, a crucial part of problem-solving: once you have understood what the problem is, what do you do about it?

Activity 1 output

- *A completed version of Table 2.1 Two examples of my own customer satisfaction and dissatisfaction.*

Readings 1, 2 and 3

Before going deeper into the topic of customer satisfaction we want to introduce the idea of problem-solving. Readings 1, 2 and 3 take you through problem-solving, which you will need to do in Activity 3. If you have already studied *Managing 1: Organisations and people*, you will be familiar with problem-solving so you need only refresh your memory by scanning Readings 1, 2 and 3.

Reading 1, *Ways of thinking about problems* in *Tools and Techniques*, sets out the difference between decision-making and problem-solving and why some problems are more difficult to resolve than others. When faced with a situation, sometimes we know instantly what to do and sometimes we struggle to understand what is happening. Sometimes our solutions to problems do not work. Sometimes they work very well. Sometimes we can take pride in the way we dealt with a problem, identifying some factor that had previously been overlooked, to arrive at an innovative solution. Why is this? The answer lies first in the nature of the problem and second in our way of approaching the problem. Note that it is not always necessary to solve a problem. The same problem may recur in a routine way and require the same solution, so all that is required is the decision to implement the same solution: there is no 'problem' to address. At other times, there will be an issue to be dealt with. Solving problems in practice is often complex and messy. You may not always be able to develop 'ideal' solutions: solutions must fit the context in which you work and the circumstances of the moment. Organisational factors, time and other resources, political agendas, swiftly changing priorities and other factors like these will influence solutions to problems.

Reading 2, *Problem-solving – a framework* in *Tools and Techniques*, sets out the problem-solving process in a clear, linear fashion. However, as you will see later, the process is an iterative one: while addressing a problem you will often have to move forward and backward through it. As you read, it would be useful to consider the way you normally go about problem-solving – or how problem-solving is conducted in your workplace – and the framework set out in the reading. Such comparisons can be uncomfortable: we try to justify our actions to show that there were no other ways. However, we need to be able to think about the possibility that we could have acted differently. Doing different things might have been more effective. It is an important way in which we learn: we see a conflict between what we know (what we did) and new information (what we might have done). We resolve this conflict by changing our thinking so that next time we act differently. This should improve our effectiveness. Reading 1, *Ways of thinking about problems* suggests that there will be many factors that prevent a systematic journey from problem identification to solution and implementation. Nonetheless, problem-solving should allow you to arrive at a situation which, if not ideal, is an improvement. Note that getting as good an understanding of the situation and the nature of the problem is a key step in finding an effective solution.

Reading 3, *Making decisions: comparing options and making choices* in *Tools and Techniques*, is useful for situations in which several options are available when you are solving a problem or simply making a decision. The reading refers you to two tools – an evaluation matrix and decision trees – which are helpful in such cases. You do not have to read about these until the need arises.

Activity 2

Allow 30 minutes for this activity.

What marketing problems do you deal with? Before you start solving a real work problem related to customer satisfaction in Activity 3, we would like you to think a bit more about what marketing means for your work and, particularly, what marketing problems you would like to be able to solve. At this stage we don't expect you to be able to identify all potential marketing problems you may be faced with. Sometimes you may not yet be aware that a particular problem might be addressed using marketing concepts, and more marketing problems will present themselves as you work through this module. For now, we merely want you to think a bit more about what marketing means in your work context, what problems (perhaps related to how you deal with your customers) present themselves and how the problem-based approach might help to understand and address these.

Now think of one or two marketing-related problems that you face at work. What is the problem in each case? In what different ways could you think about this problem – from your perspective or from your customer's perspective? What more would you need to know before being able to address the problem as well as possible? Can you think of a possible solution?

Post the answers to the above questions in the relevant thread in your activity forum. Then read what other students have posted and see whether any of them have identified a problem that is similar to yours. Have they understood it in a similar fashion? Have they come up with similar solutions?

Depending on your work context you may find this activity easier or more difficult to do. If you don't work directly with external customers, remember that a marketing problem can also arise out of interactions with other external or internal stakeholders and often relates to some kind of exchange with them.

Activity 2 output

- *A posting to your activity forum, on a marketing problem you face in your work.*

Readings 4 and 5

Have you ever bought something and thought 'Is that it?' In other words you have been left unsatisfied and disappointed? What actually makes customers happy is not always straightforward. Instead, customers often have different feelings and thoughts as to what makes them happy. As two customers' needs are never exactly the same it follows that they may also have different ways of assessing whether they are satisfied with their exchange. Reading 4, *Customer satisfaction*, explores how customers decide if they are satisfied with their exchange. A key component of customer satisfaction is what the customer expects to experience. For example, eating an ice cream on a hot day may result in instant satisfaction. Expectations refer to a promise that an individual believes will be met when they enter into an exchange.

Another component of customer satisfaction is quality. When a customer enters into an exchange they will have some expectations regarding what they are going to experience. Quality is about whether what we expect from an exchange and what we receive match. Reading 5, *Customer satisfaction and quality*, explores what quality is, how customers judge it and how organisations can assess the perceived quality of their product/service offerings and customer exchanges.

Activity 3

Allow up to 3 hours for this activity.

The purpose of this activity is to analyse and address a problem related to customer satisfaction, using the problem-solving framework. If you like, you can work on the unsatisfactory exchange that you identified in Week 1. As the exchange you explored was unsatisfactory, it is probably safe to assume that it represents a problem that needs to be resolved however, you can think of a different problem if you would prefer. Make sure the problem or task is well 'bounded' or it may be too big for this first problem-solving activity. It should also be a situation over which you have control or influence.

Normally, the identification, analysis and resolution of a workplace problem relies on bringing existing management knowledge to bear on it. In the workplace, even with a good deal of knowledge you might not actually identify a problem with any refinement until you have analysed it. When you are studying, however, you need guidance to help you identify a problem as being a particular sort of problem. Further, at this stage in the module, your analysis of situations and issues and your solutions may not cover all aspects of the situation. However, as you progress through the module, you should find that you are able to bring an increasing amount of knowledge to bear on identifying, analysing and resolving problems.

To help you with this first problem-solving activity, we offer a demonstration of the way in which an unsatisfactory exchange is addressed.

The demonstration

Executive Education runs training programmes for senior executives in large corporations. These programmes deal with the latest management issues facing organisations and are delivered by leading management academics. The programmes typically last for a week and are hosted in luxury hotels. Max Hastings, a senior manager at Executive Education, has decided that the length of the courses could be reduced with customers being offered an equivalent amount of time with online videos and online group exercises. This initiative will mean that the business can reduce the number of days for which it hires expensive hotel rooms and, as a result, it will substantially reduce Executive Education's cost-base, thereby making its operations more profitable. Max has also championed this approach among colleagues by arguing that Executive Education's mission is related to 'training' and it is not in the luxury vacation business. Some of the experienced managers believe that this move will alienate customers who enjoy the time spent in the company of their peers in the convivial atmosphere of a nice hotel.

Sandra is a newly appointed manager whose responsibility is making sure that specific training courses are delivered as promised and that individual clients are satisfied with each event. She has recently been receiving emails from dissatisfied, long-standing customers on courses who are complaining that they have only just realised the changes made to the company's offering and believe that they are not being offered a fair deal, but one that may even be unethical. In particular, they feel that if the number of days at a hotel has been reduced the company should be reducing its prices. Also, the customers value their experience of a residential learning programme, meeting other people and taking time out from family and work to learn something new. Particularly angry are long-term customers who have made block-bookings in advance. Max's response has been that the company's contracts reserve the right to replace the offered educational experience with something of equal value.

Sandra feels that something needs to be done in order not to lose future business: either Executive Education will need to reinstate the residential days or customers will have to be placated some other way. She knows that she has some authority to make changes and is not sure whether addressing the problem can be undertaken at her level or whether she should make suggestions to senior management.

Problem identification

Sandra knows that there is a problem but doesn't have enough experience to know what type of problem it is or how to solve it given the authority available to her. We have all experienced situations like this, often when we are inexperienced. Her more experienced colleague Gareth can see that there seems to be a problem: Sandra has alerted him to the fact. But it is not until she has provided some details to which he brings to bear his marketing knowledge that he knows what sort of problem it is.

Note that in problem identification it is often obvious that there is a problem, but some further investigation may be necessary to find out the exact nature of the problem.

Problem analysis

In this scenario, Sandra is aware that the customers are dissatisfied and this is arising from the loss of weekend sessions. Gareth, who has more knowledge of dealing with customers than Sandra, is familiar with the reasons this might be happening. When Sandra describes the problem in more detail, Gareth notes that she has recognised that their customers value their residential learning time and feel that this offers them a beneficial learning experience. Sandra has also noted a number of *expectations* that customers have, which include: face-to-face contact, the ability to socialise with other students, time away from the family (for some with young children a chance to get a good night's sleep), and the ease of asking their tutors questions and getting an immediate response. From this information, Gareth explains to Sandra that all these expectations are valid and, perhaps more importantly, are the very reasons why their customers are so upset! (He goes on to explain to Sandra how the students' previous experiences have been assimilated into their expectations of a good, residential, learning experience.)

Some of the recent changes introduced by the organisation seem to be removing the very things that gave customers satisfaction. In particular they note the following customer expectations:

Table 2.2 Customer expectations

Our own promises	**Reputation: our promises in the past that have been kept**	**Competitors' promises**	**Past personal experience**
Offers made in marketing literature	Previous courses that have been run	Specifications of similar courses run by competitors	Courses that managers have attended in the past

After listening to Sandra talk about the organisation's problem, Gareth tentatively identifies it as one of managing customers' expectations. However, Gareth and Sandra are not entirely sure why changing their courses has led to existing and potential customer dissatisfaction.

Gareth quickly explains to Sandra that people tend not to like change and the changes that the organisation has made may have led to expectations being disconfirmed, leading to dissatisfaction. Sandra looks puzzled so Gareth explains to her that disconfirmation typically represents information that challenges the customers' expectations. For example, their clients had a positive expectation that any training course they were going to have would be like the previous ones, i.e. residential. These previous experiences have now been challenged. More importantly, Gareth points out, is that disconfirmation can be based either on known facts and information, or from inaccurate information or misinterpretations. Consequently, all their customers may now be thinking that the online learning represents (wrongly) a drop in quality standards and, even worse, a cost-cutting and profit-generating exercise at the expense of their customers. Sandra and Gareth are certain that a greater online element in the courses does not mean lower quality, but Gareth explains that even if customers are making false assumptions this will still affect their satisfaction, so needs to be addressed.

Sandra nods her head, she has understood how important customers' perceptions of service quality are, even though, in this case, most of the customers' perceptions do not seem to be actually based upon facts or the reality of the situation. To understand further where customers' dissatisfaction may stem from, Gareth explains to Sandra that customers' perceptions of quality can be based on any one, or a combination of, the five elements of specification, conformance, reliability, delivery and cost. In this particular case, customers' negative perceptions of quality seem to stem from a problem in specification, i.e. customers had not realised that part of the residential element of the courses had been replaced with online learning, which would give them a different but equally valuable learning experience. There also seemed to be a cost element involved, i.e. due to their perception that the changes to the service represented a drop in quality, customers now no longer felt they were getting the same value for money.

Problem conclusion

Sandra and Gareth need to reach a conclusion to their problem. They decide to look again at the customer expectations and decide that the reasons why their organisation's existing and potential customers are unhappy is because of disconfirmation and a change to the specification and cost elements of perceived quality. In particular, their organisation has failed to tell their customers of the benefits to them of the changes made and why the course prices have not changed.

Problem solution

Sandra and Gareth now decide how best to solve their problem. First, they decide that whatever solutions they offer must be SMART (Specific, Measurable, Achievable, Realistic and Timed). They identify the following actions which need to be undertaken to reduce disconfirmation of customer expectations:

- address the *cost* element of perceived quality by explaining that the new structure will help the company maintain existing prices and not raise them
- address the *specification* element of perceived quality by emphasising that the online element of the new offer will reduce time away from work
- emphasise that there will still be networking opportunities for students
- highlight that the quality of the presenters will remain the same and the venues will be the same as well.

Based on these points Sandra and Gareth decide how they should resolve their problem. They recognise that they have not communicated the reasons for the change with their customers. They also believe that customers (wrongly) fear that the quality of their product will also be negatively affected. They then come up with the following SMART recommendations:

- Sandra will write a letter to all customers currently booked on a course to explain the changes to the residential and online elements of the course, emphasising that this will mean costs can be maintained at current levels, students will have less time away from work, there are additional networking opportunities arising from the online element, and the quality of the presenters and the venues will remain the same. She will ensure that each course participant is sent this letter as soon as practically possible, but at least two weeks before the start of their course.
- Sandra will then work with the team producing brochures, information leaflets and the website for Executive Education to change the relevant aspects of the information provided by the

company to prospective customers. This will be done for the next print run and, in the meantime, a leaflet with the amended information is to be inserted into all publicity going out.

Strengths, weaknesses and implications

Finally, Gareth reminds Sandra that what he recommends will not be a perfect solution. On the one hand, it is cheap to implement and should produce results quickly. The weakness of the solution (though he doesn't mention this to Sandra) is that it depends on her management skills – in particular her interpersonal skills. She will need to convince customers: this part of the solution requires sensitivity, and the morale of the whole staff team is at stake. Sandra will need to ensure that customers 'buy into' the ideas she will be presenting to them. Gareth suggests she introduces it as 'an enhancement of the value received by customers' rather than just the reduction of benefits.

To identify your own exchange problem (if you have not already done so) and to work through it until you have a solution, you may need some of the tools set out in *Tools and Techniques*. Useful ones include:

- systems maps (see 'Systems thinking')
- fishbone diagram
- multiple-cause diagrams
- network analysis.

Alternatively, as this is your first problem-based learning activity in marketing and finance, you may wish to stick with a brainstorming activity (which is also explained in more detail in *Tools and Techniques*, in the 'Decision trees' section). You can still use any of the above techniques and you can select what seems to be useful, but don't spend too long using a tool or technique that isn't helping you.

Now start working through a customer satisfaction problem arising out of your own work. As noted above, you could use the unsatisfactory exchange you identified last week or you could identify a different problem where a customer was dissatisfied with an exchange. In doing this activity you should go through the structured problem-solving process explained in Readings 1 to 3 and demonstrated above. Remember, it doesn't matter if you work on several aspects of the problem at once: possible solutions might occur to you while you are still analysing the problem; equally, a solution might have to be abandoned because you suddenly thought of an aspect of the problem you forgot to analyse. Real problem-solving is invariably more complex and iterative than any example or demonstration can convey.

To help you, we have set out the process as a series of steps with questions and tips. Complete Table 2.3 An exchange problem as you work through the steps.

Step 1: Problem identification

Think about an exchange which is causing you, or caused you, problems.

Who else was involved and what were their roles, perspectives and capabilities? In what ways did these people have an influence on the task?

Were there other people who had an influence, e.g. your own line manager?

Did you begin the task with any obvious staff or organisational constraints or potential difficulties, such as budgetary constraints or policies?

What issues arose?

Answering these questions should allow you to identify and describe the problem. You may not need all the detail you noted, but some of it is likely to be useful later.

Step 2: Analysis

Now start to analyse the problem using some or all of the concepts of customer satisfaction presented in Readings 4 and 5. You can also use concepts from previous marketing readings, such as those contained in Week 1 of this module. Exactly which concepts you use depends on the nature of your problem. Do your analysis stage by stage. For example, you might want to focus on the expectations aspect of the model by answering the following questions:

- Are your customers' expectations realistic?
- To what extent is your customers' previous experience of your or your competitors' product/service affecting their expectations?
- Were there any problems, outside of your control, that may have affected the exchange?
- How did your customers engage with you? Was it quick and efficient or slow and difficult?
- What messages have you or your organisation been giving your customers about what they can expect from you?
- Did your normal quality levels suffer for some reason during the exchange? If not then how can you improve your quality levels to prevent this problem from happening again?

Answering these questions, or similar ones that are relevant to your organisation and problem, should help you to analyse the problem. Note how you have used marketing concepts to help you to do this. This is exactly how we expect you to apply module concepts when you carry out activities in this module.

Step 3: Conclusion

Now draw together the elements of your analysis into a conclusion in the form of some statements about the nature of the problem. The points in your conclusion must be drawn from your analysis and should not contain any additional information: if additional information occurs to you, go back to Steps 1 and/or 2 and add them there.

Step 4: Solution

Now you have reached the solution phase. At this point you can be as creative as you like, but bear in mind that potential solutions to the problem will have to be acceptable to your exchange partner, any other stakeholders who have an interest in the exchange, and to the organisation in general. Your solution also needs to take account of any other constraints (for example, budget, resources, skills, timescales, whether a short-term or longer term solution is required, and so on). Solutions often need to 'fit' what seems normal and usual to an organisation, its staff, customers, consumers or clients. However, even under such constraints you can explore innovative solutions. You should also make sure that your solution is SMART.

Your potential solution, or solutions, will not be drawn from your conclusions but must address the conclusions. For example, you may decide that a potential solution is to address quality issues that affect your exchange. This may include how responsive you are to your customer needs, or how you could improve your communications with your customers and other employees. It is not enough just to state these: you need to explain how these solutions will work. For example, you may decide that to improve communication with your organisation's employees you are going to have a weekly departmental meeting to tell them about customer needs and concerns. You may also want to establish regular meetings with other managers to coordinate actions that will allow you to become more responsive to customer needs, for example by setting up a priority list of important customers to be dealt with.

As you consider possible solutions, you are likely to find that they will change and that you will abandon some possibilities. In some cases your preferred solution may raise further questions: can we afford these solutions, are they realistic, or will the organisation become resistant to my suggestions? Thus you will have a series of caveats to your preferred solution. But there will be some reasons why this solution is preferable to any others you might have considered – your justification for your choice. Thus you can say what the strengths and weaknesses of your preferred solution are. For example, it may be that it directly addresses the problem, or you may be assuming that your problem is shared by your fellow employees or they are equally concerned about it as you (or not).

Step 5: Strengths, weaknesses and implications

Now (yes, there's one final part!) you will need to think about the strengths, weaknesses and implications of your solution. If your problem turned out to be less 'bounded' than you thought, your solution may have implications for other activities or other parts of the organisation. It's best to know what these are. The realisation that there is a major implication may send you rushing back to a prior stage in the problem-solving process (but don't do that now – at this stage look at the strengths, weakness and implications of your proposed solution and note them for problem-solving activities in later weeks of the module). For example, might a manager in your organisation block your solutions because they may see it as a threat to their power and position within the organisation?

In summary, the key points of this activity are:

- identify the problem
- work through the problem, using the structured problem-solving process
- use the questions and tips provided to help you to work through the problem
- think about the implications of your solution.

Now complete Table 2.3, using the notes you have made.

Table 2.3 An exchange problem

Problem identification
Problem description
Analysis (investigation)
Conclusion to the analysis (results of the investigation)
The solution, listed as a set of SMART recommendations
Strengths and weaknesses of the recommendations
The implications of the solution, if implemented

Congratulations on completing your first full problem based activity. It may have been a satisfying experience to see how you can manage something better. At the same time, you may have found this activity quite complex and demanding. You may have found some aspects of the problem-solving process confusing at first and perhaps you found you had to go back to the readings several times to clarify things. At this stage, we would certainly not expect you to have done the process flawlessly. In fact, it is not likely that one would ever do such a process to perfection, and that is not really the point of it. Management is more often than not a process of 'muddling through', trying certain concepts to see whether they help the analysis, then trying others, thinking through different possible solutions, trying them and finding them either acceptable or inadequate. All this is part of a normal learning (and management) process. As you become more familiar with marketing concepts and problem-solving, future activities like this may become easier, but their complexity is unlikely to go away completely.

In doing this activity you are likely to have identified demands and constraints that restrict and influence your choices. You may have experienced tension between what you would like to do and what is possible. Your solution may not be the one that, in ideal circumstances, you would choose. But that doesn't matter: a 'good enough' solution that works for *your* workplace context has a high chance of success.

Activity 3 output

- *A completed version of Table 2.3 An exchange problem.*

Week 2 activity outputs

1 A completed version of Table 2.1 Two examples of my own customer satisfaction and dissatisfaction.

2 A posting to the activity forum, on a marketing problem you face in your work.

3 A completed version of Table 2.3 An exchange problem.

Learning outcomes

After completing this set of activities and readings you should be able to:

- understand and use the problem-solving process, applying module concepts
- understand and plan to resolve a problem within the organisational context and other constraints
- understand what is meant by customer satisfaction and what factors influence it
- begin to show how you would address customer satisfaction in your work context.

Week 3 Market segmentation

Introduction

You have seen that one of the issues that marketing addresses is the satisfaction of customers, which generally means meeting their expectations. Such expectations exist regardless of whether the organisation is for-profit or not-for-profit. However, customer expectation and satisfaction are not uniform but differ between different customers. Organisations *segment* a market to identify which are its most important customers and what their expectations are. Then the organisation *targets* those segments it believes will allow it to achieve its objectives, such as increasing profits or improving people's health. Then it uses *positioning* to create an image it wants the market to have of itself and its products or services.

This week we explore how segmentation, targeting and positioning are applicable to you and your organisation. The learning activities will help you to see how segmentation, targeting and positioning are carried out in your organisation and how you can use these to market yourself more effectively.

Week 3 activities

- Activity 1 Explore the market segments that you or your organisation engage(s) with, or could engage with. (Allow 20 minutes for this activity.)
- Activity 2 Identify market segments that you or your organisation should target. (Allow 45 minutes.)
- Activity 3 Develop a positioning strategy for you or your organisation. (Allow 90 minutes.)
- Activity 4 Analyse your organisation's positioning to its customers through its marketing materials. (Allow 60 minutes.)

Readings

- Reading 1 Market segmentation
- Reading 2 Market segmentation methods
- Reading 3 Segmentation as a tool for managers
- Reading 4 Targeting
- Reading 5 Positioning

You may also want to read the section on brainstorming in *Tools and Techniques* (see 'Decision trees').

Reading 1

Does your organisation give extra attention to specific customers, or group customers together to prioritise their needs? If so, then your organisation is doing some form of market segmentation. Reading 1, *Market segmentation*, explains what market segmentation is and why for-profit and not-for-profit organisations readily engage with it. As you read, make a note of your immediate thoughts about market segmentation, its relevance to you and the organisation in which you work, and whether you think the organisation does any form of segmentation.

Activity 1

Allow 20 minutes for this activity.

In this activity you will explore the market segments that you or the organisation in which you work engage with, or could do. Alternatively, you can apply this activity to your own work role, considering all the different groups of people or organisations you engage with as part of your job. The purpose of the activity is to help you to be aware of market segments. Identifying them is not always easy but different segments exist in most aspects of nearly all jobs. For example, if you work in a marketing department then your market segments would consist of your external customers, as well as internal stakeholders. If you work in a staff payments department then you could segment your market by needs, such as those of the tax office (for accurate reporting of taxes paid), the finance department (for ensuring the money is there to be paid) and employees (who want to be paid). The activity is a brainstorming exercise in which you identify as many actual or potential market segments as you can. The results of this brainstorm will be drawn on for the remaining activities this week. If you need to, first read the section on brainstorming in *Tools and Techniques* (see 'Decision trees'). In this case, allow longer for the activity.

To carry out the activity, write down whatever segments occur to you, along with any thoughts that come into your mind about these potential segments. Remember, a segment exists only when there is a behavioural difference between one group and another one. A group of people who are different from other people in a large number of ways is still not a segment unless it behaves differently in relation to the product or service you or your organisation are offering. As ideas about segments arise, try not to judge them and dismiss them. For example, access to a segment may be difficult (for example, a segment in another country), or a segment may look as if marketing efforts might not bring the expected rewards, such as profit or other benefits. However, do not judge the ideas that come to you – at least not yet!

Note all the potential market segments you have identified in a Word document. Keep your notes for Activity 2.

As you completed this task, did you realise that you dealt with so many different segments in your job? You may have thought about how the needs of these segments affect the way in which you perform your job. For example, do you give one segment more time and attention than another?

If so, why is this? Recognising which market segments we engage with provides us with an opportunity to satisfy their needs and in doing so perform our job more effectively and, often, more efficiently. You may not have realised how much time and effort you place on meeting the needs of your different market segments. The next activity allows you to explore further which market segments you need or may wish to focus your time and energy on.

Of course, you may have been surprised at how many segments you identified that the organisation in which you work does *not* engage with. If so, then you may have considered why the organisation does not engage with them. All these thoughts and considerations will be useful in Activity 2.

Activity 1 output

- *A Word document containing a list of actual and potential segments.*

Readings 2, 3 and 4

These readings will help you to understand the relationship you may have with your various market segments and how you might be able to improve how you engage with them. Reading 2, *Market segmentation methods*, explains the various approaches to segmenting a market. For example, in Activity 1 you may have segmented your market in terms of behaviours and how these vary among your customers. This approach is called behavioural segmentation and is one of several covered in Reading 1. As you read, refer to your output from Activity 1 and think about the approaches you used to segment your market.

Applying market segmentation to your current job may seem only marginally relevant. Reading 3, *Segmentation as a tool for managers*, explores how market segmentation can operate within organisations. This reading should show you that market segmentation is applicable in some form to many organisational roles. Moreover, it is not a precise science: it does not have to be done in one particular way and is often a flexible process.

Through your reading so far and in Activity 1, you may have begun to realise that some segments are more important than others. This identification process is highly relevant to market segmentation and Reading 4, *Targeting*, looks at prioritising or targeting the most important segments.

Activity 2

Allow 45 minutes for this activity.

In this activity you will consider the segments that you identified in Activity 1, select three to look at more closely and systematically and, finally, select just one. The purpose of the activity is to understand more fully the market segments you engage with, or could do, or those which are or could be most important to the organisation you work for. It is important in this activity to use your judgement. You will need to identify and prioritise those segments most likely to be beneficial to you or your organisation. This is what is meant by targeting. If you do not work directly with external customers you can still prioritise the segments you identified in Activity 1. For example, if you work in the production department of an organisation, you may have to prioritise internal jobs that are coming in, so that the most important ones are done first. If you work in fundraising, consider which segments of potential donors are most likely to provide funds and target those. If you work in a government agency with limited resources, you may need to decide which of your customers *most* needs your services and prioritise them. Deciding which segments are most important and need to be prioritised is a crucial part to many managers' jobs. Alternatively, you may decide that all your segments are equally important and an undifferentiated targeting strategy would be most appropriate. In this case, you may identify more than three segments. If so, adjust the output table to suit your needs.

Step 1: Choose from the market segments that you identified in Activity 1, no more than three existing or potential segments. The segments that you have chosen should be the ones you believe are the most important to you or the organisation where you work. In the appropriate places in Table 3.1 Importance of three market segments, describe each of these three segments and explain why you consider each segment to be important.

Step 2: Then complete the 'Reasons for targeting' row of Table 3.1. For each segment, explain why you or your organisation should spend time and resources targeting these segments.

Step 3: Finally choose the one segment that you consider to be the most important of the three and explain why you or your organisation should prioritise this segment over the other two. Enter this information in the final rows of Table 3.1.

Table 3.1 Importance of three market segments

Segment 1
Description
Why the segment is important
Reasons for targeting
Segment 2
Description
Why the segment is important
Reasons for targeting
Segment 3
Description
Why the segment is important
Reasons for targeting
Decision
The segment I or my organisation should focus on
Why

You may have surprised yourself with the results of this activity. Quite often managers and organisations have no clear understanding of who their most important customers are until someone or a team carries out an exercise similar to the one you have just done. The thinking you have done for this activity will be of value in Activity 3.

Activity 2 output

- *A completed version of Table 3.1 Importance of three market segments.*

Reading 5

Identifying market segments and deciding which ones to target is not sufficient for successful engagement with that segment. When a segment is targeted the organisation needs to create a positive image of itself and its offerings in the perceptions of the people or organisations making up that segment. This is called positioning and is discussed in Reading 5, *Positioning*, in Chapter 3. If you do not work directly with customers or other external stakeholders, or cannot influence decisions about the positioning of the organisation in which you work, it is nonetheless helpful to understand how the organisation positions itself in the eyes of important stakeholders. You can also use the idea of positioning for your own professional and career development.

Activity 3

Allow 90 minutes for this activity.

This activity asks you to position your offerings, or those of your work unit or of the organisation, using a product/service positioning map. It is designed to help you consider the image that these offerings present to customers, clients, consumers or other stakeholders in the market segment that you chose as the most important in Activity 2. This segment may consist of external or internal customers or stakeholders. Alternatively, you can work out your personal position for the purposes of your professional and career development. However, in this case you should allow more time for the activity because will not be able to use the thinking you have done in Activities 1 and 2.

To carry out Activity 3, follow the steps set out below.

Step 1: Identify the market segment you believe to be most important to you, your work unit or your organisation. This will be the segment you identified in Activity 2.

Step 2: Identify what you consider to be the most important criteria that people in that market segment take account of when buying or receiving the product or service you are offering. Make a list of these. It may be helpful to discuss this with colleagues at work. Again, brainstorming is a useful tool. There are many benefits to involving colleagues but allow longer for the activity if you decide to involve others.

Step 3: Now choose the two criteria you believe to be most important. If you consulted colleagues in Step 2, test out your choices with the same colleagues and others whom you didn't consult at that time.

Step 4: Label the axes in Figure 3.1 with these two criteria and consider what it means to have a low ranking on each of these criteria and what it means to have a high ranking. It may be helpful to use scales of 1–10 and, for each criterion, to consider what a ranking at each point represents. Again, it may be useful to consult colleagues.

Step 5: Then rank your offering, those of your work unit or of your organisation against these criteria in relation to the segment you identified in Step 1, using the scales you have just devised. The position will be where the ranking on one criterion intersects the other. If you have any difficulty working out the position, your tutor will help you.

Step 6: Now make a list of your competitors (including indirect competitors). If you have no competitors, you cannot do Steps 6 to 8 but working out your own positioning will still have helped you to understand the concept of positioning, as well as your own (or your organisation's) position in the market better.

Step 7: Rank the offerings of each competitor on each of the two criteria, using the scales you devised. You could ask colleagues to rank competitors.

Step 8: Work out the position on Figure 3.1 of each competitor. Use the same method as in Step 5. The position of each competitor will be where its ranking on one criterion intersects the other. If you have any difficulty working out the positions, alert your tutor.

Step 9: Finally, explain why you have positioned your offerings or those of your unit or organisation where you have in Figure 3.1. Write your reasons in Table 3.2. Use bullet points if this is easier, but make sure you give enough information to make each reason clear. Your notes and lists are likely to cover the main points of your thinking during this activity. Almost inevitably, and particularly if you have direct competitors, your reasons will be based on comparisons with them or their offerings.

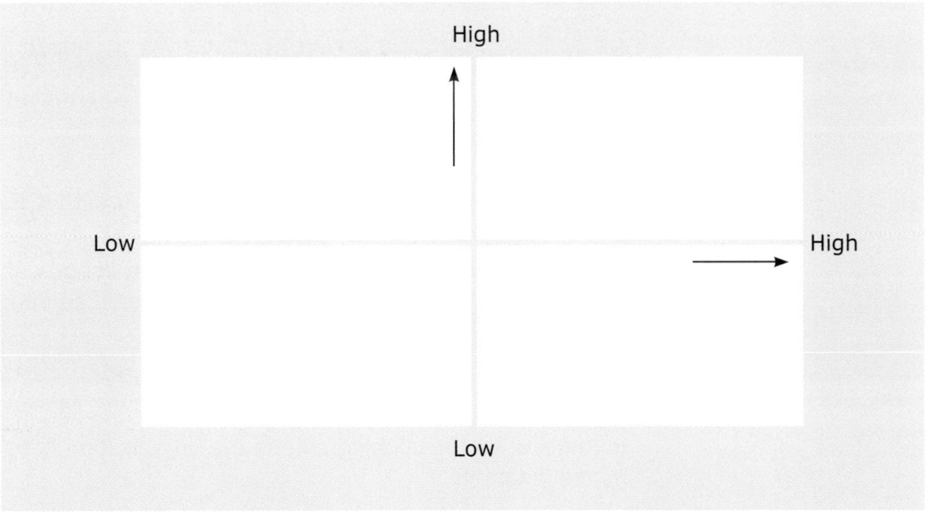

Figure 3.1 A positioning map

Table 3.2 Reasons for position

Reasons for position
1
2
…

You may be delighted with the position that your offerings or those of your work unit or organisation occupy on your positioning map. You may have found reasons for satisfaction that you had not thought of before. However, if you are unhappy with the position, then the remainder of the marketing activities in this module will help you to reposition yourself, your unit or your organisation in the minds of the market segment you identified. To improve situations, we must be open to seeing what and where things can be improved.

Activity 3 outputs

- *A completed version of Figure 3.1 A positioning map.*
- *A completed version of Table 3.2 Reasons for position.*

Activity 4

Allow 60 minutes for this activity.

In this activity, you will study your organisation's marketing material to see whether it reaches the market segments it targets. This will help you to see how segmentation, targeting and positioning need to be coordinated. To carry out the activity, gather together as many examples as you can of marketing materials produced by the organisation in which you work. These are likely to include advertisements, posters, brochures and information on the organisation's website about the organisation and its offerings.

Once you have gathered your examples, consider and respond to the following questions in Table 3.3 Analysis of marketing materials.

Table 3.3 Analysis of marketing materials

What segments are being targeted in the marketing materials? List the marketing materials and say which market segments you think are being targeted by the materials.
What particular evidence supports your view that these segments are being targeted? Include here words and phrases, or describe images, that indicate to you that the particular market segments you have identified above are being targeted.
How is your organisation positioning itself? Try here to interpret the words, phrases and images in the marketing material in terms of the positioning criteria the organisation is using in relation to each market segment.

In carrying out this activity, you may have readily identified your organisation's market segments. It may have been less obvious how your organisation is positioning itself in the minds of its customers: this can be subtle. For example, it could manifest itself in the image it is trying to convey. In the Bloomsville University example in the text, you might imagine images showing people enjoying campus life and marketing material that includes vignettes of former students who gained high-status jobs after graduating. Of course, you may have thought that the organisation in which you work is not targeting market segments effectively, or is not positioning itself correctly. This is quite a common finding. Organisations and their employees who have an incomplete understanding of their customers' expectations are not likely to be addressing those expectations as well as they could.

Activity 4 output

- *A completed version of Table 3.3 Analysis of marketing materials.*

Week 3 activity outputs

1 A Word document containing a list of actual and potential segments.
2 A completed version of Table 3.1 Importance of three market segments.
3 A completed version of Figure 3.1 A positioning map.
4 A completed version of Table 3.2 Reasons for position.
5 A completed version of Table 3.3 Analysis of marketing materials.

Learning outcomes

After completing this set of activities and readings you should be able to:

- understand what is meant by segmentation, targeting and positioning
- explain why marketers segment markets and what criteria can be used to do so
- explain how marketers target segments and what targeting strategies they may choose from
- explain how positioning relates to segmentation and targeting, and how a company can position itself in the eyes of its customers
- identify three market segments that you or your organisation should target
- locate your offerings or those of your organisation on a positioning map
- analyse the positioning of your organisation to its customers through its marketing materials.

Week 4 Understanding and influencing customer behaviour

Introduction

It should now be clear to you that the satisfaction of customers' wants and needs is central to marketing. To satisfy these needs, organisations segment and target distinct groups of customers and try to create a positive perception of products and services in the minds of potential customers by positioning.

But what of the customers, clients or consumers? They make decisions that organisations need to understand and seek to influence. For commercial and some not-for-profit organisations this means understanding how customers reach a decision about buying or using a particular product or service. Where an organisation is not trying to sell products or services, but instead trying to encourage people to change their behaviour, as, for example, in health campaigns, managers need to understand the wider influences that may encourage or inhibit behaviour change.

Because of the differences between organisations that are trying to influence the purchasing decisions of their customers, and those that are trying to promote a behaviour change, we offer two options for two of this week's activities. Thus, each of these activities has a 'buying decision' option and a 'behaviour change' option. *For these activities you need to do only one option.* Base your choice on the information set out below.

Organisation type A activity: Choose this option if you work for an organisation that offers a product or a service (for-profit and some public services will fall into this category) or for a not-for-profit organisation that is seeking donations.

Organisation type B activity: Choose this option if you work for an organisation that does not provide or sell a product or service but seeks to change a group's behaviour.

Each option is clearly indicated in the activities.

Week 4 activities

- Activity 1 Identify influences that affect your customers' decision-making (Organisation type A activity) or your customers' behaviour change (Organisation type B activity). (Allow 60 minutes for this activity.)
- Activity 2 Identify the stages of your customers' decision-making process (Organisation type A activity) or behaviour change (Organisation type B activity). (Allow 90 minutes.)
- Activity 3 Identify the role of influencers and gatekeepers on your organisation's customers' decision-making process or behaviour change. (Allow 2 hours.)

- Activity 4 Compare with one other student the respective roles of influencers and gatekeepers in both your organisation, or your part of it, and that of the other student. (Allow 45 minutes.)

Readings

- Reading 1 Understanding and influencing customer behaviour
- Reading 2 Influences on customer behaviour
- Reading 3 The organisational buying process
- Reading 4 Changing people's behaviour
- Reading 5 Who constrains and encourages customer behaviour?

Reading 1

Understanding customers and their decision-making or behaviour change processes is important for most managers. The fate of an organisation is often in the hands of customers and other stakeholders. A commercial organisation without customers and a not-for-profit organisation that does not satisfy key stakeholders are unlikely to survive. Thus, organisations – and their managers at different levels – need to understand as much as possible about the behaviour of their customers or stakeholders. Reading 1, *Understanding and influencing customer behaviour*, explores the relevance of customer behaviour and how it differs between purchasers and in different contexts. It then considers the decision-making process, from a customer perspective, in situations in which the customer has a high degree of choice.

Activity 1

Allow 60 minutes for this activity.

In Week 3 you identified the segments your organisation should target, that is, those customers that you think are the most attractive to the organisation in which you work. You may now want to remind yourself who these targeted customers are.

Organisation type A activity

For this activity, imagine you are a potential customer who falls within a segment that you think your organisation or work group should target. This customer is going to enter into an exchange with your organisation. Imagine what it is like to be this potential customer. What is the person's lifestyle, how does he or she think, what need does the person want to satisfy and why does this person believe that your organisation may be able to satisfy it? The purpose of the activity is to help you to gain insight into a customer's thinking and behaviour, and see your organisation from the perspective of this customer. Write down what you, as the customer, would think and do to reach a decision to purchase your organisation's product or service. There is no output template for this activity. Create a Word document of no more than 200 words with the title Week 4 Activity 1A.

In carrying out this activity you are likely to have covered a lot of information, perhaps identifying characteristics of your customer or your organisation's products or services that you had not thought about before. Many of the points you have noted are likely to be used by customers to reach a decision, or have an influence on the decision. Identifying these points helps you to understand your customers and their thinking.

Organisation type B activity

For this activity we want you to imagine you are a member of a group whose behaviour the organisation you work for wants to influence or change. For example, you could imagine that you are a 50-year-old man who is vulnerable to a heart attack, and who is being encouraged to stop smoking, take more physical exercise and reduce animal fats in his diet. Imagine what it is like to be this person. What is his lifestyle, how does he think, what needs does he have and how might he perceive your organisation's efforts to change his behaviour? The purpose of the activity is to help you to gain insight into a 'customer' and see your organisation from the perspective of this person.

Write down all the influences you can think of that maintain and support the behaviour that your organisation wants to change. For example, a 50-year-old man vulnerable to a heart attack may be influenced by friends who smoke, a family environment where high-fat foods are eaten regularly and a wider environment in which most people take little exercise. Aim to identify all the potential influences that affect the behaviour that your organisation wants to change.

There is no output template for this activity. Create a Word document of no more than 200 words with the title Week 4 Activity 1B.

In carrying out this activity you are likely to have covered a lot of information, perhaps identifying characteristics of the people whose behaviour you are trying to change, or discovering more about your organisation and what it is trying to achieve. You are likely to have identified a combination of internal and external influences that maintain a behaviour. Identifying these influences allows organisations to recognise what aspects of behaviour they can and cannot influence themselves to bring about a desired behaviour change in other people.

Activity 1 output

- *For Organisation type A activity, a Word document of no more than 200 words titled Week 4 Activity 1A.*

or

- *For Organisation type B activity, a Word document of no more than 200 words with the title Week 4 Activity 1B.*

Readings 2, 3, and 4

Customer decision-making is not done in isolation: customers are exposed to a variety of internal and external influences. For example, previous experience will shape a decision. We consider these influences in Reading 2, *Influences on customer behaviour* in Chapter 4.

Where the previous two readings have focused on customer decision-making, such as the process we go through to buy a television, the process by which organisations buy products or services is somewhat different. This is explored in Reading 3, *The organisational buying process*, which reviews how organisations make purchasing decisions. The reading explores the notion of a buying centre and discusses the similarities and differences between customer and organisational decision-making. These two readings should provide you with a deeper understanding of how customers make decisions and how organisations can influence this decision-making process, so that it works in their favour.

As we already indicated above, some organisations are not interested in getting customers to buy their products or use their services, or even to make decisions with respect to the organisation at all. For such organisations understanding purchasing decisions has less relevance. Instead their main purpose may be to bring about a social or behavioural change in a group or wider population. This approach is often undertaken by government organisations. In Reading 4, *Changing people's behaviour*, we explore how changing behaviour requires not focussing just on an individual but a wider group or society.

Activity 2

Allow 90 minutes for this activity.

For this activity you have a choice again. Choose Organisation type A activity if you work for an organisation that offers a product or service to customers, clients and/or consumers. Choose Organisation type B activity if you work for an organisation that tries to change the behaviour of individuals or a group.

Organisation type A activity

For this activity we would like you to go through each step of the customer decision-making process and think how it applies to the decision-making of the customer you imagined in Activity 1. The purpose of this activity is to help you to understand in more detail the customer decision-making process by applying the steps identified in Reading 1. This will allow you to identify areas where you can improve support of the customer that you, your organisation or your part of it provides in helping customers to reach their decision to purchase. Identifying the decisions made at each stage of the process offers an opportunity for you and your organisation to support that decision.

Using Table 4.1, go through each step of the customer decision-making process and note down how it applies to your customers' decision-making. To help you, you may want to construct an activity sequence flow diagram to represent the steps of the process. Then enter the information from the activity sequence flow diagram in Table 4.1. Information on activity sequence flow diagrams and how to create them can be found in *Tools and Techniques*.

Table 4.1 Steps in customers' decision-making

Problem recognition
Information search
Information evaluation
Decision
Post-purchase dissonance

Depending on the product or services your organisation provides and the nature of your 'customer', you may have found the decision-making process quite complex or relatively simple. If you found that the process was quite complex, you probably began to think about what makes it so complicated and what might be done to make it easier for customers. If so, you are thinking well!

Organisation type B activity

For this activity you will need to consider again the customer you identified in Activity 1. Using your output from Activity 1, identify all the different influences in a systematic way, using the categories set out in Reading 2, and how they interact. The purpose of this activity is to help you to understand how influences can interact to create the behaviour that you, your organisation or your part of it might want to change. Influences on behaviour are complex and often interrelated. Some are unique to an individual while others operate at group-level. Understanding how these influences act and interact to maintain behaviour is critical to understanding how to change behaviour. The aim of this activity is to encourage you to explore these interacting influences and from this begin to identify how you, your organisation or your part of it might be able to control these influences to bring about a desired behavioural change.

Write down these influences and their interactions using Table 4.2. As a first step, you could create a multiple-cause diagram and use the information from this to complete Table 4.2. Information about multiple-cause diagrams and how to create them can be found in *Tools and Techniques*.

Table 4.2 Influences on customers' behaviour and their interaction

Personal
Situational
Psychological
Social
Interactions between influences that help to maintain behaviour

In doing this activity you may have been surprised at how many influences can be grouped together into sub-groups or how these sub-groups relate to one another. This is why it is useful to think of influences in a systematic way. If you chose to draw a multiple-cause diagram you may have found this a powerful tool in helping you to identify and group the different influences.

Activity 2 output

- *For Organisation type A activity, a completed version of Table 4.1 Steps in customers' decision-making.*

or

- *For Organisation type B activity, a completed version of Table 4.2 Influences on customers' behaviour and their interaction.*

Reading 5

Have you ever been about to make a decision to do something and then stopped at the last moment? Whenever a customer is going through a decision-making process or thinking about changing behaviour, there is always the possibility of a moment of hesitancy or doubt. Being hesitant is quite natural, especially when the decision we are about to make has some implications. These implications may be financial, to do with the time required or more personal ones such as one's health. Reading 5, *Who constrains and encourages customer behaviour*, discusses how people, organisations and stakeholders can act as influencers or gatekeepers. Influencers and gatekeepers exist in all types of decision-making situations and from a manager's perspective it is important to understand how they affect your organisation and your ability to do your job.

Activity 3

Allow 2 hours for this activity.

This activity is suitable for Organisation types A and B. It requires you to identify influencers and gatekeepers, how they affect your customers and what you can do to minimise or maximise their roles. It is designed to help you understand the roles of influencer and gatekeeper more fully and how you may act to reduce or enhance their impact to achieve your desired customer objectives. If influencers and gatekeepers are not identified and managed for the benefit of the organisation, their influence can become detrimental to your objectives.

To carry out the activity, identify three influencers and three gatekeepers that affect your customers' purchase decision-making or behaviour change. Once you have identified them, describe how they exert their influence or gatekeeping role on your customers. Then make suggestions on how you can minimise or maximise their role to your benefit or that of your organisation or your part of it. Finally, identify any problems that might arise in trying to minimise or maximise their role in your customers' decision-making or behaviour change. Note that marketing theory assumes that these influencers and gatekeepers will be outside the organisation doing the marketing.

However, for internal marketing, influencers and gatekeepers that impact on your (internal) customers may well be inside your organisation, but perhaps in another department.

Use Table 4.3 for your output.

Table 4.3 Identifying and utilising influencers and gatekeepers

	Role in decision-making/behaviour change	How to minimise or maximise the person's role	Problems in minimising or maximising the person's role
Influencer 1			
Influencer 2			
Influencer 3			
Gatekeeper 1			
Gatekeeper 2			
Gatekeeper 3			

As you carried out this activity, you may have found that there are a number of influencers and gatekeepers to your customers' decision-making or behaviour change whose influence you had not previously realised. Alternatively, you may already have realised their effect on your organisation. If so, then you may also have been able to consider how you, your organisation or your part of it can control their role in your customers' decision-making or behavioural change.

Activity 3 output

- *A completed Table 4.3 Identifying and utilising influencers and gatekeepers.*

Activity 4

Allow 45 minutes for this activity.

After completing Activity 3, post a message to the relevant thread on your activity forum, in which you briefly outline the way in which your organisation uses its influencers and gatekeepers and the impact they have on your customers decision-making or behaviour. Compare your outline with that of one other student and respond to this student making three key observations on similarities and/or differences.

Activity 4 outputs

- *A contribution to the activity forum outlining the way in which your organisation, or your part of it, uses influencers and gatekeepers.*

- *A response to one student in which you set out three key observations on similarities and/or differences between the roles of influencers and gatekeepers in your own organisation and the one in which the other student works.*

Week 4 activity outputs

1 *For Organisation type A activity* A Word document of no more than 200 words titled Week 4 Activity 1A.

or

For Organisation type B activity A Word document of no more than 200 words with the title Week 4 Activity 1B.

2 *For Organisation type A activity* A completed version of Table 4.1 Steps in customers' decision-making.

or

For Organisation type B activity A completed version of Table 4.2 Influences on customers' behaviour and their interaction.

3 A completed Table 4.3 Identifying and utilising influencers and gatekeepers.

4 A contribution to your activity forum outlining the way in which your organisation or your part of it uses influencers and gatekeepers.

and

A response to one student in which you set out three key observations on similarities and/or differences between the roles of influencers and gatekeepers in your own organisation and the one in which the other student works.

Learning outcomes

After completing this set of activities and readings you should be able to:

- understand the main dimensions of consumer and organisational customer decision-making and the main differences between them
- show how these dimensions of buyer behaviour apply to customers of your own organisation
- understand the influences of outside factors and other people on the buyer decision process and behaviour change
- identify the main influences on your organisation's customers' behaviour and decision-making
- understand the role of influencers and gatekeepers in customer decision-making and behaviour change in the organisation in which you work and in another organisation
- identify influencers and gatekeepers that affect your organisation's customers and how your organisation could manage these influencers and gatekeepers to its advantage.

Week 5 Delivering value in exchanges

Introduction

By now you will have understood how organisations engage with their customers. You should be able to appreciate how organisations and customers enter into an exchange with each other to achieve a mutually satisfactory outcome. To allow organisations to maximise their exchanges with their customers you have read how markets can be segmented and segments selected depending on their importance to the organisation's needs (we called this targeting). The organisation then decides how it wants to be seen in the market (we called this positioning) and ensure that its product/ service offering meets this. In theory, organisations that pursue this approach are already on the way to being highly effective, market-led organisations motivated to meet their customers' needs. Even more importantly, if all the managers within the organisation can understand these themes and apply them to their daily engagement with their own customers (regardless of whether they are external or internal) then the managers themselves will become part of the organisation's marketing efforts.

Yet applying marketing in organisations is not this straightforward, as you may appreciate from your own experiences. Identifying which segments an organisation should target is not always precise nor is it always possible to implement procedures and products to meet a particular segment's needs. For example, some managers may be resistant to becoming part of what they see as the 'marketing machine' or simply need more training to help them perform their jobs better.

Compounding this problem are fundamental differences between a product and a service, and the wider quality implications this has for an organisation. You may know from your own experiences as a customer or as a manager responsible for delivering a service that a high level of standardised quality is often difficult to achieve. The first readings for this week explore why services are different from products and why this creates quality problems. After exploring these differences, you will read about how service quality failures occur and how, in some instances, employees can be empowered to achieve service recovery.

Meeting your customers' needs and achieving high levels of quality sometimes is not enough for customers. In many instances, customers hold significant levels of power over you as a manager or your organisation. This power may simply manifest in the customer being your largest or most valuable customer in terms of the size of their demand for your product/ service or in financial terms. In these instances, it becomes important from an organisational and managerial perspective to try and develop some type of relationship with them. The last set of readings explores the reasons why marketing encourages the development of relationships with our customers and how we can identify which customers we should develop a relationship with.

The main activity this week is problem-based.

Week 5 activities

- Activity 1 Understand the service that you deliver to your customers and how to differentiate this. (Allow 60 minutes for this activity.)
- Activity 2 Problem-based activity exploring in depth the relationship between you/your organisation and an important customer and how to improve it. (Allow 3 to 4 hours.)

Readings

- Reading 1 Value, quality and marketing relationships
- Reading 2 Understanding how services differ from products
- Reading 3 Services and resolving variability
- Reading 4 Building and sustaining quality in service provision
- Reading 5 Customer satisfaction, service failure and recovery
- Reading 6 Building good marketing relationships

Readings 1 to 5

The first four readings, all in Chapter 5, are all about how services differ from products. Even if your organisation predominately sells products or your role as a manager is only concerned with dealing with other people, you will have some encounter with service delivery. Reading 1, *Value, quality and marketing relationships*, is a general introduction to the topic of value, quality and marketing relationships. Reading 2, *Understanding how services differ from products*, explores how services differ from products and the implications of this. For example, services differ from products because they rely on individuals to create and deliver the service, such as a nurse administering first aid. Yet this reliance on individuals ensures that no two service offerings are ever the same (such as our nurse who cannot deliver an identical service to his next client) and this poses wider problems of service variability. Reading 3, *Services and resolving variability*, explores how service variability can be resolved by introducing various measures, a problem that fast food chains and banks seem to have solved. Yet service variability can often lead to quality issues in how a service is delivered and this is explored further in Reading 4, *Building and sustaining quality in service provision*. Sometimes, no matter how much effort a manager or their organisation puts into standardising a service delivery, quality issues will arise leading to unsatisfied customers. Reading 5, *Customer satisfaction, service failure and service recovery*, explores how service failure arising from poor quality can be overcome through empowering employees to act quickly.

As a manager, the relevance of some of these readings may vary depending upon the extent to which you see yourself as managing a service. However, regardless of whether you are a manager for a profit-orientated, public sector or non-profit orientated organisation some aspect of your job will involve service delivery and these readings should allow you to make better decisions. As you work through the readings, take some notes on the main points and think about how they relate to your own work.

Activity 1

Allow 60 minutes for this activity.

The aim of this activity is to allow you to explore how service delivery affects your job as a manager. In particular, you are going to explore to what extent service characteristics (intangibility, perishability, variability and inseparability) manifest in what you offer your customers. For example, if you are a manager for a payroll department then your customers would be the organisation's employees, or if you manage a distribution department then your customers may be internal as well as external. In both examples, you will be offering some level of service (for the payroll manager this would involve ensuring all employees are paid correctly and on time, while for the distribution manager it would be ensuring products are delivered undamaged and on time for the customer). Before you continue with this activity you might want to take a few minutes to think about what aspects of your job involve service delivery.

Complete Table 5.1a. You will recognise this from Reading 2, *Understanding how services differ from products*. Apply the service you provide to your customers to each of the categories in the table. Remember that all managers and organisations provide some type of service offering.

For example, a builder might think of himself as 'building houses', i.e. providing a physical product rather than a service, but he is also offering a service, i.e. building the house to the specifications of the customer. In terms of the characteristics of a service:

- The customer is also buying the *intangible* builder's skill in building the house – a service.
- Although the builder leaves physical evidence of his service, the service he is offering are his skills in building buildings, which stop once the building is completed and are thus *perishable.*
- No two buildings the builder builds can ever be the same (no matter if the same architect plans are used) and there is thus *variability.*
- Although the building built can be separated from the builder, the builder's skills are *inseparable* from the builder.

Step 1: Intangibility, perishability, variability and inseparability all offer the potential for causing problems in terms of differentiation, quality and productivity. In Table 5.1a note down how this affects the service you offer and how you resolve these problems. There are three spaces provided for problems relating to each of intangibility, perishability, variability and inseparability but we realise that there will not always be exactly three problems to be identified for each. However, you should note down at least one problem for each (remember that a problem is not always something negative but simply an opportunity to improve something). Note that the emphasis here is on how you currently resolve these service issues, not how you might do so in future. You should be as honest as you can, but need not elaborate upon what you could do differently (we shall look at that later).

Step 2: At this point you should reflect upon what you have learnt from this activity and consider what you might do differently in your job. You should summarise your thoughts in the penultimate row of Table 5.1a.

Step 3: Now consider which of the problems and solutions you identified in Step 1 you are willing to share with other students in your tutor group. Post your selection to your activity forum in a message of not more than 200 words.

Once you have done this, read at least two other students' postings and consider how their messages differ from your own. To what extent are the differences and similarities between other students and your postings attributable to the type of organisation they work for? For example, does a public sector organisation provide more or less service delivery than a profit-orientated organisation? Or can differences be attributed to the differing needs of their customers? Do not be surprised to discover that some organisations may offer differing levels of service simply because their customers demand it (and most importantly are willing to pay for it).

Summarise your thoughts of the differences between service delivery in your organisation and those of two fellow students in the final row of Table 5.1a.

Table 5.1b shows an example of how Table 5.1a can be completed. Table 5.1b continues with the example of the building firm (from the previous page). Some of the points made in Table 5.1b are fairly general, your completion of Table 5.1a can focus on more industry/profession specific methods.

Table 5.1a Problems in differentiating the services I offer my customers and how I resolve them

	Differentiation	**Quality**	**Productivity**
Intangibility	Problem: Current resolution:	Problem: Current resolution:	Problem: Current resolution:
Perishability	Problem: Current resolution:	Problem: Current resolution:	Problem: Current resolution:
Variability	Problem: Current resolution:	Problem: Current resolution:	Problem: Current resolution:
Inseparability	Problem: Current resolution:	Problem: Current resolution:	Problem: Current resolution:

What have I learnt from this activity and what might I do differently in my job as a consequence?

Differences between service delivery in my organisation and those of two fellow students (after discussion on activity forum).

Table 5.1b Problems in differentiating the services I offer my customers and how I resolve them

	Differentiation	Quality	Productivity
Intangibility	*Problem* A builder may find it difficult to differentiate his offering from his competitors because at the time of purchase customers cannot see exactly what he promises to produce. *Resolution* Builders firms can give websites and brochures showing their work on previous assignments. Websites also allow them to show videos of the process involved. Show homes can be used to provide further tangible evidence of an offering.	This may be difficult to manage because at the time the contract is drawn up between building contractor and customer, it may be difficult to determine exactly what the customers expectations are. Ordinary consumers may find it difficult to visualise plans and diagrams! *Resolution* References from previous customers can give some indication that the builder is able to meet customers expectations (which is one way of looking at quality).	This is also difficult to manage because at the time of drawing up the contract the builder may not be precisely aware of how long the project may take (particularly taking into account unforeseen delays). *Resolution* The contract could be drawn up so that risks are borne in an equitable way and people are incentivised to be efficient.
Perishability	The abilities and outputs of people in this industry cannot be stored (in some instances). This means that the builders ability to differentiate his offering depends on who he can hire at the time of undertaking any one project. *Resolution* One method of resolving this problem is to have a wide network of contractors who can be called upon when needed.	The same problem applies here as described in the box on the left. The builder will find it difficult to market a quality offering to customers, when he knows that staff who produce a high level of quality cannot be guaranteed to work on any one project and he may have to hire people whose quality of effort is not as high as he would like. *Resolution* As with the box on the left, a wide network and knowing potential referees will help.	Because the services of people who are involved in the building trade are not generally storable, there will be possible problems with productivity. For example, some work may not be possible in winter months and on any one project some specialists may need to complete some tasks before others are able to do theirs. *Resolution* Experience of scheduling work so that such problems are minimised should help, this should be clear from the firms track record.
Variability	Differentiation from competitors can be difficult because houses that the builder builds may vary in quality from each other, for example, due to variations in the staff he employs. *Resolution* One way of dealing with this is to develop methods and processes that can be used to standardise procedures. The use of tangible goods can also be used to do this.	Because of the variability in the quality of contract staff, quality of the final product may vary and this has to be managed by the builder. *Resolution* Quality control systems can be used in order to deal with this, but they can result in increased bureaucracy.	Variations in the abilities of staff members (especially if they are contract staff) may mean that productivity is difficult to manage. *Resolution* Minimum standards for employees and appropriate incentive schemes could help.

Table 5.1b continued

Inseparability	It is difficult to separate the outputs of the builder from the builder himself. This has implications for managing differentiation, because the builders ability to differentiate his offering will ultimately depend on the quality of staff he is able to hire (at least for some of the tasks that are undertaken). *Resolution* Staff training schemes.	The same issues will apply to quality as applied to differentiation. The builder may be restricted in terms of the quality of offering he is able to sell, due to the inherent skills of the staff that he has. *Resolution* He may be able to manage both quality and differentiation through stringent management and oversight of staff, but it can be difficult.	Because staff members cannot be separated from their outputs, productivity can be difficult to manage, availability of staff may affect how much can be produced and some staff members may be more productive than others. *Resolution* Effective project management.

You may have found this task harder than you thought. You may have begun to realise that actually you do offer a service, to varying levels, in your daily role as a manager. What is important to consider now is to what extent you actively aim to resolve the problems associated with the service you deliver. For example, you may not have appreciated that you do not monitor quality levels in your service offering (after all, if there have not been any complaints why bother monitoring quality? The answer is because quality can always be improved so long as the costs involved do not exceed any additional profit being made). Alternatively you may not have appreciated how much time and effort, in your role as a manager, you put into delivering services. It may be the case that you simply have been doing aspects of service delivery as part of your everyday role as a manager.

Activity 1 outputs

- *A completed version of Table 5.1a.*
- *A contribution to the activity forum.*

Reading 6

Now read Reading 6, *Building good marketing relationships* (in Chapter 5). This reading explores why some organisations want to develop a long-lasting relationship with their customers. You may have noticed if you travel how many airlines offer their business-class customers a loyalty card awarding points towards future free flights with them or how some supermarkets offer loyalty cards to their customers where points collected are converted into money-off vouchers. Both these examples illustrate how organisations aim to create long-term relationships with their customers. Long-term relationships are an even more common feature of organisations marketing to other organisations, or those offering services. Yet, as you will read, relationships with customers are not solely limited to profit-orientated organisations. Instead public sector organisations and, especially, non-profit organisations, such as charities, are recognising the importance of developing relationships with their customers. As you read, you may want to consider what type of relationships you offer your customers, what motivates you to offer and sustain a relationship with them (if at all) and whether is it worthwhile maintaining that relationship?

Activity 2

Allow 3–4 hours for this activity. As with all longer activities in this module, you can break this down into several shorter sessions if you like.

In this problem-based activity, you are going to explore one (and only one) relationship between you or your organisation and a customer. This should be a relationship which you believe can be improved. The customer you choose should be one that is important enough to you or your organisation to warrant your attention. Here are some examples of the type of relationship you might choose:

Relationship A – As a manager, you are required to deliver an output to other employees or departments within your organisation. This relationship works well for this activity if your only customers are internal ones.

Relationship B – You work for a public sector organisation, where you serve predominately external customers, such as a local government waste collection department, servicing local businesses and households. Your customers have to use your service offering and in many respects you have no competition. Lack of competition need not mean that marketing relationships cannot be improved but it – and wider organisational restrictions – may limit the extent of improvements you can or wish to make to your service delivery.

Relationship C – As a manager in a profit-orientated organisation, your dominant objective is to ensure your customers are always happy. This is regardless of whether you are a manager in marketing or in any other organisational department. As far as you are concerned, every employee in your organisation should be working towards the common goal of achieving maximum customer satisfaction. In these organisations there may be many customers who may be either from the public or other businesses. The emphasis here lies on which market segments are the most profitable and beneficial for the organisation and how marketing relationships with these segments can be improved.

Relationship D – Non-profit organisations offer an interesting contrast with public sector and profit-orientated organisations. As a manager, your work may be inclined towards helping those whom the organisation aims to support as well as/or those people and organisations who offer you support, such as donations.

Further guidance

To complete this activity you need to ensure that the relationship you or your organisation has with the customer can be improved. Ideally, you should choose a relationship where problems have occurred in the past or are still occurring. However, if you cannot do this then simply choose a relationship which can be improved. (If it cannot be improved, which is doubtful, then choose another customer where the relationship can be improved.) In deciding upon your customer and the relationship they have with you or your organisation, you may be faced with several possibilities. To make this activity as easy for you as possible you should choose just *one* relationship of which you have a lot of knowledge and/or experience.

Before carrying out this activity you will find it useful to refer back to all your activities from previous weeks. This will remind you of the various concepts that you have learnt and how they can be applied to your role as a manager or to your organisation. Once you have reminded yourself of your outcomes from previous weeks you will need to:

- be able to identify and understand exactly what is being exchanged between you or your organisation and the customer
- appreciate what the expectations are from both your customer's, and your or your organisation's perspective
- ideally, recognise what segment they could be categorised as belonging to, the reasons for placing them in this segment and what you or your organisation's expectations are of this segment
- recognise why that segment was targeted and then how you or your organisation position(s) itself within the targeted market segment that your customer exists within
- most importantly, be able to understand why the relationship between your chosen customer, and you or your organisation could be improved.

In this activity you are going to explore *one* relationship between your customer, and you or your organisation. You will need to analyse the situation, draw conclusions and plan a solution that will solve or improve the current relationship and prevent problems from occurring. Use Table 5.2 to help you structure your problem-solving. Questions to guide you are included here, but these questions do not appear in the writable version.

Table 5.2 Resolving a marketing relationship problem

Problem identification

When identifying your relationship problem you might want to consider:

- What are the symptoms?
- How do they manifest?
- What are the wider consequences of these symptoms?

Analysis

Using the readings on differences between services and products (Readings 1–4), marketing relationships and the previous week's readings, what do you think are the main causes for the relationship problems? What are the views of your customer, yourself and your organisation, and what assumptions have all of these made? To help your analysis you might want to consider the following questions:

- What were the expectations of both your customer and you or your organisation from the exchange that took place?
- To what extent were or are these expectations supported by or undermined by how you or your organisation categorised your customer through segmentation and targeting? In other words, did the segmentation category and targeting process determine how you dealt with that customer?
- To what extent did you or your organisation's positioning encourage real or unrealistic expectations in your customer's mind?

Table 5.2 continued

- To what extent can you apply SERVQUAL to identify real problems in your or your organisation's service delivery that may have contributed towards the problem?
- To what extent do you or your organisation actively try to encourage and maintain a relationship with your chosen customer?
- Finally, what do you or your organisation actually offer or provide to sustain that relationship?

Conclusion

[Add your conclusion here.]

Solution

How can the relationship problems be resolved and improved upon? You should consider as many options as possible and assess them for their relevance towards solving your problem. For example, you may have identified the problem arising from expectations and what may have been implicitly or explicitly promised. This may have arisen from your customer being identified as important to your organisation through segmentation and targeting. However, has this importance been met in realistic terms (such as meeting your demand and/or profit expectation)? Has your organisation's positioning strategies given the customer unrealistic expectations? When you are thinking about your solution you should consider the feasibility of what you are proposing and you might want to refer back to your reading *Customer satisfaction, service failure and service recovery.* While a seemingly perfect solution might be found it does not necessarily make it a feasible one! It is also possible that you will find there is no solution to the problem – or none that is in your power to bring about (for example, customer expectations may be determined to some extent by your organisation's communications, such as advertising and publicity messages. However, the service delivered may fail to match that promised for a number of reasons, which are beyond your control). If there is a possible solution, ensure that it is SMART.

Strengths, weaknesses and implications

Consider whether you have chosen a solution(s) which could actually be implemented in your organisation. If it or they can be implemented then what would be the wider implications of this? Note, this is a good place to consider ethical implications and implications for sustainability.

Completing this activity you will have started to appreciate how different elements and concepts in marketing are related and how it is generally necessary to think about marketing problems holistically in order to achieve sensible solutions. This week's activities and readings have provided you with an opportunity to understand why some relationships between your customer, and your and/or your organisation may encounter difficulties. Problems in relationships can often be attributed to a number of causes and are rarely down to one single event. By drawing upon your previous activities and readings you should have begun to appreciate how expectations can be a source of these problems and these expectations are based upon a number of marketing-related activities – for example, segmentation, targeting and positioning. You may also have realised that solving marketing problems often requires action from different parts of an organisation and it may not be possible for a single person or department to find a solution.

Activity 2 output

- *A completed version of Table 5.2 Resolving a marketing relationship problem.*

Week 5 activity outputs

1 A completed version of Table 5.1a Problems in differentiating the services I offer my customers and how I resolve them.

2 A contribution to your activity forum.

3 A completed version of Table 5.2 Resolving a marketing relationship problem.

Learning outcomes

After completing this set of activities and readings you should be able to:

- recognise how services differ from products but, ultimately, all products have some aspects of services to them
- understand how services can suffer from quality issues and how using SERVQUAL can help to identify how service quality issues arise
- appreciate how empowering employees can lead to service recovery
- identify how and why managers and organisations seek relationships with their customers and how this is determined by cost and profit considerations
- recognise that relationships are based upon expectations, with expectations occurring from inter-related marketing activities.

Week 6 The marketing mix

Introduction

You have considered how products and services differ from each other and the wider marketing implications of this. We now move on to a major component of marketing, often called the marketing mix (or, more formally, marketing strategy), which involves coordinating aspects of product, price, place and promotion. You may not be aware of it but you have already had a lifetime of being exposed to the marketing mix. The easiest way to realise how the marketing mix operates is to think of the last thing you bought. You may have had many reasons for buying that particular type of product and probably can rationalise why you bought it. However, if you view that purchase from a marketing mix perspective then you can begin to understand how the marketing mix may have affected your choice of purchase. For example, was it the product's design or colour (product) that attracted you or was it perhaps priced more competitively (price)? Maybe it was easy for you to find a shop to purchase this product (place) or perhaps you saw an advertisement that made the product appeal to you (promotion). How the marketing mix is applied varies according to whether a product or service is being offered, whether the organisation is commercial or non-profit, and so on. Nevertheless, many aspects of how the marketing mix is applied remain the same.

The readings this week explore how the marketing mix can be applied to commercial and not-for-profit organisations and the public sector. You will also read about how you can apply the marketing mix to yourself, as a manager.

This week's activities allow you to consider how you use marketing and how you could use it more effectively for yourself. This perspective acknowledges that as a manager you may wish to gain promotion in your employment or you may simply want to present a positive image of yourself amongst your peers. This option can be applied to any management role you are currently in.

Week 6 activities

- Activity 1 Identify three new tasks you could introduce as a manager and assess their attractiveness. (Allow 90 minutes for this activity.)
- Activity 2 Recognise that implementing any new activity will incur some cost to you and assess whether the cost of doing these activities is actually worth it. (Allow 60 minutes for this activity.)
- Activity 3 Identify how you can communicate your new activities to your peers and how this communication may not always be heard as you intended. (Allow 90 minutes for this activity.)

Readings

- Reading 1 Coordinating the marketing mix
- Reading 2 Product
- Reading 3 Pricing
- Reading 4 Place
- Reading 5 Promotion
- Reading 6 Sustainability and the marketing mix

Reading 1

First read *Coordinating the marketing mix* in Chapter 6, which provides a broad insight into how the marketing mix works and describes the elements of the marketing mix. As you read, think about the various products or services you have recently bought and the way in which the marketers who brought them to you used the elements of the marketing mix. For example, what aspects of the product attracted you to it and how important was the price in your decision-making? Did the company's promotional activity, for example advertising, play a role in your decision-making? You could have bought the product from different outlets, but why did you choose the one that you did? Once you have done this it is often useful to bring together all this information to understand how that product's marketing mix matched your needs. You may be surprised at how quickly you can identify how a product's marketing mix appealed and encouraged you to buy a product.

Reading 2, *Product* in Chapter 6, explores how the concept of a product differs between commercial organisations and non-profit or public sector organisations. Rather than explore all the aspects of what constitutes a product, this reading focusses mostly on how organisations and managers can determine what products or services they should be offering. This is explored through the concept of the product life cycle and two matrices (the Boston Consulting Group matrix and the non-profit analysis matrix), which can be used by managers and organisations in making important product/service decisions.

Activity 1

Allow 90 minutes for this activity.

The purpose of this activity is to apply the concept of the product portfolio analysis to a situation with which you are familiar. As not all of you will work in a position where you have any direct responsibility for deciding on the product portfolio of a commercial organisation, this activity uses the non-profit portfolio analysis matrix (described in Reading 1) and applies it to yourself and your career. Think of yourself as the marketer and the various activities you do in your work as the products/services.

Step 1

To start, think of three new activities that you could potentially perform in your job. These should be activities that you think would enhance your job profile and your employment and/or career prospects. They should be plausible within your work context but you need not worry at this stage how practical it would be for you to carry out these activities.

Enter your three chosen activities in Table 6.1.

Step 2

Now consider the external attractiveness of these three activities. How likely are they to be attractive to other people inside and outside your organisation? You can break this down into several indicators of external attractiveness, which could include something like the following:

- How many people would benefit from this activity?
- How useful would the activity be for my organisation?
- How highly would other people inside and outside the organisation rate the activity?
- Would people inside and outside the organisation consider me to be a more competent, energetic, proactive, etc., manager if I carried out this activity?

What exactly your criteria should be depends on the nature of your work/organisation and the activity you are proposing.

Note that the non-profit analysis matrix assumes that the criteria of external attractiveness will be weighted and rated, and an overall rating for the activity produced from the weighted average of the individual criteria ratings. However, in this instance, we suggest that you give an overall rating to what you believe will be the external attractiveness of each of the three activities (giving a score of high, medium or low).

Enter your criteria and the rating for external attractiveness of each activity in Table 6.1.

Step 3

Now consider the internal appropriateness of the proposed three activities. Again, it may be useful to split this up into several criteria, such as:

- How easily could you perform the activity?
- How much would you enjoy the activity?
- Does the activity fit in with your other work?
- Does the activity provide you with opportunities for learning and personal development?

Again, the precise nature of the internal criteria will depend on you, your work role and your career plans. The above are just some suggestions to get you started.

You should now rate each of the proposed activities on internal appropriateness, giving a score of high, medium or low. As for external attractiveness, we suggest you give one value for each activity, rather than rating and weighing each criterion on this occasion.

Enter your criteria for internal appropriateness and the rating for each proposed activity in Table 6.1.

Step 4

The next step is to enter the position of each of the proposed activities in terms of external attractiveness and internal appropriateness into the non-profit matrix in Table 6.1.

Step 5

After you have entered the potential activities in the matrix you should take a few minutes to reflect upon your matrix and the wider implications. Are these potential activities now so attractive? Is the matrix telling you that your proposed activities should be carried out or not? Make a note of the overall attractiveness of each activity and enter this information at the end of Table 6.1.

Table 6.1 Non-profit analysis matrix for my own work activities

Three new activities I could do at work:
Activity 1 –
Activity 2 –
Activity 3 –
My criteria for judging external attractiveness (to others):
1
2
…
External attractiveness rating (high – medium – low) for:
Activity 1 –
Activity 2 –
Activity 3 –
My criteria for judging internal appropriateness (to me):
1
2
…
Internal appropriateness rating (high – medium – low) for:
Activity 1 –
Activity 2 –
Activity 3 –

The completed matrix

		Internal appropriateness		
		High	Medium	Low
External attractiveness	High			
	Medium			
	Low			

Final assessment on which activities to carry out and which not to (with reasons):

You may have found this activity a little strange at first as we don't normally think of ourselves and our activities as products. We hope that using the matrix in this way has shown you that these tools can be applied in a number of different situations, even though applying them to oneself is not usually the purpose for which they were first developed. In doing this activity you may have thought more deeply about your work and the directions in which you could take it, and you may also have realised that not all new things that you could do at work are equally attractive from a personal and a career perspective. Assessing whether an activity should be undertaken can be painful – after all, you may have spent a lot of time thinking up the ideas – but hopefully you should have realised that proposed activities are not always worth doing. The same problems also occur for organisations when, after many resources and a long time have been spent in developing a new product/service, the idea turns out not to be feasible.

Activity 1 output

- *A completed version of Table 6.1 Non-profit analysis matrix for my own work activities.*

Reading 3

For an exchange to occur there may need to be a financial transfer between the people or organisations involved. Reading 3, *Pricing* in Chapter 6, explores how a financial price for a product/service is determined. More often than not financial pricing is associated with concepts of profit or market share. However, what happens when an organisation cannot charge a financial price for their core offering, for example, a hospital or a museum? The reading explores this question as well and considers how non-financial pricing can be used to achieve organisational objectives.

Activity 2

Allow 60 minutes for this activity.

The purpose of this activity is to consider the question of cost and pricing. You will continue to look at yourself as the marketer and the activities you carry out at work as your products. You may or may not be in a situation where your time is directly charged to the projects you are working on. Here we assume that this is not the case and that you are not necessarily in a position to extract direct non-financial 'payment' for your activities. Rather we assume that you can come to some kind of judgement about what the likely rewards would be for carrying out the activities and that you have some idea of the costs that the activities would entail for you.

Step 1

First, we want you to consider the *non-financial* cost that would be involved if you carried out the three new activities you identified in Activity 1. It will be best to use the same activities but you can think of different ones if you prefer.

For each of the three potential new activities you could carry out in your work, consider the time costs, emotional costs and opportunity costs that you would incur in carrying out that activity. How much of your time would the activity take (time cost)? How much would you like or dislike carrying out this activity (emotional cost)? And what other things that you could have done instead would you have to give up in order to carry out the activity (opportunity cost?)?

Enter this information in Table 6.2.

Step 2

Second, we would like you to consider what likely rewards you could expect from carrying out the work activities identified in Activity 1. These rewards will depend on your organisation, the nature of your work, the nature of the proposed new activities, and of course yourself. For each of the three potential new work activities note down what rewards you could reasonably expect in Table 6.2.

Then compare the likely costs and rewards for each activity and assess whether, based on this analysis, you would be well advised to go ahead with the activity. Enter your conclusions in Table 6.2.

Table 6.2 Costs and rewards associated with my proposed new work activities

	Time cost	Emotional cost	Opportunity cost
Activity 1:			
What is it?			
Activity 2:			
What is it?			
Activity 3:			
What is it?			
Likely rewards from:			
Activity 1 –			
Activity 2 –			
Activity 3 –			
Would it be advisable to go ahead with:			
Activity 1 –			
Activity 2 –			
Activity 3 –			

After completing Table 6.2 you may be surprised by the advantages and disadvantages you have identified. You might have already begun to think again about whether you want to introduce these activities. Is the cost of undertaking them too great or is the recognition too little?

Activity 2 output

- *A completed version of Table 6.2 Costs and rewards associated with my proposed new work activities.*

Readings 4 and 5

How to get your product/service to your market is a persistent problem for organisations and managers. Reading 4, *Place* in Chapter 6, explores the more traditional perspective of product distribution and how organisations often use various intermediaries to get their product distributed in the market. Intermediaries can also be used to provide a service, for example, when a utility provider, such as British Telecom, uses a third party customer-care service. It is also conceivable that non-profit organisations and public sector organisations may use intermediaries to, say, ask for donations or deliver a service. However, distribution channels in the traditional sense are most commonly considered in terms of commercial organisations and considering them from a service, public sector or non-profit organisation perspective may require some additional thought.

Sometimes no matter how much you try to manage how your product/service is delivered, problems will arise. The final part of this reading explores how conflict arises between the organisation and its distribution channels.

Reading 5 in Chapter 6 discusses the final part of the traditional marketing mix – *Promotion*. No matter how good your product/service is, it will not sell unless you have actively promoted it by telling the market that it exists and encouraging customers to buy it. From this reading you will begin to understand how promotion consists of a broad range of activities, from the obvious, such as advertising on television, to using the internet, or personal selling. The reading concludes with a simple communication model, which you should ensure that you understand.

Activity 3

Allow 90 minutes for this activity.

In this activity you will be looking at the final part of your marketing mix – promotion. As a manager it does not matter how good you are at your job or how effective your decisions are if you cannot communicate these to other people. From this perspective, communicating your achievements or actions becomes a form of promotion, although you may feel uncomfortable about promoting yourself or feel that this does not fall within your remit or your personality.

We want you to consider how you would communicate one (and only one) of your three new ideas to your peers in your organisation. To help you analyse your communication process you will use the simple communication model explained in Reading 5. In Table 6.3, note down what the aims of your communication process would be, what problems you might expect to have to solve at each stage, and how you could address these problems, as well as the implications of these proposed solutions. In other words, use the problem-solving approach.

Once you have done this you should spend a few minutes considering how you could monitor feedback about your communication and add these ideas to the table. Understanding the level of feedback you receive from a communication will allow you to understand how effective your communication message has been.

In completing the table you should consider the following points:

- *Sender.* For the purpose of the exercise this will be you.
- *Encoding your message.* This refers to how you will put your thoughts and ideas into words, specifically what words will you use: for example, will you use technical jargon or formal English or will you use easy-to-understand everyday English? These decisions can be important because any given message can be encoded in a number of different ways and how this is done will depend on who your audience is and what type of message you think will be most effective.
- *Transmission.* How do you intend to send your message to your target audience? For example, you could do this through a presentation, email, word of mouth or meetings. You should also consider the advantages and disadvantages of using your preferred methods of communication, again depending on who the target audience is.
- *Decoding your message.* How will your target audience decode your message? Will they understand what you are trying to communicate and achieve in your new activity? Or will they simply see what you are communicating as extra work for them? For this part of the communication model you need to consider how the receiver will understand your message. For example, one of the choices is whether or not to use technical jargon; if the audience consists of members of management with no technical training, the audience may not be able to understand what it is you are trying to say if you use technical terms. This would be one of the factors contributing to noise; other factors are considered below.
- *Noise.* How will other people interfere with your message? In any organisation new ideas can produce resistance and this is often manifested through rumours. It would be good to identify those peers who might offer resistance to your ideas and try to disrupt your communication process.

Table 6.3 Communicating your proposed idea to peers in the organisation

The idea or new activity I have chosen to focus on for this activity:				
Aims of communication process:				
	Encoding	Transmission	Decoding	Noise
Problems that may arise				
Nature of the problem (analysis using module concepts)				
Recommendations for solving the problem (using module concepts)				
Strengths and weaknesses of proposed solution				
How to monitor feedback about my communication:				

Activity 3 output

- *A completed version of Table 6.3 Communicating my proposed idea to peers in the organisation.*

Reading 6

The final reading for this week, Reading 6 *Sustainability and the marketing mix* in Chapter 6, considers one of the module themes – sustainability – in the context of the marketing mix. Sustainability issues often come to the fore in the marketing mix. Product and distribution are particularly relevant to sustainability, but price and promotion can also have significant impacts on sustainability, both negatively and positively. This reading will help to put the marketing mix in a wider context and you will also need it again later in the module.

Week 6 activity outputs

1. A completed version of Table 6.1 Non-profit analysis matrix for my own work activities.
2. A completed version of Table 6.2 Costs and rewards associated with my proposed new work activities.
3. A completed version of Table 6.3 Communicating my proposed idea to peers in the organisation.

Learning outcomes

After completing this set of activities and readings you should be able to:

- understand the nature of products and some of the factors that play a role in determining an organisation's product portfolio
- appreciate the main elements of pricing decisions
- recognise the variations in distribution channels and the need for managing channel conflict
- identify the various elements of promotion and how it can be supported or hindered through how you communicate your message
- understand some of the sustainability implications of the marketing mix
- apply some of the concepts of the marketing mix to yourself and your work activities.

Week 7 The extended marketing mix for services

Introduction

You have now considered how the traditional marketing mix can be applied to you and your organisation. Yet the traditional marketing mix is not fully appropriate or useful from a services perspective where there is greater emphasis on the involvement of people. Even if as a manager you do not have any direct involvement in marketing, you will invariably be involved in delivering services of some description to various stakeholders. This highlights the fact that services have become part of the fabric of working life regardless of sector or type of organisation, or indeed region of the world.

The purpose of this week's activity is to explore how you, as a manager, can apply the extended marketing mix to yourself and your department. We begin by discussing the importance of people in service delivery and how you can motivate your colleagues to deliver high levels of service quality. We shall then discuss how service management processes need to be designed to ensure smooth and efficient delivery.

This week's activity will be based around solving a work problem.

Week 7 activity

- Activity 1 Use the extended marketing mix to deliver services. (Allow 2 hours for this activity.)

Reading

- Reading 1 People, process and physical evidence

Reading 1

Reading 1, *People, process and physical evidence* in Chapter 7, discusses why the marketing of services has produced what is commonly referred to as the extended marketing mix. Issues of intangibility, inseparability, heterogeneity and perishability have produced the need for services marketing to include people, process and physical evidence. The reading then explores the central importance of employees to service delivery. Unlike a product, which can be mass produced and standardised, a service depends on a large amount of human input for its delivery. This emphasis on human input requires managers to understand how to motivate their employees.

The reading then discusses the process by which a service should be delivered in order to ensure that this is done in a smooth and efficient way and how attention to physical evidence in services can overcome some of the issues surrounding intangibility. For example, banks have traditionally operated from impressive buildings in order to reassure customers that their deposits are safe. In other situations, physical evidence can take the form of a 'thank you' sticker for a charity donation.

Activity 1

Allow 2 hours for this activity.

As a manager you will be involved in delivering a service. This may just mean that you engage with others or use a team to develop and deliver a service for internal or external customers. The purpose of this activity is to encourage you to explore how you can improve the way in which you deliver your service using the three additional elements of the extended marketing mix – people, process and physical evidence.

Step 1

In this activity, you will go through the problem-solving approach to identify first an internal or external service that you (or your team) currently deliver and how you deliver it, and then identify what issues/problems you face in doing this. It is likely that there are aspects of your current service delivery that you can identify with the extended marketing mix. If not, you might want to think about a service you have delivered in the past and which aspects, if any, of that service relate to the extended marketing mix. Either way, you should be able to identify a small problem in how you currently deliver a service.

Step 2

You should then think about the various elements of the extended marketing mix and how they can shed light on the nature of your service delivery problem(s) and their possible solutions. Think about the current service you deliver (as you identified in Step 1) and how the extended marketing mix could improve it. For example, you may be able to provide more physical evidence of your service.

Step 3

Next think about and decide on one or more possible solutions to your problem(s). Consider your current service delivery and how you might change it, or how you might incorporate opportunities to apply the extended marketing mix. Justify these solutions – say how they will improve your current service delivery. You should also consider what you will need to do to implement these changes, such as training your peers in a new way of dealing with your customers. Do you have the resources to implement these changes?

Step 4

Consider where your organisation's or your team's current practices cannot resolve the problem. You may find that you cannot change wider processes within your organisation or that attempts to introduce more physical evidence may produce criticisms of wasting money from other departments. To what extent can you change these to work in your favour, if at all?

Step 5

Focus first on the strengths, weaknesses and implications of your proposed changes to your own service delivery, then on changes which you might propose to more senior managers. In addition to implications for your immediate organisation, you might also consider implications in terms of marketing ethics and sustainability, if applicable.

Step 6

Make your proposals SMART!

Use Table 7.1 to help you structure your response.

Table 7.1 How I currently deliver a service and how it could be improved

1	Problem identification: How do I currently deliver a service?
2	Problem analysis: How can I use the extended marketing mix to improve this service delivery?
3	Problem solution: What are the proposed changes to my current service delivery?
4	Problem solution (cont.): What requires changes that are beyond my own control and what will I do about this?
5	Strengths, weaknesses and implications
6	Implementation plan for proposed changes

While carrying out this activity, you may have identified a number of opportunities or problems that you did not realise you had. How many opportunities there are to improve your service delivery will depend upon your situation. You may have found that it took you a bit of time to think through your service delivery and analyse it. If so, you will now recognise that analysing work problems with a reasonable level of depth is not always easy and can require some effort and time.

Activity 1 output

- *A completed version of Table 7.1 How I currently deliver a service and how it could be improved.*

Week 7 activity output

1 A completed version of Table 7.1 How I currently deliver a service and how it could be improved.

Learning outcomes

After completing this activity and reading you should be able to:

- understand what the extended marketing mix is
- appreciate how the extended marketing mix applies to services
- recognise how you can apply the extended marketing mix to your current role.

Week 8 Managing marketing information

Introduction

If marketing is all about maximising customer satisfaction how do managers or an organisation know whether they are achieving customer satisfaction? In all your activities and readings so far you have made well-educated guesses about what your customers need and expect. In some instances your guesses may have been very accurate but can you be 100% certain that you were right? When managers need to make decisions that have much wider implications, especially in terms of costs, having a guess at what is right will not suffice. In these instances the manager needs more accurate information on which to base a decision.

Marketing research is a set of techniques for collecting, analysing and interpreting data, which is used as input in the management decision-making processes. It allows managers to make more informed decisions based upon facts; however, this does not mean that these facts are always right! Instead, whenever marketing research is used to make a decision it is important to critique it and assess whether or not it is telling you the truth.

This week's readings and activity aim to encourage you not only to understand what marketing research is but also to be able to critique it. As a manager you may not be directly involved in gathering marketing research but the results of it are likely to have a direct effect on you.

Week 8 activity

- Activity 1 Undertake a focus group interview and assess your own performance as an interviewer. (Allow 3 hours for this activity.)

Readings

- Reading 1 The importance of information
- Reading 2 Types of marketing research
- Reading 3 Choosing respondents and gathering data
- Reading 4 Critiquing marketing research

Readings 1 and 2

Reading 1 *The importance of information* in Chapter 8, introduces you to what marketing research is and how, using an example of Coca-Cola, it can be dangerous to rely on it uncritically to make the right decision. Yet, with awareness of its limitations, managers can use marketing research to help them in a wide variety of managerial decisions.

It is unlikely that, as a manager, you will be directly involved in marketing research but it is important for you to understand the different types of marketing research. Reading 2, *Types of marketing research* in Chapter 8, explores how marketing research can be based upon widely available information (we call this secondary data) or on information gathered just for a particular project (we call this primary data). We then explore how marketing research can be defined in terms of words (we call this qualitative data) or numbers (we call this quantitative data). Understanding how marketing research data has been gathered will allow you to understand how relevant it is to you.

Activity 1

Allow 3 hours for this activity.

You can break this activity down into smaller chunks of time if you prefer.

Writing a quantitative questionnaire often relies upon an objective approach to the problem being researched. While this may be seen as relatively easy, being objective in qualitative research is a lot more difficult. What do we mean by being objective? If you are objective you have not formed or expressed your opinion in a way that is likely to influence your participants.

The purpose of this activity is to encourage you to understand how difficult but rewarding qualitative research is. This activity will also develop your active listening, a technique used in a variety of professions and one that is essential for today's manager. You will be expected to undertake a qualitative research interview, which should also provide you with insights into a customer satisfaction problem.

Active listening describes a process where you, as the researcher or manager, collaborate in a discussion by asking open-ended questions and getting feedback from the person speaking, to confirm that you understand them correctly. What you are aiming to do is provide the person speaking with a feeling of being heard.

To be an active listener, and hence an effective marketing researcher or manager, you need to ask open-ended questions. These questions encourage the speaker to express their thoughts and feelings towards the problem you want to explore, typically by using: what, when, why, if and how. For example, if you are researching children's reactions to a new toy you may ask the following open-ended question 'What did you like about Jammo the Robot?'.

Closed questions, in contrast, tend to stifle and restrict the speaker's opportunities to express themselves. These questions tend to produce one-word responses. For example, '*Did you like Jammo the Robot?*' will realistically produce a response of either 'yes' or 'no'.

The purpose of this activity is to enable you to become a better listener and ask more probing questions.

To learn more about active listening read the 'Active listening' section (pp. 79–80) in *The Manager's Good Study Guide.*

Step 1

To begin this activity you should identify a marketing problem that exists in your organisation. You may want to use the service delivery problem you analysed last week or you may want to choose another problem. Whatever problem you choose, ensure that it is relatively simple and contained, so that you have a chance of tackling it in the relatively short time available for this activity. Write your problem at the beginning of Table 8.1.

Step 2

The next part of this activity is to ask three work colleagues (or friends if you feel more comfortable with this) to pretend to be your customers. (Using actual customers may raise ethical issues.) You are interested in finding out the cause of the research problem you have just identified and have decided to conduct a focus group. Before you conduct this focus group research you need to think of some interview questions to ask your (pretend) customers. Using concepts from the previous weeks of this module, think about what the nature of the problem seems to be. Then devise a series of questions that you could ask your (pretend) customers about the problem. Limit your questions to a maximum of three or four and make sure the questions are open ended, that is, they allow people to talk as freely as possible and do not encourage short answers such as 'yes' or 'no'.

For example, if your problem is that you get regular complaints about a particular service that you deliver, possible reasons are that: you do not deliver what your customers require; your customers do not understand the nature of the service you provide; there are some operational or people problems in the delivery of the service; or various other reasons. You would then ask questions that try to elicit the exact nature of the complaint, your customers' expectations of the service, their understanding of what you can actually deliver, and so on.

Enter your questions in Table 8.1.

Step 3

You should now conduct your focus group. Find somewhere quiet, where you will not be disturbed and where you all feel comfortable. This may be where you work or in a room in your home. You should aim to run your focus group session for between 15 and 30 minutes.

Ideally, for this activity you should try and record your focus group session, as this will allow you to understand how you can improve your listening. Alternatively, you could get someone to watch you conduct your focus group and offer feedback to you. If you use someone to watch you, you might wish to give them a copy of your questions.

Step 4

As the next step, you should think about how your focus group session went. How many times did you do things which, with hindsight, might not have been conducive to your respondents talking freely or you listening effectively? For example, did you interrupt participants? Think about why you did these things and how you could avoid doing them in future.

Then think about what you did to encourage active listening, for example giving participants verbal signals such as nodding your head, or asking them to clarify or expand points they made.

Table 8.1 encourages you to think about your active listening in qualitative research and encourages you to make improvements in how you engage with other people. To help you do this you can use the following questions to guide you.

- How many times did you nod you head, say 'yes' or show you were listening?
- How many times did you seek clarification of a point your participant was making?
- How many open questions did you ask?
- How many closed questions did you ask?
- How many times were you able to let the participants keep talking without intervening?

Enter these questions (and similar ones if you like) and the answers to them in Table 8.1 (after 'Reflections on effectiveness of conducting focus group session').

Step 5

Finally, you should write down what you have discovered about your customer satisfaction problem from your focus group. Enter this at the end of Table 8.1.

Table 8.1 Focus group research on a marketing problem

My marketing problem:
The questions for my focus group session:
Reflections on effectiveness of conducting focus group session:
Findings about my marketing problem from focus group session:

After completing this activity you might be surprised how difficult active listening is! You may also be surprised at how many times you interrupted people without realising it. You may have discovered how you do not encourage people to expand upon their responses to your questions. Active listening is a skill that all managers can improve upon and hopefully this activity will have offered you an opportunity to explore this further.

Activity 1 output

- *A completed version of Table 8.1 Focus group research on a marketing problem.*

Readings 3 and 4

In the last activity you gathered together a group of people to interview in a focus group. As this was an activity you did not have to be selective over whom you interviewed but in marketing research selecting the right people is crucial. Reading 3, *Choosing respondents and gathering data* in Chapter 8, discusses the importance of choosing the right sample. The reading then introduces some useful pointers for steering and overseeing marketing research and making sure projects run smoothly.

Reading 4, *Critiquing marketing research* in Chapter 8, introduces you to ways in which you can critique marketing research. As a manager you may be exposed to various marketing research findings which will have an effect on your work. This reading explores how you can critique marketing research and assess how relevant it is to you. Marketing research is concerned with understanding why a particular behaviour or opinion has been formed, why certain events happen, and so on. It therefore involves investigating organisations' and people's beliefs, behaviours and values, and this may leave the participant feeling vulnerable. Reading 4 also explores marketing research ethics and why they are so important.

Week 8 activity output

1 A completed version of Table 8.1 Focus group research on a marketing problem.

Learning outcomes

After completing this set of readings and activities you should be able to:

- understand what marketing research is and the different types of marketing research
- appreciate what a sample is and how sampling is done
- recognise how you can critique marketing research
- understand the importance of ethics to marketing research.

Week 9 The marketing plan

Introduction

Over the past eight weeks you have covered the essential aspects of marketing: customer satisfaction, understanding customer behaviour, marketing relationships, the marketing mix and marketing information. This week we will bring all this together by looking at the concept of the marketing plan. The reading this week will introduce you to what a marketing plan is and how it can be used in different settings – commercial, public sector, not-for-profit and so on.

The key feature of a marketing plan is that it ensures that managers articulate the problem they are facing, assess the marketing environment within which the problem will have to be resolved, and also evaluate the resources that will be required in order to address the problem. Therefore, the plan enables marketers to balance the costs of their actions with the likely gains to their organisation. Our coverage of marketing planning at this stage will allow you to consider the way in which previous weeks' work can be used in a marketing plan and will also set the stage for incorporating future weeks' activities into a marketing plan.

Week 9 activities

- Activity 1 Investigate marketing planning in your own organisation. (Allow 2 hours for this activity.)
- Activity 2 Develop a marketing plan. (Allow up to 3 hours for this activity.)
- Activity 3 Explore marketing planning in different settings by sharing information with other students on the activity forum. (Allow 60 minutes for this activity.)

Readings

- Reading 1 Use of a marketing plan

You may also want to re-read the following readings:

- The module theme readings (ethics, corporate social responsibility, sustainability, climate change) in the module guide
- Reading 4 of Week 1 Exchange, fairness and satisfaction
- Reading 6 of Week 6 Sustainability and the marketing mix

Reading 1

How are all the different aspects of marketing put together? How do you make sure that the marketing activities you undertake all fit together? Marketing activities should not be considered in isolation. Rather, an understanding of your customers, segmentation and targeting of the right market, developing marketing relationships and the right marketing mix, should all be seen as part of the same marketing process. A marketing plan brings all these different elements together, sometimes for an entire organisation, sometimes just for aspects of it. Formal marketing planning is most commonly conducted in commercial organisations but is also becoming increasingly common in non-profit organisations. Reading 1, Chapter 9 *The marketing plan*, explains how marketing plans are put together and used. Marketing plans are important because they provide a template of how an organisation is going to achieve its marketing objectives and what strategy it will use.

Activity 1

Allow 2 hours for this activity (plus additional time for research if needed).

The purpose of this activity is to find out a bit more about marketing planning in your own organisation. Does your organisation have a formal marketing plan? In this activity we want you to find out what marketing planning your organisation does and what benefits it derives (or could derive) from formal marketing planning.

As explained in the reading, marketing planning is typically used when people have to bid for resources and need a formal explanation of how they intend those resources to be used and what the outcomes are intended to be. This means that in situations where resources are not acquired in such a manner, no marketing plans need exist. Moreover, in some organisations there may well be documents which are used for the purpose of acquiring resources, but they are referred to by another name.

Step 1

There are several options for this activity. Choose the one that best fits your organisation and your role in it.

Option 1

Find out whether your organisation has a formal marketing plan and what it consists of, in terms of structure and content. Either the organisation has such a document or it does not – the question is quite clear-cut. If it does then you should go straight to the description of this activity at the end of Step 1.

Option 2

If your organisation does not have a formal marketing plan, find out whether there are documents which serve the same purpose as a marketing plan, but have a different name. You can still do this activity, but you will have to undertake the additional step of relating the content of such a document to a marketing plan structure.

Option 3

If there are no documents of the sort described above, you may need to research the marketing decisions being made by the organisation, either based on your own experience or by asking the marketing manager or someone else more closely involved in the marketing process. You may also be able to deduce the marketing decisions that have been undertaken. For example, if you work in a commercial organisation your offerings may be more expensive than those sold by others because you are targeting an affluent niche market; or if you work for a charity your services may be targeted at people who can least afford commercial options.

Option 4

Bear in mind that, although we have referred above to 'your organisation', marketing plans can be developed for all sorts of situations. They could be produced for specific products and services and they can even be created for individuals. Micro-businesses, which market the services of freelance professionals, for example, typically focus on the skills and attributes of an individual person. If you are unable to find a marketing plan at the level of the organisation or a product or service, you could prepare a marketing plan for yourself – something which you may find very useful if you are considering applying for a job or for a promotion.

Describe the marketing planning process in your organisation (or for yourself if taking Option 4) in Table 9.1.

Step 2

Now think about why your organisation has the kind of marketing process that is does and which you have described in Step 1. Does this have to do with external factors (the type of sector and market you operate in, the competitive environment, etc.) and/or internal factors (the type of organisation it is, the nature of the people working in it, etc.)?

Note these thoughts in Table 9.1 (under 'Reasons why the organisation has made the decisions reflected in the marketing plan').

Step 3

Now think about whether the marketing process in your organisation could be improved and, if so, how. If not, why do you think it is best left as it is?

Note your thoughts at the end of Table 9.1.

Table 9.1 Marketing planning in my organisation

Description of a marketing plan (e.g. in terms of headings/topics/content) used in my organisation
Reasons why the organisation has made the decisions reflected in the marketing plan
(For example if the intended customers are a particular group of people, are there any reasons for this?)
Are there any areas of the marketing plan whose content could be improved?
(What improvements could be introduced?)

How easy you found this activity will depend on the nature of your organisation and your role in it. If you normally work with customers and are directly involved in marketing you may have had relatively easy access to the marketing plan and will be quite familiar with its processes. If, on the other hand, your organisation does not have a formal marketing plan and/or your role is not closely related to marketing to external customers, you may have found it more difficult to get hold of this information. In either case, thinking about why your organisation has the kind of marketing planning that it does and how it could be improved (or why that might not be necessary or possible) will hopefully have given you further insights into your organisation and what marketing planning does for different types of organisation.

Activity 1 output

- *A completed version of Table 9.1 Marketing planning in my organisation.*

Activity 2

Allow up to 3 hours for this activity.

You can break this activity down into smaller chunks if you wish.

The purpose of this activity is for you to use the problem-solving approach to develop a simple marketing plan. Again, there is a choice in this activity. *Option 1* is to analyse and plan to resolve a marketing problem faced by your organisation, using the framework in Table 9.2. Depending on your work role this option may provide immediate benefits to performance.

However, depending on the nature of your organisation and/or your role in it, you may not be able to identify a suitable cluster of marketing problems or you may find that, after starting with what you believed to be a suitable group of problems, the problems disappear or you find the activity is too difficult to make useful progress. If so, *Option 2*, which asks you to undertake the same activity with reference to the Milton Pharma case study (below) may be useful.

The purpose behind this activity is to show the close relationship between the 'marketing plan' as used by many organisations and the problem-solving approach that you have used throughout this module. As you will have seen so far, the marketing plan is simply a tool used by organisations to assess the marketing situation that they face, and in the light of that assessment to propose a marketing strategy that will achieve their objectives. In terms of the problem-solving approach, therefore, the marketing plan identifies specific marketing problems, presents an analysis and suggests a solution.

The conclusions in this particular case should be presented in the form of the strengths and weaknesses of your proposed solutions and should include a consideration of ethical and/or sustainability issues.

So you should approach this activity in terms of solving the problem (as you have done previously), and then write your answers in the format of a marketing plan, using the template provided in Table 9.2. Of course you may not have all the information that you would need for a marketing plan. Don't let that deter you but just work with the information you have.

Option 1 A marketing plan to address marketing problems in my own organisation

You should use the problem-solving approach to identify a range of marketing problems facing your organisation, analyse them and then provide a coherent solution. Unlike the other problems that you have considered in this module, the complexity with this activity is that you may well consider a *variety* of problems, all of which have to be addressed to make a coherent marketing plan. There will, therefore, be more than one solution. This is in essence what the marketing plan does – it presents the marketing strategy that an organisation intends to follow and deals with the solution to a number of different marketing problems.

As you will see from Table 9.2, the solution element of the problem-based approach correlates to the 'marketing strategy' section of a marketing plan. The key aspect of a marketing plan is that it should be consistent, especially where marketing strategy is concerned (the elements of the – extended – marketing mix). Consistency refers to the idea that your plans for 'product', for example, need to be consistent with your plans for 'pricing'. In simple terms if you anticipate marketing a high-specification product, you would expect to be charging a premium price, etc.

We don't expect you to produce a comprehensive marketing plan that covers all aspects of the marketing challenges you face, but we do expect you to cover a variety of issues. For example, it could be that it is difficult for you to deal with pricing issues, in which case you could leave out a consideration of pricing. Or you may find that your knowledge and experience of the business give you insights into the organisation's relationship-building activities and the role of process and people. You could therefore write about these topics and make sure that any solution you offer in these areas is consistent.

Option 2 Marketing plan for Milton Pharma

The case study *Milton Pharma* deals with some of the issues that faced Richard, a newly appointed first-line manager. As you read the case you will see that he faced a number of different challenges at work. In addition he is a (hypothetical) student on this module and needs to complete this activity. Your task is to put yourself in Richard's position and write the marketing plan, using the problem-based approach.

Case study – Milton Pharma

Note: This case is not set in any specific country. It has been written in order to illustrate various marketing concepts, rather than as a realistic portrayal of any healthcare system. However, the healthcare system to which it refers is one in which medical services are provided to members of the public free of charge. In addition, medicines are provided either free of charge or for a nominal fee. The healthcare system is funded by the taxpayer. The 'local doctors' to which the case refers are people whom patients visit when they first become aware they have an illness. There are no charges for such appointments. The local doctor may prescribe a medicine or may refer the patient to a local hospital.

Richard worked as regional sales manager for Milton Pharma (MP), a small pharmaceutical company which markets various dermatological products. Most of these had been developed by much larger pharmaceutical companies but had been sold to companies such as MP, because they were no longer considered to be core offerings. MP now had a portfolio of products and could position itself as a specialist dermatological products company. Richard had moved from a much larger company and could see the benefits of working for a small organisation. His job remit was now much more substantial. With his previous employer he had been given materials and told what to do with them; at MP he had much more autonomy to work with the medical and marketing departments in the company to create offerings that could meet the needs of his customers.

After five years' experience in the field, promoting products for a pharmaceuticals business, Richard had recently been appointed to the position of regional sales manager, responsible for nine sales representatives. In turn he had to report to the national sales director.

He knew he faced a challenging task. Each of those representatives was a tough personality – they had to be to make it as salespeople. But there were variations in experience and more importantly in sales success, and that was what he had to improve in order to get promoted to the next level. In order to introduce himself to the team he had organised an away-day at a local hotel and right now he was working on his presentation. He had decided to focus on a couple of issues that had come up in a group meeting with his sales director and other regional managers. He knew that he also had to provide a framework for organising the sales representatives' work in a way that was integrated with MP's other marketing activities and took into account the marketing environment.

Having spent a number of years in the field as a sales representative, Richard was aware that the role of the regional sales manager was becoming more complex, because the purchasing procedures in the national health system were changing due to economic and political pressures.

He could see that the challenge facing him was to motivate representatives both as individuals and as members of a team; he could also see that it would be difficult to meet both sales and people objectives. In addition he would need to coordinate with other departments in order to make sure that the messages his salespeople were giving customers were consistent with the messages being promoted by the firm's wider marketing campaigns.

A recent development that pleased Richard was that he had effective control over his own profit-and-loss account and the ability to deploy budgets, representatives and other resources into areas where they would be most effective. He could see that most of his time would be spent on field visits but with his supervisory responsibilities there would now be more administrative work compared with his previous role. Typically he would now be spending seven days a month in the field, with administration accounting for four days and meetings and conferences taking another three days.

Richard had already spent some time with his national marketing director who had stressed that he was expecting regional sales managers to become more involved in developing local and creative value-added strategies. He would also be expected to enhance his coaching skills because the role of salespeople was changing from being 'talking brochures' to being consultants who could solve problems for their customers.

One of the areas he wanted to cover in his talk was the changing face of pharmaceutical marketing. The processes with which his team were so familiar were changing and this would have a significant impact on what they were now required to do. In fact his own role as sales manager was also changing. There would now be more emphasis on having sales trainers work with representatives, rather than just the sales manager.

Traditionally, each of the salespeople in Richard's team had about 250 potential customers to call on, including individual doctors as well as a small number of hospitals and commercial outlets such as chemists. Hospitals were important customers: once they had agreed to buy a drug this usually led to the drug being adopted by general practitioners (local doctors) in the same area. Hospital doctors could also help with endorsing clinical data that would make MP's own claims more credible.

These customers (hospitals and local doctors) were usually seen on a one-to-one basis, with the representative having to meet the busier customers over dinner. In addition, the representatives would also have to visit smaller local hospitals and meet the medical teams and the pharmacy in order to encourage adoption of the drugs in their portfolio. Those representatives who were more experienced would be given responsibility for selling into the larger teaching hospitals. Chemists could be asked for a commitment to stock certain products that were on promotion. Effective selling skills included the representative focussing on areas where there was greatest selling potential. The introduction of laptops and sales-management software had helped this process by enabling the firm to keep track of sales.

However, a great deal of this was changing. Increasingly in his country, there had been a move towards centralised formularies that dictated prescribing practices to local doctors, and if they deviated from these there would be financial penalties. So there had been a change in who was responsible for purchasing decisions – the role of the local doctor had been reduced, and this would have implications for the amount of time salespeople spent with them. However, the local doctors still had an important role since they were still free to choose between drugs on the formulary.

In addition, salespeople had to spend more time understanding the purchasing processes in the centralised formularies and identifying the key decision-makers within them.

There were now additional benefits that salespeople needed to focus on: as well as demonstrating the efficaciousness of drugs, they also had to show that the drugs were cost-effective and delivered demonstrable benefits to the health service, from a reduction in hospital admissions to a decrease in side-effects that could demand additional medication or attention.

There would clearly be significant implications for the salesforce of MP. Local doctors would still need product information to inform their choice of on-formulary drugs; and MP would need to reinforce their products over the competition, so that their products achieved first-line prescribing status.

Another development that challenged the traditional work of the sales representative was the fact that 20% of new drug marketing was being targeted directly at the patient, and patient self-prescribing (i.e. patients themselves purchasing over-the-counter drugs to treat minor ailments) was up by 40%. This had meant that doctors needed up-to-date information to allow them to address patients' requests and suggestions.

Within the health profession there had also been new initiatives such as the 'Expert Patient Programme'. This was a new approach to the treatment of patients with chronic diseases in which patients were no longer seen as passive recipients of care and instead became key decision-makers in the treatment process. Local doctors' needs were evolving as well. So, as an extension to sales representatives' existing role of information provision, they also needed to supply doctors with a wider range of information that supported the total management of a patient's condition.

Richard knew that there were some fears amongst his team about eDetailing. This was a technology-based development, which referred to pharmaceutical companies using digital technology and interaction with the physician. The term could include, amongst other things, remote live discussion with sales representatives, scripted interactions with a website, and live interaction with a dynamic presentation of scientific and sales materials. All of these new methods of interaction between MP and doctor would have implications for the role of the sales representative and some were concerned about future employment prospects.

One of the areas Richard wanted to discuss was the notion of relationship marketing. He knew the whole team agreed that not all customers are equal. Some were clearly different from others in their attitude and behaviour. The challenge was to identify these differences and prioritise customers based on empirical evidence.

He also wanted to focus on how relationships were established. Experience told him that medical professionals demanded excellence and tended to make time to see only a few selected salespeople, if any at all. He knew that the representatives who established the most profitable relationships were those who appeared professional, were credible, and who offered a genuine service to their customers. Medical professionals often took a dim view of drug company salespeople, not because they lacked knowledge about the pharmacology of their products, but because of sloppy or pushy selling techniques. One clumsy visit could shut the door to further progress and leave the customer with a permanent dislike of salespeople in general.

Richard had heard from doctors that they needed to be certain not only that the sales representatives were fully up-to-date with the products they were selling, but also that they had the integrity and professionalism to give doctors information which was useful and relevant in the context of their practice and their prescribing formulary. Representatives also needed to be succinct, and sensitive to doctors' priorities and time constraints. The cost of getting this wrong was not that doctors would complain – they would just restrict their accessibility. One of Richard's options was to encourage employees to seek formal, accredited sales qualifications to demonstrate to customers that they were safe to let in! But he knew that some of the representatives would be very much against this and it would be a challenge to persuade them otherwise.

Another area of potential dispute would be how representatives should focus on key customers. Richard knew that some representatives believed they could compile lists of customers that would maximise sales on their territory better than any list generated by head office. However, personal experience and talking to more senior managers told him that this was not really the case.

Sales representatives could access additional sales by focussing on the target group rather than a self-generated list. It would be a mistake to presume that this would underplay the representatives' important role in the customer-targeting process. Richard anticipated allowing representatives to make adjustments and have an input into the targets for their territory; otherwise critical local knowledge, which can be a source of competitive advantage, would be missed. His national sales director was emphatic that changes and adjustments made in order to enhance the results generated from the evidence-based process should be limited. This was important because sometimes there were so many changes made to a target list that it lost its empirical origin.

This would be a tough sell to his colleagues: some representatives perceived the customer-targeting process as a necessary evil that disrupted their activities. However, Richard had read studies showing that, left to their own devices, representatives did not discriminate between customers, thereby missing opportunities to improve effectiveness. Other representatives found the ongoing changes to the target customer groups tiresome. What made it particularly difficult was the need for making updates to reflect strategic choice and the impact of the ever-changing environment. In addition, there was also the obvious question that representatives would ask: 'What's in it for me?'. Richard felt that he had some incentives to offer in this regard, including access to customers with greater potential to prescribe. In addition, there would be improved bonus-earning capacity and better customer relationships because sales propositions would be developed by the marketers with the target audience in mind. He also needed to consider similar incentives with regard to the role of ethics. There were always temptations for salespeople to take shortcuts when promoting products, but activity that was seen as unethical would have longer-term consequences for the organisation as a whole.

As well as improved targeting of customers, Richard felt that his representatives could also try more innovative means of building relationships. Having spoken to other experienced sales managers, Richard knew that the more successful representatives recognised that many of the people in doctors' surgeries and members of local management teams from the ministry of health and the prescribing units were too worried about their jobs to think about placing orders. They therefore facilitated training workshops on structure change to help get the people concerned settled and in a position to talk with the sales representative about business.

One of Richard's colleagues did one workshop a week for all the different sectors of the market. Numbers at the sessions might range from 30 people down to six or eight for a small surgery and their staff. Subjects included facilitation skills, chairing meetings, time management and personal development plans and appraisals. His colleague could also arrange for guest speakers to talk about drugs and case studies.

Richard knew that MP would like the credibility that this would engender and it would give representatives access to the customers. In fact he had heard that they would ring the representative and ask if he could provide a workshop or help them with some problem.

As you will see from the case study, there are various topics and issues that are not covered at all, whereas others are covered in some depth. This is because, for the same reasons as those given to students undertaking Option 1, we do not expect you to write a complete marketing plan. What we are expecting is an identification of the key problems facing Richard and analysis of such problems, together with some suggestions for their solution (the marketing strategy). All the material that you need to do this activity should be found in the case study itself, so you should not really need to undertake additional research, such as searching the internet for more information about pharmaceutical marketing.

Table 9.2 The marketing plan

Marketing plan	Problem-based approach
Executive summary	
Marketing objectives	Problem identification
Situation analysis	Analysis, using relevant module concepts
Solution: Market segmentation	Solution
Solution: Marketing strategy	
Solution: Short- and long-term projections	
Solution: Monitoring and evaluation	
Conclusion	Strengths and weaknesses of the proposed solutions
	Wider implications, including in terms of marketing ethics and sustainability

This is the most complex marketing activity that you have attempted in B629/BZX629. In all likelihood you found it challenging, at least in parts. Hopefully, it will have shown you that marketing problems can be fairly complex and need to be considered holistically rather than in isolation.

Activity 2 output

- *A completed version of Table 9.2 The marketing plan.*

Activity 3

Allow 60 minutes for this activity.

The purpose of this final activity in the marketing part of B629/BZX629 is for you to share your thoughts on marketing plans with others in your tutor group and thus to further deepen your understanding of how marketing planning might work in different organisations.

Step 1

Post a message on your activity forum, in which you outline in no more than 200 words how marketing planning might be applicable in different organisations, giving a brief example from your own organisation.

Step 2

Read the messages posted by other students on the activity forum, and respond to at least two of them, stating:

(a) where the marketing planning in your organisation seems to be similar to the process in their organisation

(b) where the two marketing-planning processes seem to be different, and

(c) what this says more generally about marketing planning in different organisations.

Activity 3 output

- *Your original posting on the activity forum plus two further postings in response to messages by other students.*

Week 9 activity outputs

1 A completed version of Table 9.1 Marketing planning in my organisation.

2 A completed version of Table 9.2 The marketing plan.

3 Your original posting on the activity forum plus two further postings in response to messages by other students.

Learning outcomes

After completing this set of readings and activities you should be able to:

- demonstrate an understanding of what a marketing plan is and how it brings the various aspects of marketing together
- reflect on the marketing process in different types of organisation
- apply the problem-solving approach to produce a simple marketing plan.

Week 10 The need for financial information

Introduction

Welcome to the finance part of the module. You have already seen how marketing activities have an impact on the financial situation of organisations. Now we look at how *all* the activities of an organisation affect its financial situation and why all managers need financial information to make good decisions. We also look at the various stakeholders who will be interested in evaluating the performance of the organisation and their financial information requirements.

Whether grouped together to form organisations, or in their personal lives as individuals, people typically have to make choices on how to use resources. This requires information, including financial information, about the costs and benefits of the alternative courses of action available. Once a particular course of action has been chosen, people will want to ensure that the outcomes of their choices are as expected or intended. Were the benefits as expected? Were the costs more or less than anticipated? Financial information is, therefore, necessary in making plans, taking decisions and in controlling activities to ensure that objectives are achieved.

This week we do not deal with any figures or calculations. Students are often apprehensive about the numerical aspects of finance. This is rather puzzling, since in your personal lives you are likely to have carefully and successfully made calculations about the costs of buying and selling items – such as cars and homes – and calculated interest rates and affordability. On a daily basis, you probably budget successfully. When students move from personal finance to studying finance in organisations, they say this is more difficult. Our guess is that finance specialists at work (deliberately or unintentionally) make finance too complicated. We know from what previous students have told us that we explain finance well. So, please approach your study of finance confidently! You *will* need to do simple arithmetic including addition, subtraction, multiplication, division, and percentages. If you need to revise any of these, then work through Chapter 5, Working with numbers, in *The Manager's Good Study Guide*. If necessary, use the links on StudentHome to access further materials on the Open University's website. Create good quality study time for this, and for your study of the finance part of the module. This will not be when you are tired, under pressure or subject to interruption!

Week 10 activities

- Activity 1 Share with other students what you hope to achieve by studying finance. (Allow 30 minutes for this activity.)
- Activity 2 Identify the information requirements of your organisation's various stakeholders. (Allow 2 hours for this activity.)

- Activity 3 Identify the particular financial information requirements of an organisation in financial difficulties, based on a case. (Allow 2 hours for this activity.)

Readings

- Reading 1 The importance of financial information
- Reading 2 Financial stakeholders
- Reading 3 Perspectives of financial information

Activity 1

Allow 30 minutes for this activity.

This first activity asks you to consider the following questions:

- What financial information do you deal with at home and at work?
- What benefits do you hope to gain from studying finance?

We hope that in considering these questions, you will realise that you already deal with financial information, and that this will help reinforce or establish a constructive purpose for studying finance which will provide a focus throughout the remainder of the module.

Write a short message for other students in your tutor group setting out your responses. It is advisable to say what your job is and the sector you work in, so that it is clear why you deal with (or don't deal with) financial information. For example, in many public and non-profit sector jobs, such as aspects of health care provision, you may encounter very little financial information. If, on the other hand, you are the manager of a retail store, you are likely to deal with certain types of financial information daily.

Post your message to this week's activity forum and read the messages from other students. Identify one message where you have something in common and reply to it constructively.

We hope this activity helps to clarify your reasons for studying finance and the potential professional and personal benefits you will gain. It should also have reminded you that you probably deal with financial information fairly often, at home if not at work. Thus you already have knowledge on which you can build. You are likely to have identified at least one of the many benefits of studying finance. Often the reason is to be able to make better management decisions (both professional and domestic). The activity may have made you aware of what the study of finance might involve.

One important thing to remember from this first activity is that you are not studying alone and that you are likely to have found at least one student in your tutor group with whom you have something in common concerning finance. This should be reassuring!

Activity 1 outputs

- *A contribution to this week's activity forum with responses to Activity 1 questions.*
- *A contribution to this week's activity forum in response to at least one other student.*

Readings 1 and 2

Have you ever wondered why the finance function of your organisation seems to have such influence/importance? What do these people actually do? Why should you be interested in finance? Reading 1, *The importance of financial information,* discusses managers' need for financial information in order to undertake various activities and how these various activities then impact on the financial situation of their organisation. As you read, think about the sort of financial information that would help managers achieve each of the management objectives identified – remaining solvent, making a profit, providing a quality service to the public within a financial constraint, and so on. Think also about how the activities of your particular department – and you as an individual – have an impact on the financial performance and wellbeing of your organisation. Make notes of the key points and of your thoughts on them to help you with this week's activities.

Reading 2, *Financial stakeholders,* considers an organisation as a coalition of various 'stakeholders', each of whom has a financial interest in the organisation. The reading should answer questions such as: for whose benefit is an organisation run? Is it the owners, the employees, society as a whole, the state? Various stakeholders and their financial information needs are discussed. As you read, think about the sort of decisions the various stakeholders might want to make and how financial information is necessary for them to make these decisions. Being aware of who the main stakeholder groups (typically) are and of the sort of financial information they require will help you with Activity 2.

Activity 2

Allow 2 hours for this activity.

This activity requires you to identify the various stakeholders, and their information needs, in the organisation you work for – or your part of it. It also asks you to share a summary of your findings with other students. The activity is designed to help you understand the importance of finance in the organisation you work for *and* in other organisations – those that other students work for.

Look again at Table 10.1 in Reading 2, *Financial stakeholders.* This time, using Table 10.1 below, note which stakeholder interests apply to your organisation or your part of it. Consider interests that are not mentioned in the text and add them; add new categories of stakeholders as necessary. Given the nature and purpose of your own organisation, what other (non-financial) information might be required by the various stakeholders and for what purpose?

After completing Table 10.1, write a short message of no more than 200 words summarising key points about your organisation's stakeholders and their interest in it. You will need to include in your message a sentence that identifies what your organisation does and the sector in which it operates. This will help others make sense of who its stakeholders are and their interests. Post your summary to this week's activity forum. Read the summaries of other students and compare the stakeholders and organisations for which they work with your own. What are the main differences and similarities? Are these influenced by the sector in which organisations operate?

Make a brief note of three main differences and/or similarities and whether these differences and/or similarities might be the result of organisations operating in different sectors. The note need be no longer than 100–150 words. Add this note to the last field in Table 10.1 below.

Table 10.1 Stakeholders' financial information needs

Internal
Managers
Financial information needs:
Reasons:
Employees
Financial information needs:
Reasons:
Members of management boards
Financial information needs:
Reasons:
Main external
Owners/shareholders
Financial information needs:
Reasons:
Lenders/financiers
Financial information needs:
Reasons:
Suppliers
Financial information needs:
Reasons:
Customers/clients
Financial information needs:
Reasons:
Donors (those who give money to voluntary organisations)
Financial information needs:
Reasons:

Table 10.1 Stakeholders' financial information needs continued

Other external
Government agencies Financial information needs: Reasons:
Local communities Financial information needs: Reasons:
The general public Financial information needs: Reasons:
Competitors Financial information needs: Reasons:
Three main differences/similarities with stakeholders of other organisations (information from other students' postings on activity forum)

You were perhaps surprised to find that a lot of people have a financial interest in your organisation – and that their interests are not identical. This activity should have served to revise the picture you have of the organisation you work for and to indicate how difficult it is likely to be to provide all these stakeholders with the financial information they need. In sharing your summary with other students, it will be clear that while every organisation is different, those in the same sector are likely to have similar stakeholders with similar needs. All this may seem quite distant from you in your daily work, but whenever you or your team plan budgets – and particularly when you spend more than your budget – ultimately, you are accountable to these stakeholders, not just your line manager.

Activity 2 outputs

- *A completed version of Table 10.1 Stakeholders' financial information needs.*
- *A contribution to this week's activity forum containing a summary of Table 10.1.*

Reading 3

Reading 1 discussed managers' needs for financial information and how the activities of people in the organisation have a financial impact on the organisation. Reading 3, *Perspectives of financial information,* considers how an organisation's activities – whether commercial or not – can be seen from a financial perspective. As you read, think about the organisation as a series of resource flows. Funds are received from various sources. They are used to acquire various resources (labour, materials and services) which are then used to produce outputs. Think also about the sort of financial information managers need at each stage in this process, for example, how or where to raise funds, where to acquire resources, how to ensure that resources are being used effectively and efficiently, whether the outputs are the right ones. This reading should help you to understand why financial information is needed about each part of an organisation's operations.

Activity 3

Allow 2 hours for this activity.

This activity requires you to identify specific information needs, using a scenario. The purpose is to highlight the importance and role of financial information for decision-making. The organisation in the scenario is typical in that its activities involve a flow of funds in the process of transforming inputs into outputs. The money value of the outputs must be sufficient to cover the costs of the inputs, unless the original funds' provider is willing to continually inject more cash! If an organisation wants to expand, a profit or monetary surplus must be generated to buy additional facilities, equipment, and so on. In the scenario, the organisation is in the unhappy situation of failing to cover the costs of the inputs.

Heroes Ltd

Heroes is a not-for-profit organisation that provides work for disabled people in a region of the country with a high level of unemployment. It was started some years ago by David Heeley, a successful entrepreneur, who provided the initial finance to start the business. He then transferred ownership to the employees although he continues to act as the Chief Executive Officer (CEO). Heroes produces a range of wooden kitchenware such as chopping boards and wooden toys. Little mechanisation is used in the production of items which are of high quality.

Heroes now consists of a number of workshops, each having its own product line. David Heeley suspects that some of Heroes' product lines have always been more profitable than others, although the less profitable lines have been maintained because the disabilities of some staff restrict the work they are able to do. However, the popularity of some products has declined. As a matter of policy, raw materials are all renewable and are sourced locally, although this is more expensive than purchasing from larger but more distant organisations. However, this supports local businesses. The wood supplied is of a higher quality than imported timber, which is more prone to splitting and warping because of the way in which it is seasoned.

The high quality of the products has given Heroes a good reputation and a healthy market regionally. However, David has always considered the scale of production to be too limited to consider markets that are further away. Selling over the internet would be a possibility, but would involve a method of selling with which Heroes is unfamiliar.

Given the predominantly social, rather than financial, objectives of the organisation, financial management has not been a priority. A part-time bookkeeper is employed to maintain basic accounting records (that is, information about cash balances and details of debtors and creditors to facilitate collection and payment of monies owing or owed). Although sales turnover has increased annually, last year Heroes experienced a £200k deficit of expenditure over income, which has almost exhausted its accumulated funds. David is now convinced that, unless some prudent financial management is introduced – probably resulting in some tough 'commercial' decisions – the future existence of Heroes is in danger.

He has some options in mind. These are to:

1 change the range of products sold by only producing those products that generate a surplus of revenue over cost
2 change some or all of the elements of the 'marketing mix', improving the product, changing the price, changing the way the products are promoted and distributed to increase revenue overall
3 introduce cost control methods to reduce internal waste and inefficiency, to reduce cost overall
4 purchase raw materials from cheaper (non-local) suppliers and purchase non-renewable resources where these are cheaper, to reduce cost overall
5 change the production technology by replacing labour intensive production methods (to some extent) with labour saving machinery, to reduce cost overall.

For each option identify the financial information David will need to allow him to choose one or more options. In each case the proposed action should only be implemented if the benefits are expected to exceed the costs. When you have identified the financial information needed, consider the conflicts that might arise between a particular option and Heroes' social and environmental goals. Ultimately David will implement an action only if the benefits are expected to exceed the costs. But benefits are not always financial! Which options might he reject and on what grounds? What decision, or decisions, should he make? Note that while you will be able to identify what financial information is needed, you will not be able to provide that information and will therefore not be able to make a decision based on financial information in this case. Use Table 10.2 for your responses.

Table 10.2 Financial information requirements

Option 1 Change the product range
Financial information required:
Potential conflicts with organisational goals:
Option 2 Change elements of the marketing mix
Financial information required:
Potential conflicts with organisational goals:
Option 3 Introduce cost controls
Financial information required:
Potential conflicts with organisational goals:
Option 4 Buy cheaper, non-renewable materials
Financial information required:
Potential conflicts with organisational goals:
Option 5 Change production technology
Financial information required:
Potential conflicts with organisational goals:
Least acceptable options:

The first part of this activity should have been relatively straightforward. As you worked through the options, it probably became clear not only what information was needed for each option but how financial information is vital in decision-making. You may have considered, too, the information flows needed for such information to be produced regularly for the purpose of controlling activities. If so, you are thinking well! The second part of the activity was perhaps not so easy. Some options might conflict with Heroes' primary goal of providing employment to disabled people if fewer could be employed. Other options might conflict with Heroes' purchasing policy currently guided by ethical and social responsibility criteria. However, if Heroes continues to produce a deficit the organisation might fail, providing no employment or local trade. The point of this additional part of the activity was to demonstrate to you that while financial information is vital, it will not be the only consideration. The second part of the activity probably made you pleased that you were not in David's difficult situation! Although you are not required to share your thoughts on this activity with other students, you might like to do this – just to see if they came to the same conclusions as you did.

Activity 3 output

- *A completed version of Table 10.2 Financial information requirements.*

Week 10 activity outputs

1 A contribution to the Week 10 activity forum with responses to Activity 1 questions.

2 A contribution to the Week 10 activity forum in response to at least one other student.

3 A completed version of Table 10.1 Stakeholders' financial information needs.

4 A contribution to the Week 10 activity forum containing a summary of Table 10.1.

5 A completed version of Table 10.2 Financial information requirements.

Learning outcomes

After completing this set of activities and readings you should be able to:

- understand why financial information is important to all organisations and relate this to your own organisation
- identify the need for financial information in planning, control and decision-making and recognise the importance of financial stakeholders
- begin to understand the part that finance plays in performance measurement.

Week 11 Budgets for planning and control

Introduction

What are budgets for? Last week you saw that financial information is necessary for planning, control and decision-making. It is now time to consider specifically the importance of financial information for budgetary planning and control. If there is one aspect of finance that all managers are likely to encounter on a regular basis, it is budgeting. The benefits an organisation achieves from the operation of a well-constructed budgeting system can be greatly enhanced if all managers are committed to the process of budgeting. This, in turn, requires that managers have a good understanding of the purposes of budgeting. This week, therefore, we look at the functions of budgets. We also see how budgets fit into the organisation's long-term planning process and look at the process of constructing and operating budgets.

Week 11 activities

- Activity 1 Advise an organisation's managers (based on a case) on how budgeting can contribute to solving financial problems of the organisation. (Allow 4 hours for this activity.)
- Activity 2 Identify the budgetary information required by managers in your own organisation. (Allow 3 hours for this activity.)

Readings

- Reading 1 The function of budgets
- Reading 2 Budgets and planning
- Reading 3 Budgetary procedures and structures

Readings 1–3

Why do many organisations spend so much time (and money) operating formal budgeting systems? What advantages do such systems provide? Reading 1, *The function of budgets,* discusses the role of budgets. Note the five ways in which budgets can be useful to organisations. Think about the sort of information that is necessary for each of these five functions.

Budgets are part of an organisation's overall planning and control procedures; they have an important role in linking the long-term objectives to the day-to-day activities. Reading 2, *Budgets and planning,* discusses how budgets fit into an organisation's overall planning process. Consider the four steps involved in the cycle of planning; try to think of the sort of financial information that must be provided at each step. As a manager, you may have been aware only of your own part in the wider planning and control process and, perhaps, of your own budget and the way in which you control it. Now you should be able to see how your activities fit into an organisation-wide planning and control process.

Having looked, in general terms, at the information generated by a budgeting system, it is appropriate to look in some detail at the budgeting process and the constituents of a budget. Reading 3, *Budgetary procedures and structures,* provides a description of how the organisation's budget is constructed and used, in order to fulfil the intended five functions discussed and to link the organisation's overall objectives to the day-to-day activities. After completing these three readings, you should have a good understanding of the purpose and process of budgeting.

Activity 1

Allow 4 hours for this activity.

This activity requires you to resolve a problem, using a scenario. The purpose is to highlight the benefits that budgeting brings to an organisation, by looking at the implications of not budgeting!

Garden Furnishings Ltd

Garden Furnishings Ltd is a family-owned business that manufactures garden furniture, which it sells to (predominantly large) retailers. The owners have traditionally also managed the business, but are now retiring and have appointed you as the new finance manager. The owners have always considered budgeting a waste of time – seeing it as costly and time consuming, constraining (restricting managers' ability to respond to changing circumstances), and largely irrelevant as it is not possible to predict the future. A prominent family member had been heard to say that 'in an uncertain world, the budget is out of date before the ink is dry!'

As the new finance manager, you are rather alarmed at the situation you have inherited: poor profitability and regular cash flow problems, partly as a result of the business being very seasonal, with most sales in the spring and summer. You feel that the business could be in danger of not surviving! Profit margins are very low (compared to the industry average) on most items sold, even though selling prices are similar to those of competitors.

Individual managers don't know exactly what is expected of them; consequently, each does whatever he/she thinks is appropriate. For example, although the production manager chats regularly to the sales manager, he is largely dismissive of the latter manager's views and therefore produces the amounts that he thinks are appropriate for each product. Similarly, the purchasing manager tends to buy the amount of raw materials he thinks appropriate, based on past experience of usage levels, rather than relying on forecasts by the production manager.

This lack of communication and coordination – together with the continuous low level of profit and occasions when the organisation almost runs out of cash – has led to a culture of cynicism and low morale. Some managers also feel that, while they are careful to avoid waste, others are wasteful, yet there is no positive recognition of those who behave in the organisation's best interest and no negative consequences for those who don't.

As the new finance manager, you should advise the management team how they might address the problems currently experienced, using the problem-solving method you were introduced to in Week 2 of the module and the material on budgeting presented in this week's readings.

The problem-solving method, you should recall, requires you to:

- identify the problem
- analyse the problem
- draw conclusions from your analysis
- propose a solution as a set of SMART recommendations
- acknowledge the strengths and weaknesses of your proposal
- identify any significant wider implications if your proposal were to be implemented.

If you would like to remind yourself of the elements of the problem-solving approach, you could re-read the section called Problem-solving and decision-making in *Tools and Techniques*.

You should apply this approach to problem-solving in the finance part of the module where appropriate, as in this activity. In order to focus on the finance concepts and principles, some problem situations will not require all six steps in the problem-solving process to be taken. In some, the problem may be identified for you; in others there may not be enough additional information for you to determine the wider implications of your proposed solution, or perhaps all the strengths and weaknesses of your proposal. So just address those parts of the problem-solving process that the information given and the nature of the particular problem situation allow.

Use Table 11.1 to record your output (you will be called upon to use this next week). Some questions and guidance to help you with your problem-solving are set out below.

First, you will need to identify the fundamental problem: what is the financial situation of the organisation? Then, you can start to analyse the problem: what reasons appear to be contributing to this situation? You should recognise a number of managerial issues, identified in the scenario, that are likely to contribute to the current financial situation of the business.

After completing the analysis, your conclusion should draw together the main points into a concluding statement. Do the reasons highlighted in your analysis have an underlying common theme? This conclusion should point the way to a specific solution, presented as a series of SMART recommendations. In making such recommendations, you should specify the sequence of actions that need to be taken, by whom and the timescale involved. As the finance manager, you are likely to be the prime mover in this process, but you will need support from the other managers and particularly from senior management.

Having made your recommendations, you should then identify the strengths of your proposal, how it will address the causes of the problem highlighted in your analysis. You should also acknowledge any weaknesses: what disadvantages may result for Garden Furnishings? Are the benefits likely to outweigh the costs (remember costs and benefits can be financial or non-financial)?

Finally, in considering the implications of your proposal, you should consider the impact your recommendations may have across the organisation: for example, is there likely to be a need for staff training? Is there likely to be resistance from certain vested interests who may be threatened by your proposal (and why)?

Table 11.1 Garden Furnishings: solving the problem

Problem identification
Analysis (investigation)
Conclusion to the analysis (results of the investigation)
The solution, listed as a set of SMART recommendations
Strengths and weaknesses of the recommendations
The implications of the solution, if implemented

This activity should have enabled you to link the various purposes of budgeting (coordination, control, communication, and so on) to the organisation's overall financial performance and situation. If so, then you clearly have a good understanding of the role of budgeting in managing organisations. You may have identified, for example, that the lack of co-ordination between functions (sales, production and purchasing) is likely to result in either running out of stock and lost sales or holding excessive stocks of finished goods or raw materials with money thereby invested in idle assets. There are a number of other issues highlighted in the Garden Furnishings' scenario which will also impact adversely on the financial situation of the organisation.

Activity 1 output

- *A completed version of Table 11.1 Garden Furnishings: solving the problem.*

Activity 2

Allow 3 hours for this activity.

This activity requires you to consider your own budgetary information requirements, in the organisation in which you work. (If you are not responsible for an aspect of the organisation's budget – a department or function, for example – consider the budgetary information requirements of your line manager/immediate boss.) The purpose of this activity is to provide you with an opportunity to apply to your own work context some of the ideas you have been studying. It will also serve as the basis for a full problem-based activity you will undertake next week.

What budget-related information is required by you/your line manager and for what purpose? In answering this question, think how the information could facilitate one or more of the five functions of budgets (communication, control, coordination etc.), and also how it contributes to one (or more) of the steps in the cycle of planning (preparation, authorisation, implementation, and so on).

For this activity you may have to do some research, which is why we have suggested you allow up to three hours for it. If you are responsible for an aspect of your organisation's budgeting you will need to recall and bring together all that you know about your budget, and what purposes it serves. If you are not responsible for any aspect of budgeting you will need to talk to your line manager or someone else who does have budgeting responsibility and get the required information from them.

Make brief notes summarising the budgetary information requirements and their purpose in a Word file with the title: Week 11 Activity 2 Budgetary information requirements. The note need be no longer than 400 words.

This activity may have made you think in a different way about budgeting in your organisation and how your role fits into the wider scheme of things. As you considered the various functions of budgeting, it hopefully became clear how budgeting links your/your department's activities to the organisations overall objectives. Budgetary planning and control are, therefore, an essential part of organisational management!

As you considered your/your line manager's budgetary information requirements, you may have been conscious of shortcomings in the information with respect to your needs. In Week 12, we will look at the practical issues involved in budgeting which can result in the sort of shortcomings that you have experienced.

Activity 2 output

- *A Word document noting your/your line manager's budgetary information requirements.*

Week 11 activity outputs

1 A completed version of Table 11.1 Garden Furnishings: solving the problem.

2 A Word document noting your/your line manager's budgetary information requirements.

Learning outcomes

After completing this set of activities and readings you should be able to:

- recognise the function that budgets play in the process of planning and control
- identify the procedures involved in preparing and using a budget
- apply these concepts to a case study and to their own organisation's budget.

Week 12 The practical use of budgets

Introduction

What are the practical issues that must be resolved in operating a budgeting system? Last week, you looked at the purpose and process of budgeting in fairly general terms. Now it is time to consider the detail: the practical issues involved in budgetary planning and control, including consideration of the 'human factor' – how budgets affect people and how people influence budgets. Budgeting is far from being a purely technical, financial exercise. An effective budgeting system must take into account human motivation and behaviour, including various budget 'games' that people play.

Week 12 activities

- Activity 1 Prepare a budget and discuss how budgets can be used to improve financial performance, based on a case. (Allow 4 hours for this activity.)
- Activity 2 Consider the application of budgets in your own organisation, identifying the practical problems arising. (Allow 3 hours for this activity.)

Readings

- Reading 1 Different approaches to budgeting
- Reading 2 Budgets and people

Readings 1 and 2

How are budget numbers established? Do we start with last year's figures and add a bit for inflation and any new activities, or do we start afresh each year and ask why we should spend anything at all on a particular item or how much expenditure (on say marketing or research and development) is necessary to achieve clearly specified individual goals? Reading 1, *Different approaches to budgeting,* discusses these alternative approaches to setting budgets and the different types of budget that result. Note that a choice is necessary as to whether budget figures, once set, should remain in force for the whole budget period (typically one year) or be adjusted to reflect changing circumstances. After completing this reading you should be aware of the alternative approaches to establishing budget figures that are used by different organisations and of their advantages and limitations.

Why is budgeting so problematic? Why does the process create so much ill will and resentment? What is required to get managers to take part in the budgeting process and then commit themselves wholeheartedly to achieving the targets set? Reading 2, *Budgets and people,* sets out how budgets are affected by people (and vice versa) – why they sometimes don't take responsibility for them, overestimate what they may need, fear them, try to use budgets to reflect their status, and so on. Note, in particular, that if managers are to commit themselves fully to the budgeting process, it may be appropriate to allow them to participate in setting the targets they are expected to achieve.

Activity 1

Allow 4 hours for this activity.

This activity requires you to prepare a budget for Garden Furnishings Ltd, the organisation you first encountered in Week 11, and use the information to suggest specific management actions that should be taken. The purpose is to demonstrate how the information derived from budgets can help managers to act to improve the financial situation and performance of the organisation. In Week 11, you identified problem areas where budgeting could help in managing Garden Furnishings. This enabled you to focus on the general principles of budgeting. This week's first activity requires you to actually prepare part of the budget for Garden Furnishings and suggest how the information in the budget can be used to guide management in taking specific actions.

As the new finance manager you decide to introduce a formal system of budgetary planning and control. First, you ask all the managers to attend a meeting to explain to them the advantages of budgeting. Then you work with each of them individually, gathering data to develop a detailed budget. You believe that the starting point should be the establishment of a sales budget, from which all other activities and expenditures follow. After compiling budgets for each functional area of the business – marketing, production, and so on – you have summarised these functional budgets in a master budget – see Table 12.1.

Step 1: From the master budget and additional information provided, you should now prepare a cash budget for the year. The template below (Table 12.2) provides you with the structure and content of the cash budget – all you have to do is fill in the numbers.

Step 2: When you have constructed the cash budget, suggest how the specific information now available (in the master budget and cash budget) might be used by the managers at Garden Furnishings to improve the financial performance and situation of the organisation. In doing so, you should think back to Week 11, to some of the issues that arose in Garden Furnishings as a result of not having budget information: which ones could be addressed by the information now available?

Record your thoughts and ideas briefly in a Word document of approximately 400 words, with the title: Week 12 Activity 1 Use of budget information.

Step 3: Then, post the contents of this Word document in a message to your activity forum (or attach the document to your message).

Table 12.1 Master budget for Garden Furnishings Ltd for financial year ended 20XX

	Q1	Q2	Q3	Q4	Total
Sales revenue	£216,000	£616,000	£924,000	£324,000	£2,080,000
Materials cost	£36,000	£84,000	£126,000	£54,000	£300,000
Labour cost	£72,000	£168,000	£252,000	£108,000	£600,000
Electricity and consumables	£19,200	£44,800	£67,200	£28,800	£160,000
Rent and insurance	£65,000	£65,000	£65,000	£65,000	£260,000
Cost of goods sold	£192,200	£361,800	£510,200	£255,800	£1,320,000
Gross profit	£23,800	£254,200	£413,800	£68,200	£760,000
Selling costs	£21,600	£64,800	£86,400	£43,200	£216,000
Admin costs	£85,000	£86,900	£122,750	£103,150	£397,800
Net profit/(loss)	£(82,800)	£102,500	£204,650	£(78,150)	£146,200

The following additional information is provided to enable you to convert the information concerning revenue earned and expenses incurred in the master budget, to cash inflows and outflows in the cash budget. The reason for preparing a cash budget is that cash is not usually received or paid out in the same month that sales are made (revenues earned) or expenses incurred.

1 Completed goods are sold in the same period in which they are produced. Customers are large stores who have a considerable degree of market power and do not pay smaller businesses promptly. Consequently, about 60% of sales revenue earned is received in the same quarter that sales are made, while the other 40% is received in the next quarter.
2 Materials are used in the same quarter in which they are purchased. Garden Furnishings must pay suppliers promptly to ensure continuity of supply and maintenance of credit terms; consequently 80% of the cost of materials purchases is paid to creditors in the same quarter that purchases are made; the remaining 20% is paid in the next quarter.
3 All other expenses are paid for in the same quarter in which they are incurred.
4 Opening balances for the year are:

Debtors	£120,000
Creditors	£12,000
Cash	£5,000

Currently the firm does not have an overdraft facility available.

Note: Very simply put, creditors are people to whom you owe money. Debtors are people who owe money to you.

Table 12.2 Template for cash budget

	Q1	Q2	Q3	Q4	Total
Receipts:					
Customer balance brought forward plus 60% of quarter's sales					
Payments:					
Suppliers balance brought forward plus 80% of quarter's purchases					
Labour					
Electricity and consumables					
Rent and insurance					
Selling costs					
Administration costs					
Total payments:					
Opening balance					
Net in/(out) flow					
Closing balance					

Congratulations on working through your first set of numerical calculations in the finance part of this module! If your calculations are correct, they will provide some very significant results which the Garden Furnishings management must act on. Importantly, we hope you were able to link the numbers in the master and cash budgets to some of the problems that are contributing to Garden Furnishings financial situation. If you were able to recognise these links you are well on your way to understanding budgeting!

Activity 1 outputs

- *A completed version of Table 12.2 Template for cash budget.*
- *A Word document discussing practical application of master and cash budget information to problems of Garden Furnishings.*
- *A contribution to this week's activity forum to include the contents of the Word document.*

Activity 2

Allow 3 hours for this activity.

This activity will help you to consider the adequacy of the budgeting system in your own organisation. The purpose is to reveal the difficulties that arise in operating a budgeting system in practice. In Week 11 Activity 2 you looked at the budgetary information supplied to you or your line manager and identified the purpose for which it was supplied. The various practical issues of budgeting that you have considered this week imply that no budgeting system is likely to be perfect.

- Assess whether the budgetary information you (or your line manager) are provided with is completely satisfactory and if not (as is likely to be the case) make recommendations as to how the situation could be improved.

- Use Table 12.3 to record your output. You first need to specify exactly what the limitations of the information received are. Is it, for example, the budget targets you are responsible for? Or, perhaps, that the control information you receive as feedback does not, for some reason, allow you to take the necessary corrective action?

You will then need to investigate: what are the reasons for the situation; who is responsible? After drawing your conclusions, suggest a possible remedy presented as a set of SMART recommendations. You should identify the strengths and acknowledge the possible weaknesses of your proposal, together with its wider implications – who will be affected and how?

Table 12.3 Resolving a budget information problem

Problem identification
Analysis (investigation)
Conclusion to the analysis (results of the investigation)
The solution, listed as a set of SMART recommendations
Strengths and weaknesses of the recommendations
The implications of the solution, if implemented

You may not previously have considered the causes of the limitations of the budgetary system in your organisation and how these may be addressed. If this is the case, this activity should have provided you with valuable insights. Whatever the problem you identified, it is likely to be one that is experienced in many other organisations. Budgeting is more of an art than a science and, as a result, there are many opportunities for organisations to make a less than perfect job of it!

Activity 2 output

- *A completed version of Table 12.3 Resolving a budget information problem.*

Week 12 activity outputs

1 A completed version of Table 12.2 Template for cash budget.

2 A Word document discussing practical application of master and cash budget information to the problems of Garden Furnishings.

3 A contribution to this week's activity forum based on the discussion in the Word document.

4 A completed version of Table 12.3 Resolving a budget information problem.

Learning outcomes

After completing this set of activities and readings you should be able to:

- identify the different budgeting bases used in practice (incremental, zero base, fixed, flexible and rolling bases)
- recognise the implications of the severity of budget targets for motivation and performance
- understand the impact of participation in setting budget targets on motivation and performance
- recognise how senior management's attitude towards failure to achieve budget targets can influence behaviour (in both desirable and undesirable ways).

Week 13 Measuring costs in organisations

Introduction

What are costs and what types of cost are there? You have now seen that managers need information, including cost information for planning, control and decision-making. For these management activities, it will often be necessary to group individual costs together into appropriate categories. For example, into those which can be directly traced to a particular product or service and those which cannot, or those which vary directly with the level of output and those which do not do so. To be effective in planning, control and decision-making, managers need a good understanding of the ways in which costs can be categorised and of the significance of the distinctions between the different categories.

So, this week you will start by looking at the ways in which costs can be categorised for planning, control and decision-making purposes. You will then look at a widely used business planning and decision-making tool: break-even analysis. This tool is concerned with analysing how costs (and hence profits) change as the level of output changes. To apply this tool, it is first necessary to separate an organisation's costs into those that are 'fixed' and those which are 'variable' – these terms will be explained in the first reading for this week.

Week 13 activities

- Activity 1 Perform an analysis of costs for your own organisation (or own department within the organisation, if appropriate). (Allow 3 hours for this activity.)
- Activity 2 Perform a break-even analysis, based on a case, and advise the business owner on 'marketing mix' decisions. (Allow 4 hours for this activity.)

Readings

- Reading 1 Introduction to cost concepts
- Reading 2 Contribution
- Reading 3 Break-even analysis

Reading 1

What exactly does the term 'cost' mean? What are the different types of cost and why is it necessary to classify costs into different categories? This reading discusses the main categories into which costs can be classified. Make sure you understand the difference between fixed and variable cost and between direct and indirect cost. As you read, try to think why it may be necessary to group various individual cost items together into these cost categories, perhaps by relating them to your own work experience. Note carefully the important concept of a 'cost object'. It is necessary to be clear about what the cost object is, before any of the cost categories discussed have any real meaning. When you have completed this reading, you should have a good understanding of the basic cost concepts used for planning, control and decision-making purposes.

Activity 1

Allow 3 hours for this activity.

This week's first reading has introduced you to some important cost concepts. This week's first activity requires you to apply the cost concepts to your own organisation (or your own department within the organisation, if you are too remote from some areas of the organisation to be able to obtain the necessary information). In many cases, this means that you will have to do some research about costs in your organisation and department, perhaps by asking one of the organisation's accountants or other managers. This activity should help you to understand better the nature of costs in your own organisation. Such an understanding will be necessary for two activities you will encounter in later weeks involving cost management and decision-making.

Your organisation or department presumably exists to provide some sort of product or service. What is the principal product or service provided? This product or service can be thought of as a 'cost object' – an entity to which costs relate.

Identify the main elements of cost in your organisation (or department) and then classify each element as:

- Firstly, either direct or indirect (ask yourself whether each cost identified is incurred directly as a result of producing the product/providing the service, or whether it is part of the infrastructure resources necessary to enable the organisation to exist or function efficiently)

and then

- fixed or variable (ask yourself whether producing one more unit of the product or service would cause each element of cost to change) with respect to the 'cost object' concerned.

(Remember: these categories are alternative ways of categorising the same elements of cost, so that any particular cost will be variable or fixed *and* direct or indirect).

There is no template for this activity. Record the details of your cost analysis in a Word file with the title: Week 13 Activity 1 – Analysis of costs in my organisation. Post a summary of the document (you may wish to send the document itself as an attachment) to this week's activity forum and review the summaries sent by others. You should identify the type of organisation for which you work (i.e. a manufacturing company, a service company, a charity, a public sector department, etc.). Note how the organisations of other students differ from your own in what is included in these cost categories. Have other students classified similar cost items in the same way? If not can the difference be understood in terms of the type of organisation concerned?

Activity 1 outputs

- *A Word document containing a classification of your organisation's costs.*
- *A contribution to this week's activity forum containing a summary of the Word document.*

Readings 2 and 3

Why is it necessary to separate costs according to whether they are fixed or variable? When planning and making decisions, managers often need to know how costs change as the level of the organisation's output changes. This will make it necessary to separate costs into those which are 'fixed' (and don't change as the level of output changes) and those which are 'variable' (and do change as the level of output changes). This analysis of costs makes it possible to, for example, determine the level of sales necessary to avoid making losses, or to earn a specific amount of profit/ surplus; it also facilitates the exploration of various planning scenarios, such as the effect of changing various elements of the 'marketing mix' – price, promotion, and so on. These tasks require an analysis of costs into those which are fixed and those which are variable, in order to calculate the amount of contribution resulting from a particular level of sales. Reading 2, *Contribution,* discusses the way this important concept is applied in planning and decision-making. Pay particular attention to the idea of the contribution to sales ratio and also the idea of operational gearing – and its significance in evaluating the risk associated with an organisation. As you read, try to think of ways in which the concept of contribution may be relevant to planning and decision-making in your own organisation.

Having considered the need for classifying costs according to whether they are fixed or variable and the important concept of contribution, you should be ready to apply these ideas to business planning and decision-making problems. Reading 3, *Break-even analysis,* considers an important planning, decision-making and risk management tool. As you read, think about how cost information and break-even analysis can be used to consider a whole range of different options on which to base a decision. Break-even analysis can be especially useful for supporting marketing decisions. For example, what would be the impact of increased advertising expenditure (an increase in fixed cost) on the break-even point or the level of sales necessary to achieve a particular profit target? Similarly, what would be the impact on the break-even point and profit of a reduction in selling price (a reduction in contribution per unit)? Remember also that, although a useful tool, break-even analysis has a number of limitations, which should be borne in mind in applying it. After completion of Readings 2 and 3, you should have a good understanding of why costs need to be analysed according to whether they are fixed or variable and of the significance of the concept of 'contribution' in planning and decision-making.

Activity 2

Allow 4 hours for this activity.

This activity requires you to perform a break-even analysis for a multi-product firm, calculating break-even points under a number of alternative scenarios. The purpose is to illustrate how break-even analysis can be applied in a range of business planning and decision-making situations: in this case selecting the best 'marketing mix' in order to improve profitability. You were introduced to the concept of the marketing mix in the marketing part of this module; break-even analysis enables you to evaluate some financial implications of variations in this mix.

Ray McNeil Restaurants

Ray McNeil runs a chain of restaurants. Ray is concerned that the business is not very profitable and that all the restaurants continue to operate with considerable spare capacity – the number of meals served having remained fairly constant for a number of years. Ray has prepared the following monthly budget for the business, based on past experience. He considers all costs other than food ingredients for meals to be effectively fixed costs – this assumption being reflected in the structure of his budget, shown in Table 13.1.

Table 13.1 Budget for year 1 January to 31 December 20XX

	Meal type					
	Roast	**Curry**	**Seafood**	**Salad**	**Dessert**	**Drink**
Selling price	£15	£12	£25	£10	£6	£2.0
Cost of ingredients	£3	£4	£9	£2	£1	£0.5
Contribution per meal	£12	£8	£16	£8	£5	£1.5
Average number served per month	15,000	16,000	4,000	7,000	18,000	90,000
Total contribution per meal type	£180,000	£128,000	£64,000	£56,000	£90,000	£135,000
Total contribution						= £653,000
Fixed costs						= £600,000
Net profit per month						£53,000

You have been consulted to advise Ray on how he might improve the business's profitability. From your many years of experience in the industry, you believe that a price reduction of 20% for all meals and drinks would increase the number of meals and drinks sold by 50%. Alternatively, a monthly advertising campaign on local radio stations and in cinemas and newspapers, costing £60,000 per month, is expected to increase the number of meals and drinks sold by 15% – while maintaining prices at their current levels. (It will be necessary to contract for a minimum of 12 months with the parties concerned in arranging advertising.)

Advise Ray what to do, having regard to both the profitability and the risk of the various options.

Use Table 13.2 to record your output. You will need to start by doing some calculations, both as part of the problem analysis and also as a basis for making recommendations as to how the situation can be improved. You will need to calculate break-even revenues for each of the scenarios: existing, with price reduction, with advertising campaign (refer again, if necessary, to the text for an explanation of how to do break-even calculations for a multi-product organisation). What does the break-even calculation under the existing scenario tell you about the nature of the business's problem? Which of the alternative scenarios produces a higher profit? Which has the higher risk (as indicated by the break-even level of sales)? Based on these considerations, you will need to make SMART recommendations for improving the business's profitability. What are the strengths and weaknesses of your proposal?

Table 13.2 Advice for improving profitability

Problem identification
Analysis (investigation)
Conclusion to the analysis (results of the investigation)
The solution, listed as a set of SMART recommendations
Strengths and weaknesses of the recommendations

This activity has hopefully shown how useful break-even analysis can be in evaluating business plans in terms of their potential profitability and associated risk. You may have noticed that the most profitable of the options is also the most risky, as indicated by the highest break-even point. Managerial judgement is therefore required in selecting the best course of action. Break-even analysis can't provide the final answers to business problems, but it can provide a framework for systematically considering the alternatives. While this particular activity has involved considering variations in the marketing mix, break-even analysis can be usefully applied to most business decisions that involve variations in fixed costs, variable costs or price. For example, should we buy a new machine (increasing fixed costs) in order to increase productivity (reducing variable costs)?

Activity 2 output

- *A completed version of Table 13.2 Advice for improving profitability.*

Week 13 activity outputs

1 A Word document noting own organisation's cost categories.

2 A contribution to this week's activity forum containing a summary of the Word document.

3 A completed version of Table 13.2 Advice for improving profitability.

Learning outcomes

After completing this set of activities and readings you should be able to:

- understand the fundamental cost concepts and their relevance for planning, control and decision-making
- recognise the importance of 'contribution' in planning and decision-making
- identify the break-even level of output and explore various 'what if' scenarios applying break-even analysis.

Week 14 Costing products and services

Introduction

What are overheads and how do they influence costs? You have now seen that managers need information, including cost information, for planning, control and decision-making. An important role of the finance function is providing managers with information about the cost of producing a particular product or providing a particular service. You have seen that 'cost' can be defined and measured in different ways (that is, marginal or absorption costing). The contribution approach (or marginal costing) is appropriate for special circumstances, but has dangers if used for regular decision-making. There is a danger that any action producing a positive contribution will be considered acceptable. This is likely to result in fixed costs not being covered in full in the prices charged to customers. Also, in the longer term, the level of many fixed costs can be adjusted to the level of output and so do need to be taken into account in decision-making. This week, therefore, you will look in more detail at absorption costing, which seeks to establish the 'full' cost of a product or service (including both the variable costs and a share of the fixed costs).

Week 14 activities

- Activity 1 Ascertain business segment profitability, based on a case, using traditional and activity based costing approaches. (Allow 2 hours for this activity.)
- Activity 2 Advise a business owner, based on a case, on how he can further improve profitability using an appropriate method of cost analysis. (Allow 2 hours for this activity.)
- Activity 3 Identify the main cost drivers in your own organisation or department. (Allow 3 hours for this activity.)

Readings

- Reading 1 Charging indirect costs to cost objects
- Reading 2 Activity based costing

Readings 1 and 2

Is determining the cost of making a particular product (or providing a particular service) straightforward? If not, what are the consequences or possible dangers that managers need to be aware of? Reading 1, *Charging indirect costs to cost objects,* discusses the problem of assigning overhead costs to particular products and the traditional approach to dealing with this problem. Study carefully the example of the Woodhouse Carpentry Business in order to understand the conventional approach to dealing with the problem of assigning indirect costs to products. Note how the problem is dealt with where more than one product is produced. Make sure you understand the four steps involved in charging overhead costs to products. Pay particular attention to the discussion of how a production overhead charge is calculated and applied to the products produced. The Woodhouse Carpentry example employs a 'units' approach to charging overhead costs to products, whereby overhead cost is assumed to be determined by the number of units produced. Alternative bases are also widely used to calculate the production overhead charge, including the number of direct labour hours worked, the number of machine hours worked and the direct materials cost. Note finally that *the choice* of how to charge overhead costs to products can have important consequences (good or bad). After completion of this reading, you should have a good understanding of how product costs are conventionally estimated, particularly with regard to the problem of assigning indirect (overhead) costs to products.

What are the weaknesses of the traditional absorption costing approach – and what are the implications of having inaccurate product costs? Reading 2, *Activity based costing,* discusses the principles of a comparatively new approach and how it attempts to deal with the weaknesses of the traditional approach to product (or service) costing. Note, in particular, that the conventional absorption costing approach assumes that the overhead cost of a product depends on its volume: the number of units produced or something closely related to this, such as the number of direct labour hours or machine hours consumed. Activity based costing, in contrast, recognises that the overhead cost of a product or service is not necessarily related to its volume. This is the central message of the example in the text.

Activity 1

Allow 2 hours for this activity.

In addition to calculating product costs, the alternative costing approaches you have considered can be applied to the allocation of indirect costs to different customers or to different business or market segments, in order to determine the financial performance of each. This activity involves looking at a practical example of charging overhead costs to different business segments, in this case different retail stores owned by a company. The activity does not require *you* to calculate the overhead costs to be assigned to each store; instead it takes you step by step through the process, showing you how overhead costs are assigned to a cost object (in this case a particular retail store). This activity will, however, require you to interpret and comment on the results; this will demonstrate the importance of assigning indirect costs correctly!

Step 1: Read the worked example of cost allocation below carefully.

Portal Group

Portal Group owns three retail stores. The most recent summarised financial results for the stores are as shown in Table 14.1.

Table 14.1 Store operating profit analysis

	£(000s)			
	Deptford	**Catford**	**Lewisham**	**Total**
Sales	10,000	8,000	6,000	24,000
Cost of goods sold	5,600	4,600	3,800	14,000
Gross profit	4,400	3,400	2,200	10,000
Store operating expenses	2,720	2,660	1,620	7,000
Operating profit	1,680	740	580	3,000

In addition to its direct operating expenses, each store consumes a proportion of central warehousing and head office resources. Currently, these costs are all charged to retail stores in proportion to their sales value (the 'output volume' in the context of the traditional absorption costing approach).

The central costs are as shown in Table 14.2:

Table 14.2 Central costs

	£(000s)
Storage	360
Operations and despatch	240
Delivery	600
Head Office salaries	400
Advertising	160
Total central costs	1,760

The absorption costing approach to charging central costs to retail stores

Using the current absorption costing approach, how will the central costs be allocated to each store and what will the resulting net profit figure be for each store?

Using this approach, the central overhead cost consumed by each store is assumed to depend on the level of sales. The relationship between central costs and sales value can be derived as follows:

Total central cost = (£1,760k) x 100 = 7.33% of sales value

Total sales value of stores = (£24,000k)

Consequently, the central overhead cost charged to each store will be 7.33% of the store's sales value, as shown in Table 14.3.

Table 14.3 Central costs allocation

	£(000s)			
	Deptford	**Catford**	**Lewisham**	**Total**
Sales value	10,000	8,000	6,000	24,000
Central overhead = (@7.33% of sales = value)	733	587	440	1,760

Store profitability analysis

Having determined the central overhead charge for each store, the store's profitability can then be ascertained, as shown in Table 14.4.

Table 14.4 Store profitability using absorption costing

	£(000s)			
	Deptford	**Catford**	**Lewisham**	**Total**
Store operating profit	1,680	740	580	3,000
Central overhead charge	733	587	440	1,760
Net profit	947	153	140	1,240

The activity based costing approach to charging central costs to stores

What is different about the activity based approach to charging central costs to the retail stores? With this approach, it is recognised that different elements of the central costs are caused by different activities (not necessarily sales volume). Consequently, the total central overhead charge to each store must be built up in stages. How does this process operate?

Firstly, the 'cost driver' (the determinant of the level of cost) for each element of central overhead must be identified. Assume that the accountant has identified these as follows.

Table 14.5 Cost drivers for each element of central costs

Cost	**Cost driver**
Storage cost	Storage space
Operations and despatch	Number of despatches
Deliveries	Number of delivery miles
Head Office salaries	Number of stores
Advertising	Sales value

Assume also, that the accountant has ascertained each store's consumption of each 'cost driver' as shown in Table 14.6.

Table 14.6 Store consumption of cost drivers

	Deptford	Catford	Lewisham	Total
Storage space (square metres)	40,000	30,000	30,000	100,000
Number of despatches	550	450	520	1,520
Total delivery (miles)	70,000	50,000	90,000	210,000
Number of stores	1	1	1	3
Sales value £(000s)	10,000	8,000	6,000	24,000

It is then possible to calculate charge rates for each cost driver in order to charge each store according to its consumption of the cost driver, see Table 14.7.

Table 14.7 Cost driver charge rates

Cost driver	Calculation	Charge rate
Storage space	£360,000/100,000 square metres	£3.60 per square metre
Number of despatches	£240,000/1,520 despatches	£157.90 per despatch
Number of delivery miles	£600,000/210,000 delivery miles	£2.86 per mile
Number of stores	£400,000/3 stores	£133,333.33 per store
Sales value	£160,000/£24,000,000	0.67% of sales value

These cost driver charge rates can then be used to charge the various elements of central overhead cost to stores, as shown in Table 14.8. (Some of the numbers given are approximations, reflecting rounding adjustments.)

Table 14.8 Allocation of central costs using cost drivers

Cost element	Deptford	Catford	Lewisham
Storage	40,000 x £3.6	30,000 x £3.6	30,000 x £3.6
=	£144,000	£108,000	£108,000
Operations and despatch	550 x £157.90	450 x £157.90	520 x £157.90
=	£86,843	£71,053	£82,104
Delivery	70,000 x £2.86	50,000 x £2.86	90,000 x £2.86
=	£200,000	£143,000	£257,000
Head Office salaries	1 x £133,333.33	1 x £133,333.33	1 x £133,333.33
=	£133,333	£133,333	£133,334
Advertising	0.67% x £10m	0.67% x £8m	0.67% x £6m
=	£67,000	£53,000	£40,000
Total overhead =	£631,176	£508,386	£620,438

Store profitability analysis

Having determined the total central overhead charge for each store, the store's profitability can then be ascertained, as shown in Table 14.9.

Table 14.9 Store profitability analysis using activity based costing

	£(000s)			
	Deptford	**Catford**	**Lewisham**	**Total**
Store operating profit	1,680	740	580	3,000
Central overhead charge	631	508	621	1,760
Net profit	1,049	232	(41)	1,240

Step 2: Now that you have the comparative figures for retail store profitability using the two alternative approaches, comment on the results: are they significantly different? If so, why? What are the implications for managerial decision-making?

Record your comments in a Word document with the title Week 14 Activity 1 – Comparison of alternative costing approaches. Post your comments to this week's activity forum and compare with those of other students.

We hope that this activity has helped to make clear just how much difference the choice of costing method can make and the likely implications for managerial decision-making. You have probably noticed, for example, that dramatic, urgent action appears necessary regarding one of the stores, but this was not revealed by the absorption costing approach. The activity also provides a good example of how activity based costing can be extended, beyond product costing, to the evaluation of customers, markets and (as in this case) business segments.

Activity 1 outputs

- *A Word document containing comments on the results and implications of alternative costing approaches.*
- *A contribution to this week's activity forum summarising your comments.*

Activity 2

Allow 2 hours for this activity.

This activity requires you to examine the fixed costs of Ray's restaurant business (first introduced in Week 13 Activity 2) and to suggest how an understanding of these costs can help to further improve the business's profitability. The activity is designed to show the importance, for decision-making, of understanding the cost drivers in an organisation.

Last week you looked at how the profitability of the business might be improved by varying the elements of the marketing mix. This was on the assumption that all the existing costs other than food ingredients were fixed and would not vary according to the decision alternative chosen. Now, in this activity, you are required to consider how certain of the existing fixed costs might vary, according to the decision alternative chosen. The activity does not require you to perform any calculations, but to advise Ray how a careful analysis of fixed costs might help him improve profitability.

Ray McNeil Restaurants

Continuing in your role as Ray's consultant, you decide to take the financial analysis of Ray's business one stage further and start to examine the so-called 'fixed costs' in Ray's budget – having noticed that these are much higher than the total variable cost of meals (i.e. food ingredients).

You are able to ascertain that the figure for monthly fixed costs consists of:

Table 14.10 Analysis of fixed costs

Rents and council taxes	80,000
Heat and light	20,000
Insurance	20,000
Cleaning	15,000
Purchasing	100,000
Staff training	25,000
Supervision	50,000
Baking (inc. gas and electricity for kitchen equipment)	80,000
Salaries for kitchen staff	100,000
Salaries for waiters	60,000
Central admin (bookkeeping, payroll, etc.)	50,000
Total	600,000

You discover that, although these costs are not variable in the sense of being directly proportional to the number of meals served, the consumption of many of these resources varies considerably between different menu items. For example, the oven must be switched on for baking and used for a specific period of time whether a batch of 12 or 50 meals is being prepared. The Seafood Special is produced in batches of 12, whereas curry is produced in batches of 50. (Because sales demand is uncertain and meal preparation often takes a considerable time, the restaurant produces meals in batches based on expected demand.)

Purchasing of food ingredients is a major operation, involving substantial administrative costs. Purchase orders must be raised and placed with suppliers, whether large or small amounts of ingredients are being purchased with the order. The ingredients for Seafood Special are purchased in much smaller quantities, both because they cannot be stored as they are perishable, and due to the fact that fewer such meals are served. The business does not hold large amounts of stock, as there are considerable costs involved in holding stock such as warehousing, security, interest on funds tied up. (This topic, the need to control items of working capital such as stock, will be covered in

Week 17 of this module.) There is considerable variation in the relative consumption of the purchasing function resource among the other products, too.

Staff training costs are significant because kitchen staff turnover is high and it is necessary for kitchen staff to know how to prepare all of the meals on the menu. The amount of staff training necessary varies across meals. For example, the Seafood Special is much more complicated to prepare than the salad. In addition to higher training costs, kitchen staff time required to prepare the Seafood Special is also, therefore, greater in proportion to the number of meals served.

Advise Ray how he might further improve the profitability of the restaurant business. Use Table 14.11 to record your output. In working through this activity, remember the key point from Reading 2 is that some products (or business segments) consume disproportionately (to their volume) large amounts of overhead cost. This fact is not reflected in the traditional marginal or absorption costing approaches. These traditional approaches can therefore result in inaccurate product (or business segment) costs and incorrect business decisions. In your problem analysis, you may find it useful to refer back to Table 13.1, in Week 13 Activity 2, which shows the apparent profitability of the various product lines using the current approach to cost analysis (which you should now recognise as the marginal costing approach).

Table 14.11 Further advice for improving profitability

Problem identification
Analysis (investigation)
Conclusion to the analysis (results of the investigation)
The solution, listed as a set of SMART recommendations
Strengths and weaknesses of the recommendations

Working through this activity should have demonstrated how an understanding of cost drivers can facilitate improved decision-making in an organisation, resulting in better financial performance. An important point that may have occurred to you, in undertaking this activity, is that a simple analysis of costs as either 'fixed' or 'variable' may be inadequate for understanding the behaviour of costs in an organisation. This point will be developed in the next activity, which requires you to undertake an analysis of cost behaviour in your own organisation.

Activity 2 output

- *A completed version of Table 14.11 Further advice for improving profitability.*

Activity 3

Allow 3 hours for this activity.

In Week 13 Activity 1, you identified your organisation's (or department's) main indirect costs. This week's final activity requires you to consider the cost drivers of these indirect costs. The purpose is to highlight how an understanding of cost drivers can improve decision-making or cost management, in a context with which you are familiar.

Identify a decision-making or cost management problem in your organisation (or department) which could be addressed by a better knowledge of the cost drivers. Make recommendations as to how, using the appropriate cost driver information, the problem could be solved.

Use Table 14.12 to record your output. Think about each of the various indirect costs you have identified and try to identify the cost driver for each one. Is it the volume of output (number of units of a product or service produced), or some other activity not necessarily related to the volume of output? Having identified the cost drivers, think how this knowledge could help in making decisions or managing costs and make recommendations accordingly.

Table 14.12 Application of cost driver information in my organisation

Problem identification
Analysis (investigation)
Conclusion to the analysis (results of the investigation)
The solution, listed as a set of SMART recommendations
Strengths and weaknesses of the recommendations
The implications of the solution, if implemented

In working through the activity, you may well have obtained insights which could be extremely useful for the management of your organisation. Unless your organisation is one of the very few that have attained perfection, it is likely that there is plenty of scope for improving the understanding of cost cause and effect relationships and thereby improving management decision-making and cost control. The cost driver concept is based on the identification of such relationships.

Activity 3 output

- *A completed version of Table 14.12 Application of cost driver information in my organisation.*

Week 14 activity outputs

1. A Word document containing comments on the results of alternative costing approaches.
2. A contribution to this week's activity forum summarising your comments.
3. A completed version of Table 14.11 Further advice for improving profitability.
4. A completed version of Table 14.12 Application of cost driver information in my organisation.

Learning outcomes

After completing this set of activities and readings you should be able to:

- recognise the need for product or service cost information
- understand the difficulties of estimating product or service costs – and in particular the cost of various overhead resources consumed by a product or service
- identify an organisation's main cost drivers and be able to apply this knowledge to an analysis of business problems
- identify costs attributable to different business segments using traditional and activity based costing approaches.

Week 15 Financial decision-making

Introduction

What other decisions require cost information and which costs should be included in these decisions? This week you will look at the characteristics of relevant costs and at some decision-making situations which require an analysis of relevant costs.

Decision-making involves comparing the costs and benefits of alternative courses of action. It is important for managers to understand which costs are relevant to a particular decision and which are not. The identification of relevant costs is necessary for making decisions not only in 'for-profit' organisations, but in all organisations, including 'not-for-profit' organisations. For example, managers in local government sometimes have to consider subcontracting out various services to private firms, in order to reduce costs. Managers in voluntary organisations must decide whether or not to undertake particular projects.

Increasingly, organisations must take into account the environmental and ethical implications of their actions. Organisations of all types, including 'for-profit' organisations, are beginning to place carbon reduction and climate change at the top of their agenda. There is increasing pressure from legislation and from various stakeholders to address climate change issues.

Many organisations are also now including ethical goals in their strategy formulation and decision-making processes. Ethics is the application of values such as honesty and fairness to organisational behaviour; it's about how an organisation conducts itself. Ethical standards are often set out in an organisational code of ethics or conduct. A commitment to high standards of ethics involves formally incorporating ethical objectives in organisational decision-making. Virtually all organisations, however, face financial constraints, so that a financial analysis of costs and benefits must be part of the decision-making process.

Week 15 activities

- Activity 1 Advise a local government authority whether to outsource the maintenance of local parks and gardens, based on a case. (Allow 2 hours for this activity.)
- Activity 2 Consider the appropriateness of absorption costing and marginal costing approaches to establishing selling prices, based on a case. (Allow 2 hours for this activity.)
- Activity 3 Revise concepts and methods so far. (Allow 3 hours for this activity.)

Readings

- Reading 1 Identifying relevant costs and making financial decisions
- Reading 2 Different types of decisions using relevant costs
- Reading 3 Cost information in pricing decisions

Readings 1 and 2

Why do finance people talk about 'different costs for different purposes'? Why might 'cost' be measured differently for reporting to outside stakeholders (for example shareholders) and for internal decision-making? Reading 1, *Identifying relevant costs and making financial decisions*, discusses the concept of relevant costs for making financial decisions and how such costs can be identified. In Example 15.1 in the text, 'Imelda's Choice', the difference between the (external) financial reporting approach and the (internal decision-making) relevant cost approach is considered. Pay particular attention to the various types of relevant and non relevant costs (for example opportunity costs and sunk costs) that must be considered as part of the financial aspect of decision-making. After considering the example of Imelda's Choice and the various types of relevant/non-relevant cost, look at Example 15.2, The Dream Machine, in the text.

What are the various types of decisions for which an analysis of relevant costs is likely to be necessary? Reading 2, *Different types of decisions using relevant costs*, discusses the types of decisions that commonly require relevant cost analysis. You will notice that one of the decision types identified is an outsourcing decision. This type of decision is the subject of this week's first activity. Notice, however, that in each of the decision types identified in the text, the principle of relevant cost analysis is the same: asking whether a particular cost would change depending on the alternative chosen? After reading these sections, you should have a good understanding of how to decide which costs are relevant to a particular decision-making situation and of the typical decision-making situations that require an analysis of relevant costs.

Activity 1

Allow 2 hours for this activity.

This activity requires you to advise a local government authority whether to use an outside organisation to provide services currently provided by the local government authority, based on an analysis of relevant costs of the alternatives. The purpose of this activity is to demonstrate the wide applicability of the principle of relevant cost, across all sectors, including not-for-profit organisations.

This week's first two readings explained how 'relevant cost' analysis is used for making various types of decisions. Relevant cost analysis is often used for making pricing decisions, for example, deciding whether the market price is sufficient to cover the relevant costs of providing a product or service and produce an acceptable profit/surplus – as will be discussed later in Reading 3 for this week. Alternatively, such an analysis can be used to compare the costs of providing goods or services internally with the price of obtaining those goods or services externally, as is the case with this week's first activity.

Rampsley Public Works Department

Rampsley local government authority, as part of its urgent cost-cutting procedures, is considering outsourcing certain functions to private contractors. It is proposed that in three years' time there will be a major restructuring of local government and new funding arrangements. Until then, it is essential that the local authority reduces its costs to be able to operate within its budgeted funding. Consequently the local authority is only concerned with a three-year time horizon for planning and decision-making.

One function being considered for outsourcing is the parks and gardens maintenance operations, currently provided by the Public Works Department of the local government authority.

As the Chief Financial Officer, you should evaluate the proposal to outsource this function and make recommendations, explaining your reasons, for how the parks and gardens maintenance service should be provided for the next three years. You should also indicate (if appropriate) how and why your recommendations might be different if you were considering a longer time horizon.

The local government authority's finance department has provided you with the following information to facilitate your financial analysis. The current estimated total cost per year of the parks and gardens maintenance operation, as recorded by the local authority's accounting system for financial reporting purposes, is as follows:

Table 15.1 Estimated cost per year of parks and gardens maintenance

	£
Staff	1,200,000
Insurance (equipment)	30,000
Equipment maintenance	25,000
Supplies (fertilisers etc.)	250,000
Fuel	300,000
Administration	275,000
Depreciation on equipment	125,000
Total per year	2,205,000

The staff cost is made up as follows:

- £300,000 represents temporary seasonal staff hired on weekly contracts

- £500,000 represents the cost of permanent staff who would be reemployed by the private contractor as part of the outsourcing deal, if the operation is subcontracted out
- £400,000 represents staff which would be reallocated to other tasks within the local government authority's Public Works Department.

The equipment insurance contract is such that one year's notice of termination is required. The charge for administration largely reflects services provided by other departments – e.g. finance, human resources – that would probably remain fully staffed even if the parks and gardens maintenance operation were outsourced. Currently, however, the administration cost also includes the cost of a manager within the Public Works Department, who is exclusively concerned with the parks and gardens maintenance operation. The cost of employing this manager is £45,000 per year. This individual has a clause in his employment contract that he must be paid a full year's salary in the event of his employment being terminated.

The equipment and tools used were all replaced with new items two years ago for £1,250,000 and are expected to last for ten years. This is reflected in the annual depreciation charge of £125,000. Because of its specialised nature, there is a very limited market for resale; it is estimated that the current market value is £250,000.

The private contractor has offered to perform the service for £1,750,000 per year; this price would be guaranteed for three years. In addition, it would cost the local authority £100,000 per year to administer the contract. For the purpose of this activity, ignore general inflation and possible salary increases.

Task

Use Table 15.2 to record your output. You will need to start your problem analysis by doing some calculations: what would be the savings, if any, from outsourcing the maintenance operation? You will need to determine the amount of each cost, currently charged to the operation by the local authority's accounting system for financial reporting purposes, that would be avoided if the operation were to be outsourced. Notice that, due to contractual commitments, certain costs will have to be paid in the first of the three years under consideration, even if the maintenance operation is outsourced. On the other hand, if the operation is outsourced, the equipment could be sold, resulting in cash being received in the first year but not in the second or third years. Consequently the total cost savings by outsourcing will be different in the first year from the savings in each of the second and third years.

Once you have ascertained the total cost savings from outsourcing in each of the three years, these figures should then be compared with the price charged by the external contractor. Based on this comparison and any other factors you consider important, you should make your recommendations.

You should also note a further complication. In three years' time finances will be reorganised, so the local authority is only interested in saving costs during the next three years. What happens beyond this three-year period will be ignored by the local authority in making its decision. However, the decision might be different if a longer time period is being considered. For example, if there is the need to replace equipment in future years, if the maintenance operation is kept 'in-house', this will change the relative costs of in-house provision and outsourcing.

Table 15.2 Advice on outsourcing parks and gardens maintenance operations

Problem identification
Analysis (investigation)
Conclusion to the analysis (results of the investigation)
The solution, listed as a set of SMART recommendations

You probably found this a rather lengthy activity to complete, but the time taken should have been time well spent: the activity illustrates very well how 'accounting costs' used for periodic financial reporting are not necessarily appropriate for decision-making! You may have found it relatively straightforward (if time consuming) to identify the costs that could be avoided by outsourcing. You will probably have noticed, though, that not all the costs currently charged to the maintenance operation would be avoided if it were to be outsourced. This highlights the need to analyse costs into those which are relevant and those which are not relevant to the particular decision concerned. You have probably discovered also, why the relevance of a particular cost may depend on the time period being considered.

Activity 1 output

- *A completed version of Table 15.2 Advice on outsourcing parks and gardens maintenance operations.*

Reading 3

You have now considered the principle of relevant cost analysis and looked at some of the decisions that typically involve an analysis of relevant costs. One very important decision in many organisations is the pricing decision: what price should be charged for any particular product or service? Many 'not-for-profit' organisations also face pricing decisions – often for the internal pricing of goods or services provided to other organisational units. Providing managers with cost information for pricing decisions has traditionally been a major role of the finance function in many organisations. Think carefully about the main points you have covered in this week's readings and activities so far. Reading 3, *Cost information in pricing decisions,* specifically considers cost analysis for pricing. After you have read this section, you should have an appreciation of how prices of goods and services are typically established and of the role of cost information in this process. You should also recognise that the different ways of defining and measuring 'cost' lead to different possible approaches to pricing – each with its own advantages and disadvantages.

Activity 2

Allow 2 hours for this activity.

This activity requires you to calculate selling prices, using alternative approaches to costing and pricing and to think about the circumstances where each approach might be appropriate. This will illustrate the impact that different ways of measuring 'cost' can have on decision-making.

You have seen that decision-making often involves an analysis of the financial costs and benefits of alternative courses of action. The first activity this week has involved an analysis of relevant costs to facilitate decision-making. The relevant cost, however, often depends on the timescale involved. In the short term, fixed costs may be unavoidable regardless of the course of action taken, in which case only the variable costs are relevant to the decision. In the longer term the level of most costs can be adjusted (and hence become avoidable) and so, for decisions with longer-term implications, fixed costs become relevant also. A long-standing controversy in setting selling prices based on cost, is which cost figure should be used: full cost, including fixed costs (absorption costing) or variable cost (marginal costing)? The case of Alan Brooke requires you to focus on these alternative approaches and their implications.

Alan Brooke guitar strings

Alan Brooke produces three different types of guitar strings, which sell in packs of six strings. Monthly cost and output figures for each string type are as follows:

Table 15.3 Product cost and output data

	Fine gauge	Medium gauge	Flatwound	Total
Total variable cost	£8,000	£18,000	£20,000	£46,000
Fixed cost*	£6,000	£6,000	£6,000	£18,000
Number of packs of 6 produced	4,000	4,000	4,000	12,000

* Total fixed cost is apportioned among the three products on a 'units basis', that is, according to the number of units (packs of strings) of each product produced.

Currently the company uses a full cost plus approach to setting selling prices, adding a 30% profit mark-up to full cost. The Chief Executive, however, is very worried about the low level of sales and the resulting unused production capacity (the company is only operating at about 70% of capacity). It has been suggested to her by the company's accountant that an alternative approach to pricing, based on marginal costing, be adopted. The justification provided by the accountant was that it was necessary to reduce price in order to generate more sales and any price that exceeds the variable cost would produce a positive contribution towards fixed costs which would be incurred anyway, regardless of the level of sales.

Task

Calculate the selling price per pack for each product, using, firstly, the current absorption costing approach and then, the proposed marginal costing approach. Remember that the difference between the two approaches is simply that with absorption costing a fixed cost per unit (pack) must be calculated and then the variable cost per unit added in order to arrive at a full cost figure. Once you have calculated the cost per pack, simply add the specified percentage of the cost figure as the profit mark-up. With the marginal cost approach, the logic, in this case, would be to consider any price significantly in excess of the variable cost as potentially acceptable. With the current absorption costing approach, a fixed, customary percentage is added to full cost as the profit mark-up.

Comment on the difference in cost and price: is it significant? In what circumstances would each approach be appropriate?

Record your results and comments in a Word document with the title: Week 15 Activity 2 – Comparison of absorption and marginal costing.

If your calculations are correct, you should have noticed just how much difference the different costing approaches can make to the selling price charged to customers! Remember that, in the longer term, prices must be high enough to cover all the costs and earn a satisfactory level of profit. On the other hand, there is no point setting prices higher than customers are willing to pay.

Activity 2 output

- *A Word document containing a comparison of costs and prices using absorption and marginal costing approaches to pricing.*

Activity 3

Allow 3 hours for this activity.

You have now considered the fundamental principles of budgeting (in Weeks 11 and 12) and of cost analysis (in Weeks 13, 14 and 15). It is now time to revise the key ideas you've been introduced to so far, not least because these are likely to feature in your end-of-module assessment (EMA).

You should think carefully about and try to answer the following questions:

- Why do organisations prepare budgets?
- How should a budget be structured in terms of the way costs and revenues are analysed?

- Is there any purpose in distinguishing between direct and indirect costs when presenting managers with financial information?
- Is there any purpose in distinguishing between fixed and variable costs when presenting managers with financial information?
- What conditions must be fulfilled for a cost to be relevant to a particular decision?
- What exactly is a 'cost driver'?

Activity 3 output

- *Make notes of your reflections in a Word document with the title: Week 15 Activity 3 – Revision of key ideas.*

Week 15 activity outputs

1 A completed version of Table 15.2 Advice on outsourcing parks and gardens maintenance operations.

2 A Word document containing a comparison of costs and prices using absorption and marginal costing approaches to pricing.

3 A Word document containing reflections on key module concepts.

Learning outcomes

After completing this set of activities and readings you should be able to:

- understand the principle of 'different costs for different purposes' in decision-making and financial reporting, including the concept of relevant cost
- recognise the nature of sunk costs committed costs, and opportunity costs
- analyse costs for decision-making in all types of organisation
- identify risk and the issues it poses in decision-making.

Week 16 Financial statements: the income statement and balance sheet

Introduction

What is a profit and loss account? What is a balance sheet? Are these financial statements relevant to not-for-profit organisations? You have seen that managers need financial information in order to carry out various activities. You have also seen that these activities have a financial impact on the organisation and that the various stakeholders will expect to be provided with information about this impact. This information is provided primarily through the financial statements that are prepared periodically, typically once per year. Now it is time to consider the main financial statements that are prepared for this purpose. The provision of financial information to managers to enable them to undertake various activities is conventionally known as management accounting; preparing financial statements, reporting the impact of these activities to various stakeholders (typically as part of the organisation's annual report), is known as financial accounting. This week you will look at the income statement (known as the profit and loss account in the case of a commercial organisation) and the balance sheet. In Week 17 you will consider the third major financial statement: the cash flow statement.

Week 16 Activities

- Activity 1 Prepare an income statement for a not-for-profit organisation.
- Activity 2 Prepare a balance sheet for a trading organisation.
- Activity 3 Prepare a profit and loss account for a trading organisation.
- Activity 4 Advise a business Chief Executive on maximising reported profit figure in financial statements, based on a case.

Readings

- Reading 1 Inputs, transformation and outputs
- Reading 2 Financial accounting
- Reading 3 Income statements
- Reading 4 The balance sheet

Readings 1–3

What is an 'organisation'? It is possible to view an organisation from different perspectives. Reading 1, *Inputs, transformation and outputs,* discusses how accountants are concerned with painting a picture of an organisation from a financial perspective. It is convenient, for this purpose, to think of the organisation as a process which transforms resource inputs into outputs of goods or services. Accountants attempt to measure, in monetary terms, the resources consumed in this process and thereby determine the surplus (or deficit) of income over expenditure. As you read, keep in mind the fact that this exercise is not a purely mechanical one: it involves judgement to be exercised and choices to be made. Pay attention to the way costs and revenues are measured, which involves the application of certain accounting principles or conventions. After completing this reading, you should have an understanding of the relationship between (financial) accounting and the organisation's underlying operations.

What are the main financial statements with which financial accounting is concerned and who decides their form and content? Reading 2, *Financial accounting,* firstly introduces the main financial statements that accountants prepare to summarise the financial impact of the input–output transformation process on the organisation. It then explains the need for a regulatory framework for governing financial statements – note that this includes rules about what must be included, how it should be measured or valued and also the format of such statements. As you read, keep in mind the fact that financial statements are prepared on the basis of certain accounting principles and conventions which involve judgement and choice to be exercised in determining the figures to be included. After completing this reading, you should be aware of the main financial statements that are used to show an organisation's financial performance and situation – and of why external regulation of these statements is necessary.

What does an income statement look like and how is it prepared? Reading 3, *Income statements,* provides a detailed look at the first of the financial statements identified: the income statement (typically referred to as the profit and loss account in the case of commercial organisations). Consider carefully the example of Terrestrial Trading which illustrates how a simple profit and loss account can be prepared. Pay attention to the meaning and significance of the various figures that appear in the profit and loss account – in particular gross margin, operating profit and net profit. Finally, note the examples of how the income statement differs across different types of organisation, that is, between commercial, voluntary and public sector organisations. After completing this reading, you should understand how a profit and loss account/income statement is prepared and what the various levels of profit reported indicate. You will also be aware of the variations in the income statement between different sectors of the economy.

Activity 1

Allow 2 hours for this activity.

This activity requires you to apply the accruals accounting approach (that is, using the 'matching' concept) to prepare an income statement for a not-for-profit organisation. This will illustrate the application of certain important accounting principles (in particular the matching principle) and demonstrate how accruals accounting differs from cash accounting in the not-for-profit sector.

Smallville Sports and Social Club

Shown below as Table 16.1, is the receipts and payments account for Smallville Sports and Social Club.

Table 16.1 Receipts and payments account for year ended 31 December 20XX

Subscriptions from members	£24,000
Net income from snack bar*	£9,000
Total receipts	£33,000
Rent of clubhouse	£15,000
Fundraising and publicity	£5,000
Travel expenses	£3,000
Furnishings	£6,000
Total payments	£29,000
Excess of receipts over payments	£4,000

* Snack bar receipts £25,000; payments for bar stock £16,000.

Now consider the additional information below.

1 Subscriptions due but unpaid at 31 December 20XX were £5,000.

2 Of the subscriptions received during 20XX, £3,000 related to the previous year.

3 All snack bar receipts were in cash, but bar stock was purchased on credit terms. At the beginning of 20XX, £1,500 was owed to suppliers and this was paid during 20XX. At the end of 20XX, £2,000 was still owed to suppliers for goods purchased and consumed during 20XX.

4 At the beginning of 20XX, snack bar stock (valued at cost) was £7,000; at the end of 20XX it was £8,500.

5 All other expenses were paid for in cash during the year.

6 The payment for furnishings was made on the last day of the year and the club has decided not to provide for depreciation on these assets this year. You can therefore ignore depreciation in constructing your income and expenditure account.

Task

- From the information given above, and the extra details provided below, prepare an income and expenditure account for Smallville Sports and Social Club.
- After you have prepared this financial statement, explain the arguments for preparing an income and expenditure account (using accruals accounting) rather than a receipts and payments account (using cash accounting).
- Record your results and comments in a Word document with the title: Week 16 Activity 1 – Smallville accounts.

Additional guidance

- The information you have been given above means that the receipts or payments figures need to be adjusted to derive the income and expenditure figures. Point 5 suggests that no adjustment is necessary for other expenses. Try, first, to make the adjustments necessary to transform 'receipts' into 'income'. Then try to make the adjustments necessary to transform 'payments' into 'expenditure'. You will find the following extra information is needed to complete this task.
- Income adjustments. Points 1 and 2 mean that the subscriptions figure needs adjustment in order to derive the income figure from the receipts figure. Point 1 will have the effect of making income earned greater than cash received; point 2 will have the opposite effect.
- Expenditure adjustments. Point 3 means that the amount paid in cash for stock in the year is not the same as the value of stock purchased (consequently, to calculate cost of goods sold, for the income and expenditure account, you will need to adjust the cash paid figure to derive the purchases figure).
- Point 4 means that the value of stock sold to customers is not the same as the value purchased (look at Reading 3 again for an explanation of how the cost of goods sold should be calculated).

If you have been able to prepare the income and expenditure account, you have gained a good understanding of how accruals accounting differs from cash accounting! Accruals accounting is being increasingly adopted across all sectors to provide a 'true and fair view' of an organisation's financial performance, for which cash accounting is considered inadequate. You should have noticed that the surplus of income over expenditure figure (income and expenditure account) is not the same as the net cash flow figure (receipts and payments account) and this has important implications, as you will see in Week 17 when cash flow management is considered.

Activity 1 output

- *A Word document containing an income and expenditure account and comments on accruals accounting.*

Reading 4

What does a balance sheet look like and how is it prepared? Reading 4, *The balance sheet*, gives you a much more detailed look at this financial statement. Think carefully about why balance sheets are prepared: what do they tell various users about the organisation? Make sure also that you understand the various categories that appear in this financial statement: what are fixed assets and current assets; what are long-term and current liabilities? Think also about some of the relationships revealed – for example that between the amount of current assets and current liabilities. What might this reveal about the financial position of the organisation?

Note finally how the balance sheet will be different for different types of organisation. After completing this reading, you should have an understanding of how a balance sheet is prepared and of what it tells users (and also of its limitations – what it doesn't tell them!).

Activity 2

Allow 1 hour for this activity.

The next two activities require you to construct a set of financial statements. The best way to understand financial statements and be able to interpret them in a meaningful way is by knowing how the information contained in them is derived. This knowledge can only really be acquired by preparing such statements. That is the purpose of these activities.

First read the information below carefully.

Musical Instruments Business (1)

A group of musicians have established a company selling medieval period musical instruments by mail order and appointed themselves company directors. The musicians have raised £750,000 of the capital required themselves and borrowed a further £500,000 in the form of a long-term bank loan. In order to establish the business, they have undertaken the following transactions.

- Bought premises for £850,000 (paid by cheque).
- Bought furniture and fittings for £100,000 (paid by cheque).
- Bought (on credit) stock of instruments for resale for £300,000.
- Bought a motor van for £20,000 (paid by cheque).

The remaining £280,000 of the total initial funds provided is deposited in the business's bank account.

The directors are not sure of the effect of these various transactions on the new enterprise and would like to see some sort of analysis showing its financial situation. The bank providing the long-term loan also demands to see this information! You have been approached to help with this problem.

Task

Prepare an opening balance sheet showing the opening financial position of the organisation (use the horizontal format, as for the Terrestrial Trading example in Reading 4). Remember a balance sheet is really just a list of assets, liabilities and owners' capital, which is the difference between total assets and total liabilities. For each of the transactions identified, you should determine the impact on the business' sassets, liabilities and owners' capital.

Record your results in a Word document with the title: Week 16 Activity 2 – Balance Sheet for Musical Instruments Business.

If you have correctly drafted the balance sheet for the Musical Instruments Business, it will, of course, balance! The fact that it balances, however, is not a guarantee that it is correct, since compensating errors are possible where errors have been made that affect both sides of the balance sheet equally.

Activity 2 output

- *A Word document containing a balance sheet for Musical Instruments Business.*

Activity 3

Allow 2 hours for this activity.

This activity requires you to prepare a profit and loss account for Musical Instruments Business, summarising the results of the business's first year of trading.

Again, read the information below carefully, first.

Musical Instruments Business (2)

During the first year of trading, the following transactions occurred:

- instruments costing £1,400,000 were sold on credit terms for £2,000,000
- more instruments were purchased on credit terms for £1,500,000
- wages and other expenses of £300,000 were paid in cash
- cash totalling £1,250,000 was received from debtors
- cash totalling £1,400,000 was paid to creditors
- interest (paid cash) on the long-term loan was 10%.

At the end of the year, the directors decided to make a provision for bad debts of 5% of the year end debtors' figure.

Closing stock (valued at cost) was £400,000.

An allowance for depreciation is to be made as follows:

- buildings, 2% of cost = £17,000
- furniture and fittings, 10% of cost = £10,000
- motor van, 20% of cost = £4,000.

Task

Prepare a profit and loss account, for Musical Instruments Business, for the first year of trading (using the format shown for Terrestrial Trading in Reading 3). You will again need to apply your understanding of accruals accounting in distinguishing between income/expenditure and cash received/ paid and also distinguishing between purchases and cost of goods sold.
In Week 18, you will be introduced to some tools that can be used to systematically analyse and interpret financial statements. For now, though, simply examine the profit and loss account for a general impression and identify any significant features or characteristics you observe. Did the business make a profit? Was it a large profit? What other features stand out (if any)?

Record your results and comments in a Word document with the title: Week 16 Activity 3 – Profit and loss account for Musical Instruments Business. You will need to refer to this in your response to one of Week 17's activities.

You may have found it reasonably straightforward to prepare the profit and loss account for Musical Instruments Business, if you have a good understanding of the accruals accounting principle. You have already had some practise in applying this principle in preparing financial statements in this week's first activity. How easy did you find it to evaluate the financial performance of the business?

Activity 3 output

- *A Word document containing a profit and loss account and comments for Musical Instruments Business.*

Activity 4

Allow 2 hours for this activity.

This activity requires you to advise a business's Chief Executive on how to maximise the profit figure reported in the business's financial statements. The purpose is to illustrate how the generally accepted accounting conventions and principles, employed in preparing financial statements, impact on profit measurement.

As usual, read the information below, first.

Catering services business

Robin Williams is the owner and Chief Executive of a business that provides catering services. He believes that the business has considerable growth potential but needs to raise additional funds to finance the additional assets that will be required. Consequently, he intends to approach a venture capitalist who he hopes will provide extra capital. Robin is aware that the venture capitalist will look carefully at the recent financial performance of the business – especially the current financial year, which will end in a few weeks' time. Robin wants to present the year's performance in as favourable a light as possible; his rough estimate is that sales revenue will be about £1,500,000 and net profit before tax about £200,000.

He has identified a number of imminent transactions and is considering possibly delaying them until after the financial year end – depending on the impact that each transaction will have on this year's profit and loss account. He is uncertain about this, as he is not familiar with the various accounting principles and conventions that are employed in determining profit. He is aware, however, that delaying some transactions could have operational consequences for the business.

The transactions being considered by Robin are as follows.

- Spend £50,000 on advertising, which Robin estimates will increase sales by 20% in the next financial year (although he is not certain of the relationship between advertising and sales).
- Take out goods worth £5,000 for his own use.
- Sell goods for £50,000 on credit (at a 30% gross profit margin) if the customer is granted an extra month's credit period in which to pay. (This means that the cash will certainly not be received until after the current financial year end.) Without the additional credit period, the customer would not be prepared to purchase the goods before Robin's year end.
- Replace a motor van which is used for delivering goods to customers' premises but is in a poor state of repair. This would cost £30,000 for a vehicle with an estimated useful life of 6 years and zero scrap value at the end of that period.
- Purchase plastic containers and paper napkins for catering jobs at much lower prices than normal, if purchased immediately for cash, due to abnormal but temporary market conditions. Total outlay involved would be £25,000. It is certain, however, that these stocks will not be used before the end of the current financial year.

Task

Advise Robin what to do, giving reasons for your recommendations. Use Table 16.2 to record your output. In making your recommendations, you should explain the impact of each transaction on the current year's profit and loss account, the particular accounting principle or concept this impact reflects and also any likely operational consequences of delaying the transactions until after the year end. Think carefully about the meaning of each of the conventions or principles in terms of the cost or revenue figures to be included in the financial statements. Then consider each transaction in turn.

Note for guidance: Although there are many accounting conventions and principles, the transactions in this activity will only be affected by one or more of: accruals/matching, revenue recognition, prudence, entity concepts.

Table 16.2 Advice on maximising reported profit figure

Problem identification
Analysis (investigation)
Conclusion to the analysis (results of the investigation)
The solution, listed as a set of SMART recommendations
Strengths and weaknesses of the recommendations
The implications of the solution, if implemented

You may have found this activity rather demanding, but it demonstrates well how some important accounting concepts and principles affect the preparation of the financial statements. It also illustrates the nature of accounting profit and how this may differ from the cash generated during the same period. This topic will be developed in greater depth in Week 17. You may have noticed that the objective of maximising the current period's reported profit figure, as determined by various accounting concepts and principles, can conflict with the normal operating activities of the business and with the longer-term wellbeing of the organisation.

Activity 4 output

- *A completed version of Table 16.2 Advice on maximising reported profit figure.*

Week 16 activity outputs

1 A Word document containing an income and expenditure account and comments on accruals accounting.

2 A Word document containing a balance sheet for Musical Instruments Business.

3 A Word document containing a profit and loss account and comments for Musical Instruments Business.

4 A completed version of Table 16.2 Advice on maximising reported profit figure.

Learning outcomes

After completing this set of activities and readings you should be able to:

- understand some of the most important accounting principles that are used in the preparation of financial statements
- recognise the importance of the profit and loss account/income statement to various user groups
- prepare a simple profit and loss account/income statement
- recognise the importance of the balance sheet to various user groups
- prepare a simple balance sheet
- relate these financial statements to not-for-profit organisations.

Week 17 The cash flow statement, cash flow and working capital management

Introduction

What is the relation between cash flow and working capital? You have now seen that profit will not usually be the same as the net inflow of cash within a particular period of time. It is quite possible to earn a profit/surplus but not generate enough cash to pay the organisation's liabilities as they become due. This is actually a very common cause of failure among small and start-up businesses. An important part of the financial management of an organisation, therefore, consists in ensuring that assets are used in such a way as to generate sufficient cash. This involves careful management of the organisation's working capital (stock, debtors and creditors and any other short-term assets or liabilities it may have).

Various stakeholders, especially funds providers, will wish to evaluate an organisation's ability to generate cash. An important source of information enabling such an evaluation is provided by the cash flow statement. This week, therefore, you will look at the importance of managing cash flow, how cash flow is represented by the cash flow statement and how an organisation can manage its working capital, to ensure it generates the necessary flow of cash.

Week 17 activities

- Activity 1 Identify factors influencing cash balances held by an organisation. (Allow 1 hour for this activity.)
- Activity 2 Prepare a cash flow statement and use the information to assess an organisation's financial performance. (Allow 2 hours for this activity.)
- Activity 3 Identify and provide a solution to a working capital management problem in your own organisation. (Allow 4 hours for this activity.)

Readings

- Reading 1 Cash flow
- Reading 2 Cash flow statements
- Reading 3 Managing the working capital cycle

Reading 1

Is profitability (or in the case of not-for-profit organisations, a surplus of income over expenditure) sufficient to ensure the financial health of an organisation? Reading 1, *Cash flow,* discusses the cash flow cycle and demonstrates that costs and revenues, as defined by accruals accounting (that is, applying the matching concept), are not the same as cash outflow and inflow during a particular period of time. As you read, think carefully about the flow of finance through an organisation and how this results in the need to ensure 'liquidity' as well as an excess of income over expenditure in all types of organisation. After completing this reading, you should have a good understanding of why profit/surplus of income over expenditure is not the same as a positive cash flow and an insight into why cash flow management is so important.

Activity 1

Allow 1 hour for this activity.

This activity requires you to identify the factors that influence how much of its assets an organisation is likely to hold in the form of cash (including bank balances). The purpose is to highlight the need to manage cash balances in an organisation. In this week's first reading, you have seen that, over a period of time, all organisations need sufficient cash inflow to cover their cash outflows.

Task

Identify the factors that influence the amount of cash/bank balances an organisation will wish to hold at any particular point in time.

Make a brief note (this need be no more than 400 words) in a Word document with the title: Week 17 Activity 1 – Managing cash. In identifying the factors influencing the level of cash/bank balances held, you will need to consider the following:

- Why do organisations hold some of their assets in the form of cash?
- What are the costs of holding too much cash?
- What are the costs of having too little cash?
- To what extent are the reasons for holding cash similar to those for holding stock?

In working through this activity you should have gained a valuable insight into an important aspect of the financial management of an organisation: managing the cash/bank balances. You may have recognised the serious consequences of not getting it right! In Reading 3 you will look in greater depth at the management of working capital, which emphasises further the need for an organisation to carefully manage its current assets. First, though, you will consider how the cash flow statement can represent an organisation's cash generation over a period of time.

Activity 1 output

- *A Word document containing notes on factors determining the level of cash balances.*

Reading 2

What is the purpose of a cash flow statement? Reading 2, *Cash flow statements,* discusses the nature and role of the cash flow statement in summarising an organisation's cash generation during a period of time (usually one year): where it came from, where it went. It also provides examples of cash flow statements for various types of organisation, including not-for-profit organisations. As you read, think about what the cash flow statement tells you that the profit and loss account and balance sheet do not. Finally, the reading illustrates the construction of a cash flow forecast, an important tool in managing an organisation's cash flow – think about the use to which such information may be put. After completing this reading, you should have an understanding of why a cash flow statement is necessary (in addition to the profit and loss account and balance sheet) and of how a cash flow forecast can be constructed to aid an organisation's management in managing cash flow.

Activity 2

Allow 2 hours for this activity.

This activity requires you to construct a cash flow statement and use the information provided by it. The purpose is to highlight the factors that determine an organisation's liquidity.

Refer back to the transaction details and other information given for Week 16 Activity 3, which you used to prepare a profit and loss account for the first year of trading for Musical Instruments Business. You will need this information for Activity 2, in order to prepare a cash flow statement for the business.

During the first year of trading, the directors of Musical Instruments Business have frequently experienced serious cash shortages – even though the enterprise has made a profit.

Task

Advise them how to improve the business's liquidity. Use Table 17.2 to record your output. You will need, firstly, to prepare a cash flow statement for the business, for the first year of trading (using the format given in this week's Reading 2 and the information about the business's transactions in Activity 3 from Week 16) and use the information this provides to make your recommendations. Not all of the different categories of cash flow given in the text example – Terrestrial Trading Company – will appear in the first year of trading for Musical Instruments Business. The template below (Table 17.1) provides you with the structure and content of the cash flow statement: all you have to do is fill in the numbers.

Table 17.1 Cash flow statement for Musical Instruments Business first year of trading

	£
Cash received from customers	
Cash paid to suppliers	
Cash expenses	—
Cash flows from operations	
Bank interest paid	—
Net cash flow	

Table 17.2 Advice on improving liquidity for Musical Instruments Business

Problem identification
Analysis (investigation)
Conclusion to the analysis (results of the investigation)
The solution, listed as a set of SMART recommendations
Strengths and weaknesses of the recommendations
The implications of the solution, if implemented

This activity should have provided another illustration that profit does not equal cash (the profitability of an organisation does not automatically result in its liquidity). The cash flow statement you have prepared should indicate the main source of this organisation's lack of liquidity. Such information should enable management to take appropriate remedial action, as well as enable other stakeholders (such as the providers of funds) to form an opinion about the financial management of the organisation. You may have noticed, in preparing the cash flow statement, that the net cash outflow for the year exceeded the business's cash/bank balances at the beginning of the year (as shown by the balance sheet you constructed previously); how do you think it financed this deficit? Presumably through an additional injection of funds: perhaps in the form of a bank overdraft. You were not provided with this information in the activity; if you had been, you could have extended the cash flow statement to include this cash inflow from fund providers.

Activity 2 output

- *A completed version of Table 17.2 Advice on improving liquidity for Musical Instruments Business.*

Reading 3

How can managers help to ensure the liquidity of an organisation? The previous two readings this week introduced you to the cash flow cycle and how this can be represented by a cash flow statement. Reading 3, *Managing the working capital cycle,* discusses the importance of managing working capital in order to generate sufficient cash to meet the organisation's liabilities as they fall due for payment. It also introduces a number of performance indicators (in the form of ratios) which are widely used in managing the various elements of working capital.

Pay particular attention to the working capital/cash cycle and why it is important to ensure that the time cash spends in the cycle is as short as possible. Think also about the implications of having too little or too much working capital: what would be the consequences of having too little stock or debtors? Note, finally, the importance of timing of cash receipts and payments.

After completing this reading, you should have an understanding of why organisations have working capital and also of why it is important not to have too much.

Activity 3

Allow 4 hours for this activity.

This activity requires you to consider a working capital management problem in your own organisation. The purpose is to illustrate the importance and relevance of working capital management in all organisations, in all sectors.

Virtually all organisations have working capital, although not all may have all the elements of working capital. A not-for-profit organisation that does not make sales on credit may not have debtors – although some may, for example a local government authority will be owed money for local taxes and rents at any particular point in time. Virtually all organisations will have creditors and most will have stocks of consumable materials and stationery, even if they are not trading organisations. A hospital, for example, will have stocks of medicines and consumable materials such as needles, bandages and surgical gloves.

Identify a problem, actual or potential, in your own organisation, relating to one element of working capital management (stocks, debtors, creditors or cash/bank balances) and make recommendations as to how it could be resolved or the situation improved. Use Table 17.3 to record your output. If you are not directly involved in managing a particular element of working capital, as may well be the case, consult someone in your organisation who is. For example, the office or administration manager may be responsible for managing stationery stock; someone in the finance/accounts office will be responsible for managing payment of suppliers (creditors).

Table 17.3 Solution to a working capital problem in my organisation

Problem identification
Analysis (investigation)
Conclusion to the analysis (results of the investigation)
The solution, listed as a set of SMART recommendations
Strengths and weaknesses of the recommendations
The implications of the solution, if implemented

You may have found this activity rather challenging if you are not directly involved in managing one of the elements of working capital in your organisation. We hope, though, that you found it interesting and instructive. You will probably have seen how at least one element of working capital has a significant influence on your organisation's cash flow. The activity may well have provided insights which are potentially useful to management in your organisation for improving its liquidity. You may wish to consider taking the activity further and pass your recommendations on to someone directly involved in managing the relevant aspect of working capital, if you are not. You should, of course, deal with this situation diplomatically and sensitively, as your actions may appear to constitute a criticism of those concerned!

Activity 3 output

- *A completed version of Table 17.3 Solution to a working capital problem in my organisation.*

Week 17 activity outputs

1. A Word document containing notes on factors determining level of cash balances.
2. A completed version of Table 17.2 Advice on improving liquidity for Musical Instruments Business.
3. A completed version of Table 17.3 Solution to a working capital problem in my organisation.

Learning outcomes

After completing this set of activities and readings, students should be able to:

- recognise the importance of cash flow
- understand the relationship between cash flow and working capital
- identify and explain the main liquidity ratios used in managing working capital
- understand the nature and purpose of the cash flow statement.

Week 18 Analysis and interpretation of financial statements

Introduction

How can useful information about the financial performance and financial position of an organisation be extracted from the income statement and balance sheet? This week you will be introduced to some simple tools that can be used for analysing and interpreting the information provided by these financial statements.

Week 18 activities

- Activity 1 Perform ratio analysis and interpretation of financial statements of a business, based on a case. (Allow 2 hours for this activity.)
- Activity 2 Perform ratio analysis and interpretation of financial statements of a not-for-profit organisation, based on a case. (Allow 2 hours for this activity.)
- Activity 3 Perform analysis and interpretation of financial statements of your own organisation. (Allow 3 hours for this activity.)

Readings

- Reading 1 Percentages and ratios
- Reading 2 Financial performance ratios

Readings 1 and 2

Why are ratios important in interpreting quantitative information? Reading 1, *Percentages and ratios,* discusses how ratios and percentages represent important relationships, thereby converting raw data into meaningful information. As you read, think about how each of the ratios or percentages identified help to provide deeper insights into quantitative information. After completing this reading, you should have an understanding of why ratio analysis lies at the root of most quantitative interpretation by managers.

What ratios can be applied to the analysis of financial statements? Perhaps the most important financial ratio for evaluating commercial organisations is return on capital employed (ROCE), sometimes known as return on investment (ROI). Reading 2, *Financial performance ratios,* discusses the elements that contribute to return on capital employed and how it can be further analysed into a pyramid of secondary ratios. Collectively, these ratios can reveal a good deal about the financial performance and situation of an organisation. As you read, think carefully about what each of the ratios identified tells you about an organisation that the individual figures involved do not!

Can the pyramid of ratios be applied in not-for-profit organisations? It depends! The final part of Reading 2 discusses the use of ratio analysis in the not-for-profit sector. Note that for many not-for-profit organisations, the concept of 'return' on capital employed (that is, profit/capital employed) is not meaningful and nor, therefore, is the analysis of such a figure into the various secondary ratios. For example, debtors turnover can only be calculated where there are sales on credit. Stock turnover can only be calculated where stock is bought and sold. Note, also, that it is nevertheless important to apply appropriate cost management ratios in evaluating performance, as funds available will almost certainly be limited. The principle that ratios and percentages can reveal important relationships still applies. As you read, try to think of examples of cost ratios that might be important in a not-for-profit organisation – perhaps a local government authority or a charity. After completing this reading you should have an understanding of some of the tools that are widely used to evaluate the financial performance and position of various organisations. You should also be aware of how ratio analysis can be adapted to the needs of the not-for-profit sector.

Activity 1

Allow 2 hours for this activity.

This activity requires you to calculate some ratios and use them to interpret the financial statements of a business organisation. The purpose is to highlight what the financial statements can potentially reveal about an organisation.

You will need to refer back to the profit and loss account you prepared in Activity 3 from Week 16 for the Musical Instruments Business and use it in conjunction with the balance sheet (given in Table 18.1 in a simplified version of the vertical format used for Terrestrial Trading – the example given for ratio analysis in Reading 2) at the end of the first year of trading. Hypothetical industry averages for the main performance ratios are also shown below to provide a performance standard against which Musical Instruments Business may be compared.

Table 18.1 Balance Sheet for Musical Instruments Business at end of first year

	£(000s)	£(000s)
Fixed assets		939,000
Current assets:		
Stock	400,000	
Debtors	712,500	
	1,112,500	
Creditors falling due within one year		
Trade creditors	(400,000)	
Bank overdraft	(220,000)	
Net current assets	620,000	492,500
Long-term loan		(500,000)
Net assets		931,500
Representing:		
Capital		750,000
Retained profits		181,500
Shareholders' funds		931,500

Industry average ratios:

Return on capital employed = 33%

Return on sales = 15%

Stock turnover = 4 times per annum

Debtors turnover = 5.25 times per annum

Creditors turnover = 5.15 times per annum

Current ratio = 2.0:1

Quick ratio = 1.5:1

The directors of Musical Instruments Business believe, based on anecdotal evidence from contacts within the industry, that their business is underperforming in terms of profitability, as well as suffering from liquidity problems.

Task

Advise the directors on the actions they should take to improve the financial performance of the business. Use Table 18.2 to record your output. In order to make your recommendations to the directors you will need to calculate, for Musical Instruments Business, each of the ratios for which the industry average has been identified. (Some of these ratios were introduced this week, but others were introduced in Week 17 when you looked at working capital management.) Comparison between each ratio for Musical Instruments Business and the industry average should highlight the problem areas to guide your recommendations to the directors.

Table 18.2 Advice on improving Musical Instruments Business financial performance

Problem identification
Analysis (investigation)
Conclusion to the analysis (results of the investigation)
The solution, listed as a set of SMART recommendations
Strengths and weaknesses of the recommendations

You probably found it relatively straightforward to calculate each of the ratios. The real value of such an activity comes, of course, in the interpretation of what the numbers are telling you. If your calculations and interpretation are correct, you will have recognised that the financial management of Musical Instruments Business has not been as good as it might have been! This is, however, a relatively new business and such problems are not uncommon with new businesses – and do not necessarily prove fatal!

Activity 1 output

- *A completed version of Table 18.2 Advice on improving Musical Instruments Business financial performance.*

Activity 2

Allow 2 hours for this activity.

This activity requires you to calculate some ratios for a not-for-profit organisation and use the information to evaluate its overall financial performance. The purpose is to illustrate how the principles of ratio analysis can be adapted and applied to non-commercial organisations.

Corporate social responsibility (including minimising carbon emissions and other damaging environmental impacts) and ethical behaviour are increasingly important. A major objective of commercial organisations is, nevertheless, profit. Consequently, the evaluation of their performance involves an analysis of profitability and the variables that influence profitability: asset utilisation and sales margin, as indicated by the pyramid of ratios. In not-for-profit organisations, such as charities, profit is not the objective, but the financial statements can still provide very useful information about how such an organisation is being managed and the extent to which it is achieving its objectives.

The trustees of Benign Organisation, a registered charity in the US, are concerned about the managerial ability of the Chief Executive Officer (CEO) who joined the organisation a year ago from the commercial sector. Given below in Tables 18.3 and 18.4 are the charity's financial statements.

Table 18.3 Income and expenditure account for Benign Organisation for year ended 31 December 20XX

	20XX	**20XX–1**
	$(000s)	**$(000s)**
Income:		
Child and community sponsorships	27,828	25,097
Other donations	5,989	4,644
Contributions from official bodies	5,570	7,018
Net income from trading operations	165	263
Miscellaneous income	1,588	1,820
	41,140	38,842
Contributions from European partners	3,808	3,531
Total income	44,948	42,373
Expenditure:		
Direct charitable expenditure		
Grants to other organisations	8,226	7,615
Development and emergency expenditure	14,930	15,186
Education and research	3,836	2,969
Support costs	7,393	7,383
	34,385	33,153
Other expenditure		
Fundraising	8,433	7,012
Administration	1,001	1,194
	9,434	8,206
Total expenditure	43,819	41,359
Net income	1,129	1,014
Fund balances brought forward at 1 January	20,598	19,584
Fund balances at 31 December 20XX	21,727	20,598

Table 18.4 Balance Sheet for Benign Organisation as at 31 December 20XX

	20XX	**20XX–1**
	$(000s)	**$(000s)**
Fixed assets	3,396	3,144
Investments	73	—
Current assets:		
Stock	16	5
Debtors	4,449	3,812
Bank deposits	12,850	13,000
Cash at bank	3,532	4,326
	20,847	21,143
Creditors:		
Amounts falling due within one year	(2,589)	(3,689)
Net current assets	18,258	17,454
Net assets	21,727	20,598

Table 18.4 continued

Funds:		
Restricted funds	16,060	15,640
Designated funds:		
Fixed assets	1,457	1,262
Emergency	200	150
General fund	4,010	3,546
	5,667	4,958
Total funds	21,727	20,598

Task

Based on the information provided by the statements in Tables 18.3 and 18.4 advise the trustees what action to take with respect to the CEO. Use Table 18.5 to record your output. The performance of the CEO in this case is to be evaluated via the analysis and interpretation of the financial statements of the organisation. These statements summarise the financial performance and situation, for which he is ultimately held responsible. The analysis and interpretation of a voluntary organisation's financial statements proceed along similar lines to those of a business organisation: calculate the relevant ratios for the organisation, compare them over time and to the sector average and think about what these comparisons are telling you. For voluntary organisation's such as Benign Organisation, the relevant ratios will be different from those of a business organisation; details of these ratios, together with sector averages (for the US), for comparison are in this week's Reading 2.

Formulae for the relevant ratios are:

- programme expenses = (charity programme expenditure/total expenditure) x 100
- admin expenses = (administration expenditure/total expenditure) x 100
- fundraising expenses = (expenditure on fundraising/total expenditure) x 100
- working capital ratio = (working capital (= net current assets)/total expenditure)
- revenue growth = ((total income this year – total income last year)/ total income last year)) x 100
- fundraising efficiency = expenditure on fundraising/voluntary donations*
- programme expenses growth = ((direct charitable expenditure this year – direct charitable expenditure last year)/direct charitable expenditure last year)) x 100

* Strictly speaking this ratio compares amount spent on fundraising with voluntary donations only – not income from all sources. In the income statement for Benign Organisation, this consists of 'Child and Community Sponsorships' and 'Other Donations'.

Table 18.5 Advice to trustees concerning CEO

Problem identification
Analysis (investigation)
Conclusion to the analysis (results of the investigation)
The solution, listed as a set of SMART recommendations
Strengths and weaknesses of the recommendations
The implications of the solution, if implemented

In your analysis of the financial statements of Benign Organisation, you may have found the ratio calculations slightly more challenging than those you performed previously for Musical Instruments Business. Again, though, it is your ability to interpret these ratios that is most important. If your analysis and interpretation are correct, you will probably have recognised that there is cause for concern and that some sort of remedial action is necessary!

Activity 2 output

- *A completed version of Table 18.5 Advice to trustees concerning CEO.*

Activity 3

Allow 3 hours for this activity.

This activity requires you to apply the financial analysis tools you have been introduced to, to your own organisation. This will give you further practise in analysing and interpreting financial statements and may provide some revealing insights into your organisation. Obtain a set of financial statements for your own organisation (or where this is not possible, another organisation of your choice) – most large organisations have them available on the internet. Examine these carefully. What aspects do you recognise from your studies of financial statement analysis? Note the various elements and what they tell you – for example, what information is provided outside the income statement and balance sheet in the form of narrative or notes? What are the main features, points of interest or areas for concern? Calculate and comment on any ratios you think are appropriate. Do they reveal a satisfactory performance and financial situation? What problems or dangers are revealed?

Make brief notes (of between 400 and 500 words) in a Word document with the title: Week 18 Activity 3 – Analysis and interpretation of own organisation's financial statements.

The nature of the organisation for which you have undertaken a financial statement analysis will have a significant influence on the information presented and on the important ratios/relationships. Nevertheless, you have probably been able to extract some meaningful information about the financial performance and situation of the organisation which is of relevance to various stakeholders. This may have led you to seeing your own organisation in a different light!

Activity 3 output

- *A Word document containing notes on financial performance and situation of own organisation.*

Week 18 activity outputs

1 A completed version of Table 18.2 Advice on improving Musical Instruments Business financial performance.

2 A completed version of Table 18.5 Advice to trustees concerning CEO.

3 A Word document containing notes on financial performance and situation of own organisation.

Learning outcomes

After completing this set of activities and readings you should be able to:

- understand the importance of ratios and percentages in analysing and interpreting quantitative information
- calculate the individual ratios that make up the pyramid of ratios and interpret their meaning
- perform a simple analysis and interpretation of an organisation's financial statements
- apply ratio analysis to not-for-profit organisations.

Week 19 Performance management

Introduction

What financial and other information will help to monitor and improve performance in your organisation? You have now seen that managers need financial information to carry out various activities in pursuit of the organisation's objectives. You have also seen that various stakeholders require periodic information on how the activities undertaken by management have impacted on the organisation's overall financial performance and position. This week you will look at how financial (and other) information is used by managers to monitor the performance of the various parts of an organisation to ensure organisational objectives are met.

The three financial statements you have looked at in the finance part of the module (the income statement, balance sheet and cash flow statement) are concerned with the performance and financial position of the organisation as a whole; they are prepared primarily for external stakeholders and are prepared relatively infrequently – typically annually. Managers will also be interested in internal performance measurement at much more frequent intervals – monthly, weekly or even daily. They will wish to monitor the various parts of an organisation – divisions, business segments, operating units, departments, and so on – on a regular and relatively frequent basis to ensure that each part is acting in a manner which is consistent with the organisation as a whole achieving its objectives.

Internal performance measurement may include various financial performance indicators such as those you encountered in Week 18. ROCE and the various secondary ratios that influence it can be applied to the evaluation of individual business segments as well as to the organisation as a whole. Increasingly, however, it is recognised that relying solely on financial information does not give a complete picture – and may indeed encourage the wrong sort of behaviour from those being measured! A well-known aphorism states that 'what gets measured gets managed'. This reflects the well-attested fact that managers tend to concentrate on those aspects of their performance that they know are measured and reported. Long-term success of the organisation usually requires a focus on a number of non-financial variables such as employee satisfaction, research and development, and so on. Such focus can only be achieved by systematically monitoring performance in these areas.

Organisations are increasingly coming under pressure to ensure that they act in a manner that is both ethical and environmentally sustainable. For commercial organisations it will be very difficult to achieve or maintain a competitive advantage without responding to this pressure. Consequently, it is becoming increasingly necessary to measure and manage both environmental impact and ethical behaviour. Performance indicators used often now include those relating to an organisation's carbon footprint and the degree of compliance with a code of ethics (including dealings with customers, suppliers, employees, and so on). It is essential that organisations formally include measures of social and environmental impact and ethical behaviour in their performance measurement and management systems. The challenge is to develop appropriate key performance indicators (KPIs) for measuring the impact of the organisation's activities on the environment, local communities and other stakeholders.

Week 19 activities

- Activity 1 Identify performance measures used in your own organisation and problems arising from their use. (Allow 2 hours for this activity.)
- Activity 2 Advise business organisation's managing director on implementation of a responsibility accounting system, based on a case. (Allow 2 hours for this activity.)
- Activity 3 Identify critical success factors and key performance indicators for a commercial organisation. (Allow 1 hour for this activity.)
- Activity 4 Identify performance indicators for each of the four Es (economy, efficiency, effectiveness and equity) for a not-for-profit organisation. (Allow 2 hours for this activity.)

Readings

- Reading 1 Internal performance measurement
- Reading 2 Responsibility accounting
- Reading 3 The Balanced Scorecard
- Reading 4 The four Es: economy, efficiency, effectiveness and equity

Reading 1

Why is performance measurement a necessary part of organisational management? Reading 1, *Internal performance measurement,* discusses why an important role of an organisation's finance function is measuring and reporting the performance of each part of the organisation and its manager/s. As you read, think about why it is usually necessary to measure non-financial performance indicators as well as financial performance indicators, and also about how these might conflict with each other. Think also about why a standard of comparison is necessary for meaningful performance evaluation and about the possible difficulties of obtaining an appropriate standard.

After completing this reading, you should have an understanding of why internal performance measurement is an important part of organisational control and why it is often highly problematic!

Activity 1

Allow 2 hours for this activity.

This activity requires you to consider (internal) performance measurement in your own organisation. The purpose is to highlight the need for and problems of performance measurement in a context with which you are familiar.

Identify two or three (internal) performance measures that are used in your own organisation, or an organisation with which you are familiar. When you have selected the performance measures, identify one or more problems that arise as a result of the use of these measures in performance evaluation. The problems you identify may relate to people behaving in undesirable ways in order to meet performance targets. Alternatively, they may relate to the level at which targets are set, or the degree to which those held responsible can actually influence achievement of performance targets.

Make brief notes (these need be no more than 400 words) in a Word document with the title: Week 19 Activity 1 – Performance measures and problems arising in my organisation.

You may have selected performance measures that are used within your own department to monitor a particular activity, or performance measures that are used higher in the management hierarchy to monitor the overall performance of an organisational segment (perhaps your department). Depending on your choice, you will probably have identified different problems arising; in either case, though, you will probably have recognised that the practical application of internal performance measurement is far from straightforward.

Activity 1 output

- *A Word document containing notes on performance measures and problems in own organisation.*

Reading 2

Why does delegation of decision-making authority occur and what are the consequences? Reading 2, *Responsibility accounting,* discusses an important aspect of organisational control which is concerned with holding particular managers responsible for particular areas or aspects of the organisation's operations. As you read, think about the nature of the different types of responsibility centre identified. Try to think of examples of each type in your own organisation. Think also about how the interests of one responsibility centre may conflict with those of another, and with those of the organisation as a whole.

Note that the principle of controllability is fundamental to a good system of responsibility accounting: managers should only be evaluated according to those factors they can control. It is important to remember that the concept of a responsibility centre relates to an area of managerial responsibility, rather than a particular organisational segment. This makes responsibility centre performance evaluation problematic, as it is quite possible to have a good manager in a disadvantaged organisational segment and vice versa.

After completing this reading, you should have an understanding of the concept of responsibility accounting and of the main types of responsibility centre that are used in a system of responsibility accounting. You should also be beginning to develop an awareness of the potential problems that may arise in operating a system of responsibility accounting.

Activity 2

Allow 2 hours for this activity.

This activity requires you to select appropriate responsibility centre types and anticipate the likely performance measurement problems arising from their use. The purpose of the activity is to illustrate:

- how individual responsibility centres may act in a way that maximises their performance, but impacts adversely on the performance of other responsibility centres or the organisation as a whole
- how linkages between the responsibility centres may make it difficult to evaluate the performance of each centre individually.

Spellman Co. Ltd

Spellman Co. Ltd is a medium-sized business that sells new and second-hand pasteurising, homogenising and freezing equipment to ice cream manufacturers. It also provides service and repairs to both its own and external customers. For the new machines market, it acts as a distributor for a single large Japanese-based manufacturer (also providing after-sales service, maintenance and repairs). For the second-hand market it buys all the major manufacturers' products on the open market. Spellman allows customers purchasing new equipment to exchange their old equipment in part settlement – often giving very good prices, above the market price for the old equipment, to encourage the purchase of new equipment. The old equipment is then serviced, checked and sold on the second-hand market.

The machinery used in the ice cream manufacturing business typically has a life of 20–30 years, if properly serviced and maintained. Consequently, there is a large second-hand market, with many firms (especially smaller firms and new firms) willing to buy and use second-hand machines for ice cream manufacture.

As a result of rapid growth and increased complexity (with more customers, transactions and staff to manage), the business is experiencing a number of problems resulting from the centralisation of power, whereby all decisions are currently made by the managing director (MD) and costs and revenues are aggregated at the level of the business as a whole. The MD is finding it impossible to have sufficiently detailed knowledge of each business segment (concerning customer needs, competition, and so on) and this often results in poor quality decision-making. This concentration of decision-making authority also results in slower decisions in a fast moving environment, as everything has to be passed up the chain of command. Competent, knowledgeable staff feel frustrated and demotivated at being unable to use their initiative and apply their specialised knowledge. The lack of separable parts of the organisation, with responsible managers, means the various business segments cannot be evaluated in terms of their financial performance.

Task

Advise the MD how he can restructure Spellman to improve the situation, also making him aware of the problems that might arise if your recommendations are implemented.

Use Table 19.1 to record your output. In order to make your recommendations to the MD, you will first need to consider the type of responsibility centre that is appropriate for each of the three main business areas: new equipment sales, second-hand equipment sales and service and repairs. To identify the appropriate responsibility centre type for each activity, you will need to consider whether the responsibility centre manager can significantly influence the revenues, costs and investments associated with his or her area of the business. Once you have identified the appropriate responsibility centre type for each activity, identify possible problems that may arise as a result of the way the centre's performance is measured and evaluated. How, for example, might a cost centre manager act in such a way as to keep his/her costs down but potentially have an adverse impact on other responsibility centres or the organisation as a whole?

Table 19.1 Advice on responsibility accounting system

Problem identification
Analysis (investigation)
Conclusion to the analysis (results of the investigation)
The solution, listed as a set of SMART recommendations
Strengths and weaknesses of the recommendations
The implications of the solution, if implemented

You probably found it quite challenging to identify the appropriate responsibility centre types for each of the main business areas of Spellman Co. Ltd. This illustrates how, in practice, defining responsibility is seldom clear-cut: whether a manager can control revenues or costs in a particular area is often a matter of degree rather than absolute. If you were able to identify several possible problems arising as a result of the way the responsibility centres are measured and evaluated, you are well on the way to understanding the difficulties associated with a system of responsibility accounting. These problems are often unsolvable, but managers need to be aware of them and to adopt a flexible approach to evaluating performance.

Activity 2 output

- *A completed version of Table 19.1 Advice on responsibility accounting system.*

Reading 3

What are the consequences of an overemphasis on measuring and reporting financial performance indicators? Reading 3, *The Balanced Scorecard,* discusses the need for a range of non-financial as well as financial performance indicators to ensure attainment of long-term organisational objectives.

Think about the possibility of introducing an additional measurement perspective, concerned with corporate social responsibility (CSR) issues: climate change, sustainability and ethical behaviour. Organisations are increasingly coming under pressure from both legislation and stakeholder demands to perform in these areas and it is unlikely that they will achieve or maintain competitive advantage without high performance on CSR factors. Consequently, such factors should be reflected in the organisation's balanced scorecard. You should also think carefully, however, about the inherent problems of such a multi-measure approach.

After completing this reading, you should have an understanding of the need for a range of financial and non-financial performance indicators to facilitate a properly balanced evaluation of performance – and of the problems arising with such an approach!

Activity 3

Allow 1 hour for this activity.

This activity requires you to identify some of the performance indicators that might be included in a balanced scorecard. The purpose is to provide a practical illustration of the construction of a scorecard, including the importance of linking performance measures to organisational strategy.

Consider a commercial airline operating a five-perspective balanced scorecard (including a CSR perspective). Identify two critical success factors and associated key performance indicators for each balanced scorecard perspective.

The critical success factors you identify are likely to depend on which market segment the airline is competing in: the low price or superior service quality segment. You will need to make an explicit choice of segment in order to identify the factors that are critical to the airline's ability to compete successfully. Think back to your study of the 'marketing mix' in the marketing part of this module and consider the relative importance of each element in the mix when selecting critical success factors for the customer perspective of the scorecard. In considering appropriate critical success factors and key performance indicators remember, also, that a commercial airline is a particularly significant organisation in terms of environmental impact!

Make brief notes (these need be no more than about 400 words) in a Word document with the title: Week 19 Activity 3 – Critical success factors and key performance indicators for airline scorecard.

In identifying critical success factors and associated key performance indicators, you probably started by selecting an appropriate competitive strategy for the airline, as this choice will determine customer expectations, which, in turn, determine the critical business processes. These, in turn, determine the key areas for learning and innovation. Performance management is critical for each of these perspectives in order to meet the expectations of financial stakeholders. If you were thinking broadly along these lines in arriving at your choice of key performance indicators, you have gained a good understanding of the balanced scorecard approach to performance measurement and management. If you have identified key performance indicators for a corporate social responsibility perspective, you probably recognised how these conflict with some other performance areas!

Activity 3 output

- *A Word document containing notes on critical success factors and key performance indicators of an airline.*

Reading 4

How can the performance of an organisation (or organisational segment) be evaluated when it is not possible to assign a monetary value to its outputs (that is, to quantify the benefits it produces)? Reading 4, *The four Es: economy, efficiency, effectiveness and equity,* discusses possible approaches to performance evaluation when the profit measure is absent, as in the public sector and not-for-profit sectors.

As you read, think carefully about the significance of each of the four Es and also about possible conflicts between them (for example between effectiveness and efficiency). After completing this reading, you should have an understanding of a widely used framework for evaluating value for money performance. You should also have an understanding of how some of the four Es may be achieved at the expense of others, making the overall evaluation of performance difficult!

Activity 4

Allow 2 hours for this activity.

This activity requires you to identify appropriate value for money performance indicators for a particular not-for-profit organisation: a hospital. The purpose is to highlight some of the difficulties in assessing value for money performance and in particular the conflicts that often arise between the objectives of economy, efficiency, effectiveness and equity.

In measuring performance in the public sector, it is important to consider the resource inputs, the services provided (intermediate outputs) and the impact of these services (final outcomes). Consider, for example, the cancer unit of a hospital that provides services such as chemotherapy to patients. The main inputs, outputs and outcomes are shown in Table 19.2.

Table 19.2 The four Es

Resource inputs	Services provided (= outputs)	Impact (= outcomes)
Beds, staff, drugs, laboratory services, clinical equipment, etc.	Chemotherapy sessions, malignancy removed, post-survival treatment	Normal lifestyle, quality of life, readmissions, death

(Adapted from Coates et al., 1996, p. 221)

In the context of the cancer unit:

- Economy is concerned with procuring beds, staff, drugs, laboratory services, and so on at the minimum cost for an acceptable quantity and quality of resource.
- Efficiency is concerned with using the minimum amount of resources – staff, drugs, laboratory services, and so on – to provide a specified volume and quality of service, for example chemotherapy sessions.
- Effectiveness is concerned with whether the treatments provided – chemotherapy, malignancy removal, and so on – are having the desired impact, for example survival, resumption of normal lifestyle, and so on.
- Equity is concerned with ensuring, for example, that all members of the community have equal access to the services provided.

Identify two appropriate performance indicators for each of the four Es for the hospital's cancer unit. What possible conflicts may arise between these measures and how could the cancer unit's managers deal with these conflicts?

Make brief notes (these need be no more than about 500 words) in a Word document with the title: Week 19 Activity 4 – Performance indicators for hospital cancer unit.

You probably found it reasonably straightforward to identify performance indicators, although you may have found the identification of indicators of effectiveness (outcomes) less easy. In this particular case you may also have found it relatively straightforward to identify possible conflicts between measures whereby a high level of performance in one area can often be achieved at the expense of performance in another. Suggesting what managers should do about this was probably less easy.

You should keep in mind that the ultimate purpose of performance measurement is performance evaluation and this requires an appropriate standard of comparison: the comparison of actual results with what should have been achieved.

Establishing an appropriate standard of comparison is particularly difficult where means–end relationships are not well understood, that is, where it is difficult to predict with any certainty the outcomes occurring from particular actions. The relationship between resource inputs and services provided (for example chemotherapy sessions) may be predictable with a reasonable degree of certainty. The relationship between chemotherapy sessions and restoration of normal quality of life for patients, on the other hand, is far less predictable. This is one of a number of problems that managers face in attempting to exercise organisational control.

Activity 4 output

- *A Word document containing notes on hospital cancer unit performance indicators.*

Week 19 activity outputs

1. A Word document containing notes on performance measures and problems in own organisation.
2. A completed version of Table 19.1 Advice on responsibility accounting system.
3. A Word document containing notes on critical success factors and key performance indicators of an airline.
4. A Word document containing notes on hospital cancer unit performance indicators.

Learning outcomes

After completing this set of activities and readings you should be able to:

- recognise the need for internal performance measurement
- understand the concept of responsibility accounting and recognise the main types of responsibility centre used in a system of responsibility accounting
- understand the need for a range of non-financial as well as financial performance indicators in performance evaluation and the application of the balanced scorecard
- recognise the common problems arising from performance measurement
- apply the four Es framework for performance evaluation when the profit measure is absent.

References

Coates, J. B., Rickwood, C. and Stacey, R. J. (1996) *Management Accounting for Strategic and Operational Control*, Oxford, Butterworth-Heinemann.

Acknowledgements

Grateful acknowledgement is made to the following source:

Cover image: © Fotosearch

Contents

CD-ROM

The accompanying CD-ROM contains:

Task files
Suggested answers.

Introduction

The Advanced ECDL Word Processing module is for those who have already completed the ECDL qualification or have intermediate word processing skills. You do not have to have studied or passed ECDL to take the stand-alone Advanced modules.

Unlike ECDL, which requires you to take modules that cover a selection of software packages, Advanced ECDL is more specialised; you study each module separately, and it is then tested and certificated separately. The Advanced qualification syllabus develops word processing skills that are not required for ECDL.

This book assumes that you have word processing skills at ECDL or Intermediate level and covers the additional skills that are required to enable you to achieve the Advanced ECDL word processing module. Included with the book is a CD that contains:

- the files you will need for the Tasks
- the answers to those Tasks.

The Tasks have been presented in a way that enables you to learn the skills in context with other skills, rather than as stand-alone exercises. These skills build up through the book with the more complex elements of the syllabus covered towards the end.

CD-ROM

To access the files on the CD-ROM:

1 Insert the CD into your CD-ROM drive.
2 The CD-ROM will run automatically.

Some machines may not support autorun and the CD-ROM will not start automatically. If this is the case:

1 Go to 'My Computer' and double-click on your CD-ROM drive.
2 The CD-ROM should now run automatically.

If it does not run, but instead displays a list of the files on the CD-ROM, then:

Double-click on the file default.htm. This will start the user interface screen

Note: If you are running the program from the CD-ROM, you must have the CD-ROM in the drive (including when you are trying to exit).

HEINEMANN BOOK CONTENTS PAGE

FEATURES	PAGE	TASK
AutoShapes	53	4
Bookmarks	140	9
Borders and shading	46	4
Captions/Automatic	74 &137	5
Columns	2	1
Columns / Break & Changes	38	3
Comments	123	8
Convert text to table	63	5
Create chart from table or Excel w'sheet	67	5
Cross-Reference	143	9
Field codes/Update	27 & 113	2
Footnotes & Endnotes	33	3
Forms	23 & 116	2
Index	15	1
Macros	104	7
MailMerge	99	7
Master Documents	128	9
Password	18 & 32	1
Sections	36	3
Styles	78 &132	6
Table calculations	65	5
Templates	96	7
Text boxes	42	4
Text effects	50	4
TOC	81	6
Track Changes	120	8
Watermark	10	1
Widow/orphans	9	1

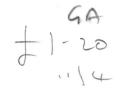

Heinemann Educational Publishers
Halley Court, Jordan Hill, Oxford OX2 8EJ
Part of Harcourt Education Ltd

Heinemann is the registered trademark of Harcourt Education Limited

First published 2004

09 08 07 06 05 04
10 9 8 7 6 5 4 3 2 1

British Library Cataloguing in Publication Data is available
from the British Library on request.

ISBN 0 435 46298 9

Designed by Artistix, Thame, Oxon
Typeset by TechType, Abingdon, Oxon
Original illustrations © Harcourt Education, 2004

Cover design by Tony Richardson at the the Wooden Ark Ltd

Printed in the UK by Thomson Litho Ltd

Acknowledgements
I would like to thank everyone at Heinemann who has offered advice, guidance and support. For my boys, Ryan and Adam.
Christine Blackham

The publishers would like to thank Duncan Grey, Project Gutenberg for permission to reproduce the Samuel Pepys diary extracts. The text can be seen at the Sanuel Pepys website at http://www.pepys.info and the whole of the text is also available from Project Gutenberg.

The Health and Safety (Fees) Regulations © Crown Copyright 1989.

Screen shots reprinted with permission from Microsoft Corporation.

Every effort has been made to contact copyright holders of material reproduced in this book. Any omissions will be rectified in subsequent printings if notice is given to the publishers.

Websites
Please note that the examples of websites suggested in this book were up to date at the time of writing. It is essential for tutors to preview each site before using it to ensure that the URL is still accurate and the content is appropriate. We suggest that tutors bookmark useful sites and consider enabling students to access them through the school or college intranet.

Tel: 01865 888058 www.heinemann.co.uk

Getting started

Style conventions

Text in **bold** denotes Word menu or selection options.

PC setting conventions

Drop-down menus

It will be easier to follow the instructions if you set the drop-down menus on your machine to show all the options rather than the most recently used options.

Method

1 Right-click on the menu bar (underneath the blue bar at the top of the screen), select: **Customize**. The Customize dialogue box appears.

2 Click on the **Options** tab, then click in the tick box to select: **Always show full menus**.

3 Click on: **Close**.

Handy Hint

If you are unsure which options are available to you as you work through the tasks, remember that right-clicking on an object will nearly always provide you with a drop-down menu of possibilities.

Toolbars

You may also want to see all the icons on the Standard Toolbar and Formatting Toolbar, rather than the shared row.

Method

To give each toolbar a separate row:

1 Use the method as above, but this time select: **Show standard and formatting toolbars on two rows**.

2 Click on: **Close**.

You should get three rows at the top of your screen, as shown in Figure 1.

Figure 1 Select a separate row for each toolbar

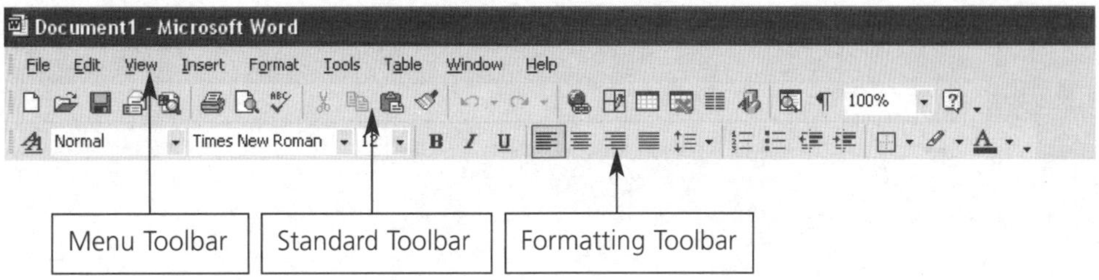

Measurements

The instructions in this book and the assignment are in centimetres. If your machine is set to work in inches, use the following method to change your machine setting.

Method

1. On the main menu toolbar, click on: **Tools**, then select: **Options**.
2. In the Options dialogue box, select the **General** tab.
3. From the **Measurement units** drop-down menu, select: **Centimeters**.

Dialogue boxes

As you go through the tasks, you will be working with dialogue boxes. These boxes have blue bars across the top and most have a selection of tabs that contain various Word functions. For example, Figure 2 shows the dialogue box for the AutoCorrect function.

Figure 2 The AutoCorrect dialogue box

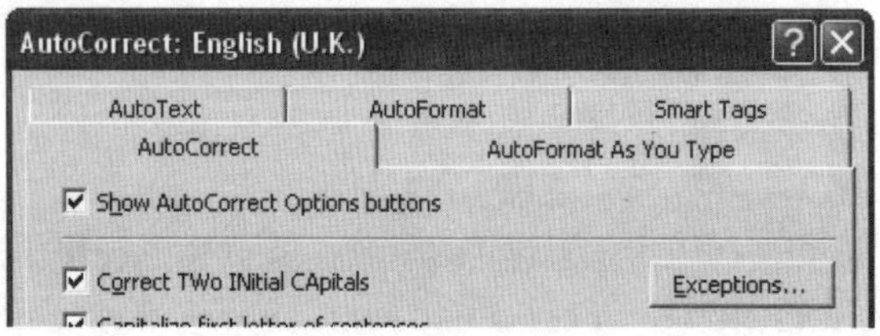

The functions displayed in a dialogue box are not appropriate to use all the time, but it is important that you become aware of what is behind the tabs.

Method

1. From the main menu bar, click on **Tools,** then select: **AutoCorrect Options**.
2. Click on the tabs to see the range of settings that you could apply to your document.

Task 1 Daniel Defoe handout

In this task, you will cover the following skills:

- Select different viewing options.
- Create multiple column layouts.
- Modify column width and spacing.
- Apply text effect options.
- Use paragraph shading and border options.
- Apply widow and orphan controls to paragraphs.
- Add a watermark to a document.
- Use text wrapping options.
- Create footnotes and endnotes.
- Create or edit an index.
  - o Select text for the index.
  - o Create the index from the marked entries.
- Add password protection to a document.
- Print odd and even number pages only, and a defined selection.

Scenario

You have been given a file that contains text from a Daniel Defoe book. The owners of the file have requested that you produce a document to be handed out at a meeting.

Unfortunately, the file was originally produced on a word processor that was not able to format, and what you have received is unformatted text. As this is a first meeting and the attendees are new to the group, the Chair of the meeting would like it updating. Your task is to transform the text into a document that will capture their attention.

1.1 Select different viewing options

Method

1 In Word, **Open** the file **Text for Task 1** from the Task Files folder on the CD-ROM.

2 As you can see when you click on the **Print Preview** icon, the document is 8 pages.

3 **Save** your document as: **Task 1**.

4 You need to work with the document in **View**: **Print Layout** so that 'what you see is what you get'. There are three other views that could have appeared on your screen. Your document should look like Figure 1.1.

Figure 1.1 Opening a saved file in View: Print Layout

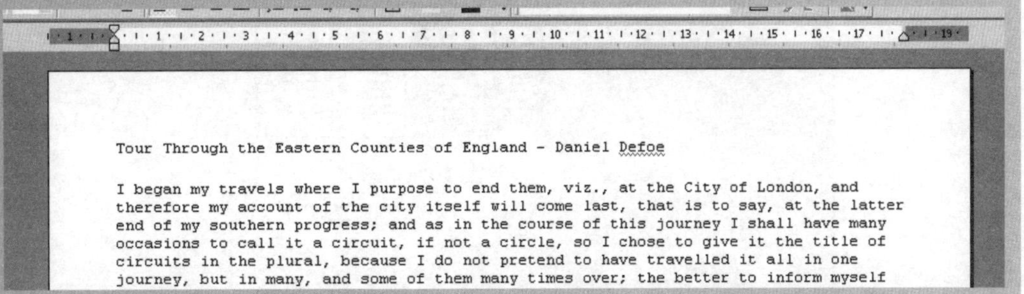
Tour Through the Eastern Counties of England - Daniel Defoe

I began my travels where I purpose to end them, viz., at the City of London, and therefore my account of the city itself will come last, that is to say, at the latter end of my southern progress; and as in the course of this journey I shall have many occasions to call it a circuit, if not a circle, so I chose to give it the title of circuits in the plural, because I do not pretend to have travelled it all in one journey, but in many, and some of them many times over; the better to inform myself

You should be able to see the text in a line across the page and be able to see the outside edges of the 'paper', i.e. there is a grey background.

5 Try changing the view to look at the different options. Click on: **View** and then select in turn: **Normal**, **Web Layout**, **Print Layout** and **Outline**.

6 Leave your document in **Print Layout** view.

1.2 *Create multiple column layouts*

The first formatting you are going to do is to put the document into newspaper columns, i.e. vertical columns of text so that the reader does not have to read across the full page width. You will set the text in two columns per page.

Method

Make sure that the I-beam cursor is on the page. Two methods are given below:

METHOD 1:

- Click on: **Format: Columns**, then select: **Two** (see Figure 1.2).

Figure 1.2 Selecting two text columns in Format: Columns

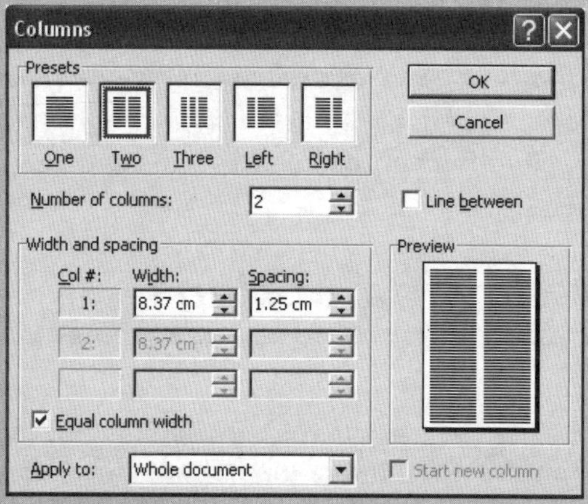

- Click on: **OK**. The document should now be in two columns.

METHOD 2:

- Click on the **Columns** icon on the Standard Toolbar.

Figure 1.3 Click on the Columns icon on the Standard Toolbar

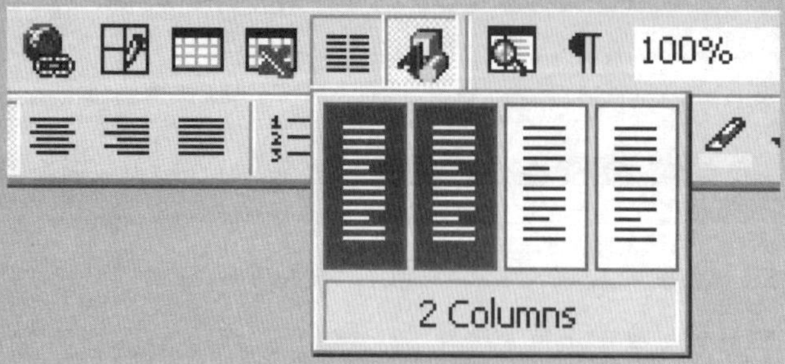

Practise this skill using both methods.

Set the document to three columns.

Now set the document to two columns with a wider right-hand column. To do this you need to use the first method to make the Columns dialogue box active.

Method

1 Click on: **Format**: **Columns**.

2 Remove the 'tick' from the **Equal Column Width** box. Once you have done this, you can use the up and down arrows to change the column widths. The **Preview** box will show you what is happening.

Figure 1.4 Adjusting column width in Format: Columns

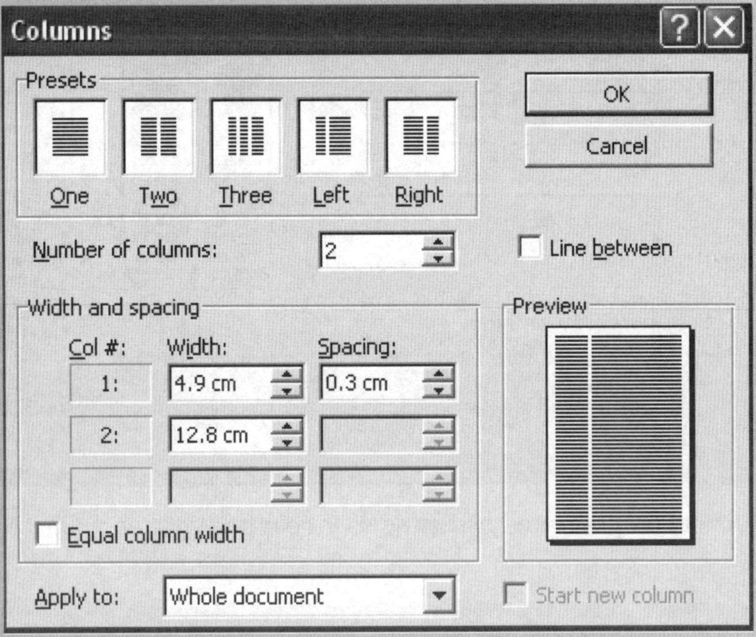

3 Set the document back to 2 columns of equal width, i.e. make the **Equal Column Width** box active. Set the **Spacing** between the columns to 1.27 cm. This is the default setting.

Handy Hint

If you wanted to apply column formatting to a section of your text, rather than the whole document, you can make this choice from the Apply To drop-down menu in Format: Columns.

You should have two columns of text including the heading.

1.3 *Change column width and spacing*

It now looks as though the columns are too wide. You will modify this and put a line down the centre of the columns to separate them.

Method

1 Click on: **Format**: **Columns**.

2 Make the selections as shown in Figure 1.5. Look at the Preview box to check the changes.

Figure 1.5 Changing the column width and checking the changes in the Preview box

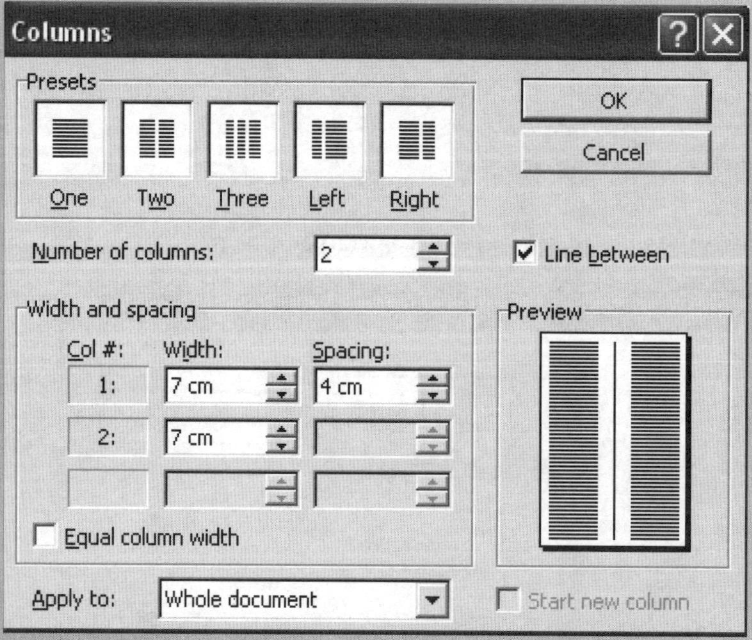

3 Click on: **OK**.

The text could be presented as newspaper columns with each line of text the same length.

Method

1 Hold down the **Ctrl** key and press: **A** to select all the text in the document.

2 Click on the **Justify Alignment** icon .

3 Click anywhere on your document to remove the 'reverse video' effect caused by selecting all the text.

The title heading of the document is currently in the first column. It should run along the top of the page above the two columns.

Method

1 Select the heading text.

2 Select: **Format**: **Columns**: **One**.

3 Click on: **OK**.

Figure 1.6 Setting the heading text to one column

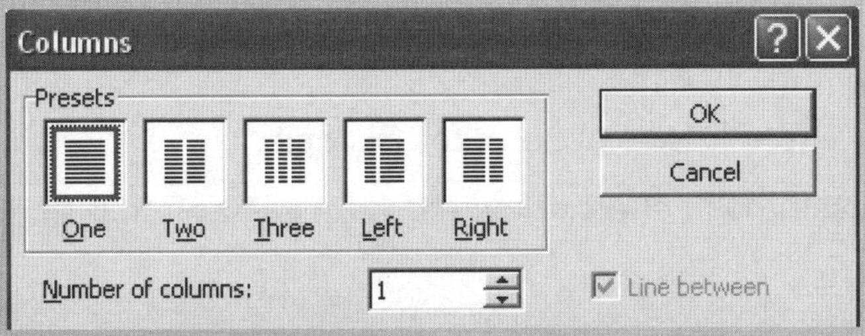

4 If you now click on the **Show/Hide** icon ¶ , you will see that the instruction **Section Break (Continuous)** has been added and the heading is running across the page.

5 Apply this formatting to the first paragraph using the same method.

6 Deselect: **Show/Hide**.

1.4 *Apply different effects to text*

You are going to change the font of the heading to Arial, 16 point, bold, with a shadow effect.

Method

1 Select the title text using the I-beam cursor or by triple-clicking.

2 Right-click (you must make this a quick click) to get the correct pop-up menu.

Handy Hint

If your right click is too slow, you will get the Move/Copy pop-up menu, which does not have the Font option.

Or:

3 Select **Format** from the main menu bar, then **Font**.

4 Make the following selections:

- **Font:** Arial
- **Font Style:** Bold
- **Size:** 16
- **Effects:** Shadow

Figure 1.7 Applying text effect options from the Font menu

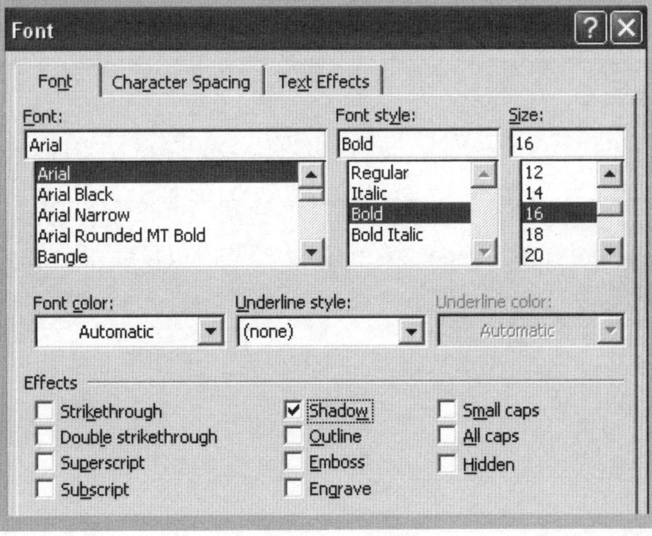

5 Look in the **Preview** box to see how your selections have affected the text.

6 Click on: **OK**.

Try more of the various Effects options, for example:

- Apply the Strikethrough effect to the second paragraph that starts with the words, 'I hope it will'.

Method

1 Select all the text in the paragraph either by triple-clicking or by using the I-beam cursor.

2 Select: **Format** from the main menu bar, then select: **Font**: **Strikethrough**.

3 Click on: **OK**.

- Apply the Superscript effect to the 'rd' in the date on the first line of the third paragraph.

Method

1 Select 'rd' after the number 3.

2 Select: **Format** from the main menu bar, then select: **Font**: **Superscript**.

3 Click on: **OK**.

- Apply a Subscript effect to 'Daniel Defoe' in the heading.

Method

1 Select 'Daniel Defoe'.

2 Select: **Format** from the main menu bar, then select: **Font**: **Subscript**.

3 Click on: **OK**.

- Try the Underline style drop-down menu on the heading. You can underline the words only and apply different styles, for example dotted, dashed or a combination of both. Do not add this effect to your work.

1.5 *Apply paragraph shading and borders*

You are now going to format the first paragraph with shading and a border.

Method

To apply the shading:

1 Triple-click in the first paragraph (or use the I-beam cursor to select the text).

2 Select: **Format** from the main menu bar, then select: **Borders and Shading**.

3 Click on the **Shading** tab, then select: **Gray-25%**. Apply to: **Paragraph**. <u>Do not click on OK.</u>

Method

4 Click on the **Borders** tab, then select:

- **Setting**: Box
- **Color:** Blue
- **Width:** $2\frac{1}{4}$ pt

Handy Hint

Take time when selecting the colour – hold the cursor still over the colour and you will get a pop-up text to confirm exactly which colour you are selecting.

5 Make sure that the **Apply to** box shows: **Paragraph**.

6 Click on: **OK**.

Figure 1.8 Applying a border around a paragraph

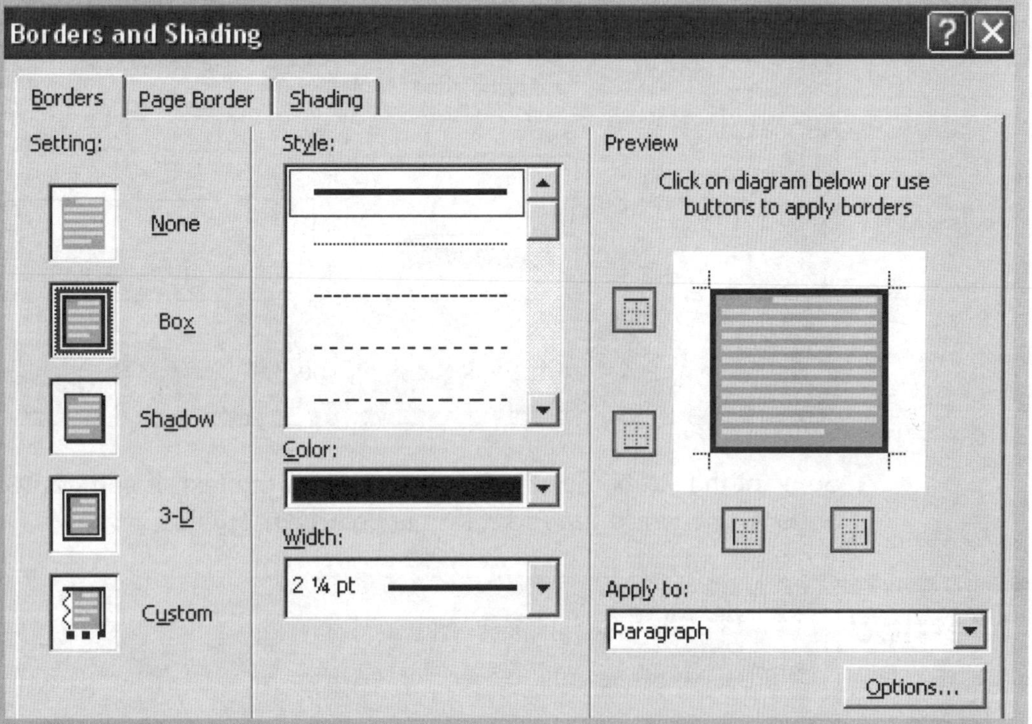

Handy Hint

The same method can be used to apply a border to any amount of text. For example, to apply a border around the whole page you would select the **Page border** tab.

Your borders do not have to be straight lines: you can choose to have Art around the edges of your document.

Method

1. Click on: **Format** from the main menu bar, then select: **Borders and Shading**.
2. Click on the **Page Border** tab, then click on the drop-down **Art** menu. Look at the various options and make a selection. An example is shown in Figure 1.9.

Figure 1.9 Using the Art drop-down menu on the Page Border tab

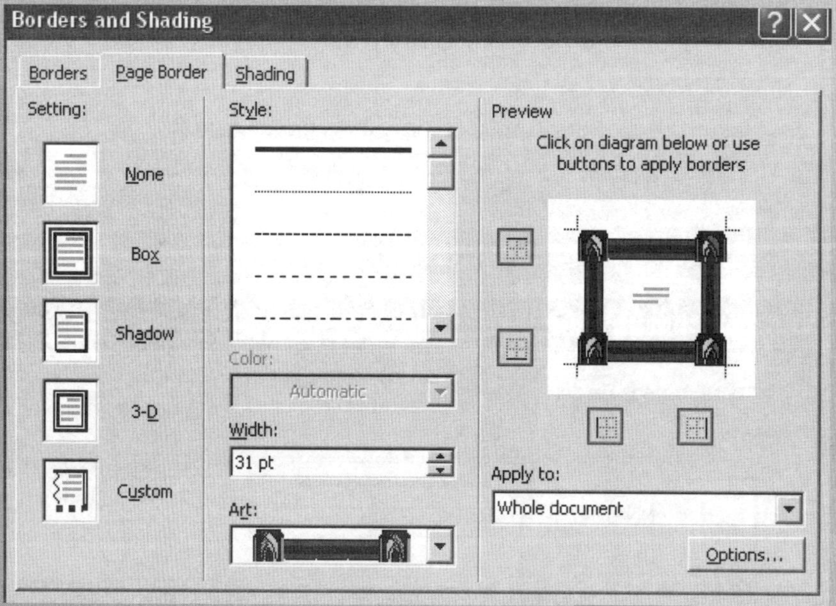

3. You will need to click on: **OK** to apply your selection.

Some of the Art borders flow over the top of the text. If you wanted to use these Art options, you would have to reformat your text. Try this:

Method

1. Select: **File** from the main menu toolbar.
2. Select: **Page Setup**.
3. Select the **Margins** tab and change the **Top**, **Bottom**, **Left** and **Right** margins, for example to 2.5 cm.
4. Apply to: **Whole document**, then click on: **OK**.
5. Click on the **Undo** icon to revert back.

As these Art borders are not appropriate for our purposes, make your final selection as follows.

Method

1. Click on: **Format** from the main menu bar, then select: **Borders and Shading**.
2. Click on the **Page Border** tab, then click on the drop-down **Art** menu. Select: **None**.
3. Select the following options:
   - **Setting**: Box
   - **Color:** Green
   - **Width:** $\frac{3}{4}$ pt
   - **Apply to:** Whole document

1.6 *Use widow and orphan controls*

You will see when you scroll through your document that you may have a line left on its own at the bottom of the column (orphan) or a line on its own at the top of a column (widow), i.e. it has become separated from the rest of the paragraph. To stop this happening you need to apply the widow and orphan control.

Method

1 Select all the text (**Ctrl** + **A**).

2 Click on: **Format** from the main menu bar, then select: **Paragraph**.

3 Select the **Line and Page Breaks** tab.

4 Select: **Widow/Orphan control**.

Figure 1.10 Selecting Widow/Orphan control in Format: Paragraph

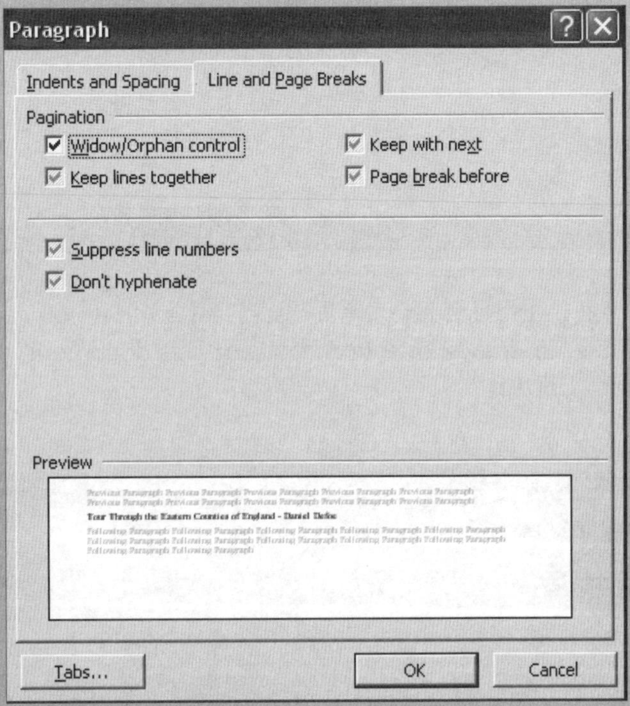

Handy Hint

If you have grey ticks in the boxes (as in the illustration above) then some of the text has already been formatted. Click in the Widow/Orphan control tick box until you get a black tick indicating that all the selected text has the formatting applied.

5 Click on: **OK**.

Click down on your document and scroll through your document again. You should not see any 'lonely' text.

1.7 *Insert a watermark*

The literary group would like a watermark added to the centre of the document to prevent it being photocopied and 'passed off' by anyone else.

Method

1. Select: **View**: **Header and Footer**.
2. Run the pointer tool over the icons in the pop-up dialogue box until you see **Show/Hide Document Text**.
3. Click on the **Show/Hide Document Text** icon

Figure 1.11 Selecting the Show/Hide Document Text icon

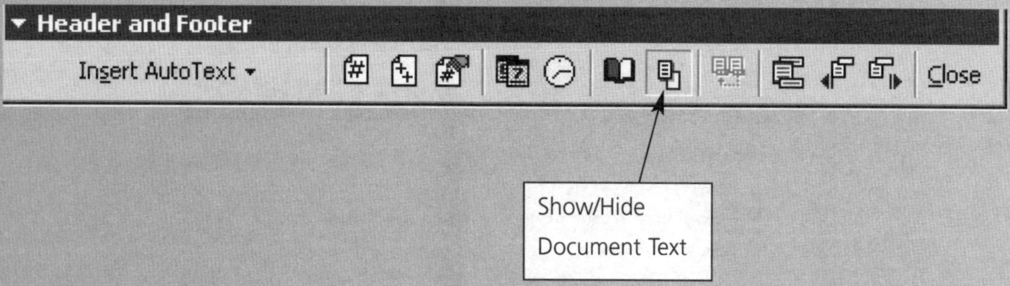

Don't panic! The text in the document will disappear so that you can work on inserting, for example, an image or a text box. For this document, you are going to insert an image from ClipArt.

Method

1. Select: **Insert**: **Picture**: **ClipArt**. The ClipArt task pane appears on the right-hand side of the screen. In the **Search For** box, key in **books**.
2. Click on: **Search**.
3. Click on your selection to insert the ClipArt into your document.

Figure 1.12 Inserting a picture from ClipArt

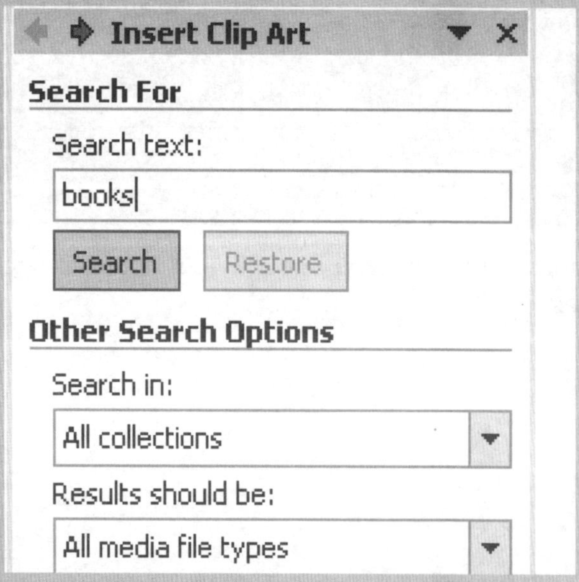

The image should now be in the header.

4 Close the **ClipArt** dialogue box by clicking on the 'X' in the right-hand corner of the task pane.

5 Click on your image to select it. This ensures that the **Picture Toolbar** is active. Click on the **Color** icon, then select: **Washout**. The image should now have changed to appear grey.

Figure 1.13 Selecting Washout from the Color icon on the Picture Toolbar

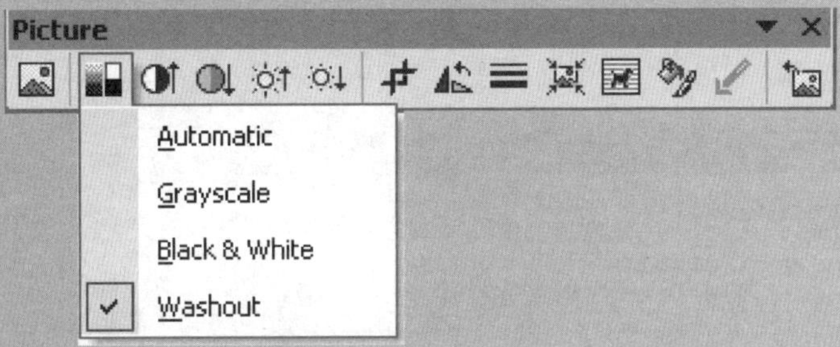

The image needs placing in the centre of the page: at the moment it is at the top of the page. You may find that the image you have chosen will not move when you click down (hold the mouse button down) and drag. This is because the image is formatted to be 'in line with text'. In this case, you will have to change the formatting of the image.

1.8 *Apply text wrapping*

Method

1 Double-click on the image to access **Format Picture**.

2 Select the **Layout** tab, then select: **Behind text**. This selection will allow the text to flow over the image and allow you to move the image.

Figure 1.14 Selecting Behind text to flow text over a chosen image

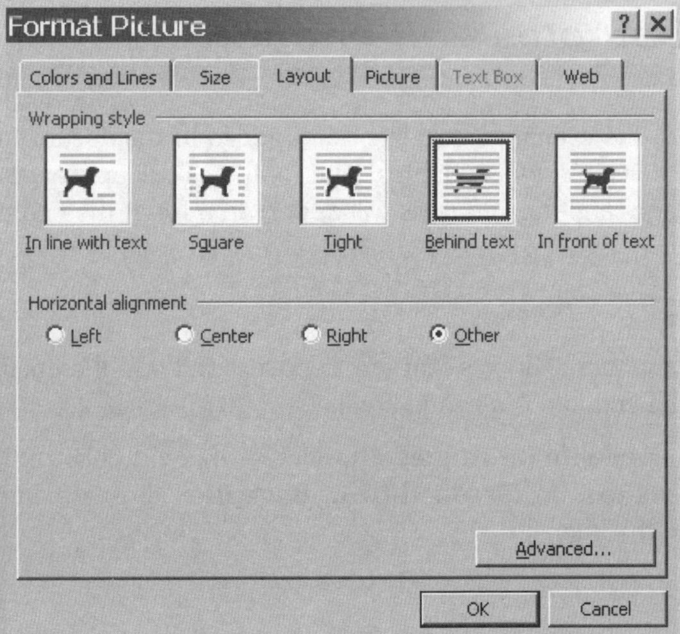

You can also centre the image vertically and horizontally using the Format Picture dialogue box, rather than making a 'best guess'.

Method

1. In the **Format Picture: Layout** dialogue box, click on the **Advanced** button (Figure 1.14).
2. Select the **Picture Position** tab.
3. Make the selections shown in Figure 1.15. You will need to click on the **Alignment** radio buttons (the small circles) before accessing the drop-down menus.

Figure 1.15 Centring an image vertically and horizontally in Format Picture

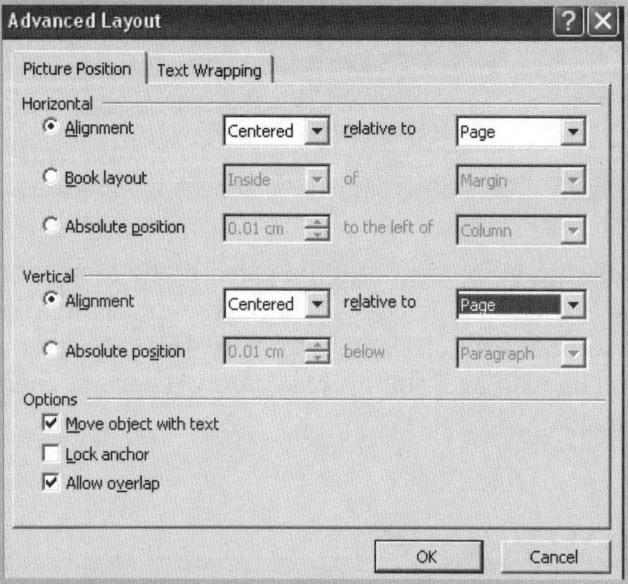

4. Click on: **OK** to clear the **Advanced Layout** dialogue box, then click on: **OK** to clear the Format Picture dialogue box. The image should now be in the centre of your page.
5. Click on: **Close** on the **Header and Footer** dialogue box. The image should move to the back of the text and appear on every page.

1.9 *Insert footnotes and endnotes*

The speaker for the evening would like notes added to the document. Two footnotes need to be included and two endnotes. The footnotes will appear at the bottom of the relevant pages and the endnotes will appear in a list at the end of the document.

Endnotes

Following are the two endnotes that are to be inserted into the document. The position of each endnote is given in brackets.

- **Maps are available on request** (position at the end of second paragraph).
- **Extra copies can be obtained from Reception** (position after the word 'England' in the title).

Method

1 Click in the text at the appropriate point, i.e. at the end of the second paragraph after the words 'opportunity to see them' to insert the note reference marker.

2 Click on: **Insert** from the main menu toolbar. Select: **Reference** then select: **Footnote** – this will access the **Footnote and Endnote** dialogue box.

3 Under **Location**, select the radio button **Endnotes**.

Handy Hint

You can change the symbol if you wish, but you will have to remember to change it for subsequent endnotes.

Figure 1.16 Inserting an endnote using the Footnote and Endnote dialogue box

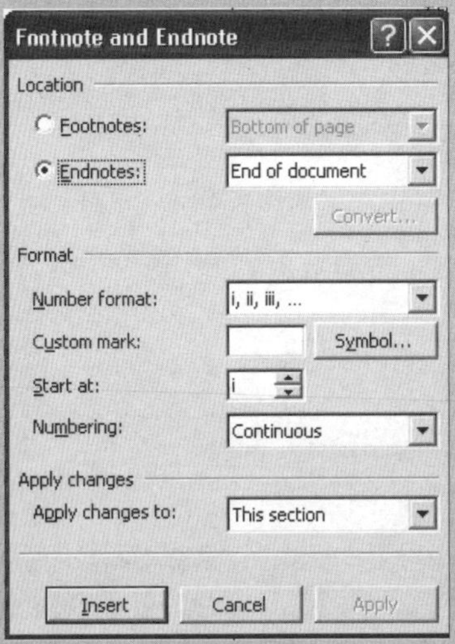

Handy Hint

You could reposition the endnotes (or footnotes) and change the formatting at this point if you wished. For this task, we want the endnote to fit the options shown below.

4 Select the following endnote options (as illustrated in Figure 1.16).

- **Location**: end of document
- **Numbering**: continuous
- **Number format**: set to Roman numerals.

5 Click on: **Insert**.

6 The cursor will move to the end of the document. Key in the text you want to appear, i.e. **Maps are available on request**. If you now run the cursor over the position of the Endnote at the end of the second paragraph (use **Ctrl** + **Home** keys to get to the top of the document), you will see a symbol attached to the cursor and the Endnote text on-screen. You will find this much easier to do if you have your screen set to Normal View rather than Print Preview.

Handy Hint

If you wish to delete the endnote (or footnote) for any reason, you do this by selecting the note reference marker in the main body of the document and pressing the Delete key.

Repeat this method for the second endnote, i.e. **Extra copies can be obtained from Reception**. You will notice that Word recognises that the second endnote you inserted should go before the first endnote.

Footnotes

Following are the two footnotes that are going to be inserted and positioned at the bottom of the page. The exact position of each footnote is given in brackets.

- **of an ancient Roman Catholic family** (position after the name 'Fanshaw').
- **Mr Martin Creswell** (position after the word 'Newbrugh').

Method

To find the position quickly where the footnotes are to be inserted:

1 Click on: **Edit** from the main menu toolbar, then select: **Find**.

2 In the **Find what** box, key in the word 'Fanshaw'.

3 Click on: **Find Next**. The cursor moves directly to the word and highlights it.

4 Close the Find and Replace dialogue box by clicking on the '**X**' or the **Cancel** button.

Figure 1.17 Using the Find what box to access a position quickly

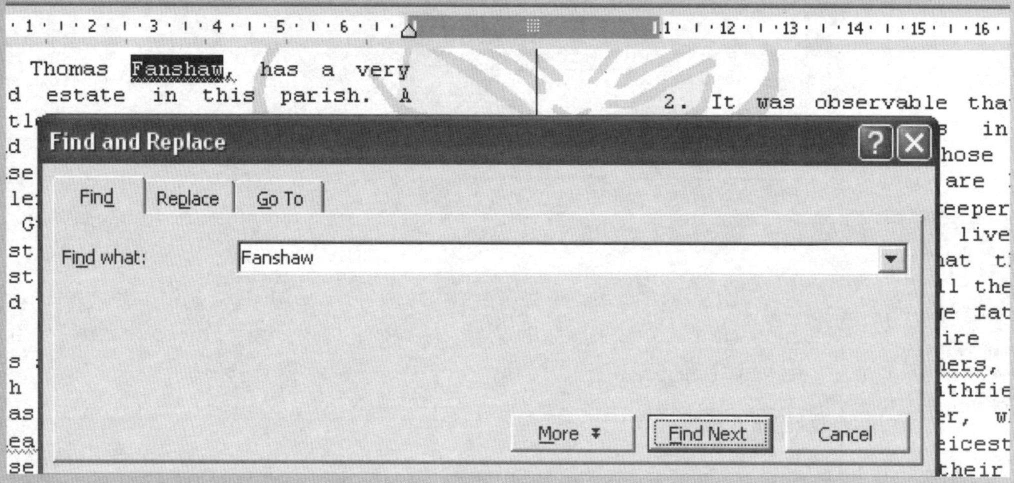

Method

To insert a footnote:

1 Position your cursor after the 'w' in Fanshaw and click.

2 Click on: **Insert** from the main menu toolbar, then select: **Reference**. Select: **Footnote**.

3 Select: the **Footnotes** radio button.

4 Click on: **Insert**. The cursor will move to the bottom of the page.

5 Key in the text you want to appear.

Repeat this method for the second footnote.

Handy Hint

You will need to click in the body of the text if you want to use Find again. If you don't, Word will look in the footnote area only for the new word and the search will fail.

Check that your footnotes and endnotes appear in the document by moving the pointer close to the Footnote/Endnote markers in the text.

1.10 Create an index

Part of the discussion on the Daniel Defoe document is going to focus on the geography of the area in the novel. Being able to focus quickly on certain geographical features will help the speaker to make his or her point. You can mark these items using an index.

Indexes are similar to producing a table of contents, in that Word will automatically search and produce a list for you. You will see later that tables of contents are produced from text that has a specified style applied to it, whereas an index is defined by determining the exact words you want to appear in your index and hence the words you want Word to search for.

There are two parts to producing an index. The first part is to select (mark) the text; the second is to create the index from the marked entries.

Select text for the index

Method

1. Click on: **Insert** from the main menu bar, then select: **Reference**. Select: **Index and Tables**.
2. Select the **Index** tab.
3. Click on: the **Mark Entry** button.

You should now have the Mark Index Entry dialogue box on-screen.

The next step is to mark the words you want to be indexed, i.e. 'rivers', 'canals', 'villages', 'marshes' and 'towns'. You may need to use Find and Replace if you cannot immediately see these words.

Handy Hint

You can use the Mark Index Entry and Find and Replace dialogue boxes on-screen at the same time. You can move between the two without closing either, and can highlight the selected words on the main document at the same time.

Method

1. Find the word 'river' using **Edit**: **Find**. It does not matter if the word that you highlight is not the first occurrence of the word in the document.
2. Click in the **Main Index Entry** box. The word 'rivers' should appear in the box.
3. In page number format, select **Bold** and **Italic**. This determines the style in which the page numbers appear in the index.
4. Click on: **Mark All**. This tells Word that you want <u>all</u> instances of the word 'river' marking.

Have a look at your document now. Word has automatically turned on the Show/Hide facility. You should be able to see the 'XE' marker in brackets after the selected words.

Figure 1.18 Selecting index items using the Main Index Entry dialogue box and the Find and Replace dialogue box

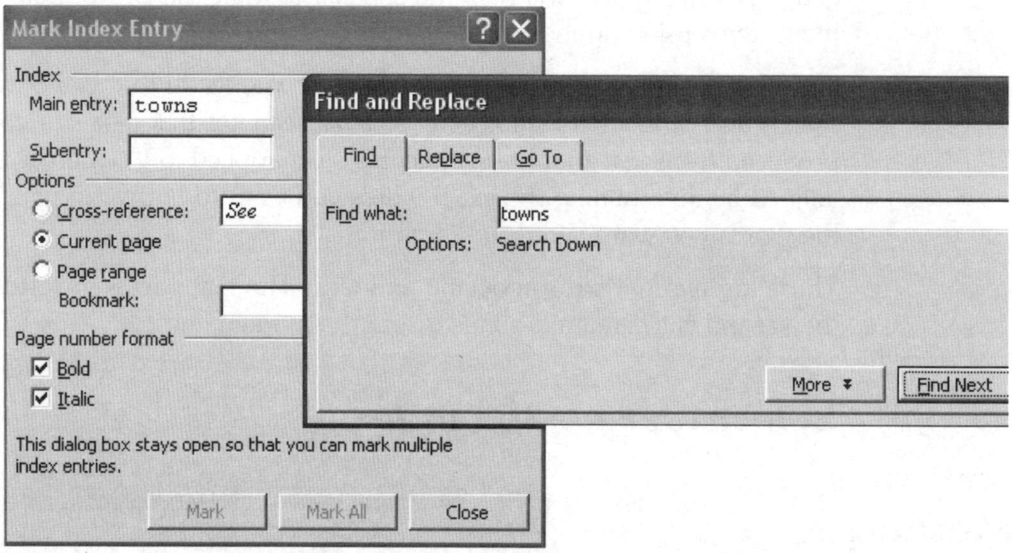

5. Click on your document. The Mark Index Entry box should remain on-screen so that you can continue to use it.

Method

1. Find the word 'canals' using **Edit**: **Find**.
2. Click in the **Main Index Entry** box, and 'rivers' will change to 'canals'.
3. Click on: **Mark All**.
4. Repeat this sequence (steps 1 to 3), marking the words 'villages', 'marshes' and 'towns'.
5. Click on: **Close** to remove the Index and Tables dialogue box.
6. Click on: **Cancel** to close the Find and Replace dialogue box.

The first part of creating an index in Word is complete.

The second part, creating the index from the marked entries, is the easier part. The most important instruction to remember is that you must position the cursor at the point where you want the index to appear.

Create the index from the marked entries

Method

1 Click at the end of the document but before the endnotes.

Handy Hint

If you click after the endnotes, the index will not work. The reason for this is that the endnote has an instruction that it should appear at the end of the document.

2 Click on: **Insert** from the main menu bar, then select: **Reference**. Select: **Index and Tables**.

3 Select the **Index** tab.

4 Click on: **OK**.

You should now have an index positioned at the end of the text and before the endnotes. This is the default index. You can amend this by going back into Index and Tables and changing the options.

Method

1 Click on: **Insert**: **Reference**: **Index and Tables**, then select the **Index** tab.

2 Select the **Right align page numbers** option.

3 Using the **Tab leader** drop-down menu, select the dotted line.

4 Using the **Formats** drop-down menu, look at the different formats shown in the **Print Preview** box. Select: **Fancy**.

5 Click on: **OK**.

6 Click on: **Yes** to replace the selected index. Your index should now look something similar to Figure 1.19.

Figure 1.19 Setting the index style on the Index tab in Index and Tables

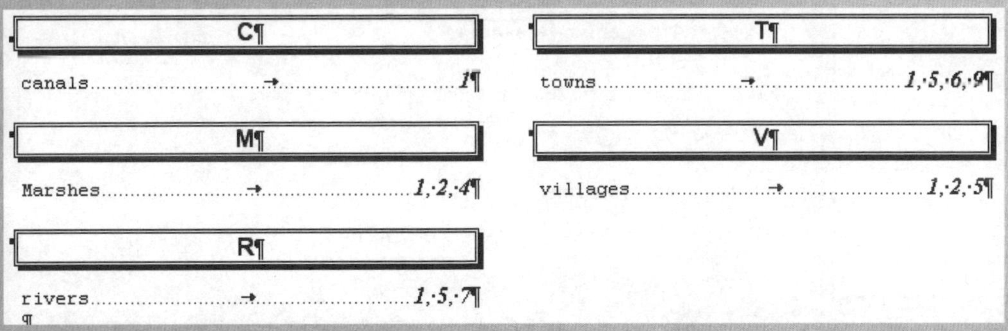
C¶
canals → 1¶
M¶
Marshes → 1,·2,·4¶
R¶
rivers → 1,·5,·7¶
¶
T¶
towns → 1,·5,·6,·9¶
V¶
villages → 1,·2,·5¶

You can see easily from Figure 1.19 that 'canals' only appears once in the document, whereas 'towns' appears four times. [Note: Depending on how your PC is set up, your page numbers may be different.]

1.11 *Add password protection to a document*

As your work area is a shared area, you may want to be totally confident that your work will not be lost or modified. One way you can do this is to add a password to your document.

Method

With your document on-screen:

1. Click on: **File**: **Save As**.
2. Click on: **Tools**, then select: **Security Options**.

Figure 1.20 Click on Tools, then select Security Options

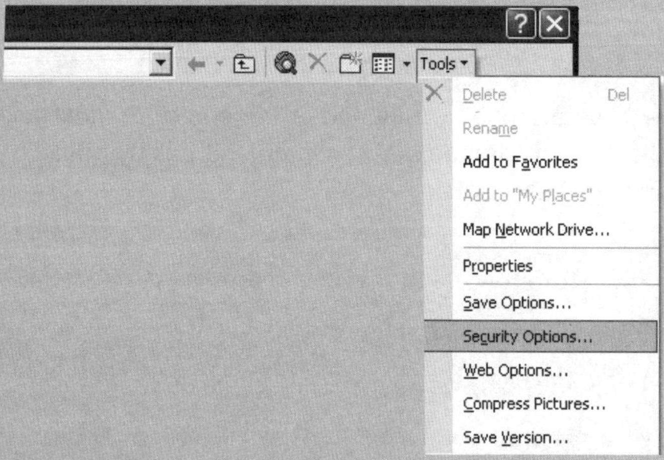

3. You can choose two passwords: one to open the document and one to modify the document. The second password will allow others to view the document but not to modify it.

Figure 1.21 Entering passwords to open and modify the document

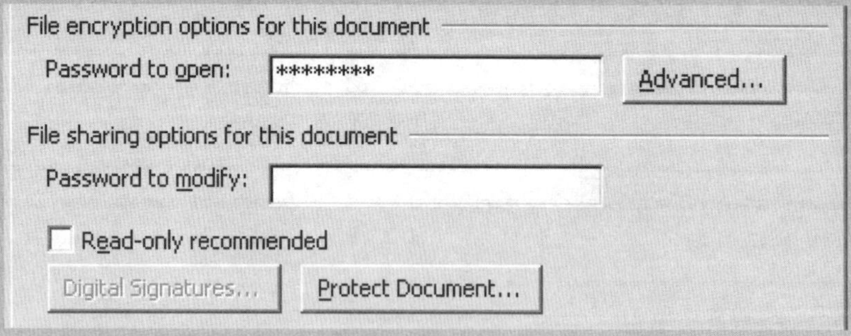

Handy Hint

CAUTION: Passwords appear as asterisks. Be very careful that you key in correctly and remember that passwords are case sensitive.

4. Key in your password.
5. Click on: **OK**. You will be asked to confirm the password to re-open the file.
6. Click on: **OK**.
7. Save your document as: **Task 1**.
8. To check that your password is working, close the document and re-open it.

Handy Hint

CAUTION: Write down your password (or use a password you know you will remember) so that you can access your document.

1.12 *Print a selection of pages*

You will print the first and last page of your document to check style and layout.

Method

1. Click on: **File**: **Print**.
2. In **Page Range**, select the **Pages** radio button and key in: **1,9** (if 9 is your last page, otherwise key in your last page number).
3. In **Zoom**, select from the **Pages per sheet** drop-down menu: **2 pages**. Printing in this way will save time, paper and ink.
4. In **Printer**, check that the name of your printer is selected from the **Name** drop-down menu.

Figure 1.22 Selecting print options in File: Print

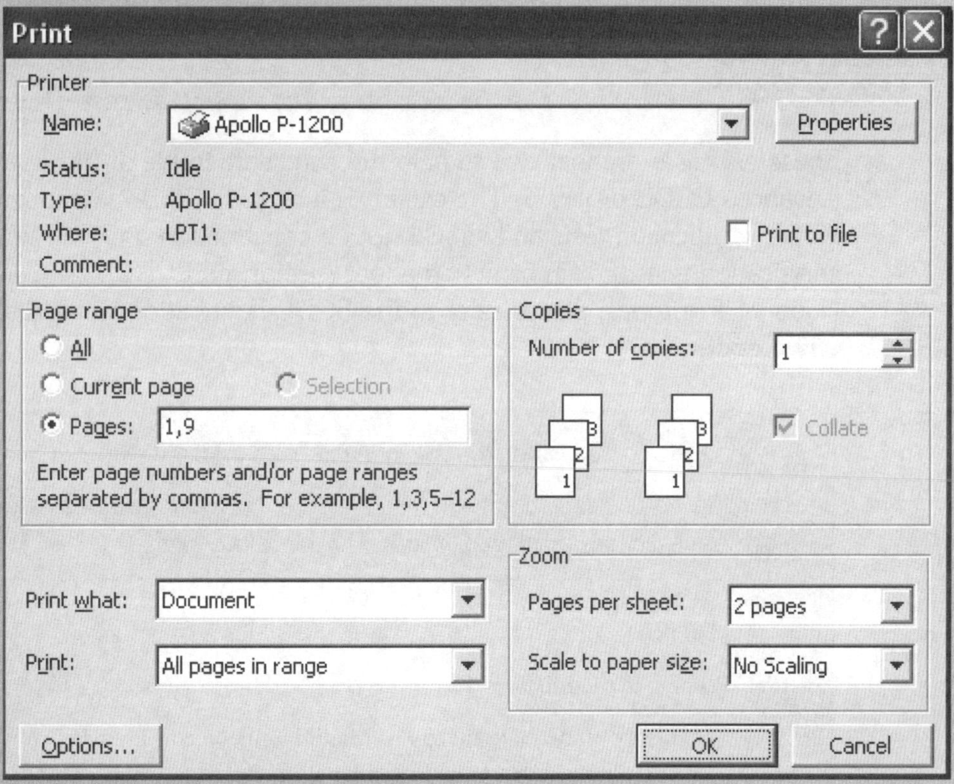

When selecting pages for printing:

- A comma is used to select individual pages. For example, if you wanted to print pages 1, 3 and 8, you would key in 1,3,8.
- A hyphen is used to indicate a range of pages. For example, if you wanted to print the first page and the last 3 pages of a 9-page document, you would key in 1,7-9.

Look at the following print options:

- The **Print what** drop-down menu allows you to select which element of your file you want to print, for example, Document properties.
- The **Print** drop-down box allows you to print all the pages (default). Alternatively, you can select to print odd number pages or even number pages only.

Handy Hint

In Print, the Options button allows you to format your printing output to your own requirement. Draft output and Reverse print order are two very useful selections:

- Draft output saves on ink.
- Reverse print order saves you having to re-order your pages after printing. However, the disadvantage of Reverse print order is that it can slow down the printing process.

Practice Task *Task 1*

These exercises are included to help the candidate in his or her training for the Advanced ECDL program. The exercises included in this material are not Advanced ECDL certification tests and should not be construed in any way as Advanced ECDL certification tests. For information about Authorised ECDL Test Centres in different National Territories, please refer to the ECDL Foundation website at **www.ecdl.com**.

Open the File named **Madrid** from your Task Files folder.

The following text should appear. It is for a flyer that you have been asked to produce for a local travel agent's holiday to Madrid.

> MADRID
>
> Panoramic Madrid
>
> The history of the majestic city of Madrid will come to life when you allow your guide to introduce you to its incredible past. Once an Arabian Fortress, this city is now a thriving cultural centre bursting with monuments, galleries and museums. You will even see Santiago Bernabeu Stadium, home of the famous Real Madrid football team.

Artistic Madrid

Introducing one of the world's greatest art galleries. The Prado Museum holds major works from all the great schools of European art, including paintings by Rubens, Rafael, Goya and El Greco. Let our guides take you there. Then move on to explore the 18th-century Royal Palace.

Toledo, El Escorial, Valley of the Fallen

Journey south of Madrid into a long forgotten world as you discover the ancient city of Toledo, once the medieval capital of Spain. Become familiar with the life of a monk as you tour El Escorial Monastery, and spare some thought for the dead of the Spanish Civil War in the Valley of the Fallen - the history of this country will simply amaze you.

Madrid by Night

At night, Spaniards put on their dancing shoes and step out for an evening of fun, feasting, and friendly flirting. After a panoramic drive to see the city lights, you'll join the locals at the Florida Park nightclub. Enjoy a fabulous tapas meal, a flamenco show, and all-night dancing.

1 Display the text in landscape with four columns of equal width.

2 Change the spacing between the columns to 2 cm.

3 Display the text fully justified.

4 Apply pagination, widow and orphan control.

5 Centre the heading 'MADRID' so that it appears above columns 2 and 3.

Handy Hint

Before you align the heading, highlight the word 'MADRID' and format to one column. This inserts a section break.

6 Place a 3 pt shadow border around each subheading. Apply to text.

Handy Hint

If the subheading is on two rows, you will need to apply the border to Paragraph, not Text.

7 Change the subheadings to Arial, bold, blue, 14 pt.

Handy Hint

If you need to reformat the borders, because the subheading has gone onto two lines, you will need to remove the border from the 'text'.

8 Change the heading to bold 48 pt.

9 Apply an outline effect to the heading.

10 Shade each subheading with yellow.

Handy Hint

If you have done this correctly, the yellow colour will not 'fill' the border but will flow outside the box.

11 Insert an appropriate image for a coach holiday from ClipArt and set the image as a watermark in the header.

Handy Hint

Key in 'bus' in the Search for Clips box.

12 Format the coach image so that text flows over the top and bottom.

13 Resize the image so that the height is 7 cm.

14 Position the image at the bottom right-hand side of the page.

15 Ensure that you can see the watermark.

16 Expand the character spacing on the heading to 200%.

Handy Hint

Format: Font.

17 Insert an appropriate image from ClipArt that represents sunshine.

18 Position the image at the top of column 2, and resize if necessary. Apply a text wrap so that the text does not flow over the image.

Handy Hint

Apply the text wrap before you move the image.

19 Insert column breaks to ensure that each subheading starts at the top of the column.

Handy Hint

Position the cursor in front of the subheading and select: Insert: Break: Column Break: OK. If the image moves around, drag it back into position.

20 Adjust the size of the text in column 1 so that the text fills the column without pushing text out from the other columns.

21 Create the footnote 'See leaflet 6' after the word 'dancing' at the bottom of the fourth column.

22 In Symbol, apply the heart as a Custom Mark.

23 Spell-check your work.

24 Print the current page only.

25 Save your work as **Task 1 Answer**.

26 Use your place of birth as a password to protect the document.

Task 2 Staff planner

In this task, you will cover the following skills:

- Create a form.
- Use available form field options.
  - o Text form field.
  - o Drop-down menu.
- Protect a form.
- Edit a form.
- Use merge cells options in a table.
- Insert a field code.
- Delete a field code.
- Lock or unlock a field.
- Use split cell options in a table.

Scenario

While the Daniel Defoe document is with the Literary Group for checking, you have been tasked with drawing up the staff-evening rota for the next month. The rota is for part-time staff working on a very flexible basis. This means that the document is constantly being amended as staff change their working hours. To make the planning easier you can insert into a form all the names of the staff available at a particular time of day, and then select them as and when changes occur.

2.1 *Create a form*

Method

1. Open a New Blank Document by clicking on the icon.
2. To bring up the Forms toolbar, select **View** from the main menu bar, then select: **Toolbars**: **Forms**.
3. Run the pointer tool over the icons on the Forms Toolbar to see the options you have available.

Figure 2.1 Options on the Forms Toolbar

For this exercise, you will need to start with a table.

Method

1. From the Forms toolbar, select the **Insert Table** icon.
2. Select the maximum table size it will allow, i.e. a 4 x 5 table. Select by clicking in the bottom right-hand cell.

Handy Hint

If you know exactly the size of table you require, you can create a larger table, i.e. with more rows and columns, by holding down the left mouse button and dragging diagonally from the first cell until you have the size you want.

3 Key in the text for the table, as shown below. Use the tab key to move around the table.

	Week 1	Week 2	Week 3	Week 4
Monday	G Forrest	G Forrest	G Forrest	G Forrest
Tuesday	G Forrest	G Forrest	G Forrest	G Forrest
Wednesday	G Forrest	G Forrest	G Forrest	G Forrest
Thursday	G Forrest	G Forrest	G Forrest	G Forrest
Friday	G Forrest	G Forrest	G Forrest	G Forrest

To create an extra row, insert the cursor in the bottom right-hand cell and press the tab key.

2.2 *Use form field options*

Text form field and drop-down menu

The names of the members of staff that work evenings need entering into the form. These are:

- G Forrest
- R Solangi
- A Ahmed
- P Wong
- Y Brown
- H Johnson

Method

1 Click in the cell for Week 1, Monday.

2 On the **Forms** toolbar, click on: **Drop-Down Form Field**.

Figure 2.2 The Drop-Down Form Field on the Forms toolbar

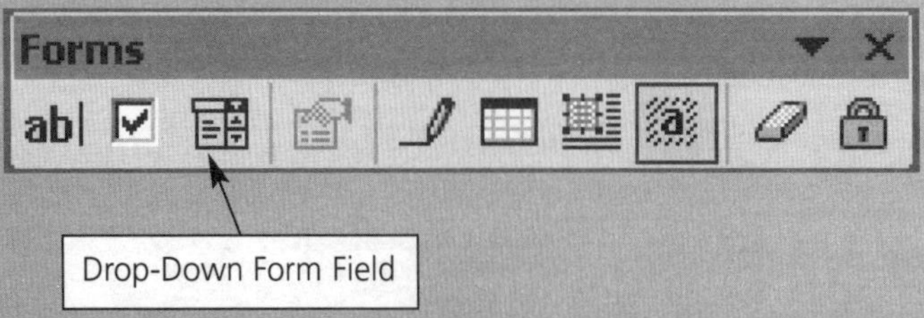

3 A shaded area will appear in the cell. Double-click in the shaded area and a **Drop-Down Form Field Options** dialogue box will appear (see Figure 2.3).

4 Key in the names of the staff in the **Drop-down item** box. After keying in each name, click on: **Add** (or press the **Enter** key) and the name will appear in the **Items in drop-down list** box.

Figure 2.3 Entering names in the Drop-down item box

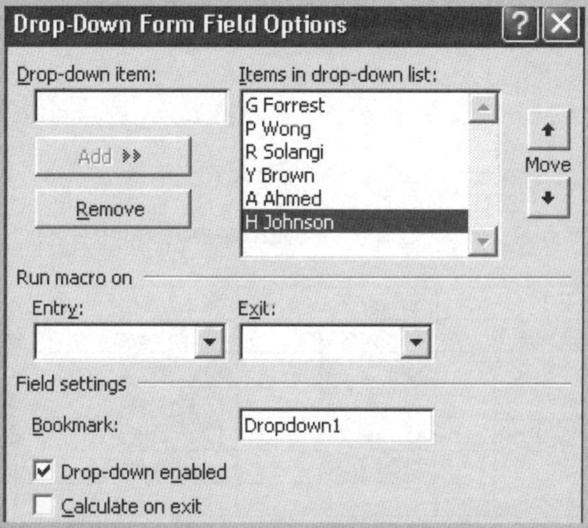

5 Click on: **OK**. You will see the first name in the shaded box.

Rather than spending time putting all the names into the other days and weeks, you can save time in the following way.

Method

1 Highlight the shaded cell by using the black pointer that appears at the left-hand side of the cell and clicking once.

2 Right-click once to access the pop-up menu, then select: **Copy**.

3 Highlight all the remaining cells up to Friday, Week 4.

4 Right-click once to access the pop-up menu, then select: **Paste Cells**. Your table should look like the one below.

	Week 1	**Week 2**	**Week 3**	**Week 4**
Monday	G Forrest	G Forrest	G Forrest	G Forrest
Tuesday	G Forrest	G Forrest	G Forrest	G Forrest
Wednesday	G Forrest	G Forrest	G Forrest	G Forrest
Thursday	G Forrest	G Forrest	G Forrest	G Forrest
Friday	G Forrest	G Forrest	G Forrest	G Forrest

The table is still not working as a form with drop-down fields yet. You have to 'protect the form' to make the drop-down menus active.

2.3 *Protect a form*

Method

1. If you have closed the Forms toolbar, access again by selecting **View**: **Toolbars**: **Forms**.
2. Click on the **Protect Form** icon (the icon that looks like a lock).
3. A drop-down arrow should appear. From this, you can select the staff names. Each of the cells in the table works independently, i.e. the arrow only appears in the cell when you click down into it.

Figure 2.4 Using the Protect Form icon to activate a drop-down menu

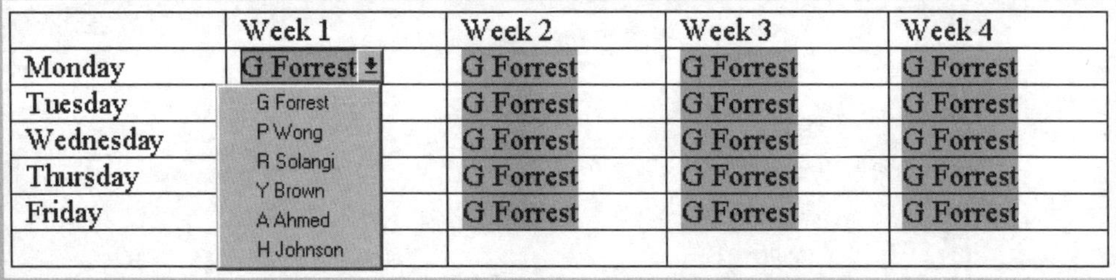

	Week 1	Week 2	Week 3	Week 4
Monday	G Forrest	G Forrest	G Forrest	G Forrest
Tuesday		G Forrest	G Forrest	G Forrest
Wednesday		G Forrest	G Forrest	G Forrest
Thursday		G Forrest	G Forrest	G Forrest
Friday		G Forrest	G Forrest	G Forrest

2.4 *Edit a form*

If you want to make changes to the drop-down menu, i.e. edit the form, you will have to unlock (unprotect) it by clicking once more on the Protect Form icon.

2.5 *Merge cells in a table*

The last row needs to be one column and the date and time fields need inserting.

Method

1. Make sure that the document is unprotected by clicking on the **Protect Form** icon on the **Forms** toolbar.
2. Select the last row of the table by moving the mouse pointer to the left of the row, outside the table. When the cursor changes to a white arrow, click and the row should be selected.
3. Right-click to access the pop-up menu, then select: **Merge Cells**.
4. Click into the last row. It should now appear as one cell.
5. Key in the words 'Last updated by' followed by a colon.
6. Hold down the **Ctrl** key and press the **tab** key twice to insert two tabs.
7. Key in the word 'Date' followed by a colon.
8. Hold down the **Ctrl** key and press the **tab** key twice to insert two tabs.
9. Key in the word 'Time' followed by a colon.

Handy Hint

You cannot insert tabs in tables unless you use both the Ctrl key and the tab key.

2.6 *Insert a field code*

Now that you have entered tab spaces between the texts on the last row, you can insert fields that automatically update whenever you open the document.

Method

To insert the date field:

1 Click in the table after the word 'Date:'.

2 Select: **Insert** from the main menu toolbar, then select: **Field** to access the Field dialogue box.

3 In **Categories**, select: **Date and Time**.

4 In **Field names**, select: **Date**.

5 Click on: **OK**. The date should now appear in the row.

Figure 2.5 Inserting the date field using the Field toolbar

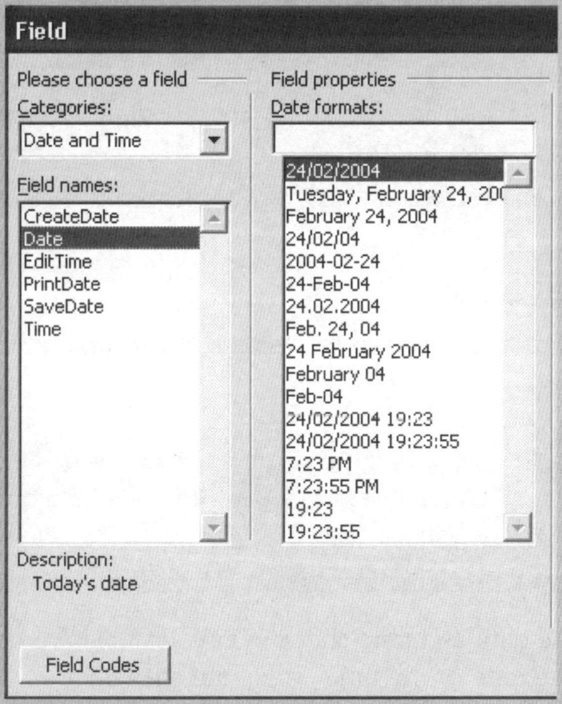

Method

To insert the time field, repeat steps 2–3 above, then:

1 In **Field names**, select: **Time**.

2 In **Date formats** select: **h:mm:ss am/pm**.

Figure 2.6 Selecting the date formats

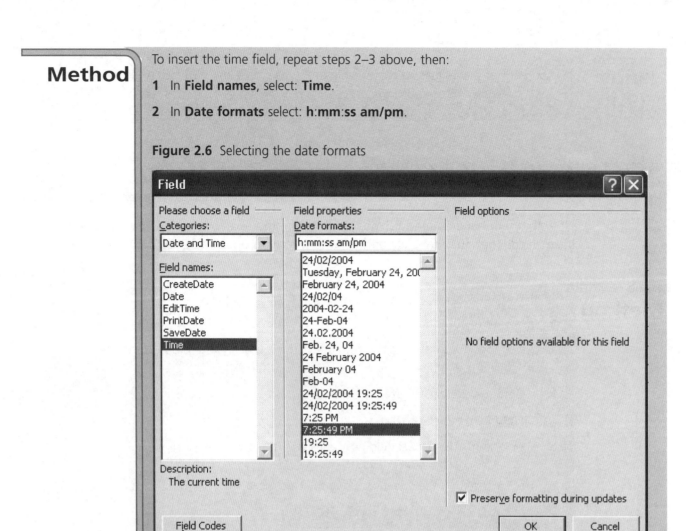

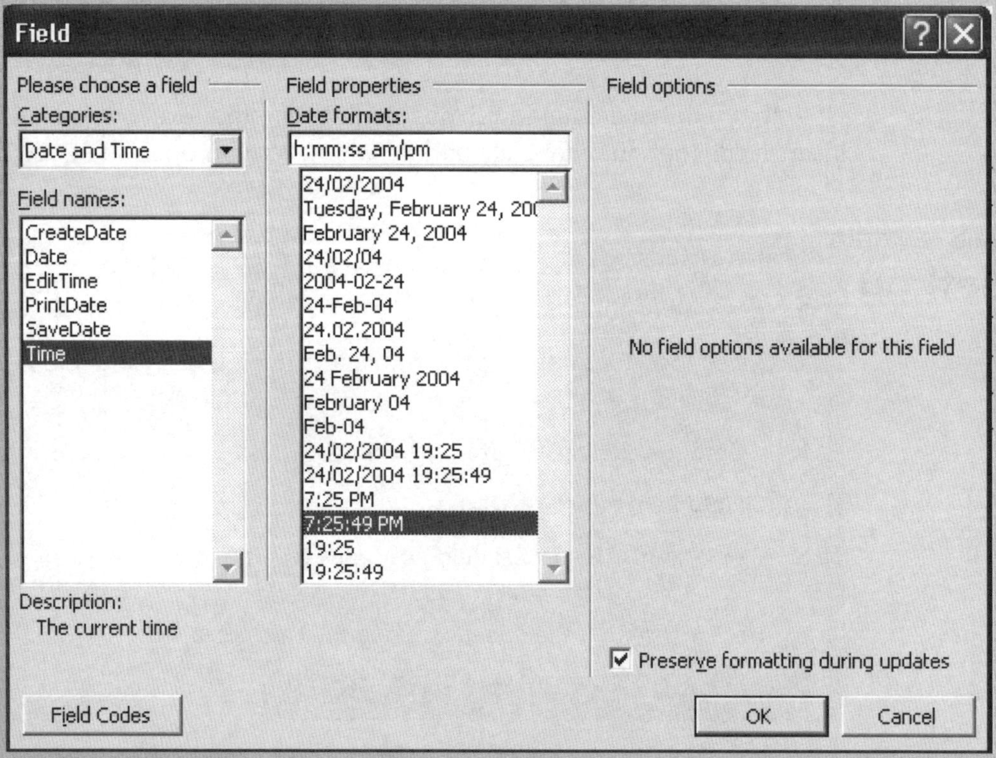

3 Click on: **OK**.

2.7 *Delete a field code*

Method

If you want to remove a field, for example if you inserted your field in the wrong position or selected the wrong field, you can delete it very easily. Double-click on the field to select it, then press the delete key on your keyboard.

You should now have the date and time showing in your table. You can see the fields if you click into either the date or the time – they are shaded.

2.8 *Lock and unlock a field*

To stop the fields automatically updating when the document is opened, i.e. so that you know when the table was last updated, you can lock the fields.

Method

Click in the 'Date:' field and press: **Ctrl** + **F11**. This action will lock the field.

If you right-click on the field now, you will see that Update Field is shaded out.

To unlock the field:

Method

Click in the field and press: **Ctrl** + **Shift** + **F11**.

Check if you can update the field using right-click and selecting **Update Field**. Then re-lock the field.

Handy Hint

The F9 function key also updates fields. Click in the 'Time:' field and press F9. The time should have been updated.

2.9 *Split cells in a table*

It would also be useful to have an extra box in the table, for writing comments on the hard copy (the printout). To make the box, you can split the existing cells.

Method

1 Select all the cells that contain drop-down fields. Be careful not to select any other cells, e.g. the row and column headers.

2 Click on: **Table** on the main menu bar, then select: **Split Cells**. A Split Cells dialogue box should appear. In the **Number of columns** box, the number should be: 8. In the **Number of rows** box, the number should be: 5.

Figure 2.7 Splitting cells in the Split Cells dialogue box

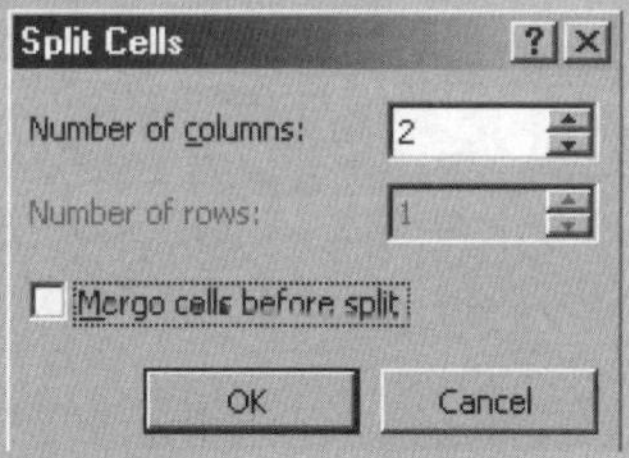

3 Deselect the **Merge cells before split** option by clicking to remove the tick. The **Number of Columns** changes to 2, the **Number of Rows** is shaded out.

4 Click on: **OK**.

You should now have an extra box next to each drop-down field.

There is always the possibility that someone else may update the document in your absence. You therefore need an area on the form where that person could insert his or her initials. The best way to do this is to insert a text field that the person updating can see.

Method

1 Position the cursor to the right of the text 'Last updated by:'.

2 On the Forms toolbar, click on the **Text Form Field** icon.

Handy Hint

You should have a shaded area inserted after the colon. If you do not, click anywhere inside the table and then, on the Forms toolbar, click on the Form Field Shading icon.

If the Last updated by field has caused the time field to go to the next row, select the row and choose a smaller font size.

3 Save your document as **Staff rota**.

Practice Task — *Task 2*

These exercises are included to help the candidate in his or her training for the Advanced ECDL program. The exercises included in this material are not Advanced ECDL certification tests and should not be construed in any way as Advanced ECDL certification tests. For information about Authorised ECDL Test Centres in different National Territories, please refer to the ECDL Foundation website at **www.ecdl.com**.

You work in a restaurant and one of your responsibilities is to decide which set menu is to be offered. The set menus are already prepared, but the season, time of day and availability of fresh food will affect the choice of menu throughout the year. Ten set menus are rotated every 12 weeks.

1 Create a table that has 3 columns and 13 rows.
   - Label column 2, 'Lunchtime'. Label column 3, 'Evening'.
   - Label rows 2 to 13, 'Week 1', 'Week 2', etc.

2 Create a drop-down menu for Week 1, Lunchtime. The text for the list is: Menu 1, Menu 2, Menu 3, etc. up to Menu 10.

3 Duplicate (copy and paste) the list for the Evening of Week 1 and for Weeks 2 to 12, for both Lunchtime and Evening.

4 Save your work as: **Task 2 Answer**.

5 Insert a row at the top of the table.

Handy Hint

Table: Insert: Rows Above.

6 Merge the two adjacent cells at the top of column 1 and column 2, and insert a date field.

7 Insert one row at the bottom of the table. Merge the cells at the bottom of columns 2 and 3 and insert a field that shows the File Name.

8 Protect the form and check that your drop-down form fields are working.

9 Using Pale Blue and Light Green colours, shade each Week row alternately.

Handy Hint

Format: Borders and Shading: Shading.

You need to unprotect the form first.

10 Apply the 'cake' (third selection) Art border to the page.

11 Insert a heading above the table, 'Set Menu Planner'.

Handy Hint

If you didn't leave room at the top of the page, move the table by dragging the square handle that appears in the top left-hand corner of the table when you run the cursor over the table.

For the heading:

- choose Goudy Old Style, 24 pt
- centre the heading
- centre the text within the table.

Handy Hint

You can centre the heading text and the table text by holding down the Ctrl + A keys to select both, then clicking on the Center icon.

12 Change the height of the rows to 0.8 cm.

Handy Hint

Table Properties: Row, then specify the height (approximately 0.8 cm).

13 Insert a footer that will show the date the document was last saved.

Handy Hint

View: Header and Footer, then switch to Footer.

If you press the Enter key after you have inserted the field, the field will move up the page and out of the border area.

14 Save your work as: **Task 2 Answer**.

Task 3 Daniel Defoe handout revisited

In this task, you will cover the following skills:

- Remove password protection from a document.
- Modify existing footnotes or endnotes.
  - o Accessing footnote text.
  - o Amending footnote text.
  - o Accessing multiple footnote text.
- Modify format and positioning of footnotes or endnotes.
- Create sections in a document.
  - o Break types.
  - o Section break types.
- Modify column layouts.
- Insert a column break.
- Print a defined number of pages per sheet.

Scenario

The document that you developed for the Literary Discussion Group in Task 1 has now been returned after checking, and there are amendments to be made.

3.1 Remove password protection

The group thought that the password protection would cause problems if the people who had the password could not be contacted. To remove the password, you will need to open the document; you will be asked for the password.

Open your saved copy of Task 1. You will need the password to open the document.

If you have lost your work, or cannot remember the password to open your document, there is another copy on the CD in the 'Suggested Answers' folder. The file is named: Task 1 password protected. The password is 'password'.

Method

To resave the document without the password, i.e. to remove the password:

1 Click on: **File**, select **Save As**.

2 On the **Save As** menu bar, click on: **Tools**, then select: **Security Options**.

In the **Password to open** box, you will be able to see your password as asterisks, i.e. ******. **Delete** the asterisks.

3 Click on: **OK**.

4 Click on: **Save**.

The document should now be saved with the existing name but without the password protection. To check this, close the document and re-open it. If you were asked for the password, you need to repeat the above procedure.

3.2 *Modify existing footnotes or endnotes*

Note: the method for modifying footnotes and endnotes is exactly the same.

The Literary group would like the footnotes amended.

Accessing footnote text

Method

As there are only two footnotes, you can use the following method. This method takes you directly to the footnote text:

1 Select: **View**: **Footnotes**, to access the View Footnotes dialogue box.

If you do not have any footnotes in your document, you will not be able to select this option.

Figure 3.1 The View Footnotes dialogue box

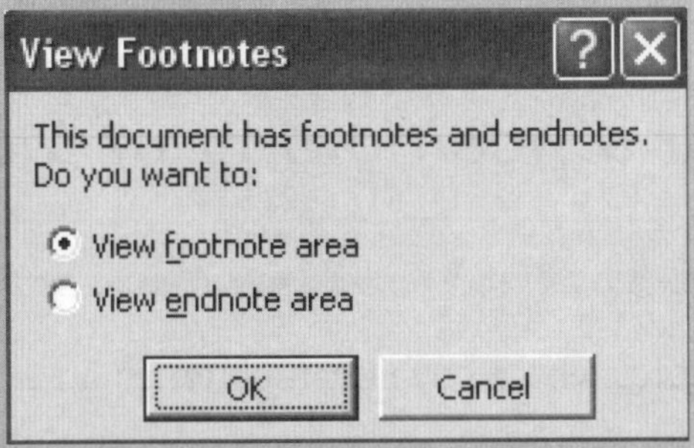

2 Select: **View footnote area**.

3 Click on: **OK**. The cursor will now move to the first footnote.

Amending footnote text

You can amend the text in the footnote just as you would in the main body of the document, i.e. you can select the text to change the font or font size. You can also add symbols and automatic numbering.

Method

1 Delete the word 'Roman' from the first footnote.

2 Click anywhere in the document, to exit the footnote area.

Accessing multiple footnote text

Method

If there had been more footnotes, it would have been easier to:

1 Click on: **Edit**.

2 Select: **Go To**.

3 From the **Go to what** box, select: **Footnote**.

Figure 3.2 Accessing footnotes from the Go to what box using Edit: Go To

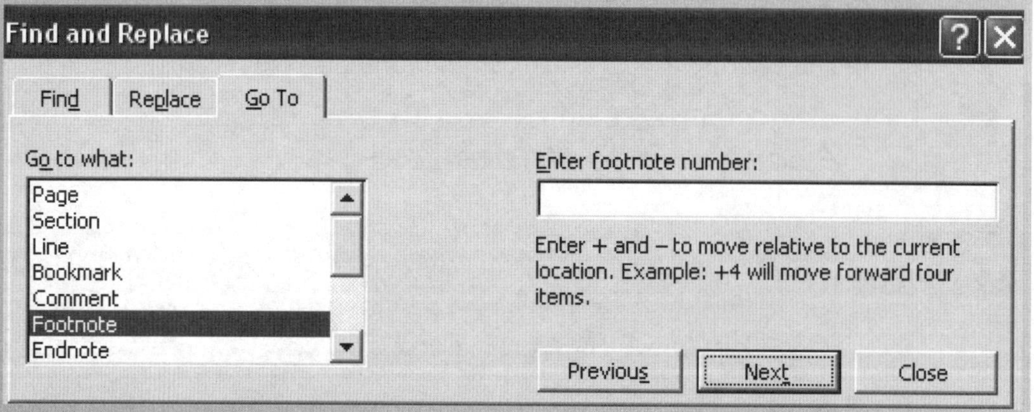

4 Select the **Previous** and **Next** buttons to move around the footnotes in the document.

Try this method now to see how it works.

3.3 *Change format and positioning of footnotes or endnotes*

On reflection, one of the footnotes would have been better as an endnote.

Method

1 Go to the second footnote, 'Mr Martin Creswell'. Right-click on the text.

Handy Hint

Take care that you don't click on a spelling error, underlined in red. Right-clicking on a spelling error brings up a different menu (see Figure 3.3). Word anticipates that you want to use Spellcheck and offers you this menu.

Figure 3.3 Be careful not to access the Spellcheck menu

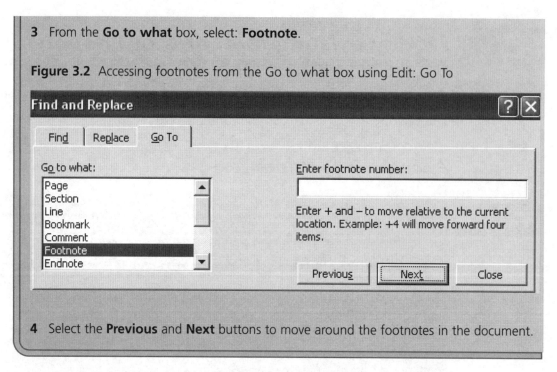

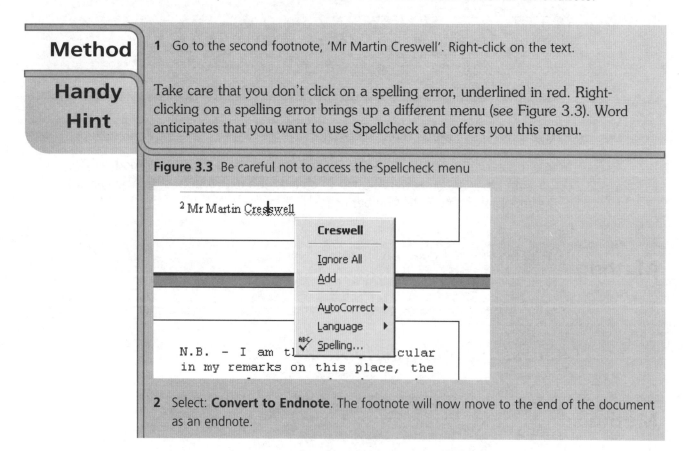

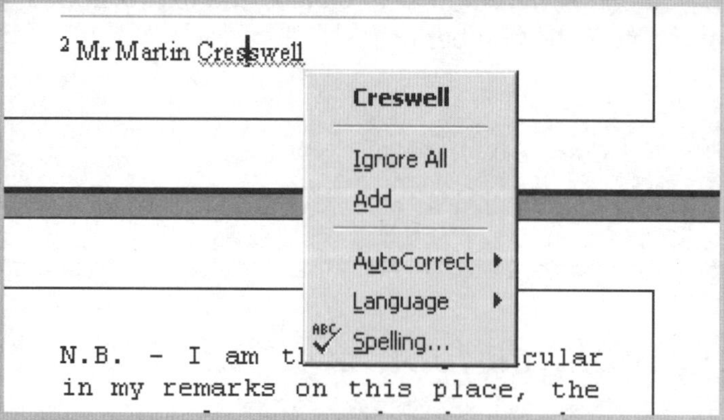

2 Select: **Convert to Endnote**. The footnote will now move to the end of the document as an endnote.

Figure 3.4 Right-click on the footnote to select: Convert to Endnote

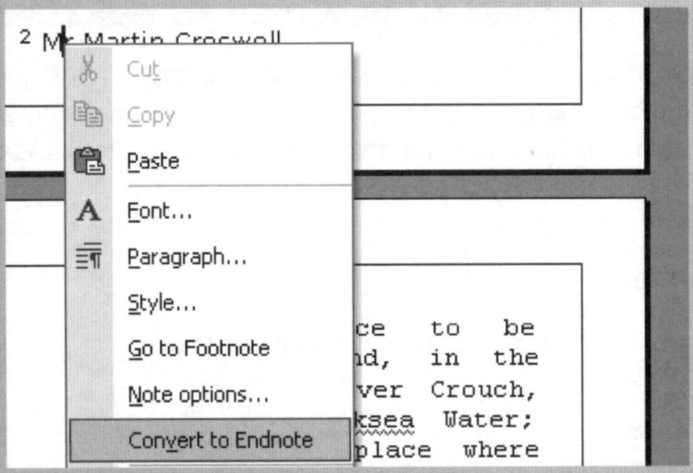

Go to the end of the document to check that this has worked. You will see that the endnote marker in the main body of the text has automatically changed to: iii.

You can also move the footnotes and endnotes around the document by highlighting the marker in the text, right-clicking and then dragging to the correct position.

Figure 3.5 Highlight the footnote or endnote marker, then right-click and drag to another position

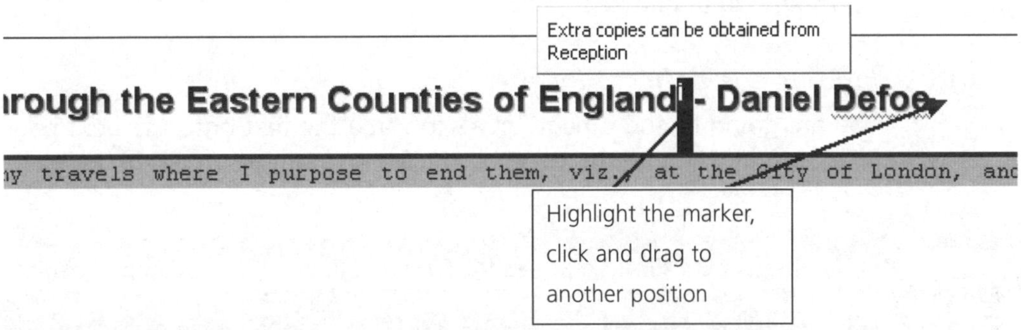

Method

1 Highlight the marker.

2 Click and drag the marker for the first Endnote, from its position after the word 'England' to the end of the heading, after the word 'Defoe'.

3 A Paste Options drop-down menu appears.

4 Select: **Keep source formatting**.

Handy Hint

If you find clicking and dragging a problem, don't forget that you can use Cut and Paste from the pop-up menu when you right-click, or from the icons on the standard toolbar.

Right-clicking on any of the listed endnotes at the end of the document gives you a pop-up menu. If you choose Go to Endnote, the cursor moves to the marker for that endnote. Try this on one of the endnotes.

3.4 Create sections in a document

A comment has come back from the Literary Group that the text looks too long. While nothing can be done about the number of words, the document can be formatted so that it appears in different sections and helps to break up the text for the reader.

Break types

There are three break types, i.e. what you want to break:

- Page break.
- Column break.
- Text wrapping break.

Section break types

In addition, there are four section break types, i.e. where you want the text to restart.

- Next page.
- Continuous (same page).
- (Next) even (numbered) page.
- (Next) odd (numbered) page.

Finding the point to insert the break

You are going to add a page break to force the text onto the next page. First, you need to find the point in the text where you want to insert the break.

Method

1 Select: **Edit**: **Find**, to access the Find and Replace dialogue box, then select the **Find** tab.

2 In the **Find what** box, key in: 'Several little'.

Figure 3.6 Using the Find what box in Edit: Find

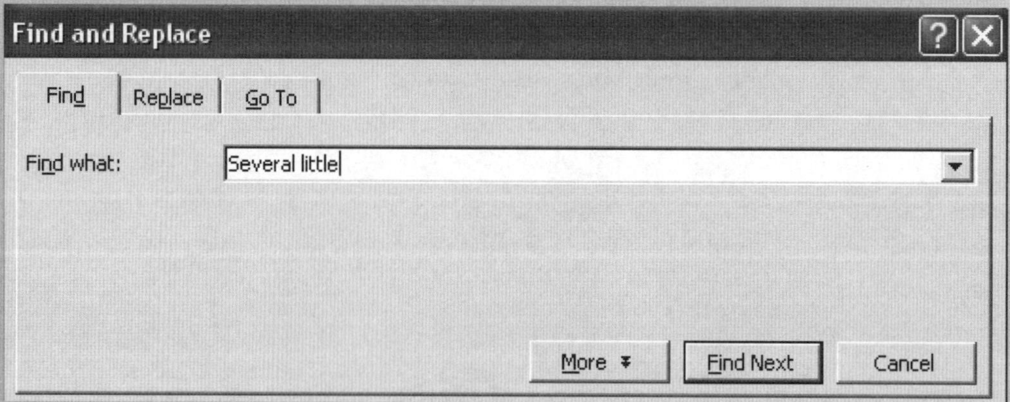

3 Click on: **Find Next**.

4 To close the **Find and Replace** dialogue box, click on: **Cancel**.

The cursor should now be at the start of the paragraph that begins 'Several little observations'. The words 'Several little' will be highlighted. Click down at the start of the paragraph before the word 'Several'.

Handy Hint

If you do not remove the highlighting before you put in the page break, you will lose the highlighted words.

Inserting the page break

Method

To insert the break you can either:

- Hold the **Ctrl** key and press the **Return** (**Enter**) key.

Or:

- Click on: **Insert**: **Break**, to access the Break dialogue box, select: **Page break**, then click on: **OK**.

The text should have moved to the top of the following page.

Adding column breaks

You are now going to convert a section of the text from 2 columns to a single column that spans the width of the page.

Method

1 Select the text from the top of this new page to the end of the paragraph numbered 3, i.e. to 'just above Gravesend'.

Handy Hint

The easiest way to do this is to hold down the shift key and use the arrow keys (down and right) to select the text. This gives you much more control.

2 You will now set the text into one column. This can be done in two ways:

- Select: **Format**: **Columns**, to access the Columns dialogue box. Select '1' in the Number of columns box, or click on the single column icon.
- Click on the **Column icon** on the standard toolbar and select: 1 column.

Figure 3.7 Using the Column icon to select 1 column

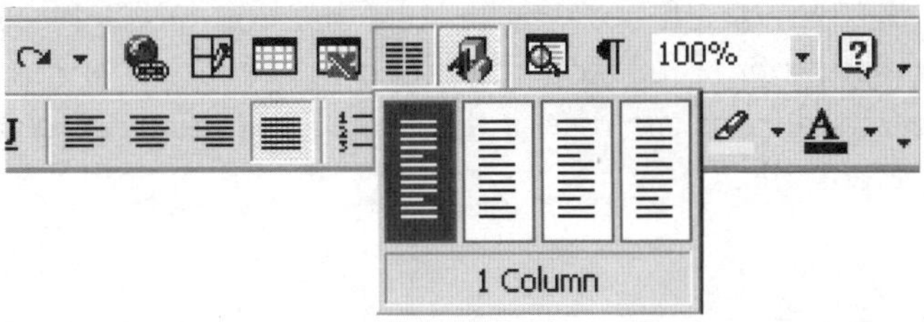

The text beginning 'Several little …' and the paragraphs numbered 1 to 3 should now run across the page.

Handy Hint

If the last line that ends 'Gravesend' is force justified, i.e. if the words are spaced out across the page, press the Enter key (insert a return) after the word 'Gravesend' (see Figure 3.8).

If there is too much space between the paragraphs, click down in front of the word 'The' and press the backspace key. The text should move up the column (see Figure 3.8).

Figure 3.8 Move text up a column using the backspace key

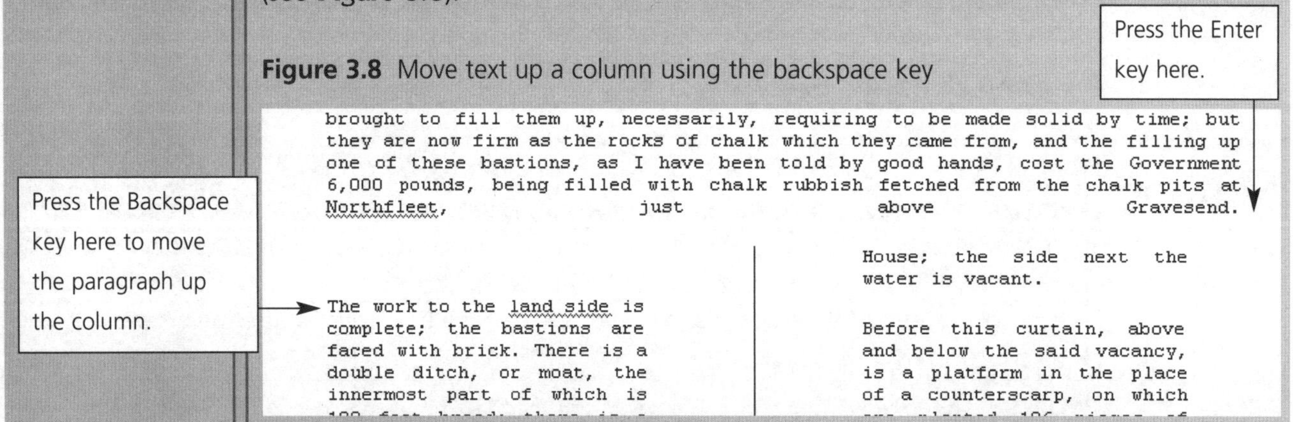
Press the Enter key here.
Press the Backspace key here to move the paragraph up the column.

brought to fill them up, necessarily, requiring to be made solid by time; but they are now firm as the rocks of chalk which they came from, and the filling up one of these bastions, as I have been told by good hands, cost the Government 6,000 pounds, being filled with chalk rubbish fetched from the chalk pits at Northfleet, just above Gravesend.

The work to the land side is complete; the bastions are faced with brick. There is a double ditch, or moat, the innermost part of which is

House; the side next the water is vacant.

Before this curtain, above and below the said vacancy, is a platform in the place of a counterscarp, on which

Be careful not to press the backspace too many times – you will remove the section break instruction that you have just put in.

Repeat the above method with the text that starts 'From hence I went' (use Edit and Find to access this text). Start this on a new page (insert a page break) and apply one column format to the paragraph.

3.5 *Change column layouts*

Scroll through the document and format three more paragraphs. You can choose any three.

- Format the first paragraph to 1 column.
- Format the second paragraph to 2 columns.
- Format the third paragraph to 3 columns.

Handy Hint

Triple-click on the text to select the whole paragraph.

Don't forget that you must highlight the section of text. If you do not, you will format the whole document. If you forget, the undo icon is the best option.

When you select the paragraph text, make sure that you highlight <u>all</u> the text in the paragraph, including the final full stop. If you do not, you will end up with one line of the paragraph detached from the rest of the text. Triple-clicking to select the paragraph will prevent this.

3.6 *Insert a column break*

One method of leaving space without starting a new page, for example for a picture, is to force the text to the top of the next column. To do this you can add column breaks.

Method

1. Insert the cursor on the first page at the front of the paragraph that starts, 'I set out the'.
2. Click on: **Insert**: **Break**, to access the Break dialogue box, then select: **Column break**. Do not select any Section break types – they are not appropriate. You want the text to start in the next column.
3. Click on: **OK**.

The text should move from column 1 to the top of column 2 on the first page. Column 1 should be blank after the word 'them' (see Figure 3.9).

Figure 3.9 Inserting a column break

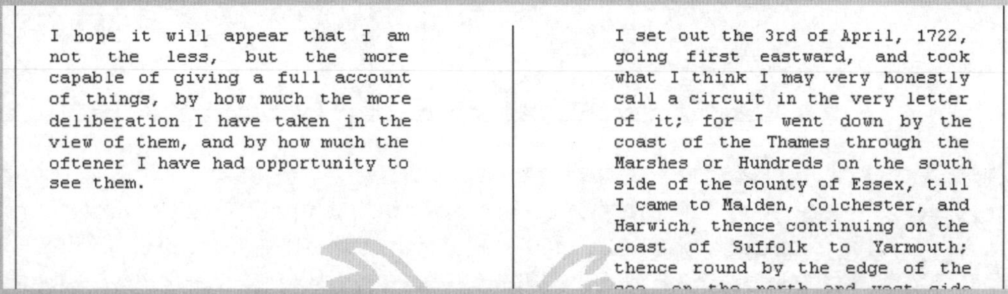
I hope it will appear that I am not the less, but the more capable of giving a full account of things, by how much the more deliberation I have taken in the view of them, and by how much the oftener I have had opportunity to see them.

I set out the 3rd of April, 1722, going first eastward, and took what I think I may very honestly call a circuit in the very letter of it; for I went down by the coast of the Thames through the Marshes or Hundreds on the south side of the county of Essex, till I came to Malden, Colchester, and Harwich, thence continuing on the coast of Suffolk to Yarmouth; thence round by the edge of the

4. Save your work as: **Task 3**.

3.7 *Print more than one page per sheet*

Method

1. Select: **File**: **Print**, to access the Print dialogue box.
2. In **Page range**, click to select: **All**.
3. In the **Zoom** box, from the **Pages per sheet** drop-down menu, select: **4 pages**.
4. Click on: **OK**.

Figure 3.10 Printing 4 pages per sheet

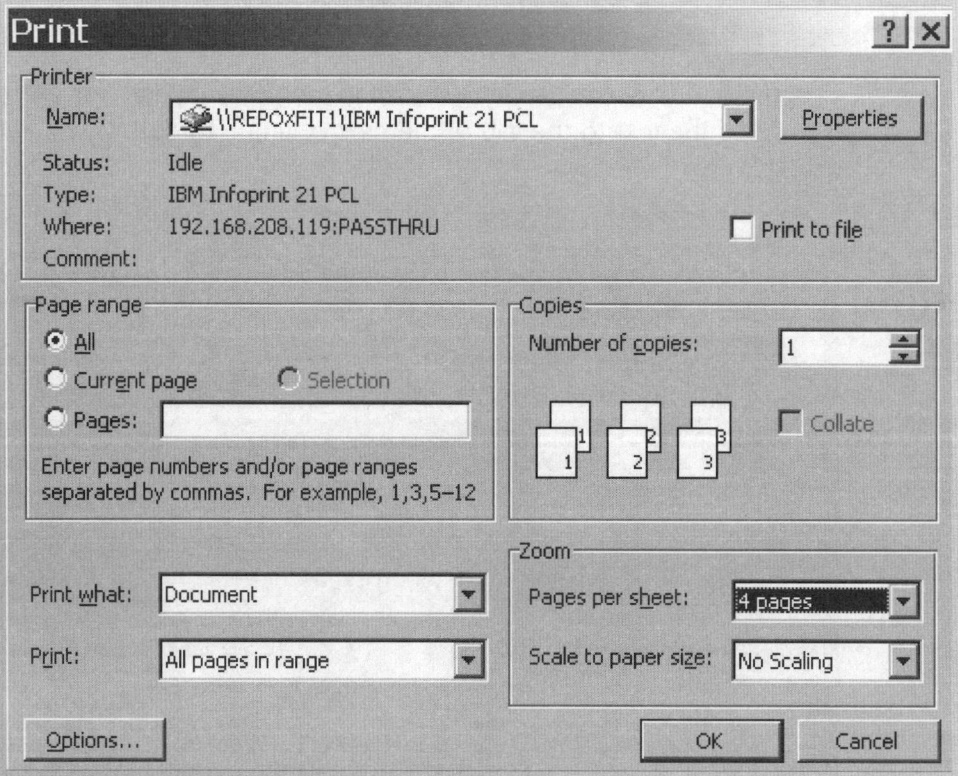

Handy Hint

If you were printing several copies of a multi-page document, in the Print dialogue box you could tick to select the Collate option in the Copies box. It takes longer to print using this option, but less time than collating the printed pages by hand.

Practice Task — *Task 3*

These exercises are included to help the candidate in his or her training for the Advanced ECDL program. The exercises included in this material are not Advanced ECDL certification tests and should not be construed in any way as Advanced ECDL certification tests. For information about Authorised ECDL Test Centres in different National Territories, please refer to the ECDL Foundation website at **www.ecdl.com**.

Method

1 Remove the password from the document you saved as 'Task 1 Answer' at the end of Practice Task 1.

2 Save your work as: **Task 3 Answer**.

3 Amend the footnote to read: See Leaflet 3.

4 Convert the footnote to an endnote.

5 Create a section break at the end of column 2 that forces columns 3 and 4 onto the next page.

6 Change the Page Setup to Portrait.

Handy Hint

Apply to 'Whole Document'.

7 Remove the column breaks.

Handy Hint

Do not remove the page break.

8 Format the document to 2 columns.

Handy Hint

Make sure that the position of the cursor on the page is away from the heading.

9 Increase the body text to 20 pt.

10 Reposition the sun image to the top of column 1, underneath the heading.

11 Increase the size of the image to fill the column width and to force the second subheading into column 2.

12 Reposition the watermark if it has moved off the page.

13 Add the following header: HOLIDAYS BY COACH. (Use: **View**: **Header and Footer**.)

- Use Arial Black font, 12 pt.
- Use a shadow effect on the font.
- Right align.

14 Print both pages onto one sheet of paper.

15 Save your work as: **Task 3 Answer**.

Task 4 Advertisement flyer

In this task, you will cover the following skills:

- Insert or delete text boxes.
  - o Insert text boxes.
  - o Delete text boxes.
  - o Text wrapping.
  - o Copy and position text boxes.
  - o Inserting text.
- Link text boxes.
- Apply border and shading options in text boxes.
- Edit, move or re-size text boxes.
  - o Move text boxes.
  - o Change text box size.
  - o Standardise text box size.
- Use text orientation options.
  - o Rotating text.
  - o Changing the shape of the rotated text box.
  - o Formatting options.
- Apply animated text effect options.
- Use available text design gallery options.
  - o The WordArt Toolbar.
- Use pre-defined shape options.
  - o AutoShapes.
- Group or ungroup pre-defined shapes.
  - o Grouping.
  - o Ungrouping.
  - o Fix the position of grouped objects.
- Send pre-defined shapes in front of or behind text; send pre-defined shape to back or to front.
- Modify image borders.

Scenario

The next task is to produce an A4 flyer to advertise the next Literary Discussion Group meeting.

You will be using tools that are readily available through the Drawing Toolbar. Make sure that you have this toolbar showing at the bottom of your screen. If not:

- *Click on View: Toolbars: Drawing. The toolbar should appear at the bottom of the screen. The first item is Draw.*

Key in the following text on a new page. Leave the text as default. Leave one clear line space between each line of text.

Literary Discussion Group
Next Meeting 7.30pm
(Put next Friday's date here)
Tour Through the Eastern Counties of England
Daniel Defoe
Library Reading Room

4.1 *Insert and delete text boxes*

Insert text boxes

After the line 'Tour Through the Eastern Counties of England', you are going to insert two text boxes.

Method

1 Position the cursor on the blank line underneath the text.

2 Click on: **Insert**, then select: **Text Box**. Press the **Delete** key to remove the drawing area box. The mouse cursor now changes to a black cross.

Another way of doing this is: on the **Drawing Toolbar**, click on the **Text Box** icon .

3 Click down and drag the cursor from top left to bottom right, until the box is approximately 5 cm x 5 cm. Use the horizontal and vertical rulers as a guide.

Figure 4.1 Inserting a text box

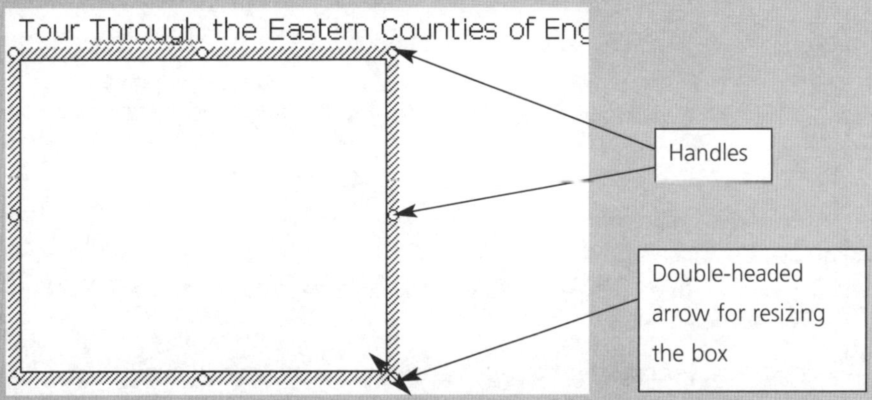

4 Release the mouse.

Delete text boxes

Method

To delete the text box, right-click over one of the handles to select the box. From the pop-up menu, select: **Cut**.

Handy Hint

The text box is selected when the border is shaded, as in Figure 4.1.

If you right-click anywhere else on the text box, other than over the handles, you will get different pop-up menus.

The I-beam cursor should be flashing in the text box. If the text box is sitting on top of the remaining text, you will need to wrap the text.

Text wrapping

Method

To wrap the text:

1 Right-click on the shaded area around the text box to access the pop-up menu. (If you click inside the box, you will not get the Format Text Box option.)

Figure 4.2 Right-click to access the pop-up menu

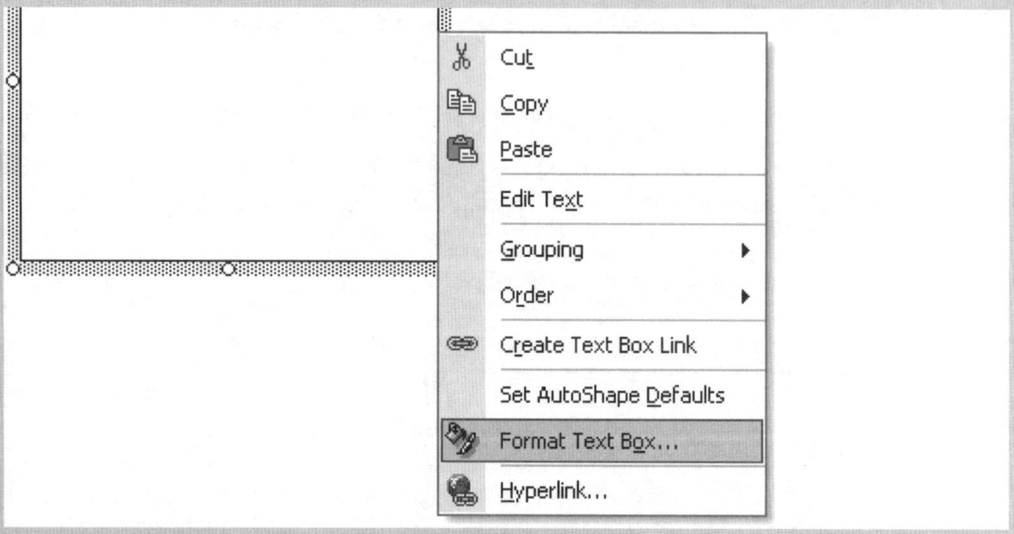

Another way of doing this is to select **Format** from the main menu toolbar, then select: **Text Box**.

2 Select: **Format Text Box**, to access the Format Text Box dialogue box.

3 Select the **Layout** tab.

4 Click on the **Advanced** button, to access the Advanced Layout dialogue box.

5 Select the **Text Wrapping** tab.

6 In Wrapping style, select **Top and bottom**. This option will force the text to flow to the top of the image and continue below it, i.e. the text will not flow over or under the image.

Figure 4.3 In Wrapping style, select Top and bottom in the Advanced Layout dialogue box

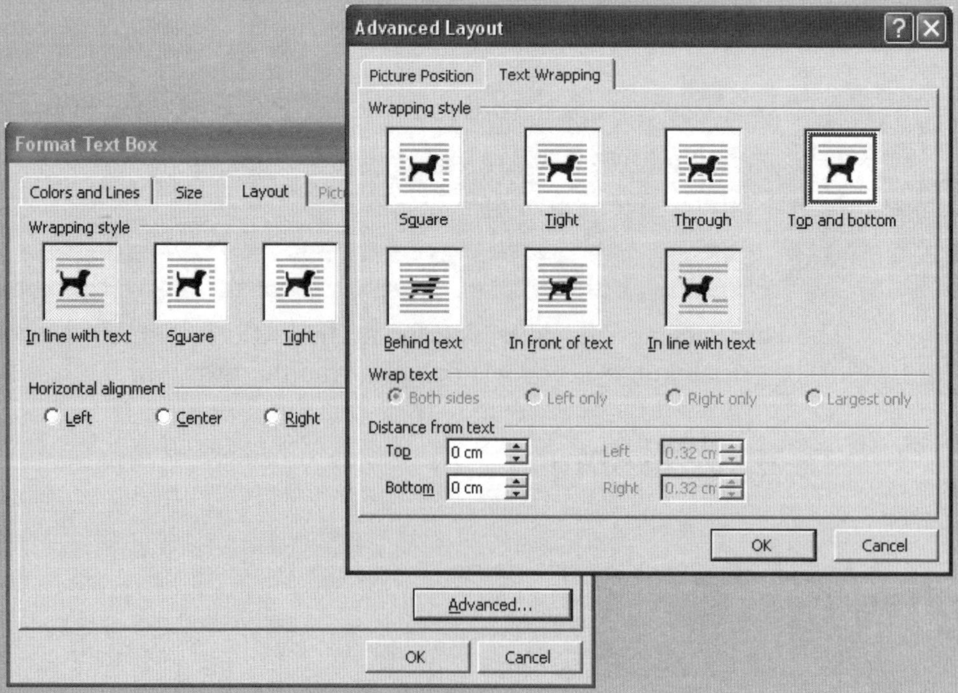

7 Click on: **OK** to close the Advanced Layout dialogue box, then click on: **OK** to close the Format Text Box dialogue box.

The text should now appear underneath the box.

Copy and position text boxes

Rather than repeat the above process to create a second identical box, you can make a copy of the original box.

Method

1 Right-click on one of the text box handles, then select: **Copy**.

2 Click outside the box.

3 Right-click and select: **Paste**.

Note: if you do not click outside the box before selecting Paste, you will end up with the second text box inside the first.

Move the second text box somewhere to the right of the first one. It does not matter at this stage exactly where.

Method

Click on the edge of the text box, avoiding the handles. Hold the left mouse button down and drag the box to the right.

Note: if you drag the handles, you will resize the box.

Figure 4.4 Click and drag to position the second text box

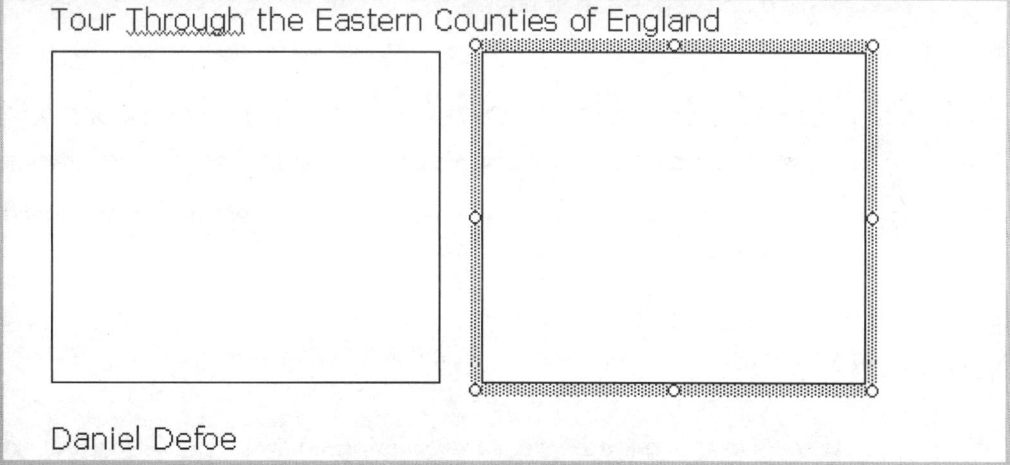

Inserting text

The first paragraph from the Daniel Defoe document is to be entered into the boxes.

Method

1 From the folder: Task Files, open the file: **Text for Task 1**.

(This unformatted file is being used, rather than your saved Task 1 document, because the copy process will copy the formatting you have already applied.)

2 Triple-click on the first paragraph to select, then right-click to access the pop-up menu. Select: **Copy**.

3 Bring your A4 flyer back on screen. Unless you closed the file, you will be able to select the document from Window on the main toolbar.

4 Click in the first text box on the A4 flyer, then right-click and select **Paste**. The pasted text will be in one box, but you will not be able to see it all.

4.2 *Link text boxes*

To force the text into the next box, you need to create a link.

Method

1 Move the cursor over any of the 'handles' on the first text box. A double-headed arrow should appear.

2 Right-click to access the pop-up menu, then select: **Create Text Box Link**. The cursor turns into a small jug.

3 Move the cursor over the second text box. As you do this, the jug tips and shows letters tumbling out (to indicate the remainder of the text).

4 Left-click in the second text box and the overflow text from the first text box should appear.

Don't worry at this stage that you cannot see all the text. The boxes are going to be resized and repositioned later.

4.3 *Apply borders and shading to text boxes*

To apply the same border and shading to both text boxes, you need to select them both before you apply the formatting.

Method

1 Click in the first text box. Hold down the **Shift** key and click in the second text box. There should be shaded borders around both boxes. You can release the shift key.

2 Select: **Format**: **Borders and Shading**, to access the Format Text Box dialogue box.

3 Select the **Colors and Lines** tab.

Experiment with the options.

- Change the **Fill** colour – don't forget the **More Colors** option where you can choose a **Standard color** or create your own **Custom color**.
- Check the effect of using the sliding bar to change the transparency.
- Change the colour, style and weight of the **Lines** – in this instance, the formatting is applied to the borders of the boxes.

Method

Figure 4.5 Experiment with the options using the Format Text Box dialogue box

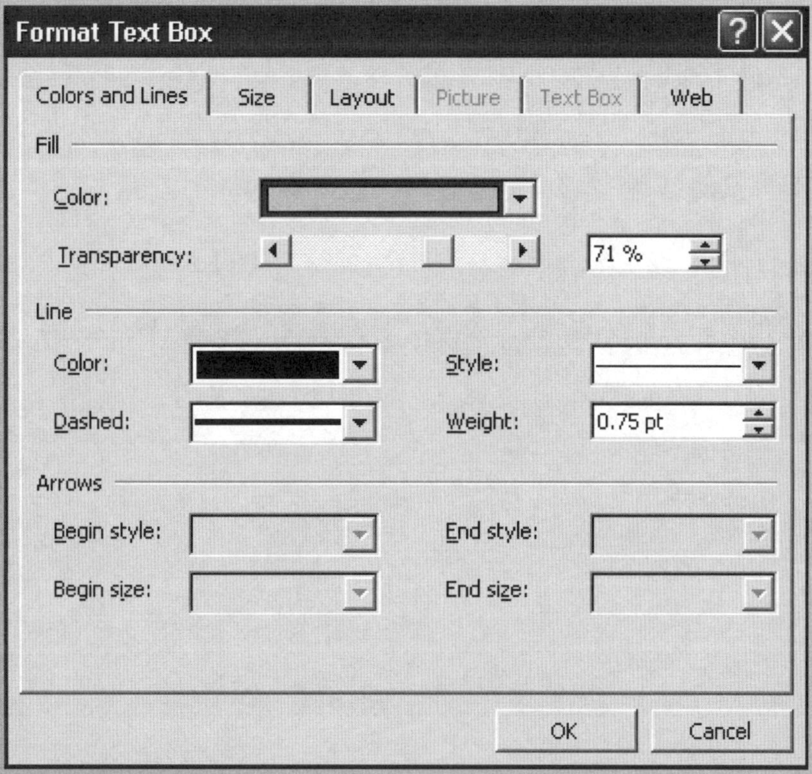

4 Click on: **OK** to see the effect of your selections.

5 Repeat the above method and make your final selections, as follows:

- **Fill**: Light Turquoise.
- **Line**: Light Green, Solid, 4.5 pt.

4.4 *Edit, move and re-size text boxes*

Move text boxes

Try moving the text boxes around the page – click and hold the mouse button down on the edge of the boxes and drag. You will see that no matter where the box is on the page, the text remains with the boxes, even if you put the second box in front of the first.

Change text box size

Now try changing the size of the text boxes. Make the first box bigger or smaller by clicking on any of the square 'handles' while holding down the left mouse button, and drag. The text will flow from one box to the other.

Standardise text box size

Now would be a good time to make both text boxes the same size.

Method

1 Select both the text boxes: click in the first box then hold down the **Shift** key and click in the second box.

2 Right-click to access the pop-up menu, then select: **Format Text Box**.

3 In the **Format Text Box** dialogue box, select the **Size** tab.

4 In **Height**, select: **6 cm**. In **Width**, select: **6 cm**.

Figure 4.6 Select text boxes size in the Format Text Box dialogue box

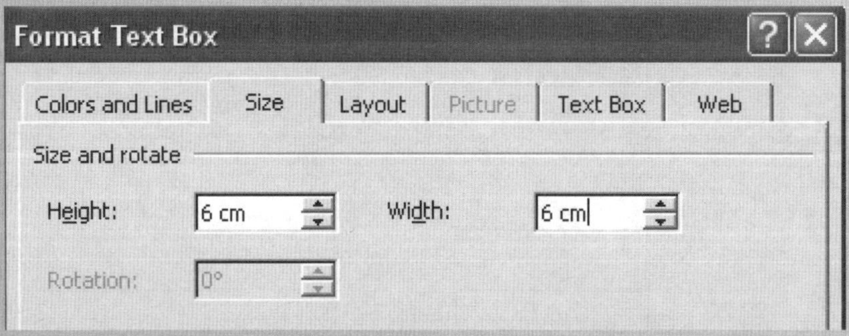

5 Click on: **OK**.

The boxes are now the same size. However, you can still change the size if you click and drag the handles.

The text should be Courier New, 10 pt. If the text is not this format, click in either box and select all the text by using Ctrl + A. Then format the text using the formatting toolbar.

4.5 *Change text orientation*

Rotating text

The Literary Group would like their name to run down the left-hand side of the flyer. This involves rotating the text. To be able to rotate or move text independently from the rest of the text on the page, you need to put the text to be rotated into a separate text box.

Method

1 Triple-click to select the text: **Literary Discussion Group**.

2 Click on **Insert** from the main menu bar, then select: **Text Box**.

Note: 'Literary Discussion Group' will appear in a text box.

3 Click on: **Format**, then select: **Text Direction**.

4 In the **Text Direction** dialogue box, select the first vertical option, i.e. the text reads from the bottom to the top (see Figure 4.7).

Figure 4.7 Selecting text direction

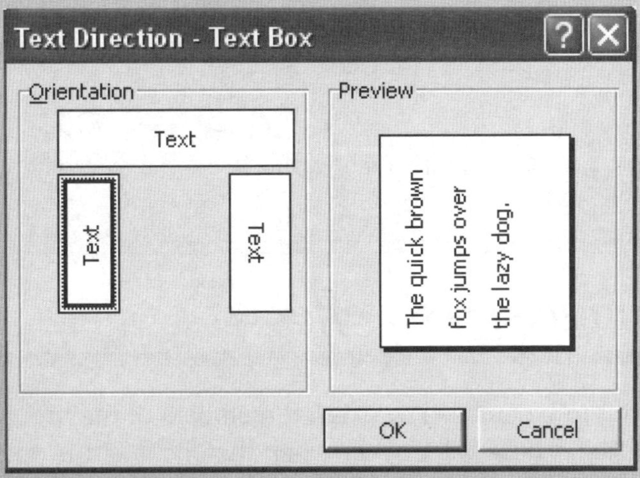

5 Click on: **OK**. The text is now rotated 90 degrees.

Formatting options

Formatting text

Method

Select the text. You will notice when you click into the rotated box that the I-beam cursor is rotated 90 degrees. This means that you can format the text without changing the text direction back to horizontal. Make the following changes:

- Set the font to: **Arial, 48 pt, Bold**.
- Click on the **Center** icon on the **Formatting Toolbar** to centre the text within the box. The icons have been rotated, but they are still in the same position on the toolbar.

The text box is too small. Click on the centre handle at the bottom of the box and drag down to the bottom margin.

Formatting text box border

You will now change the colour and style of the line around the text box, and fill it with colour.

Method

This is the same method that you used for the linked text boxes.

1 Select the text box by clicking inside.

2 Click on: **Format**: **Text Box**. In the Text Box dialogue box, in **Colors** and **Lines**, make the following selections:

- **Fill**: Turquoise, transparency 50%.
- **Line**: Blue, dash, 0.75 pt.

Handy Hint

Hold the cursor still over the selections to access the pop-up text.

3 Click on: **OK**.

Formatting text colour

Method

Make sure that the cursor is in the rotated text box area.

Change the colour of the text by first selecting the text (**Ctrl** + **A**) and then clicking on the **Font Color** icon on the Formatting Toolbar. From the drop-down menu, select: **Indigo**.

4.6 *Apply animated text effects*

As the flyer is going to be emailed to existing members of the group, animated text effects can be applied. These will appear when the document is opened as an email attachment.

Method

1 Select the title of the discussion, i.e. **Tour Through the Eastern Counties of England**.

2 On the main menu bar, click on: **Format**: **Font**, to access the Font dialogue box.

3 Select the **Text Effects** tab. Click on each of the animations in turn. You can view the effect in the **Preview** box at the bottom of the Font dialogue box.

4 Select: **Sparkle Text**.

Figure 4.8 Selecting animated text effects

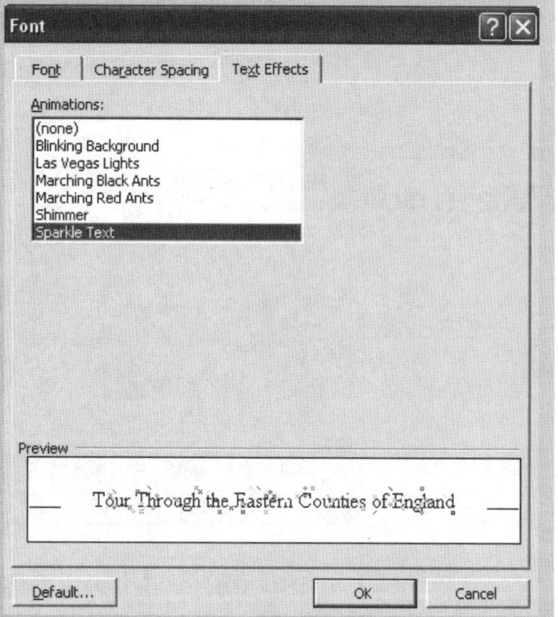

5 Click on: **OK**.

6 In the Font dialogue box, click on the **Font** tab. Now make the following changes:

- Font color: Red.
- Size: 36 pt.

Click on: **OK**.

7 Now change the case to upper case. Select: **Format**: **Change Case**, to access the Change Case dialogue box. Select: **UPPERCASE**.

Figure 4.9 Using the Change Case dialogue box

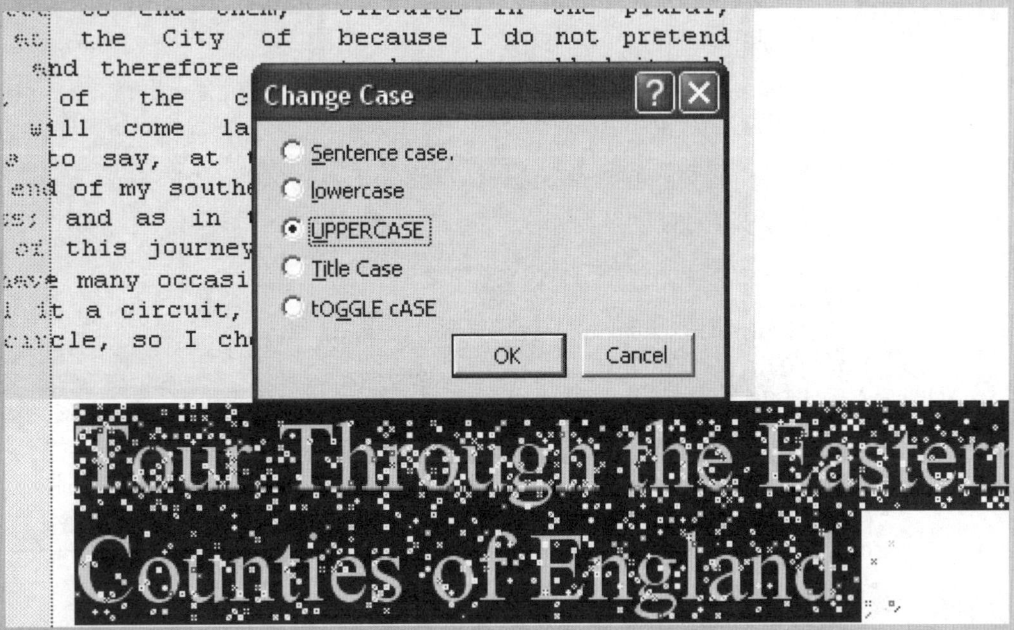

8 Click on: **OK**. The text is now in capitals.

You may have found, as with the example in Figure 4.9, that the heading has moved down the page and the text boxes have moved to accommodate the new text size. Don't panic! The easiest items to move on your document are the text boxes (because of the formatting applied earlier).

Method

1. Select both the linked boxes: click in one box then press **Shift** and click in the second box.
2. Click on the edge of one of the boxes and drag them further down the page. The headline will now return to the top of the page.

A more fiddly method is to select the headline text and then left click and drag the text to the top of the page. You may find that, using this method, you still have to move the text boxes.

4.7 *Use text design gallery options*

The flyer is starting to take shape now, so we shall consider some more formatting options.

The WordArt Toolbar

To add 'Everyone Welcome' to the bottom of the flyer, we will use the WordArt Toolbar.

Method

1 Select: **View**: **Toolbars**: **WordArt**. The WordArt Toolbar will appear at the bottom of the screen.

2 Position the cursor on a line after 'Library Reading Room'. Click on the first icon on the toolbar.

3 Select the fifth option on the fourth row. Click on: **OK**. The Edit WordArt Text dialogue box will appear.

4 Key in the words: 'Everyone welcome'.

Figure 4.10 Keying in words in Edit WordArt Text

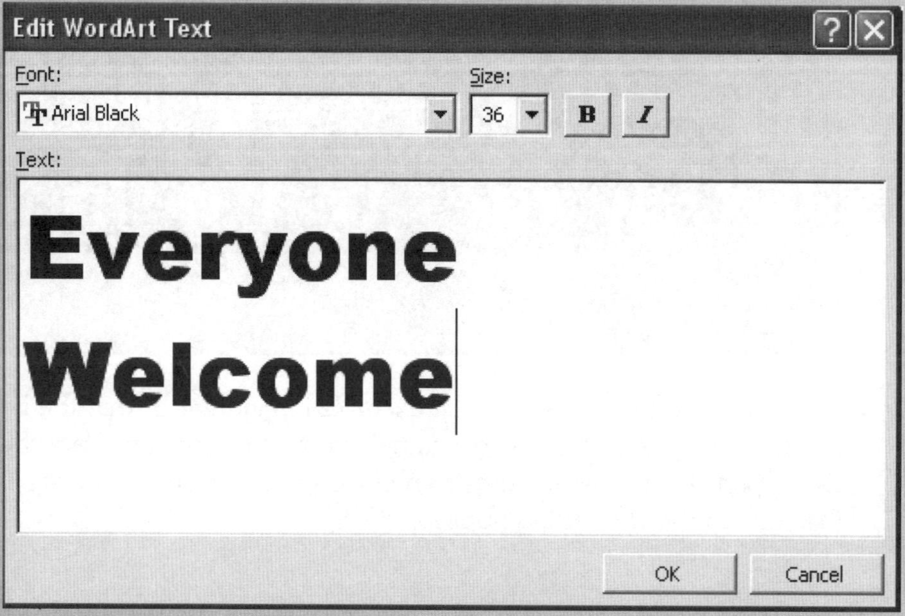

5 Click on: **OK** to return to the flyer. See what your selection looks like.

6 Click on the text and run the cursor over the WordArt toolbar.

Figure 4.11 The WordArt Toolbar

Experiment by selecting each of the icons in turn. Don't forget that you can click the 'undo' button on the main menu toolbar to return to your original selection.

4.8 *Use pre-defined shapes*

Included with Word are shapes that have been prepared for you to amend to your requirements. These options are called AutoShapes and are accessed through the Drawing Toolbar.

AutoShapes

Method

1 Select: **View**: **Toolbars**: **Drawing**.

2 Click on: **AutoShapes**.

3 Select **Block Arrows**, then click on: **Curved Left Arrow** (see Figure 4.12) and drag the cursor so that the curved arrow is in position on the right-hand side of the flyer, just above the WordArt text (see Figure 4.13).

Figure 4.12 Selecting arrow shapes in AutoShape

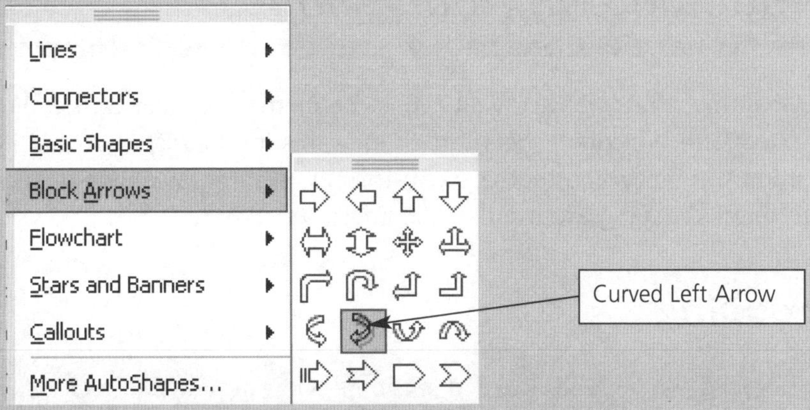

This takes practice. If you get it wrong, just delete the arrow with the delete key and start again.

4 Right-click on the arrow, then **Copy** and **Paste**, to create a second arrow. Position the arrows so that the lower arrow is in front of the higher arrow (see Figure 4.13).

5 On the **AutoShapes** drop-down menu, select: **Block Arrows**: **Left Arrow** (the second option on the first row). Click and drag to position this arrow to the left of the lower curved arrow (see Figure 4.13).

Figure 4.13 Click and drag on the arrows from the AutoShape drop-down menu to position in the document

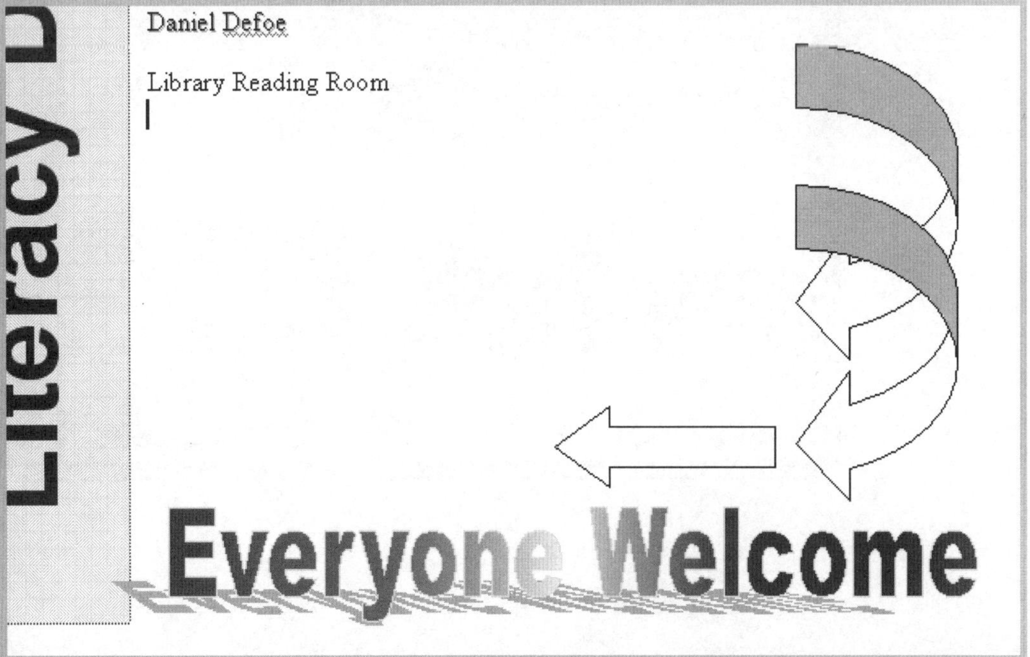

The block arrow pointing left needs to point to the words 'Library Reading Room'.

Method

1 Triple-click to select the text 'Library Reading Room', then to place into a text box select: **Insert**: **Text box**.

2 Click on the text box and drag into position. You will need to modify the shape of the text box by dragging the handles.

3 Now remove the line border from around the text box: **Format**: **Text Box**, then click on the **Colors and Lines** tab. From the drop-down menu, select: **No Line**.

4.9 *Group and ungroup shapes*

You may find that your arrows have some element similar to the WordArt you chose for 'Everyone Welcome'. You can change this if you wish, but first it would be better to group the arrows so that you can format all three at once and stop the AutoShapes moving around the document independently.

Grouping

Method

1 Hold down the **Shift** key and select the two curved arrows and the left arrow by clicking on them in turn. (This is exactly the same method that you used to select the linked text boxes.)

2 Right-click: this should be a quick click to get the correct pop-up menu. Select: **Grouping**, then select: **Group**.

Figure 4.14 Fixing the position of AutoShapes using Grouping: Group

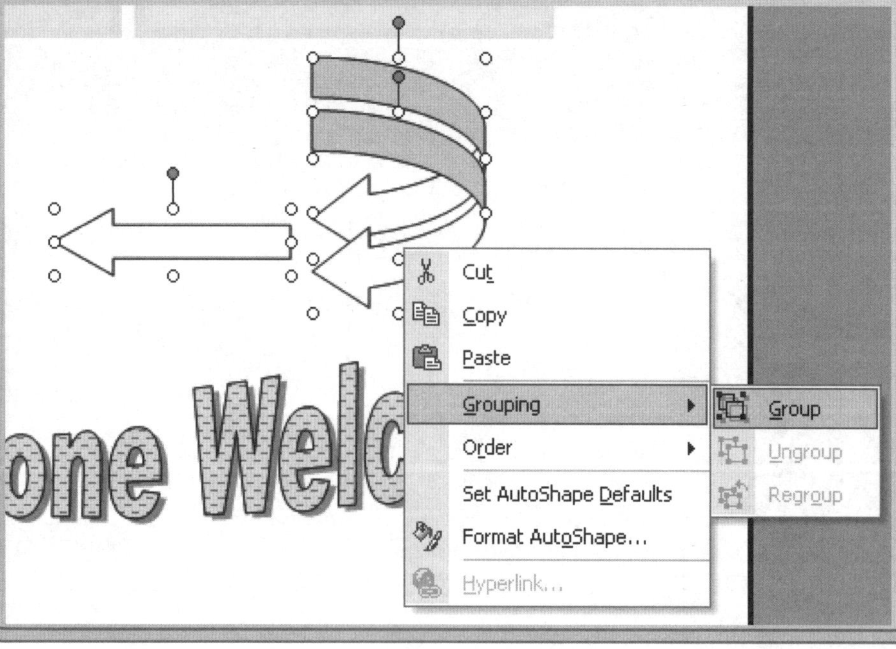

Ungrouping

If you later wanted to ungroup the AutoShapes, you follow the same method, selecting **Grouping**, then select: **Ungroup**.

Handy Hint

If you find right-clicking particularly difficult when handling AutoShapes, left-click in the AutoShape and make the selections from the Drawing toolbar. Click on the Draw drop-down menu to access the Group and Ungroup options.

You should have one set of handles around the outside of all three AutoShapes. These gouped AutoShapes now work just as any other image or picture until they are ungrouped.

Fix the position of grouped objects

The AutoShapes will still move around the document as you make amendments to, for example, the text or the text boxes. The way to stop this happening is to format the AutoShapes (objects) so that they do not move with the text.

Method

1. Click on the arrows, hold down the **Shift** key and click on the 'Everyone Welcome' text.
2. Move the cursor over a handle and right-click, select: **Format Object** to access the Format Object dialogue box. Another way to access the Format Object dialogue box is to left-click and select: **Format**: **Object** on the main menu bar.
3. Select the **Layout** tab, then click on the **Advanced** button. The Advanced Layout dialogue box appears.

Figure 4.15 Fixing the position of grouped objects using the Advanced Layout dialogue box

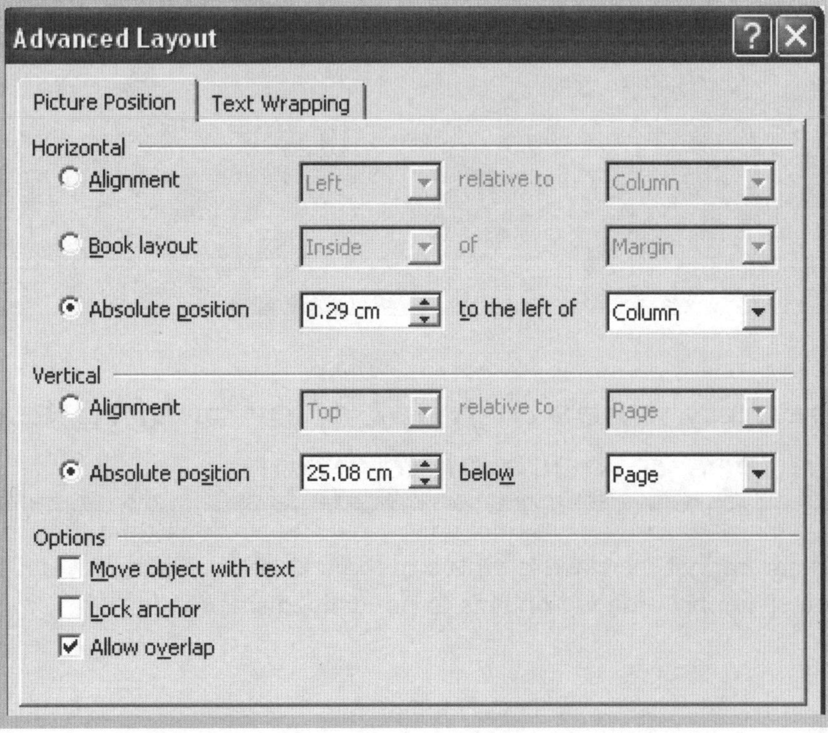

4 Click on: **Picture Position** tab.

5 Under **Options**, deselect the **Move object with text** box.

6 Click on: **OK** twice to remove the dialogue boxes. You may need to re-position the AutoShapes after clicking on the second OK.

You won't see any obvious changes but if you insert any line spaces now, or re-size the text boxes, the 'Everyone Welcome' text and the arrows will not move.

You will now make some changes to the font and add a second shape – the Cloud Callout – to the flyer.

Method

1 Change the 'Library Reading Room' and 'Daniel Defoe' text to Times New Roman, 18 point.

2 Click and drag the text box and/or the WordArt/AutoShape into position.

3 You will add the Cloud Callout to the end of the extract text in the boxes. Click on the **AutoShapes** drop-down menu from the Drawing toolbar, then select: **Callouts**: **Cloud Callout**.

Figure 4.16 Inserting a Cloud Callout using the AutoShapes drop-down menu

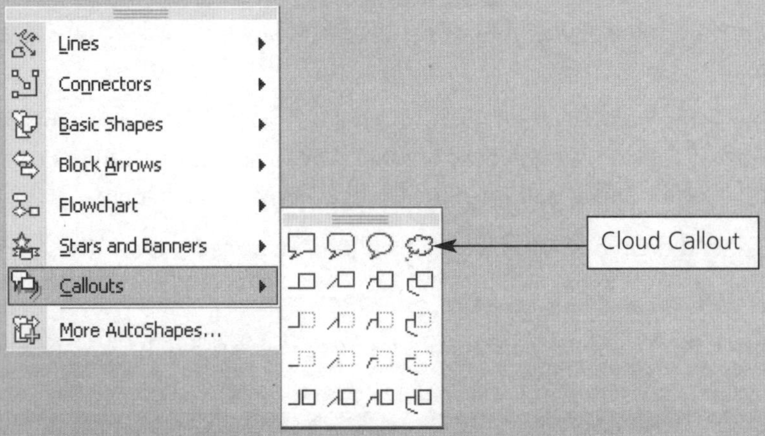

4 Click on and drag the end of the Cloud Callout so that it rises out from the text 'Daniel Defoe'. The shape of the cloud can be changed by dragging the handles. If you click on the diamond-shaped handle at the end of the cloud, you can adjust to 'point' in a different direction. Your work does not have to look exactly like Figure 4.17.

4.10 *Send shapes in front of or behind text; send shapes to back or to front*

To ensure that the cloud is on top of the text boxes, i.e. that it is in front of the text, you can apply ordering options to pre-defined shapes.

Method

1 Click on the Cloud Callout.
2 Click on: **Draw**.
3 Select: **Order**.

You will see a range of options. What you have on screen will determine which of the options will have an effect. If your cloud is behind the text, you need to select **Bring in Front of Text**.

Figure 4.17 Setting an AutoShape in front of text using Draw: Order

Try these options out on the Cloud Callout:

- Bring to Front.
- Send to Back.
- Bring Forward.
- Send Backward.
- Bring in Front of Text.
- Send Behind Text.

4.11 *Change image borders*

The Cloud Callout may have picked up some formatting, for example, the same formatting as the other AutoShapes. You need to change the format of the cloud to a white fill with black lines.

Method

1. Right-click over one of the handles, then select: **Format AutoShape**: **Colors and Lines**.
2. Select the following options:
   - **Fill**: White.
   - **Line**: Black, solid, 1 pt.
3. Format the 'Next Meeting' and 'Date' text to 26 pt and centred.
4. Check that the different elements are still in place. If not, select them and drag into position.
5. Save the document as: **Flyer**.

You may have noticed that the 'formatting' dialogue boxes, e.g. Format Object, Format Picture, Format Text Box and Format AutoShape, are all fairly similar in that they contain the same tab headings. The content of these headings are explored as you work on different tasks throughout the book.

You are not restricted to formatting and making modifications using the above dialogue boxes: you can also add and modify borders to pictures using Borders and Shading, for example.

Method

1. Open a new blank document and insert an image from ClipArt, i.e. **Insert**: **Picture**: **ClipArt**. In the **Search Text** box, key in: **photographs**.
2. Make a selection from the **Photographs** category. If you do not have this category, make a selection from any of the other categories. Select a photograph.

   You should have an image on-screen with black square handles.
3. Right-click on the image and select: **Borders and Shading**. The Borders dialogue box appears.
4. Make the following selections:
   - **Setting**: Box
   - **Style**: see Figure 4.18
   - **Color**: Violet
   - **Width**: 6pt

   (Note: Not all the Style options have the choice of 6 pt; if this is not available, choose the widest width available.)
5. Make sure that the **Apply to** box has **Picture** selected.

Figure 4.18 Adding a border to a picture using the Borders dialogue box

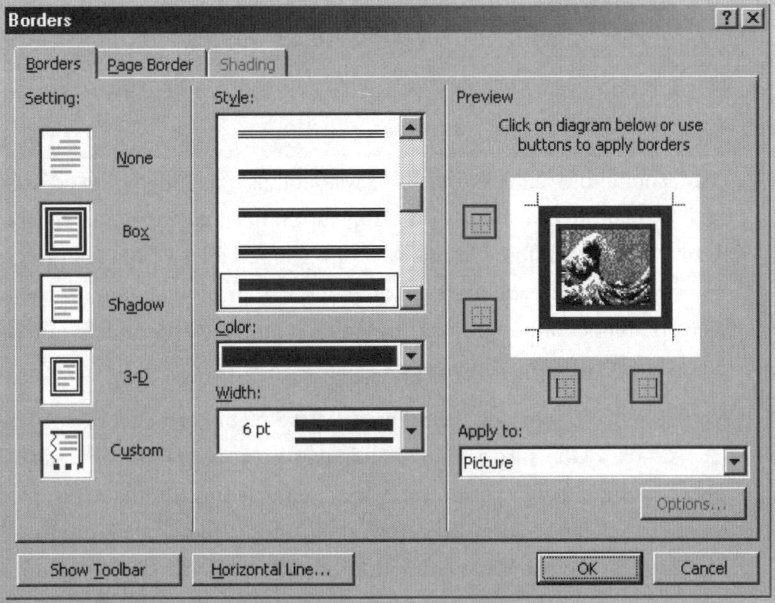

6 Click on: **OK**. Your picture should now have a border around it.

7 Amend the border by right-clicking on the picture, then select: **Borders and Shading**. Change the **Setting** to **Shadow**. Click on: **OK**.

You can also apply formatting options to the picture using the Picture toolbar that appears when you insert the picture. Click on the picture and check out the effects that using Image Control, Contrast, Brightness, etc. has on the picture.

When using the cropping tool, don't forget to position the cursor over the handles on the picture. To reset the picture to the original form, click on the final icon on the toolbar: Reset Picture.

Practice Task *Task 4*

These exercises are included to help the candidate in his or her training for the Advanced ECDL program. The exercises included in this material are not Advanced ECDL certification tests and should not be construed in any way as Advanced ECDL certification tests. For information about Authorised ECDL Test Centres in different National Territories, please refer to the ECDL Foundation website at **www.ecdl.com**.

You are going to create an A4 handout on the ***Phantom of the Opera*** by Gaston Leroux.

The flyer is going to be portrait, with one image and a border. To give you a starting point, look at the suggested Task 4 Answer on page 149. Your completed document may look quite different from the one in the book: this is not important, provided that you have used all the Word functions that the Task requires.

WordArt and Drawing Tools will be used for the subheading and the text border:

- Subheading: 'Prologue'
- Text border: 'In which the author of this singular work informs the reader how he acquired the certainty that the opera ghost really existed'

Below is the main body of text, which will be inserted in to linked text boxes. The file is stored in your Task Files folder as: Opera_Text.

> The Opera ghost really existed. He was not, as was long believed, a creature of the imagination of the artists, the superstition of the managers, or a product of the absurd and impressionable brains of the young ladies of the ballet, their mothers, the box-keepers, the cloak-room attendants or the concierge. Yes, he existed in flesh and blood, although he assumed the complete appearance of a real phantom; that is to say, of a spectral shade.
>
> When I began to ransack the archives of the National Academy of Music I was at once struck by the surprising coincidences between the phenomena ascribed to the 'ghost' and the most extraordinary and fantastic tragedy that ever excited the Paris upper classes; and I soon conceived the idea that this tragedy might reasonably be explained by the phenomena in question. The events do not date more than thirty years back; and it would not be difficult to find at the present day, in the foyer of the ballet, old men of the highest respectability, men upon whose word one could absolutely rely, who would remember as though they happened yesterday the mysterious and dramatic conditions that attended the kidnapping of Christine Daae, the disappearance of the Vicomte de Chagny and the death of his elder brother, Count Philippe, whose body was found on the bank of the lake that exists in the lower cellars of the Opera on the Rue-Scribe side. But none of those witnesses had until that day thought that there was any reason for connecting the more or less legendary figure of the Opera ghost with that terrible story.
>
> GASTON LEROUX

1 Open a new document and create three text boxes, size 9 cm x 7 cm.

Handy Hint

Create box 1, copy and paste to produce box 2 and 3. Arrange the boxes as in the suggested answer on page 149.

Set Zoom to: Whole Page.

2 Insert the file: Opera Text into the first text box.

3 Link the text boxes and drop the text into the remaining 2 text boxes.

4 Apply Lavender shading to the boxes.

5 Apply a Dash Dot border, Plum colour, 1.5 pt weight.

6 At the top of the page as the heading, key in: Phantom of the Opera. Use sentence case. Format as follows:

- Font: GiGi
- Style: Bold
- Size: 48 pt
- Colour: Red
- Effect: Emboss
- Underline: Dotted
- Align: Centre

7 Using WordArt (select the last option on the third row), insert in uppercase the word: PROLOGUE. Format to: Showcard Gothic font, 40 pt. Position the WordArt centrally below the heading.

The remainder of the text you are going to run around the outside of the page to form the border.

8 Using a text box, insert in uppercase the words: IN WHICH THE AUTHOR OF THIS SINGULAR WORK INFORMS.

Handy Hint

From the Zoom drop-down menu, select: Whole Page.

9 Apply the following formatting:

- Chiller font, 36 pt, bold.
- Choose a deep red colour from More Colors: Standard.
- Order the text box to: Send Behind Text.
- Remove the border (if you have one).
- Rotate the text so that the base of the letters is to the right. Resize the box to accommodate the text.
- Place this text box down the left-hand side of the page.

10 Using a text box, insert the words: THE READER HOW HE ACQUIRED. Place this text box at the top of the page.

Handy Hint

Select the previous text box, copy and paste, change the wording, rotate, resize and reposition. This will save you the work of formatting the font again.

11 Using a text box, insert the words: THE CERTAINTY THAT THE OPERA GHOST REALLY EXISTED. Rotate the text so that the base of the letters is to the left. Place this text box down the right-hand side of the page.

12 In the top corners of the page, to indicate the direction of the border text, insert: AutoShapes: Bent Arrow. Fill each of the corner arrows with the same colour as the border text.

Handy Hint

Copy and rotate the first arrow to produce the second arrow. To do this, click on the first arrow, then select: Draw: Rotate or Flip: Rotate Right.

13 Search for Eiffel Tower images in ClipArt. You may have a different image from the suggested answer. You may also be asked if you want to convert the image to a Microsoft Drawing object. Click on Yes.

- Format the picture to: Square layout.
- Position in the bottom right-hand corner of the page.
- Remove the sky.

Handy Hint

Ungroup the image, click anywhere on the page away from the image, click on the portion you want to delete. This is much easier to do if you zoom the page to 200%.

14 Reformat the image as a group.

Handy Hint

Use the white pointer tool from the Drawing toolbar and draw a box (a marquee) around the separate parts to select them all.

15 Change the font in the body text boxes to: Arial, 12 pt.

Handy Hint

Select the text in all three boxes by clicking in the second box and using Ctrl + A keys.

16 Re-position the text boxes so that they form a square with the image. (See suggested answer.)

17 Apply to the heading the text effect: Blinking Background.

18 Save your work as: **Task 4 Answer**.

Task 5 The Narrowboat Company

In this task, you will cover the following skills:

- Convert tabbed text into a table.
- Sort data in a table.
  - o Alphabetic or numeric.
  - o Ascending or descending order.
- Perform addition calculations on a numeric list in a table.
- Create a chart
  - o Create a chart from a table.
  - o Create a chart from pasted worksheet data in a document.
- Modify an embedded worksheet in a document.
- Modify the formatting of a chart.
  - o Modify a chart created from a table.
  - o Modify a chart created from pasted worksheet data.
- Position a chart in a document.
- Add or update a caption to an image, table or worksheet.
- Apply a numbered caption to an image, figure, table or worksheet.
  - o Update existing captions.

Scenario

You are going to prepare a stock sheet for a company that sells narrowboats.

5.1 *Convert text into a table*

From your Task Files folder, open the file: **Task 5**. Click on the Show/Hide icon ¶. You will see that the page contains a block of tabbed text that could be displayed as a table.

Method

1 Select the text from 'LOCATION' to '54,750'.

2 Click on: **Table** on the main menu toolbar, then select: **Convert**: **Text to Table**. The Convert Text to Table dialogue box will appear.

Figure 5.1 The Convert Text to Table dialogue box

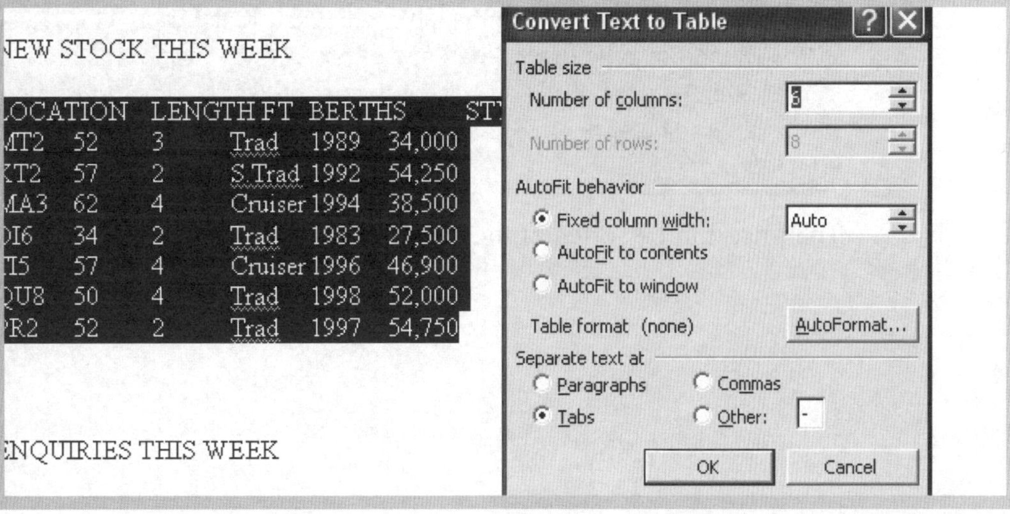

If you have selected the text correctly, Word should have recognised the Table size as 6 columns and 8 rows. If not, you need to amend the number of columns box.

3 Click to select: **Fixed column width**. This option displays the table across the full width of the page.

4 Click on: **OK**.

5 Repeat the above procedure on the smaller section of text below the heading 'ENQUIRIES THIS WEEK'. This time, in the Convert Text to Table dialogue box, select: **AutoFit to contents**. This option displays the table to fit the longest length of text in the column.

The figures have been entered incorrectly. Click in the table and amend the figures as below.

Figure 5.2 Amend the figures in the table as shown

ENQUIRIES THIS WEEK

Traditional	12
Semi Traditional	21
Cruiser	18

5.2 *Sort data in a table*

One of the most important questions customers ask when buying a narrowboat is what is the size. To make answering enquiries more efficient, the table needs to be sorted into order of length.

Method

1 Click anywhere in the table.

2 Click on: **Table** on the main menu toolbar, then select: **Sort**. The Sort dialogue box will appear (see Figure 5.3).

3 From the **Sort by** drop-down menu, select: **column 2** and the **Descending** radio button.

4 There is a header row on the table, i.e. LOCATION, LENGTH FT, etc. To prevent Word trying to sort the top (header) row of text with the rest of the table, click on the radio button **Header row**. You will see that in the Sort by drop-down menu, you now have the heading of the row you are sorting, i.e. LENGTH FT.

The price can be sorted at the same time.

Method

1 From the **Then by** drop-down menu, select: **PRICE £**. You will notice that Word automatically recognises whether you have text or numbers in the column when the radio button Header row is selected.

2 Select: **Ascending**.

3 Click on: **OK**.

Figure 5.3 Using the Sort dialogue box to sort data in a table

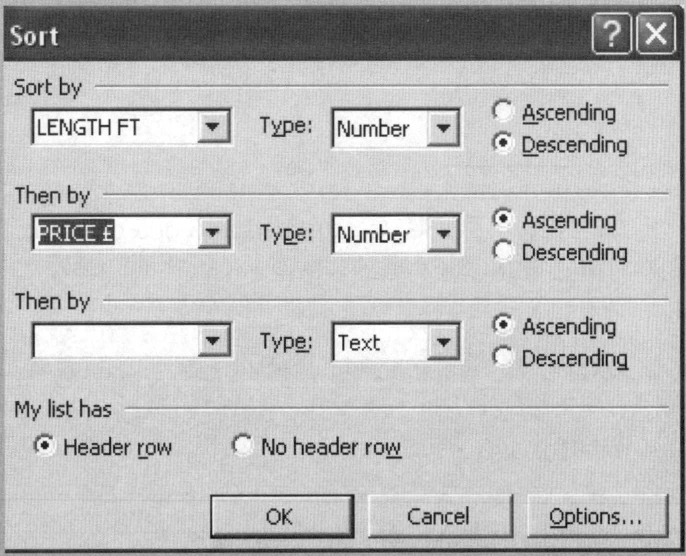

The two 57 ft boat prices should now be listed in ascending price order.

5.3 *Perform addition calculations on numeric data in a table*

The Narrowboat Company has bought more boats than usual this week. As all the stock is bought using a bank overdraft, a check needs to be made to ensure that the budget of £300,000 is kept to.

Large amounts of data calculations should be made using a spreadsheet, but you can perform a quick calculation using Word. The calculation must be done inside the table, so you need to create another row to accommodate this.

Method

1 Click in the cell at the end of the last row, i.e. the bottom right-hand corner.

2 Press the **Tab key**, or click on: **Table**: **Insert**: **Rows Below**.

You should now have a new row.

In the first column, key in the text: 'VALUE OF NEW STOCK'.

Figure 5.4 Key in the text: VALUE OF NEW STOCK

LOCATION	LENGTH FT
MA3	62
TI5	57
KT2	57
MT2	52
PR2	52
QU8	50
DI6	34
VALUE OF NEW STOCK	

The text 'VALUE OF NEW STOCK' is squashed into one column. To spread the text along the row you can merge the cells in the adjacent columns.

Method

1 Highlight the text in column 1 and the two blank cells to the right.

Figure 5.5 Highlight columns 1 to 3

DI6	34	2	Trad	1983
VALUE OF NEW STOCK				

2 Click on: **Table**: **Merge Cells**.

The text 'VALUE OF NEW STOCK' should now appear in one row.

Handy Hint

Always sort your table before you perform any merge operations.

Note: you cannot sort merged cells. It is important to remember that if you want to sort a table after you have merged cells, you must select only the unmerged rows that you want to sort, not the whole table. This will mean that you have to perform several sort operations to sort the table. If you try to sort the whole table, Word will move the merged cells to the bottom of the table.

To insert the calculation:

Method

1 Click in the last cell in the PRICE £ column, on the VALUE OF NEW STOCK row.

2 Click on: **Table**: **Formula**. The Formula dialogue box appears.

The default **Formula** is: =SUM(ABOVE). You can make further selections using the **Paste function** drop-down menu but not all the selections are appropriate (see Figure 5.6). If you make an obviously wrong selection, you will get the message: **!Syntax Error** in the selected cell of the table.

Figure 5.6 The Formula dialogue box

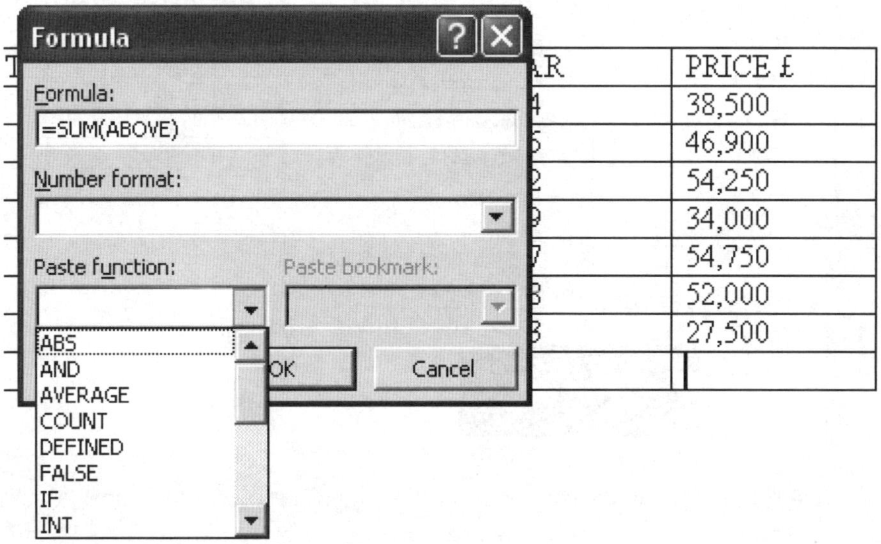

You can also change the number format: have a look at the options in the **Number format** drop-down menu. The default is appropriate for this document, but you do have other choices.

Leave the dialogue box at default and click on: **OK** to total the column. The total is greater than the overdraft limit! Fortunately, the company has received an unusual amount of enquiries for boats this week. This good news would look even better if presented as a graph.

5.4 *Create a chart from a table or pasted spreadsheet data*

Create a chart from a table

The graph can be created from the ENQUIRIES THIS WEEK table.

Method

1 Select the data in the table by either of the following methods:

- highlight using the mouse
- click in the table, then select: **Table**: **Select**: **Table**.

2 Click on: **Insert** from the main menu bar, then select: **Picture**: **Chart**.

Figure 5.7 Click on Insert from the main menu bar, then select Picture: Chart

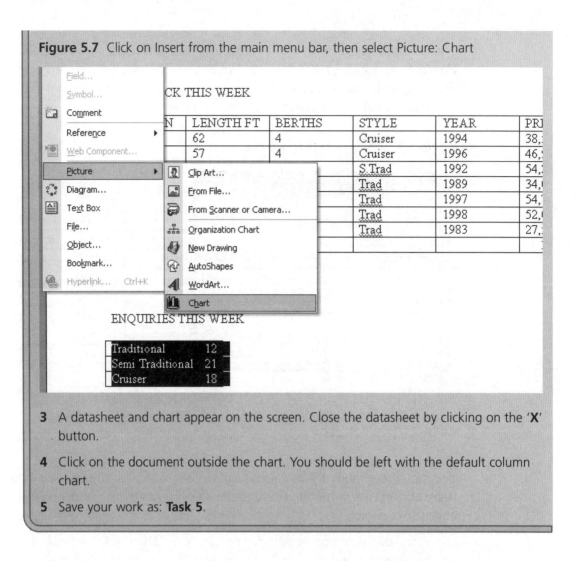

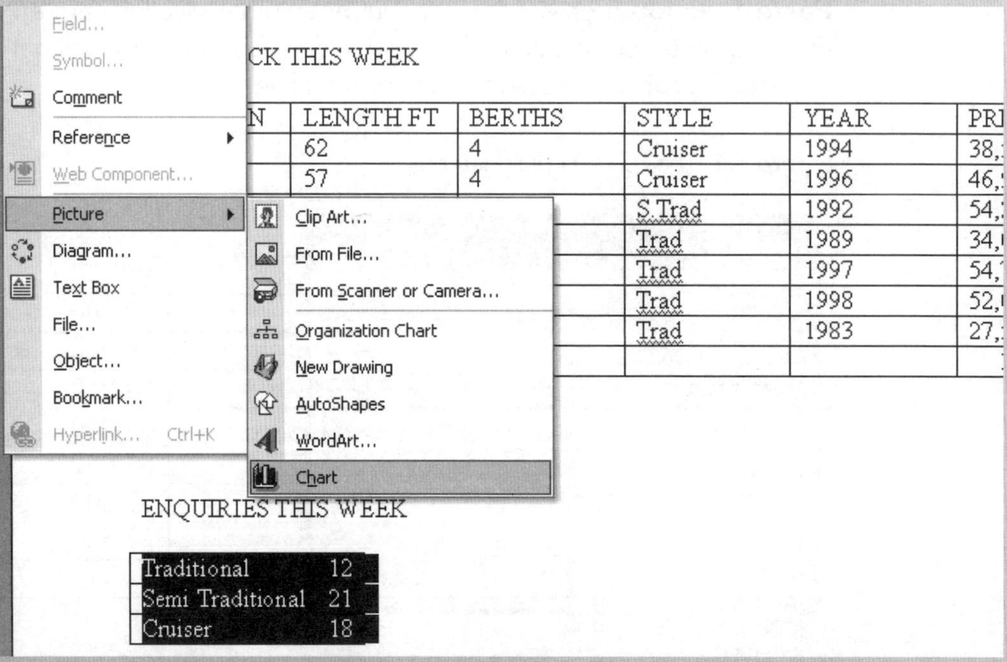

3 A datasheet and chart appear on the screen. Close the datasheet by clicking on the '**X**' button.

4 Click on the document outside the chart. You should be left with the default column chart.

5 Save your work as: **Task 5**.

Create a chart from pasted spreadsheet data

The above chart has been created in Word. You can also create charts from Excel. This involves putting the data into an Excel spreadsheet and then copying the data into Word.

Copying data from Excel into Word

Method

1 Open: **Excel**.

2 Key in the following data as illustrated in Figure 5.8:

Traditional 18
Semi Traditional 24
Cruiser 52

3 Highlight to select the cells from A1 diagonally to B3.

4 Right-click and select: **Copy**.

Figure 5.8 Key in the data in Excel, then right-click and select: Copy

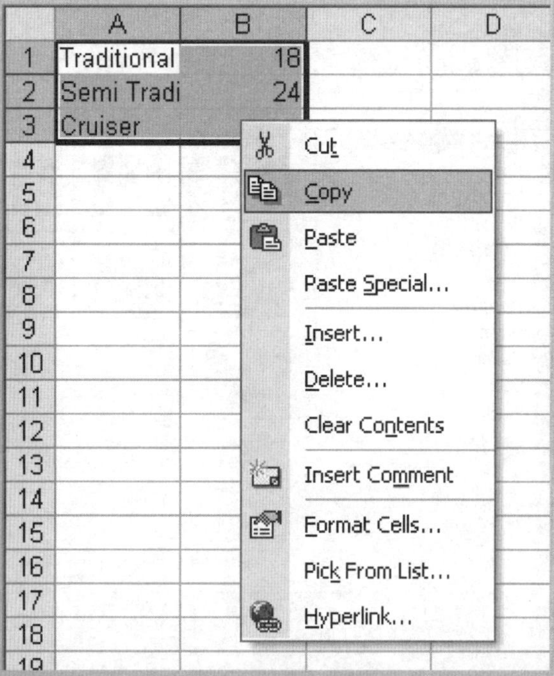

5 Open a new Word document.

6 Select: **Edit**: **Paste Special**. A Paste Special dialogue box appears.

7 In the **As**: box, select: **Microsoft Excel Worksheet Object**.

8 Click on: **OK**.

Note: it is important that you select Paste Special and not simply Paste. Paste Special pastes (embeds) the spreadsheet into the document, not just the data. If you double-click on the embedded spreadsheet, you will see that the row and column headings are visible.

Also, if you click to select the **Paste link** radio button, when you double-click on the embedded worksheet this will link you back to the original Excel Worksheet. While this is a useful tool, it is not always appropriate and can prove very frustrating as you jump unnecessarily from Word to Excel.

Creating a chart from pasted Excel data

To create a chart from this data:

Method

1 Double-click on the embedded worksheet.

2 Select: **Insert**: **Chart**.

3 Select: **Column**: **Next**: **Next**: **Next**: **Finish** (see Figure 5.9 and 5.10).

Figure 5.9 Select the chart type

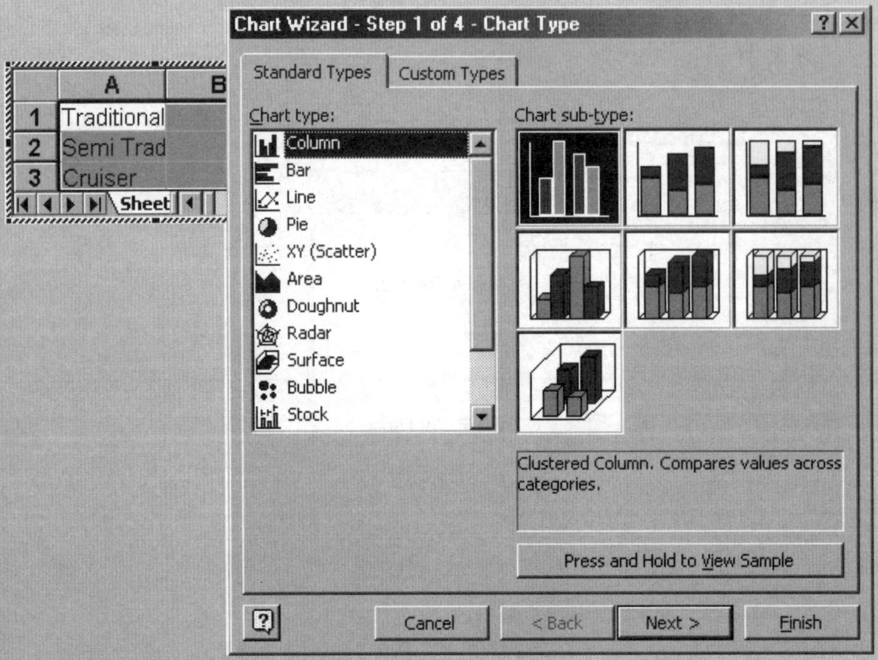

Figure 5.10 The finished chart

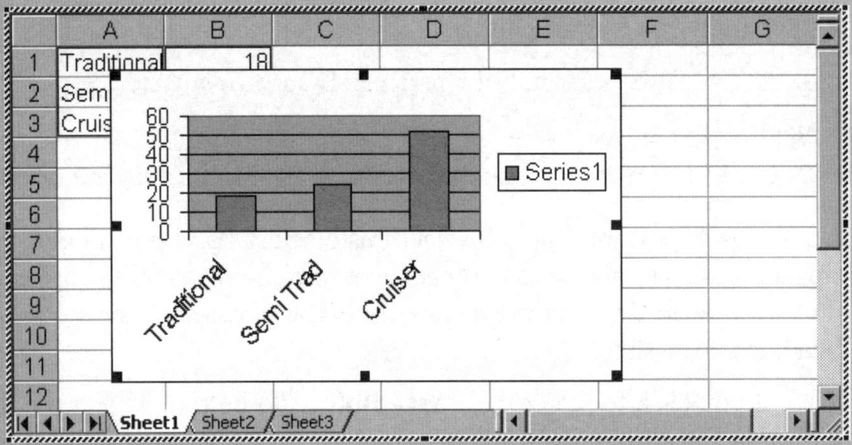

You should be able to see the chart in the embedded worksheet. To see the entire chart, you can drag out the bottom right-hand handle of the worksheet.

Click down outside the worksheet to deselect it.

5.5 *Modify an embedded worksheet*

If you use the above method to create a table from data pasted in Word from an Excel worksheet, and then need to change the data, double-click on the data. Excel formatting icons appear at the top of the screen and the embedded worksheet is made available for editing.

If the chart is covering the numbers, you will need to move it to one side by clicking on the chart (make sure that you have the 4-headed arrow) and dragging to a new position.

Method

1 Make the following changes. You will see the chart update as you are inputting the new data:
- Traditional: 12
- Semi Traditional: 21
- Cruiser: 18

2 Save your work as: **Task 5a**.

5.6 *Change the formatting of a chart created from a table or pasted spreadsheet data*

Open: **Task 5** again and double-click on the chart. The main menu toolbar will show tools for formatting the chart.

The various elements of the chart can be selected from the drop-down menu (see Figure 5.11). These can then be formatted by clicking on the icons. If you click on the drop-down menu at the end of the toolbar, you will see more icons, for example, Fill and Gridlines.

Figure 5.11 Using the Chart Toolbar to format a chart

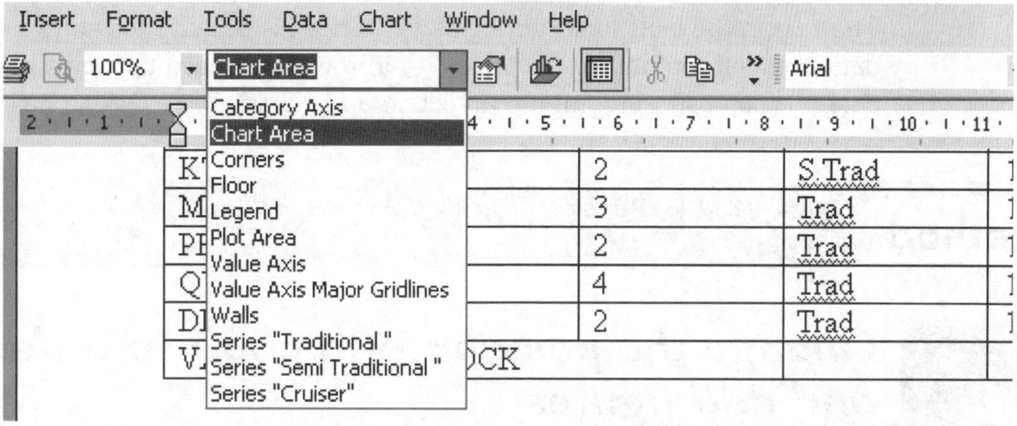

Try some of the options to see the effects.

Handy Hint

If you make several changes that you don't like, and the Undo button won't undo any more, you can close without saving and reopen the file.

The Narrowboat Company always use pie charts, so the column chart needs to be changed accordingly.

Modifying chart type

Method

1 To select the chart, double-click on the chart. You should have a shaded box around the chart and a toolbar at the top of the screen with chart formatting icons.

2 Click on the **Chart Type** icon, then from the drop-down toolbar options menu select: **Pie Chart**. (You may have to click on the drop-down menu at the end of the toolbar to see the Chart Type icon.)

Note: make sure that you have not selected any of the individual elements of the table, e.g. a single column, because you will end up with just that column shown as a pie chart.

You should get a chart that looks like this:

Figure 5.12 Changing the table to a pie chart

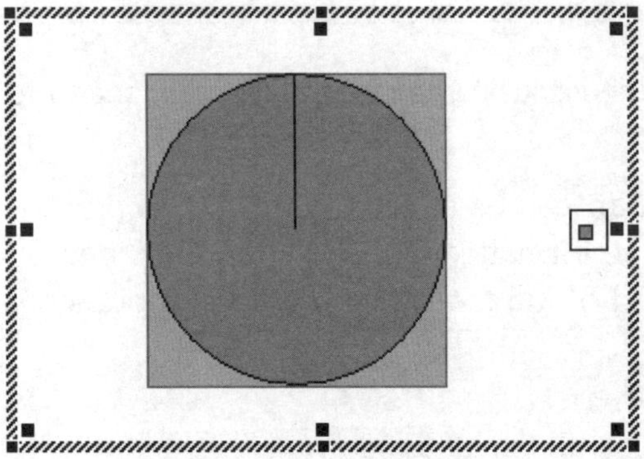

The reason the table looks wrong as a pie chart is because the software reads the data from left to right for the table, i.e. in rows. You need the software to read the data in columns to present it correctly in a pie chart.

Method

On the Chart Toolbar, click on the **By Column** icon.

5.7 *Change the position of a chart in a document and add figures*

Now delete the 'ENQUIRIES THIS WEEK' table from the page by clicking in the table, then selecting: **Table: Delete: Table**.

Deleting the table will not affect your graph as the data required to produce the graph is now stored in the datasheet table. To see the datasheet, double-click on the chart then click on: **View: Datasheet**.

Changing the chart position

Now the table has been deleted, the graph can be moved into position underneath the heading 'ENQUIRIES THIS WEEK'.

Method

1 Click once in the graph – you should get a box with square handles.

2 Click on the **Align Left** icon on the formatting toolbar.

Handy Hint

If you double-click to select the chart (i.e. so that the chart has a shaded border), you will not have access to the formatting toolbar.

Adding figures to the pie chart

The pie chart does not make any sense without figures. To add figures to the chart:

Method

1 Double-click on the pie chart to select it.

2 Double-click on the pie chart area. Right-click and select: **Format Data Series**.

3 Select the **Data Labels** tab.

4 Click on the box **Value**. This will pick up the data from the datasheet.

Figure 5.13 Adding data to a pie chart using the Format Data Series dialogue box

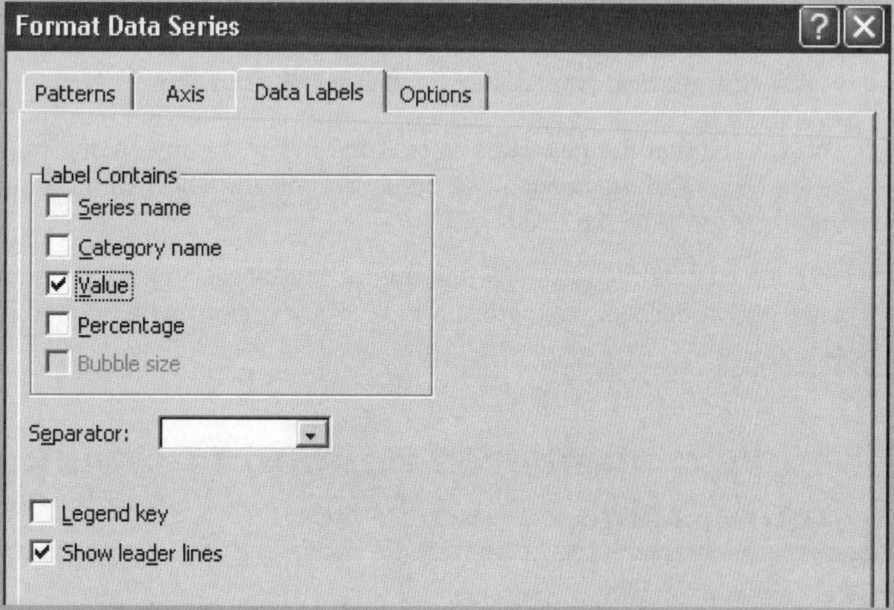

5 Click on: **OK**. The number of enquiries should appear next to the appropriate pie segment.

5.8 *Add and update an image, table or worksheet caption*

At the top of the document is an image that the Narrowboat Company uses as a logo. The caption underneath the image needs to be updated.

Method

1 Right-click on the image, then from the pop-up menu select: **Caption**. A Caption dialogue box appears.

2 Click on: **New Label**. A New Label dialogue box appears.

3 In the **caption** box, key in: **The Narrowboat Company**.

4 Click on: **OK**.

Figure 5.14 Changing a picture caption using the Caption dialogue box

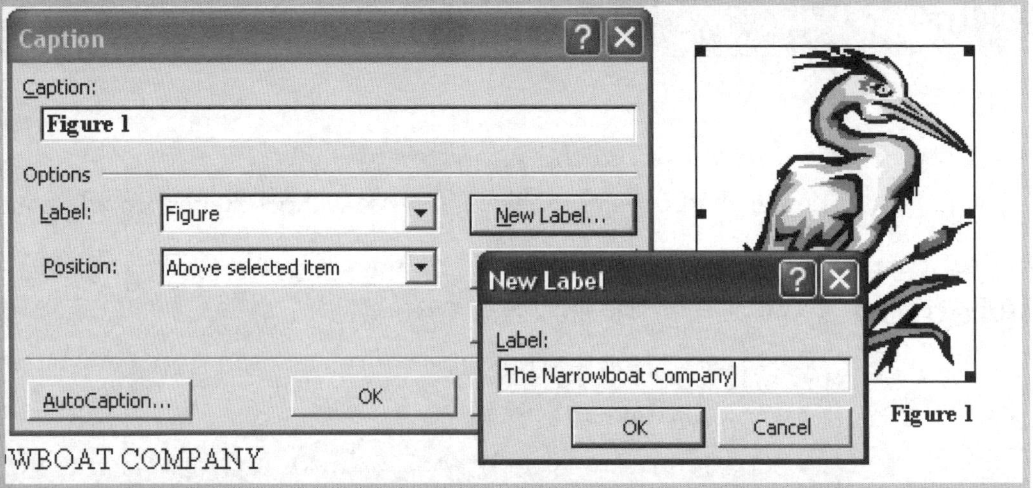

5 From the **Position** drop-down menu, select: **Above selected item**.

6 Click on: **OK**.

You will see that the new caption is at the top of the image and the old caption is still at the bottom of the image. The number 1 after the new caption indicates that this is the first caption in the document.

You can change the format of the numbering by clicking on the numbering button in the Caption dialogue box. Have a look at the options when you apply the next caption.

5.9 *Apply a numbered caption to an image, figure, table or worksheet*

Now you are going to add a caption to the NEW STOCK THIS WEEK table.

Method

1 Select the table, i.e. **Table**: **Select**: **Table**.

2 Right-click to access the pop-up menu, then select: **Caption**. The Caption dialogue box appears. This offers you the next caption, i.e. **The Narrowboat Company 2**, as the caption.

3 Click on: **OK**. The caption is added to the table.

Now add a caption to the pie chart. This caption will be: **The Narrowboat Company 3**.

Method

1 Right-click on the pie chart to access the pop-up menu.

Handy Hint

Do not double-click to select the pie chart, because you will not get the pop-up menu you need.

2 Select: **Caption**. The Caption dialogue box appears offering you the caption.

3 Click on: **OK**.

On further thought, you don't need a caption for the NEW STOCK THIS WEEK table. Delete the caption by selecting and pressing the Delete key.

Update existing captions

Although you have deleted caption 2, the image (company logo) and the pie chart still have caption 1 and caption 3 attached to them. You need to update the captions.

Method

1 Select the caption text: **The Narrowboat Company 3**.

2 Right-click to access the pop-up menu, then select: **Update Field**. The caption should change to: The Narrowboat Company 2.

Handy Hint

You can amend or delete the captions by clicking into them on the page. However, if you delete the number your caption will not be included when you update. If you click the I-beam cursor just before the number, you will see that the number is in a grey field area.

Save your work as: **Task 5**.

Practice Task

Task 5

These exercises are included to help the candidate in his or her training for the Advanced ECDL program. The exercises included in this material are not Advanced ECDL certification tests and should not be construed in any way as Advanced ECDL certification tests. For information about Authorised ECDL Test Centres in different National Territories, please refer to the ECDL Foundation website at **www.ecdl.com**.

You have been asked to produce details of holidays lasting 7 and 8 nights.

1 Key in the following text for the 7-night holidays. Use the Tab key to move from column to column. Do not set up the text as a table. Do not put more than one tab between the columns.

7-night·holidays¶
12·Apr–9·May→340¶
10·May–23·May → 210¶
24·May–6·Jun→420¶
7·Jun–20·Jun → 360¶
21·Jun–·4·Jul → 398¶
5·Jul–18·Jul → 440¶
30·Aug–5·Sep→337¶

2 Convert the text to a table and AutoFit to contents. Do not include the table heading.

Handy Hint

Separate text at tabs.

3 Create a column chart that shows the dates and the prices for 7-night holidays.

4 Position the chart underneath the table.

5 Make the following amendments:

- Change the colour of the background to yellow.
- Remove the gridlines.
- Change the chart to a bar chart.

6 Insert an extra row at the top of the table to contain the column headings, and add a column to the right of '7 nights'. Key in the following details:

Dates	7 nights	Extra night (£)
12 Apr–9 May	340	18
10 May–23 May	210	21
24 May–6 Jun	420	28
7 Jun–20 Jun	360	34
21 Jun–4 Jul	398	39
5 Jul–18 Jul	440	44
30 Aug–5 Sep	337	26

7 Insert an extra column to the right of the 'Extra night' column.

- Insert the heading: 8 nights.
- Using a formula, calculate the cost of the 8-night holiday for each time period.

Handy Hint

Each time, check that the formula is: =SUM(LEFT). If not, key in the correct formula.

8 Select the number format that gives you the £ symbol and the total to 2 decimal places.

9 Insert a row at the bottom of the table.

10 Using a formula, calculate the average cost of the 7-night holidays and the average cost of the 8-night holidays.

Handy Hint

Look in: Paste function. The formula you need to create is =AVERAGE(ABOVE).

11 Select the number format that gives you the £ symbol and the total to 2 decimal places.

12 Sort the holidays into Ascending order of cost for 8 nights.

Handy Hint

Select the rows you want to sort, otherwise Word includes the last row of the table in the sort.

13 Above the table, insert a picture that represents holidays.

14 Add the caption above the image: Holidays in the Sun.

15 Amend the 7-nights price for 7 Jun–20 Jun to £460. Don't forget to update the Formula field in the 8-nights column.

Handy Hint

Right-click in the cell containing the formula.

16 Update the chart with the new price by amending the datasheet.

Handy Hint

Double-click on the chart to access the datasheet.

17 Save your work as: **Task 5 Answer**.

Task 6 Literature for children

In this task, you will cover the following skills:

- Create new character or paragraph styles.
  - o The Style drop-down menu.
  - o Creating a new style.
  - o Applying a new style.
- Create a table of contents.
  - o Add page numbers to a document.
  - o Creating a table of contents.
- Apply formatting options to a table of contents.
  - o Leader options.
  - o Add a heading to a table of contents.
- Update and modify an existing table of contents.
  - o Remove existing contents.
  - o Add new contents.
- Create a simple drawing using the drawing options.
  - o Using the Drawing Toolbar.
  - o Create a basic drawing using AutoShapes.
  - o Group the elements of a drawing.
  - o Add colour to a drawing.
  - o Add 3-D effects to a drawing.

Scenario

Open the file from the folder 'Task Files' called: ***Task 6****. The file contains Robert Louis Stevenson's,* A Child's Garden of Verses. *The verses are already in numerical order, but to make it easier for the Literary Group members to go directly to the verse under discussion, a contents page would be useful.*

6.1 Create new character and paragraph styles

As you can see when you scroll through the document, it contains a variety of text fonts and sizes. In order to set up a table of contents, specific styles have to be applied to the text so that Word knows what to look for when setting up the contents page.

The Style drop-down menu

Styles can be used to format a number of sections of text that are not adjacent to each other, e.g. if you wanted all your subheadings in 16 pt, bold, italic, you could create the style and then for all the subsequent subheadings you simply select the style from the drop-down menu.

The Style drop-down menu is the first drop-down menu on the formatting toolbar. Click on this menu now and you will see that it already contains default styles.

Creating a new style

Method

1 Click into the first verse title, i.e. 'Bed in Summer'.

2 Click on: **Format** from the main menu toolbar, then select: **Style's and Formatting**. A task pane appears at the right-hand side of the screen.

3 Click on: **New Style**. The New Style dialogue box appears.

4 In the **Name** box, key in: **Verse Title**.

5 In the **Style based on** box, select: **(no style)**. (You need to scroll to the top of the list of options.) No style is selected because the other option is to have your new style based on an existing style; this may not be exactly what you want.

Figure 6.1 Formatting text style using the New Style dialogue box

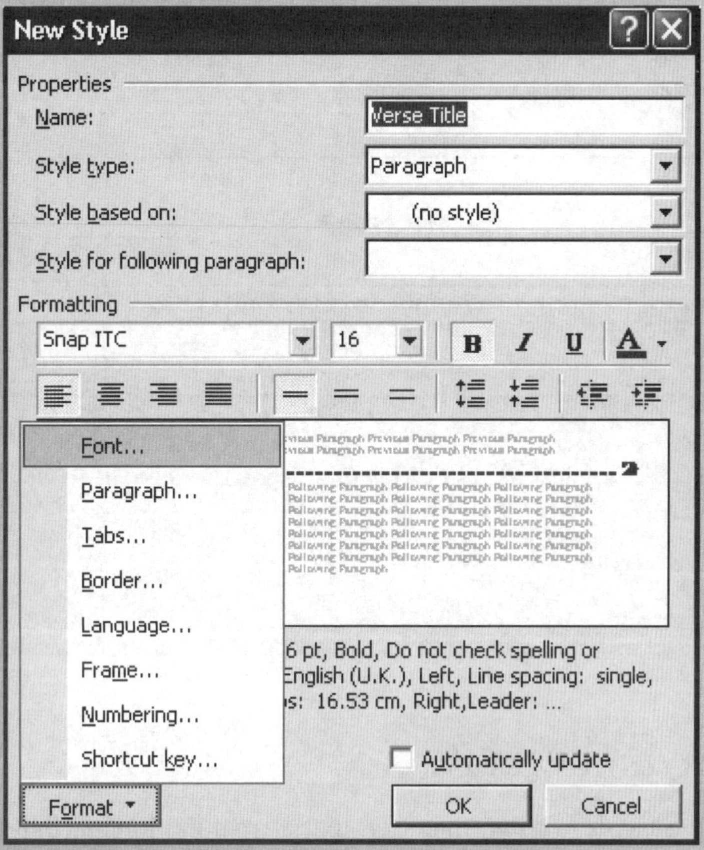

6 Click on the **Formatting** drop-down menus to make the following selections:.

- **Font**: Snap ITC
- **Font style**: Bold
- **Size**: 16 pt
- **Font color**: Red
- **Effects**: Shadow

7 Click on the **Format** button to access the Font dialogue box.

Figure 6.2 Selecting formatting options in the Font dialogue box

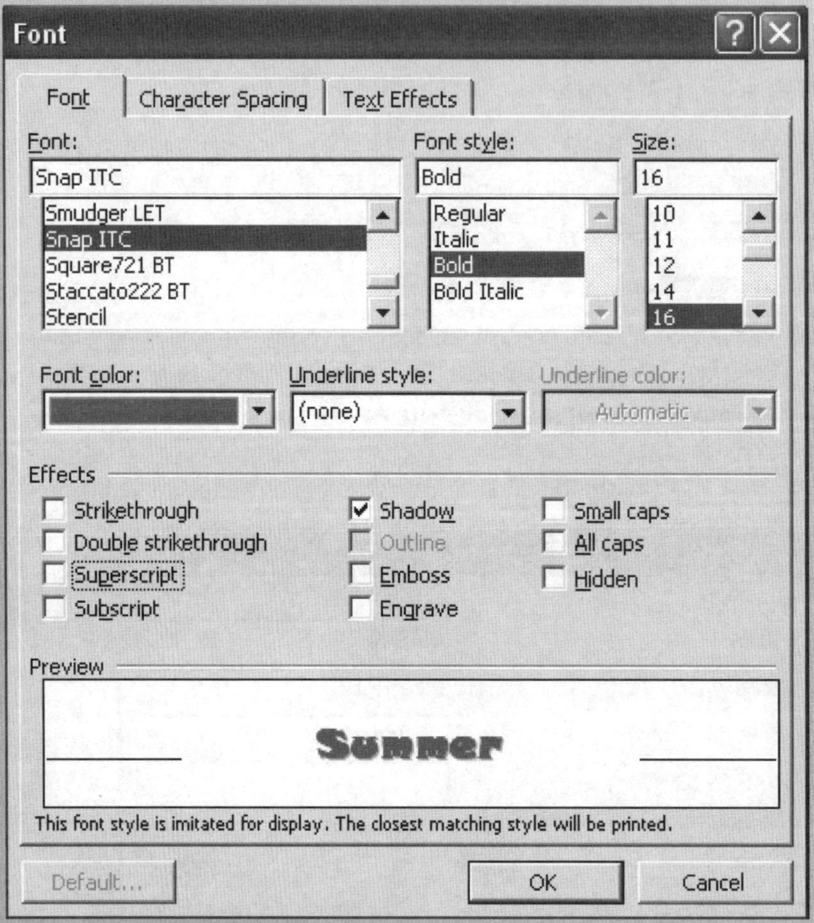

8 Click on: **OK** to exit the Font dialogue box, then click on: **OK** to exit the New Style dialogue box.

9 Verse Title should now appear in the Styles and Formatting task pane.

Applying a new style

Check in the Style drop-down menu on the Formatting toolbar that the new heading style you have created, i.e. Verse Title, appears in the list.

Figure 6.3 Accessing a chosen style in the Style drop-down menu

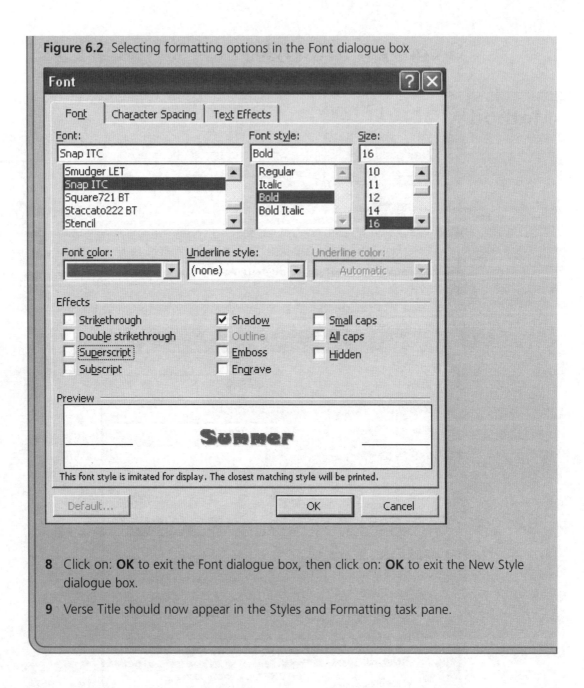

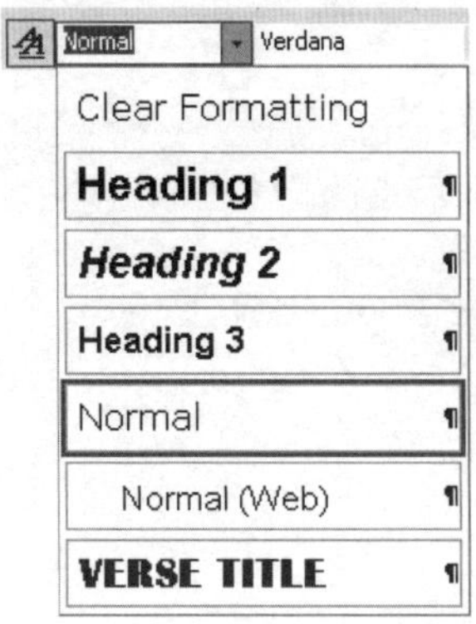

There is no quick way to do the next part. In the Word document, you need to click into each of the verse titles and then select your new style from the Styles and Formatting task pane. Continue until all the verse titles have the Verse Title style applied.

Handy Hint

Beware! If you miss applying the Verse Title style to any of the verse titles, that title will not appear in your table of contents.

6.2 *Create a table of contents*

A table of contents is a list created from formatted text that has a specified style applied to it. Typically a table of contents will be found at the front of the book, e.g. as a list of chapters and page numbers. Word picks up the style, in order, and lists the formatted text with the page on which it appears.

Add page numbers to a document

Before you create a table of contents (TOC), it is necessary to add page numbers to the document.

Method

1 To insert page numbers at the bottom of the pages, select: **Insert**: **Page Numbers**. The Page Numbers dialogue box will appear.

2 Deselect the option: **Show number on first page**. (The first page is eventually going to be the front cover.)

3 Click on: **OK**.

Figure 6.4 Inserting page numbers using the Page Numbers dialogue box

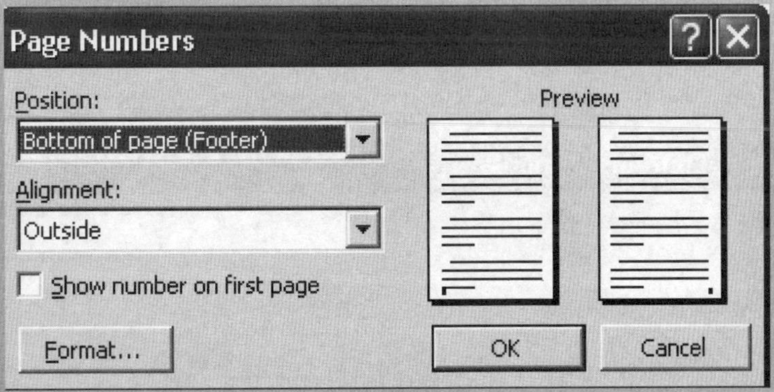

Handy Hint

In the Page Numbers dialogue box, from the Alignment drop-down menu, choosing Outside will place the page numbers at the bottom of the pages alternating from left to right (even numbers on the right). This means that when a document is produced back to back, the page numbers will show on the outside edge of the booklet.

Creating a table of contents

You are now going to create a table of contents for *A Child's Garden of Verses*.

First, you need to create a space at the beginning of the document to accommodate the Contents page.

Method

1 Position the I-beam cursor at the start of your document, i.e. before the 'I'. (Use the **Ctrl + Home** keys.)

2 Select: **Insert**: **Break** to access the Break dialogue box.

3 Click to select: **Page break**.

4 Click on: **OK**.

Handy Hint

An alternative way to insert a page break is to hold down the Ctrl key and press Enter.

Method

1 Position the cursor at the top of the new page 1.

2 Click on: **Insert** from the main menu bar, then select: **Reference.** Select: **Index and Tables**. An Index and Tables dialogue box appears.

3 Select the **Table of Contents** tab.

4 Click on the **Options** button at the bottom of the dialogue box. The Table of Contents Options dialogue box appears.

5 Scroll down to the bottom of the **TOC level** list; you should find Verse Title (see Figure 6.5).

6 As you only want one TOC level, i.e. all the verses listed underneath each other and left aligned, next to the Verse Title style, key in the number 1. A tick appears next to Verse Title.

Figure 6.5 Setting a table of contents using the TOC level

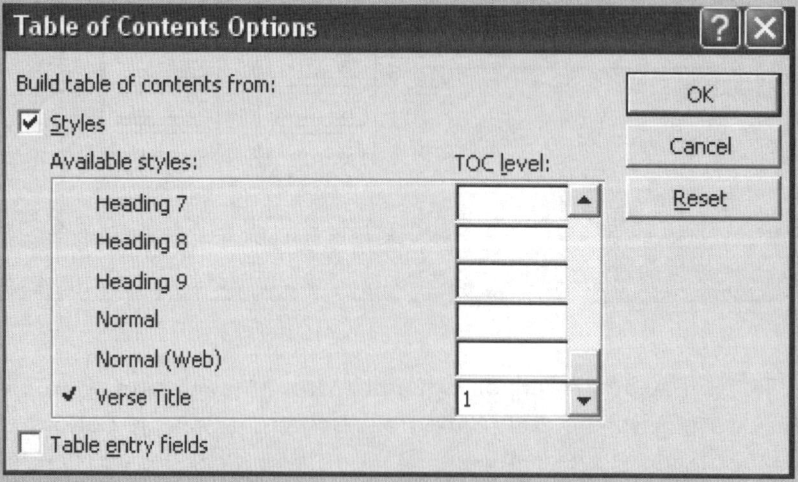

7 Click on: **OK** twice, to exit the two dialogues boxes. You should now have a table of contents on your first page.

The verse titles on the contents page are now linked to the verse titles in the main body of the document. Hold down the Ctrl key and click on one of the titles; the cursor should go straight to that verse.

6.3 *Apply formatting to a table of contents*

Leader options

The contents page would be easier to follow if the leader dots were a solid line.

Method

1 Press: **Ctrl + Home** to take you to the top of the contents page. This method also selects the table of contents, which you need to do before altering the leader dots.

2 Click on: **Insert** from the main menu toolbar, then select: **Reference**. Select: **Index and Tables**.

3 In the Index and Tables dialogue box, select the **Table of Contents** tab.

4 From the **Tab leader** drop-down menu, select the **solid line** option.

Figure 6.6 Using Tab leader in the Index and Tables dialogue box

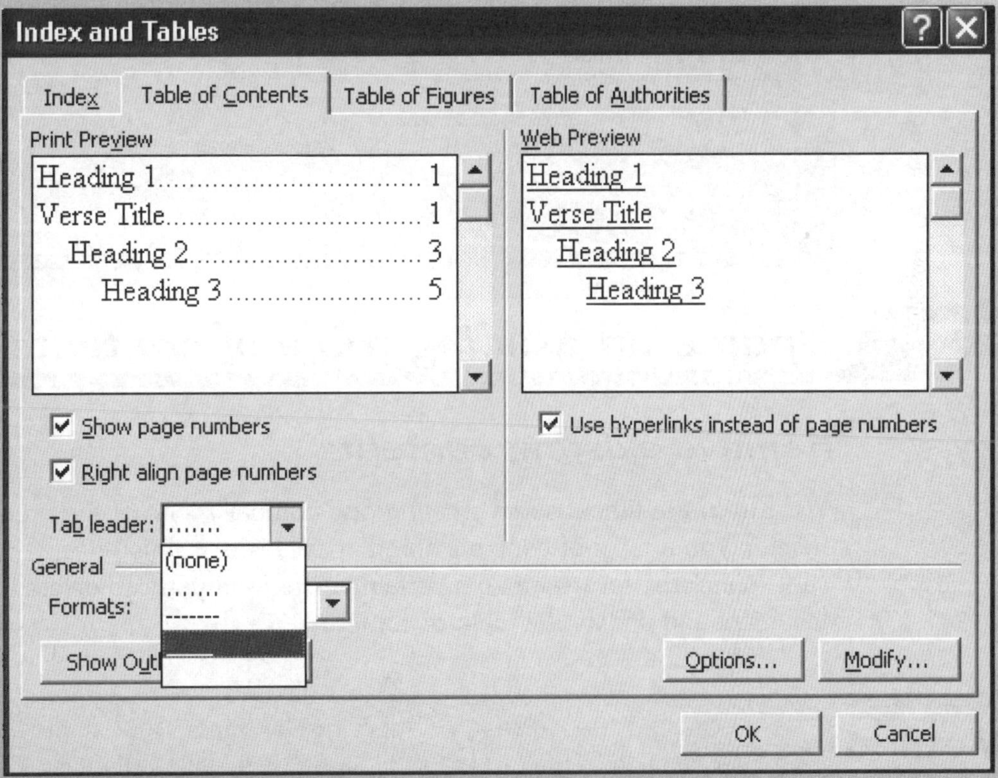

5 Click on: **OK**.

6 A dialogue box will appear, asking '**Do you want to replace the selected table of contents**'. Click on: **Yes**. The contents page is now amended.

Add a heading to a table of contents

To finish the page, you can add the heading 'Contents' above the table of contents.

Method

1 Use the **Ctrl + Home** keys to get to the top of the page.

2 Press: **Enter** twice to create two line spaces.

3 Key in the word: **Contents**.

4 Increase the character spacing of the word Contents, as follows:

- Click on: **Format**: **Font**.
- In the Font dialogue box, select the **Character Spacing** tab.
- In the **Scale** box, change the per cent to: **300**. (300 is not listed in the drop-down menu, so you will need to key '300' in the scale box.)
- Click on: **OK**.

Figure 6.7 Formatting a heading on the Character Spacing tab in the Font dialogue box

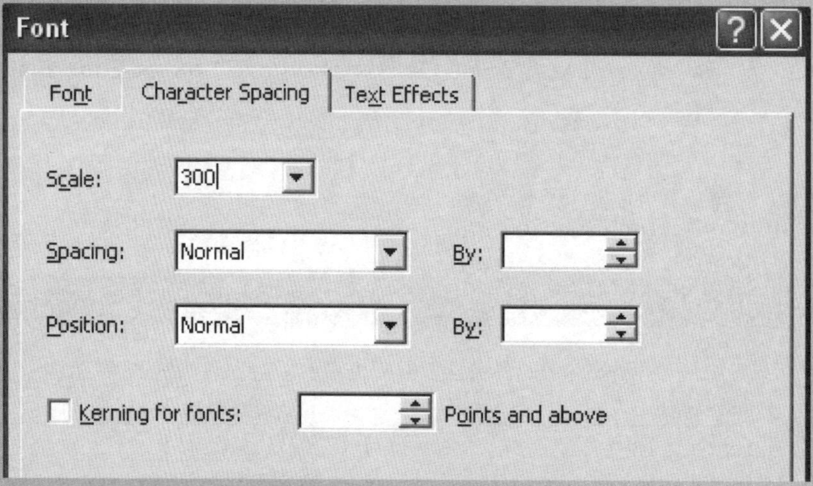

6.4 *Update an existing table of contents*

Remove existing contents

Apart from the time it saves creating one manually, one of the greatest advantages of setting up a table of contents automatically is that if you decide that you don't want to include, for example, a certain verse, then you can delete it from your document and update the table of contents.

Method

1 Select and delete: **Verse XIV**: **Where go the boats?** You can get quickly to this verse by holding down the **Ctrl** key and clicking on the title in the table of contents.

Figure 6.8 Select and delete the chosen verse

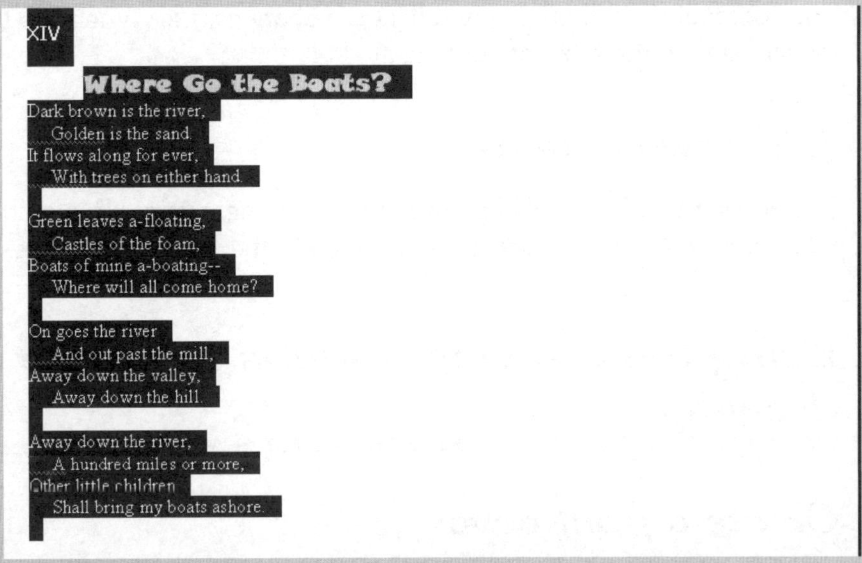

2 Right-click on your first page (the table of contents). The table of contents is now shaded and a pop-up menu has appeared.

3 From the pop-up menu, select: **Update Field**.

Figure 6.9 From the pop-up menu, select: Update Field

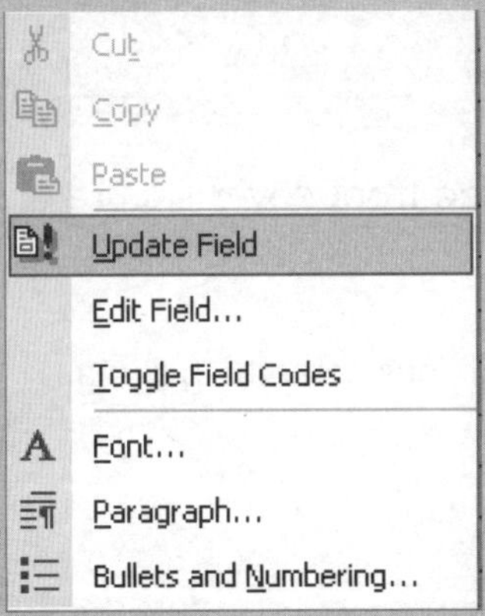

4 An Update Table of Contents dialogue box appears. You will be asked which part of the table of contents you want to update: either **Update page numbering** only or **Update entire table**. As you have changed more than the page number, i.e. you have deleted part of the document, select: **Update entire table**.

Figure 6.10 Selecting a chosen update option in the Update Table of Contents dialogue box

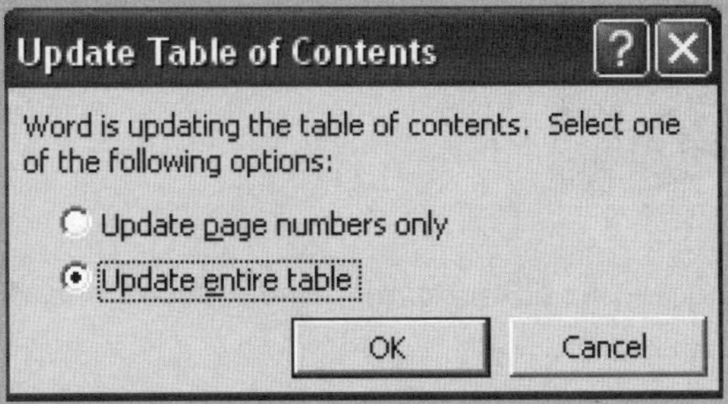

5 Click on: **OK**.

6 Save your work as: **Task 6**.

The contents page should now reflect the changes, i.e. 'Where go the boats?' is no longer listed in the table of contents.

Add new contents

The above method can also be used to include new verse. Remember to apply the relevant style to the text you want included in the table of contents.

6.5 Using the drawing options to create a simple drawing

Create a front cover

Open the **Task 6** document (if it isn't open already). Go to the top of the document (**Ctrl + Home** keys). The document needs a front cover now. To create a new first page, insert a page break in front of the contents page (press **Ctrl + Enter**).

Handy Hint

Don't forget to update your table of contents. All the verses will now be on different page numbers.

You are going to create a simple boat for the front cover. Figure 6.11 is an example of what your finished work may look like.

Figure 6.11 The boat for the front cover will look something like this

Creating a drawing that is going to fill the whole page is easier to do if you can see the whole page you are working on.

Method

Click on: **Zoom** from the standard toolbar and select: **Whole Page**.

Figure 6.12 Click on Zoom: Whole Page to view the whole page you are working on

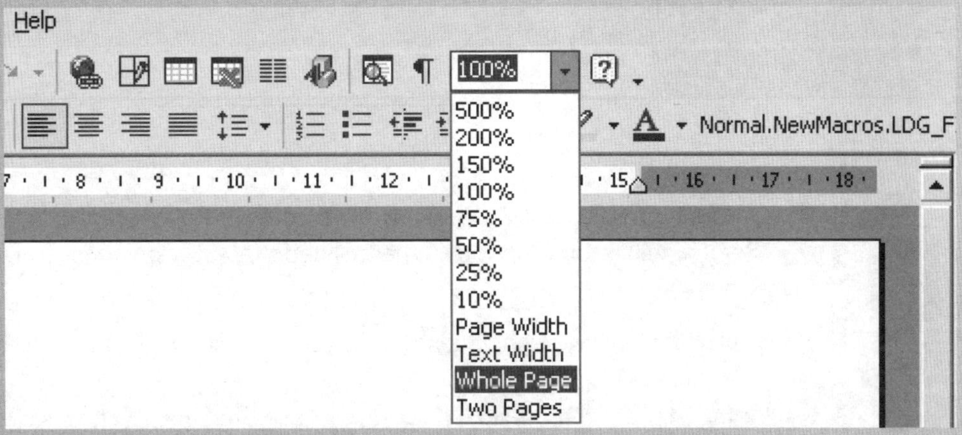

Using the Drawing Toolbar

To create the drawing, you will be using tools from the Drawing Toolbar only. Make sure that you have this toolbar visible at the foot of the screen. If not:

Method

Click on: **View**: **Toolbars**: **Drawing**. The Drawing Toolbar is positioned at the bottom of your screen.

Figure 6.13 The Drawing Toolbar

Handy Hint

Caution: the following instructions assume that you click and drag from top left to bottom right.

Create a basic drawing using AutoShapes

The first shape is going to be the hull of the boat.

Method

1 Click on the **AutoShapes** drop-down menu, then select: **Basic Shapes**. Select the third option on the top row: **Trapezoid**.

2 Click on the page at approximately 16 cm on the vertical ruler. Drag the black cross across the page until you get a basic 'hull' shape (see Figure 6.14).

Figure 6.14 Using the Trapezoid AutoShape to create the boat hull

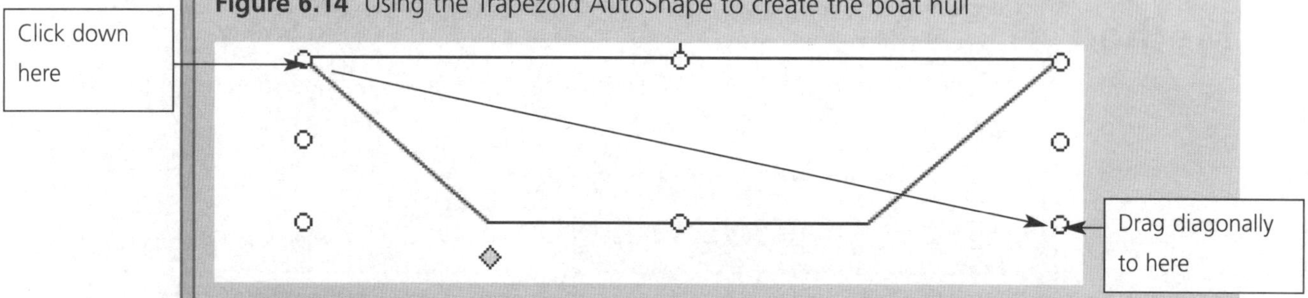

3 For the mast, select the **Line** tool which is located to the right of AutoShapes. Click on a central point along the top of the hull and drag upwards until you get a vertical line that represents a mast.

Handy Hint

Keep referring back to the finished illustration (Figure 6.11 on page 86).

4 For the sails, from the **AutoShapes** drop-down menu, select: **Basic Shapes**, then select the fourth option on the second row: **Right Triangle**. Click near the top of the mast (leave room for a flag) and drag right to form the right-hand sail.

Handy Hint

If you don't like your first effort, it is easier to adjust the shape using the handles than to try again.

5 For the sail on the opposite side, select the same Right Triangle AutoShape. For the left-hand sail, you need to flip it. Draw the triangle first, then from the **Draw** drop-down menu, select: **Rotate or Flip**: **Flip Horizontal**.

Figure 6.15 To flip the sail, from the Draw drop-down menu, select: Rotate or Flip: Flip Horizontal

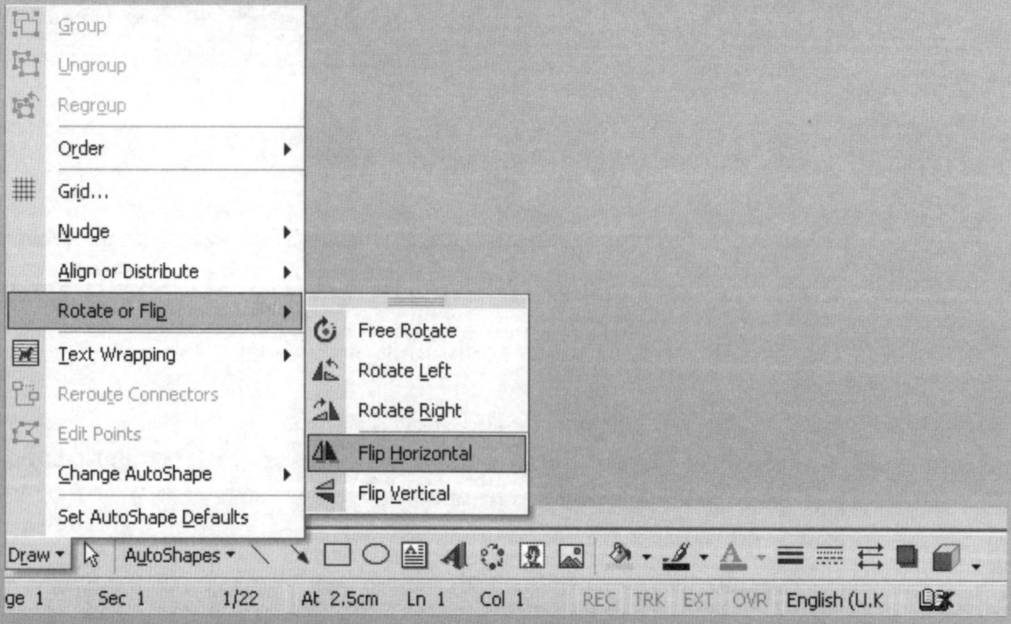

6 For the flag at the top of the mast, from the **AutoShapes** drop-down menu, select: **Stars and Banners**, then select the third option on the last row: **Wave**.

Figure 6.16 To create the flag, from the AutoShapes drop-down menu, select: Stars and Banners: Wave

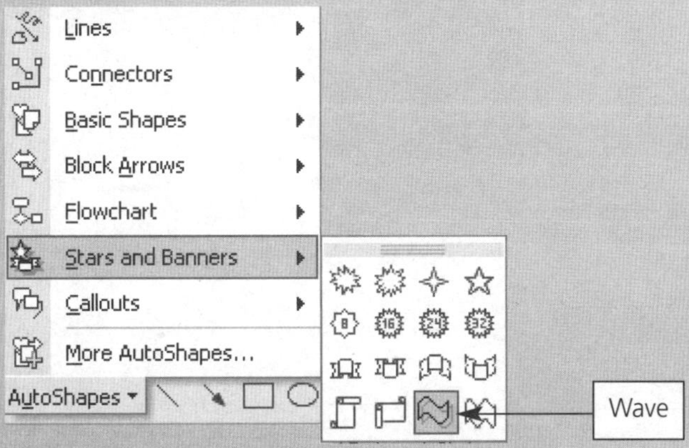

7 At the top of the mast click and drag right.

You should now have a simple line drawing of a sailing boat that looks approximately like Figure 6.17.

Figure 6.17 The sailing boat shape should look like this

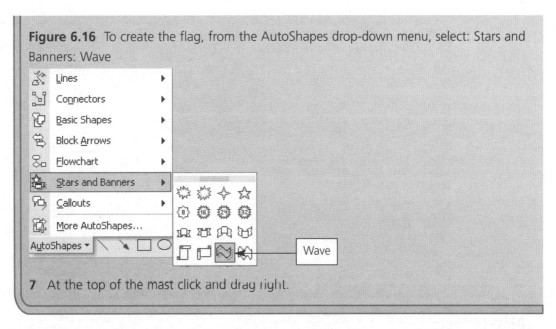

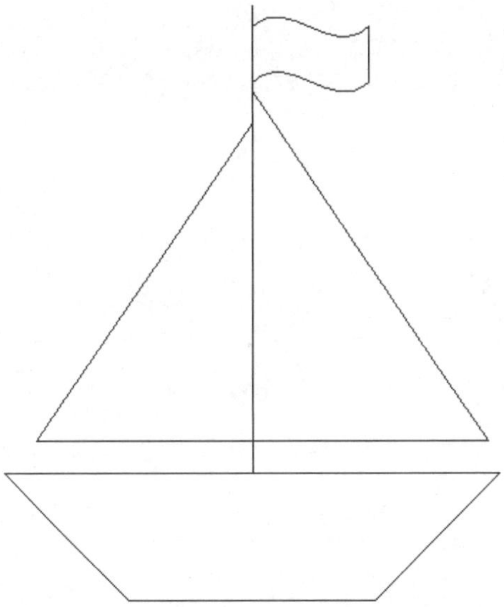

If the size and/or shapes are not quite right and you want to adjust them, click on the shape you want to adjust and resize by dragging the handles.

Group the elements of a drawing

To keep all the elements of the boat together, you can group them.

Method

1 On the Drawing Toolbar, click on: **Select Objects** (the white pointer tool), then draw a large box around all the parts of the boat.

Handy Hint

You are really drawing a box around the handles, not the shapes that you can see on-screen, so make sure that your box is big enough.

Figure 6.18 Group the elements of the drawing using Select Objects

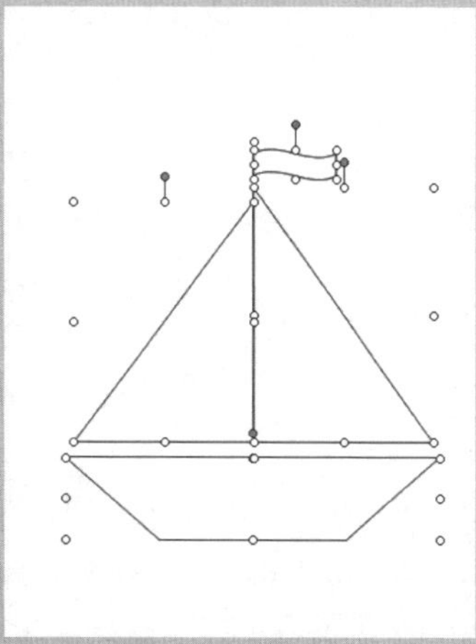

Handy Hint

This method is faster than holding down the Shift key and selecting each AutoShape individually.

You should now have all the AutoShapes selected. If not, try again but draw a larger box to make sure that you pick up all the handles.

2 Click on: **Draw**, then select: **Group**. One box and one set of handles will appear around the boat.

If you click anywhere in the boat and drag the drawing, the whole boat should move.

To include the sea in the picture:

Method

1 From the **AutoShapes** drop-down menu, select: **Stars and Banners**, then select the last option on the last row: **Double Wave**.

2 Click at the point where you want the waterline to be and drag from the left-hand side of the page to the bottom right-hand corner.

Figure 6.19 To create the sea, select: AutoShapes: Stars and Banners: Wave

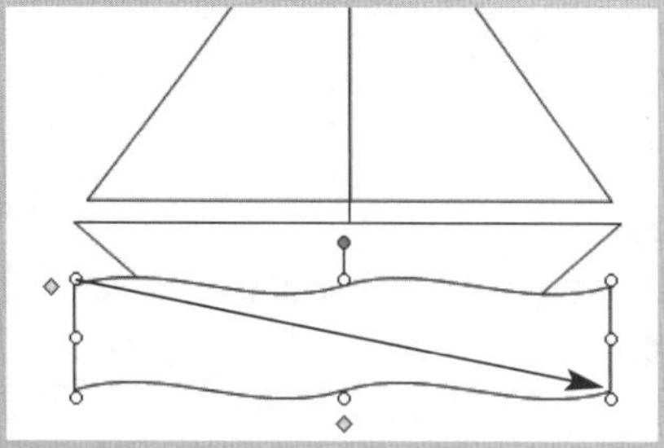

To put the wavy text inside the 'sea':

Method

1 Click on the **Insert WordArt** icon .

2 Select the blue wave text from the fourth row.

3 Click on: **OK**.

4 Key in: **Poetry for Children**.

Figure 6.20 In WordArt, key in: Poetry for Children

5 Click on: **OK**.

The text will appear on the screen. Right-click on the WordArt and select: **Format WordArt**. Select the Layout tab. Select: **Square**. Click on **OK**. Click and drag the WordArt into position in the sea. Drag out the corner handles to resize.

Handy Hint

Dragging with the corner handles maintains the original proportion of the WordArt.

To create the sun:

Method

From the AutoShapes drop-down menu, select: **Basic Shapes**: **Sun**.

Handy Hint

To keep the image circular, hold down the Shift key when you drag out the drawing.

Add colour to a drawing

You can now add colour to your picture. You are going to use the **Fill Color** icon, the **Line Color** icon and the **Font Color** icon from the Drawing Toolbar. Run the I-beam cursor over these icons at the bottom of your screen, to see the icon labels.

Method

Click on the document in the **Sun AutoShape**. From the **Fill Color** pop-up menu, select: **Yellow**. (To access the pop-up menu, you will need to click on the down arrow next to the icon.)

Before you can repeat this process for the rest of the picture, you will need to ungroup the boat AutoShapes.

Method

Right-click on the drawing to access the pop-up menu, then select: **Grouping**: **Ungroup**.

Don't forget to use more Fill Colors and Fill Effects. For the sea:

Method

1 Select: **Fill Color**: **Dark Blue**, then select: **Fill Effects**.

2 In the Fill Effects dialogue box, select the **Gradient** tab, then select: **Horizontal**.

3 Using the **Dark to Light** scroll bar, change the density of the colour.

Figure 6.21 In Fill Effects, change the destiny of colour using the Dark to Light scrollbar

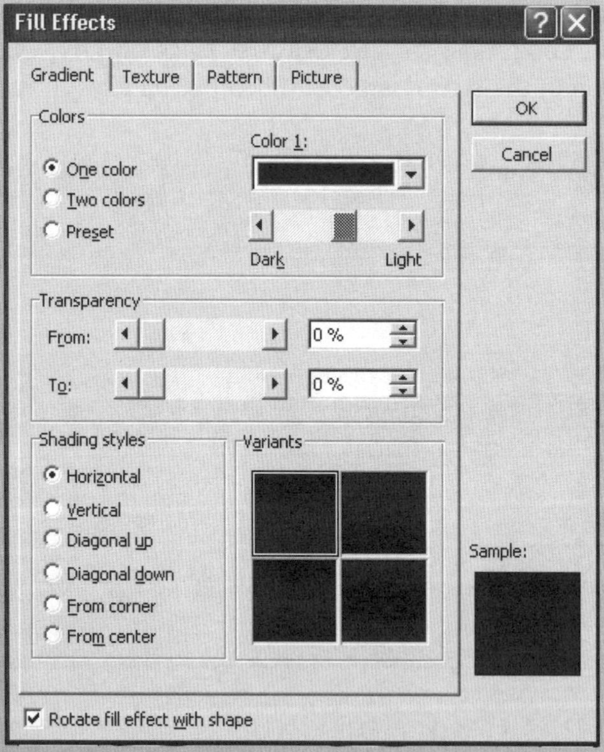

4 Once you are happy with the boat, **Group** the whole page.

5 Save your work.

Add 3-D effects to a drawing

To add 3-D effects to the drawing:

Method

1 Click on the drawing.

2 From the Drawing Toolbar, select the **3-D Style** icon .

3 Experiment by clicking on the different effects. If you don't like your choices, click on the **Undo** button to go back. You can get even more effects from the **3D-Settings** menu.

Figure 6.22 The 3-D Settings menu

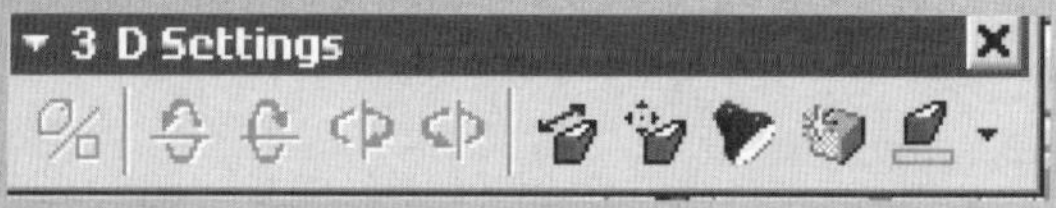

When you have made your final selection(s), save your work as **Task 6**. Click on the **Print Preview** icon then select: **Multiple Pages** to view your work. You will see that you have completed a substantial piece of work of approximately 23 pages.

Practice Task

Task 6

These exercises are included to help the candidate in his or her training for the Advanced ECDL program. The exercises included in this material are not Advanced ECDL certification tests and should not be construed in any way as Advanced ECDL certification tests. For information about Authorised ECDL Test Centres in different National Territories, please refer to the ECDL Foundation website at **www.ecdl.com**.

Method

You are going to set up a document that contains a selection of Aesop's fables. The document will have a front cover and a table of contents at the end. The main body text of the fables is to be input by an operator at a later date.

1 From the Task Files folder, open the file: **Aesops Fables**.

> The bat and the weasels
>
> A bat who fell upon the ground and was caught by a weasel pleaded to be spared his life. The weasel refused, saying …
>
> The ass and the grasshopper
>
> An ass having heard some grasshoppers chirping, was highly enchanted; and, desiring to possess them …
>
> The lion and the mouse
>
> A lion was awakened from sleep by a mouse running over his face. Rising up angrily, he caught him and was about to kill him, when …
>
> The boy hunting locusts

A boy was hunting for locusts. He had caught a goodly number, when he saw a scorpion, and mistaking him for a locust, reached out …

The mole and his mother

A mole, a creature blind from birth, once said to his mother: 'I am sure that I can see, mother!' In the desire to prove to him his mistake, his …

The traveller and his dog

A traveller about to set out on a journey saw his dog stand at the door stretching himself. He asked him sharply: 'Why do you stand …

Hercules and the wagoner

A carter was driving a wagon along a country lane, when the wheels sank down deep into a rut. The rustic driver, stupefied and aghast …

The bear and the fox

A bear boasted very much of his philanthropy, saying that of all animals he was the most tender in his regard for man, for he had such …

The dog in the manger

A dog lay in a manger, and by his growling and snapping prevented the oxen from eating the hay which had been placed …

2 Save your work as: **Task 6 Answer**.

3 Apply a password to the document to:

- Protect your work (use your first name)
- Modify your work (use your surname). This password will allow the operator access to your work.

4 Create a style for the subheadings:

- Choose any font or colour.
- Choose a 16–20 font size.
- Ensure that you give your style a name that is easily identifiable in the Style drop-down menu.

(The suggested answer has been created in Papyrus 18 pt font.)

5 Create a style for the body text of the fables. Choose a font smaller than the subheadings.

(The suggested answer has been created in Lucida Bright, 12 pt font.)

6 Format Paragraph to 1.5 line spacing with a first line indent.

7 Apply the new styles to the text by selecting them from the Style drop-down menu.

8 Create a blank page 1.

Handy Hint

Insert a page break at the top of the first page.

9 Insert page numbers at the top of the page. Apply lower case Roman numerals and centre. Do not show page numbers on the first page.

10 Create a table of contents to start on a new page after the last fable. Apply a classic or distinctive format, with page numbers and dotted tab leaders.

The fables will appear on page 2 or 3 until the remainder of the fables are keyed in and the table of contents has been updated.

11 Key in the following fable at the top of page 2.

> The Stag, The Wolf, And The Sheep
>
> A STAG asked a sheep to lend him a measure of wheat, and said that the wolf would be his surety. The sheep, fearing some fraud …

12 Update the table of contents.

To create the front page you are going to use the drawing tools.

13 Create an abstract picture using AutoShapes. (See a finished example in the answers section.)

14 Use WordArt to insert the title: Aesop's Fables.

15 Apply Fill, Order and Rotate to the AutoShapes.

16 Group the AutoShapes wherever possible.

17 Print 4 pages per sheet.

18 Save your work.

Task 7 Letters to speakers

In this task, you will cover the following skills:

- Create a new template based on an existing document or template.
- Change basic formatting and layout options in a template.
  - o Insert a date field.
  - o Save a new template.
- Edit a mail merge data source or data file.
  - o Amend a data file.
  - o Produce a form letter.
  - o Using merge fields.
- Apply automatic text formatting options.
  - o Amend AutoText options.
  - o Apply letter case options in AutoCorrect.
- Merge a document with a data source or data file using given merge criteria.
  - o Access a data file using Mail Merge.
  - o Make selections from a data file.
- Sort data source or data file records.
- Record a simple macro.
  - o Assign a keyboard shortcut to a macro.
  - o Recording the macro.
  - o Assigning a toolbar shortcut to a macro.
- Run a macro.
  - o Run a macro using a keyboard shortcut.
  - o Run a macro assigned to a toolbar.
- Assigning a macro to a custom button on a toolbar.
  - o Add a macro button to an existing toolbar.
  - o Create a macro toolbar.
- Copy a macro.
- Edit or update a field code entry.
  - o Remove Form Field options.
  - o Update date and time manually.
- Use automatic text entry options.
- Use available form field options: check box.
- Delete items in a form.

Scenario

The Literary Discussion Group would like to send out letters to their regular speakers, to invite them to put forward topics for the next round of meetings. They have provided a file with the names of the speakers, their addresses and their favourite venues. They would like a system setting up so that they can use their file to pick out the most appropriate people for the venue. This will involve producing a merged document (the finished letters) using the data from the supplied file and a form letter (a standard letter).

7.1 Create a new template

A letter heading for the Literary Discussion Group has not been provided. This means that you will need to create a template that can be used each time the Literary Discussion Group wants to send out letters.

Microsoft Office has a selection of templates for users to amend according to their own available specifications. You access these from the **File** menu on the main menu toolbar.

Method

1 Click on: **File**: **New**. The New Document task pane appears.

2 Select: **General Templates** from **New form Template** (Click once on the icon).

3 Select the **Letters & Faxes** tab, then select: **Contemporary Letter**.

4 In the **Create New** box, click on the **Template** radio button.

Figure 7.1 Creating a new template in File: New

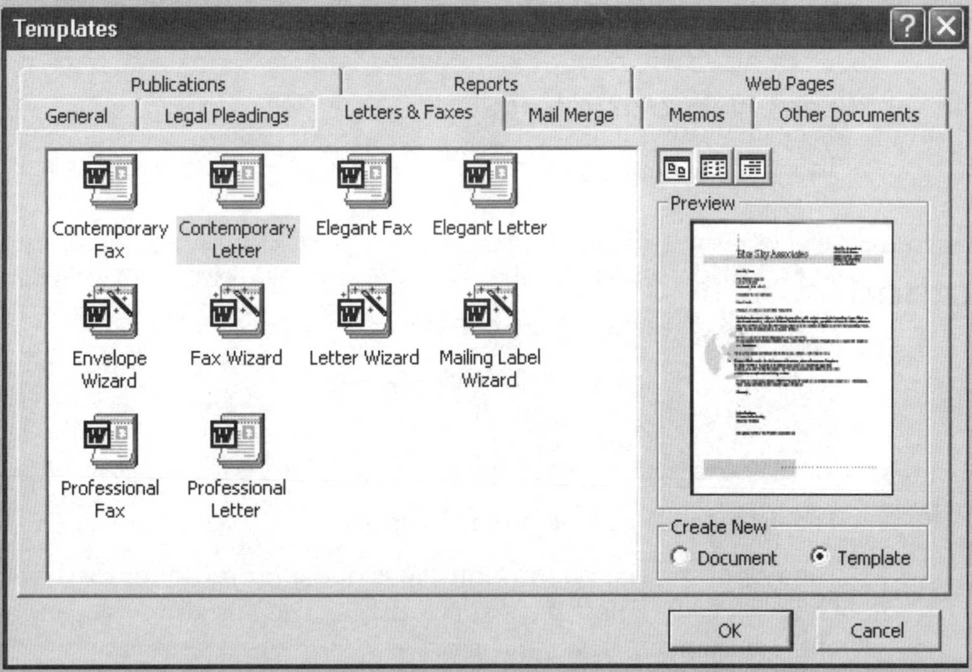

5 Click on: **OK**. The template to be amended appears on screen.

6 Click in the top right-hand corner box where the words **Click here and type return address** appear.

7 Key in the address of the Literary Discussion Group (see Figure 7.2). Change the font size to 12 pt.

8 Triple-click on: **Company name here**. Insert: **Literary Discussion Group**.

Figure 7.2 Key in the Literary Discussion Group details on the template

7.2 *Change formatting and layout of a template*

Next, the date needs to go onto the template. The date needs to update each time the template is opened. There is already a date field underneath the shaded bar, but it is not in the format you would like and it needs removing.

Method

To remove the field, highlight with the I-beam cursor to select, then press the **Delete** key.

Insert a date field

To insert the date:

Method

1 Click on: **Insert** from the main menu bar, then select: **Date and Time**.

2 Select the option: **XX month XXXX**.

3 Select the **Update Automatically** box.

4 Click on: **OK**.

The date should now be on the template.

The rest of the text on the template is not appropriate for the Literary Discussion Group's needs. Select the text and delete. There is also a 'slogan' box at the bottom of the document. Delete this too.

Save a new template

To save your new template:

Method

1 Select: **File**: **Save As**. The Save As dialogue box appears.

Figure 7.3 The Save As dialogue box

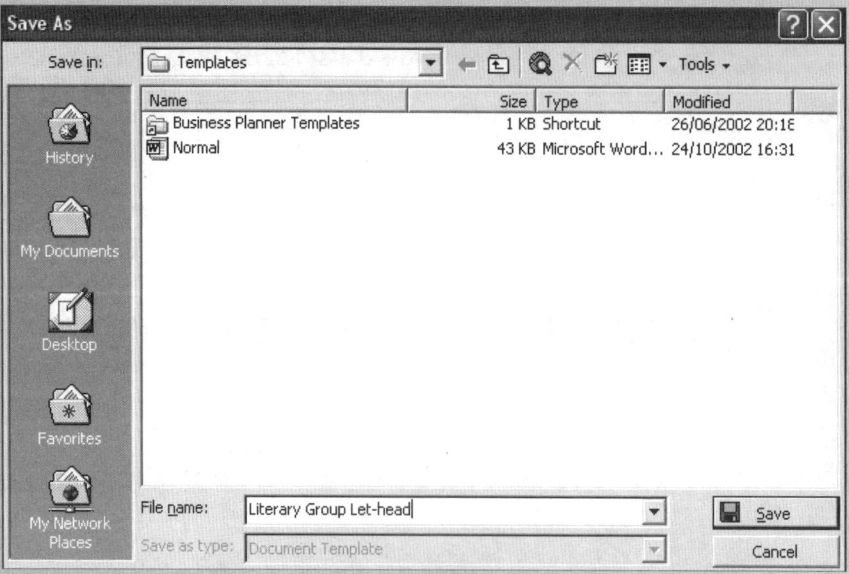

2 Name the file: **Literary Group Let-head**. In the **Save As Type** drop down menu, select **Document Template**.

3 Click on: **Save**.

4 Click on: **File**: **New**. Select: **General Templates** from the task pane. Select the **General** tab in the **Templates** dialogue box. You should see your new template in the list.

The Literary Group Let-head file will open as a document template, but you will be able to save it as a Word document. The original template will remain unchanged.

Figure 7.4 The new template appears in the General tab in the Templates dialogue box

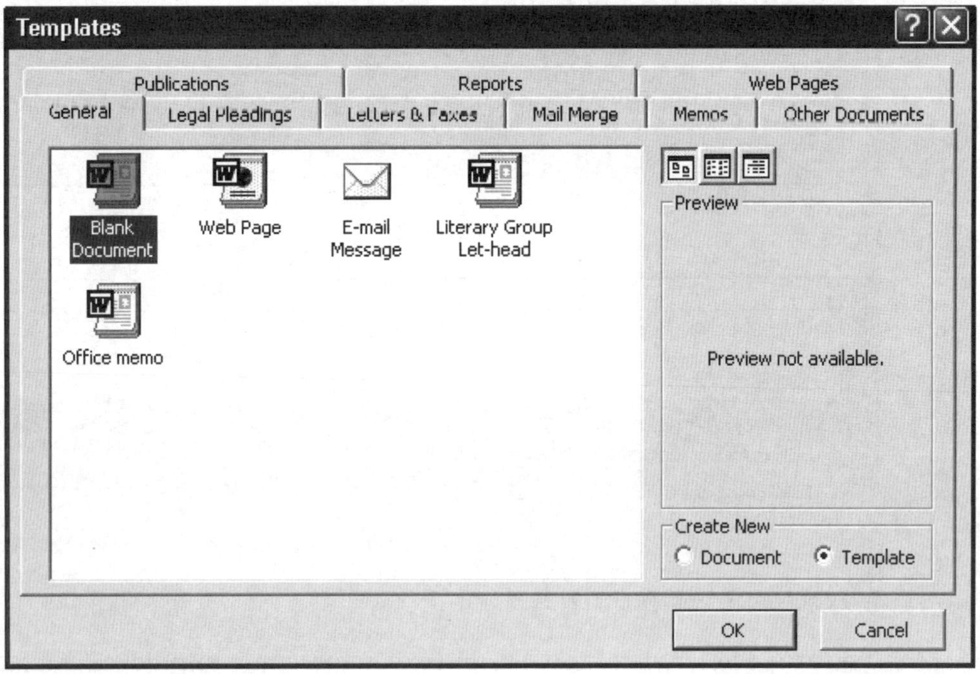

7.3 *Edit a mail merge data source and data file*

Amend a data file

Before you can produce the letters, you need to make some amendments to the data file that you have received from the group.

Method

1 Open the file: **Mail Merge Data** from the Task Files folder.

2 You are to add a new record. Click in the last cell and press the tab key. A new line should appear. Key in the following details:

Mrs Lynn Westerly
98 Wharfe Road
Barnoldswick
Lancs
BB3 2RJ
Kenwood Hall

One of the records needs to be deleted. Julie Platt is entered twice: once as Ms and once as Mrs. Julie would like to be addressed as Mrs. To delete the unwanted record:

Method

1 Click anywhere on the line to be deleted.

2 Select: **Table** from the main menu toolbar, then select: **Delete**: **Rows**. The row will disappear.

Handy Hint

You must use this method: if you simply highlight the text and press the delete key, you will remove the words but not the row, i.e. you will be left with blank cells as shown in Figure 7.5.

Figure 7.5 You will be left with a blank row if you highlight the text and press the delete key

Mrs	Julie	Platt	56 Cross Avenue	Nelson	Lancs	BB9 1DR	Earby Library Room
Mr	Steven	Mossley	89 Booth Avenue	Rastrick	Yorks	YO3 4TB	Earby Library Room

3 Save the file using the same name.

Produce a form letter

Using the Literary Let-head Template, you are going to produce the form letter. This is the document that will combine (merge) with the data file containing the names of the speakers. The reason for using a data file and a form letter is that you can use the two over and over again, making different selections from the data file each time.

Method

1 Open the Literary Let-head Template on-screen. Leave at least one clear line space below the date.

2 Click on: **Tools**: **Letters and Mailings**: **Mail Merge Wizard**. Make sure that the **Letters** radio button is selected in the Mail Merge task pane. Select: **Next – Starting Document**.

3 Select: **Use the Current Document** on the task pane. Select: **Next – Select Recipients**.

4 Select: **Use an Existing List** on the task pane. Click on: **Browse**. Select the Mail Merge Data file from the Taskfiles folder. Click on: **Open**.

5 The Mail Merge Recipients dialogue box will appear. If the data in the dialogue box is the correct file, click on: **OK**. Click on: **Next – Write Your Letter**.

6 You can at this point select Address Block and you will be offered several default formats for the address. You are going to add the fields individually. Click in the document under the date where the first line of the recipient's address is to go.

Figure 7.6 Selecting the fields

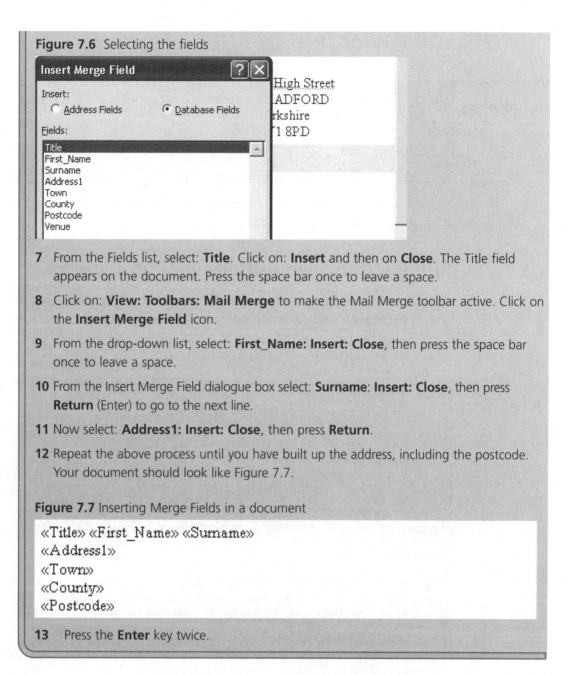

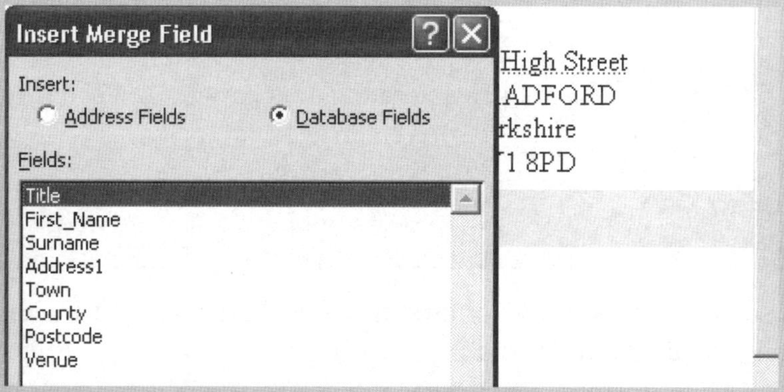

7 From the Fields list, select: **Title**. Click on: **Insert** and then on **Close**. The Title field appears on the document. Press the space bar once to leave a space.

8 Click on: **View: Toolbars: Mail Merge** to make the Mail Merge toolbar active. Click on the **Insert Merge Field** icon.

9 From the drop-down list, select: **First_Name: Insert: Close**, then press the space bar once to leave a space.

10 From the Insert Merge Field dialogue box select: **Surname**: **Insert: Close**, then press **Return** (Enter) to go to the next line.

11 Now select: **Address1: Insert: Close**, then press **Return**.

12 Repeat the above process until you have built up the address, including the postcode. Your document should look like Figure 7.7.

Figure 7.7 Inserting Merge Fields in a document

«Title» «First_Name» «Surname»
«Address1»
«Town»
«County»
«Postcode»

13 Press the **Enter** key twice.

7.4 *Apply automatic text formatting*

Amend AutoText options

Before you start to enter the text for the letter, this would be an appropriate time to look at the settings that you can apply so that Word automatically formats your text.

Method

1 Click on: **Format**, then select: **AutoFormat**. The AutoFormat dialogue box appears.

2 Click on: **Options**. An AutoCorrect dialogue box appears.

3 Click on the **AutoText** tab to see the default list of AutoText entries. You may have seen these in action: when you type 'Yours' at the end of a letter, you are offered the word 'truly' as the next word.

4 Scroll down the list and you will find 'Yours truly' is the last entry. To remove this, select: **Yours truly** from the list and click on: **Delete**.

Similarly, you can add your own AutoText:

Method

1 In the **Enter AutoText entries here** box, add the AutoText entry: **Yours sincerely**.

2 Click on: **Add**.

3 Click on: **OK**.

You will see that you are now offered this AutoText option at the end of the letter when you type the word 'Yours'.

Apply letter case options in AutoCorrect

If you produce documents that contain listed items on separate lines, you may wish to stop Word automatically inserting a capital letter at the start of each listed item. Apply this setting to your machine.

Method

1 In the AutoCorrect dialogue box, click on the **AutoCorrect** tab.

2 Click to deselect: **Capitalize first letter of sentences**.

3 Click on: **OK** twice to exit the dialogue boxes and to apply the AutoText and AutoCorrect settings.

4 Now key in the following letter (Figure 7.8), inserting the Merge Fields as you go along.

Figure 7.8 Insert Merge Fields while entering text into a Form Template

Dear «First_Name»

The next round of meetings is now being planned for «County». As you very kindly volunteered to give a talk on a topic of your own choice I would be grateful if you would forward your ideas to me so that I can check that you are not going to clash with another speaker.

We omitted to make this check last year and it proved very embarrassing for everyone concerned. Once again let me thank you for your very kind offer and I look forward to meeting you again on the evening.

Yours sincerely

Peter Smithson
Secretary

5 Now save this file as a document. Save as: **Form Letter**.

(Note: you may need to change the folder from Templates.)

7.5 Merge a document with a data source or data file using certain criteria

Access a data file using Mail Merge

You are about to bring together the information you want from the data file, i.e. all the speakers for Yorkshire, and sort the letters into order of surname.

Method

Click on: **Next: Preview your Letters**. All the recipients will be merged with the letter. You can view the letters by clicking on the arrows at either side of Recipient in the task pane.

To filter out all the speakers from Yorkshire and to sort into alphabetical order of surname.

1 Click on: **Edit recipient list** on the task pane. The Mail Merge Recipients dialogue box appears (Figure 7.9).

2 Click on the drop-down menu next to the field **County**. Select: **Yorks**. All the addresses in Yorkshire will be listed. You can see that the data is filtered by the blue arrow on the drop-down menu.

3 To sort the surnames simply click on the **Surname** field. Click on **OK** to close the dialogue box.

When you preview your letters this time you should only have addresses in Yorkshire.

Figure 7.9 Selecting the Yorks field

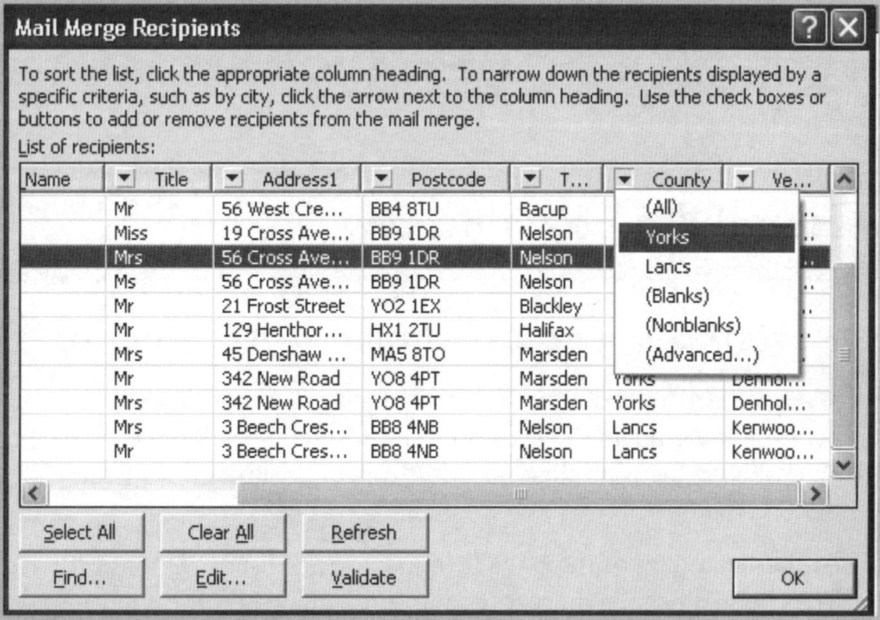

Now select the speakers from Lancashire.

Method

With the letters to Yorkshire addresses on screen:

1 Click on: **Edit recipient list**.

2 Click on the **County** field. Select: **All** from the drop-down box.

3 Click on the County field again and select: **Lancs**.

You will have a new set of letters addressed to speakers in Lancashire. You now have two sets of letters: one for speakers in Lancashire; one for speakers in Yorkshire.

To select, for example, all the addresses in Nelson and Marsden:

1 Click on the **Edit recipient list**.

2 Click on: **County**, then select: **All** to clear the previous filter.

3 Click on the **Town** field. Select: **Advanced**.

4 In the Query Options box (Figure 7.10), select: **Town Equal to Nelson** or **Town Equal to Marsden**.

5 Click on: **OK** to remove the dialogue boxes.

Figure 7.10 Selecting all the addresses in Nelson and Marsden

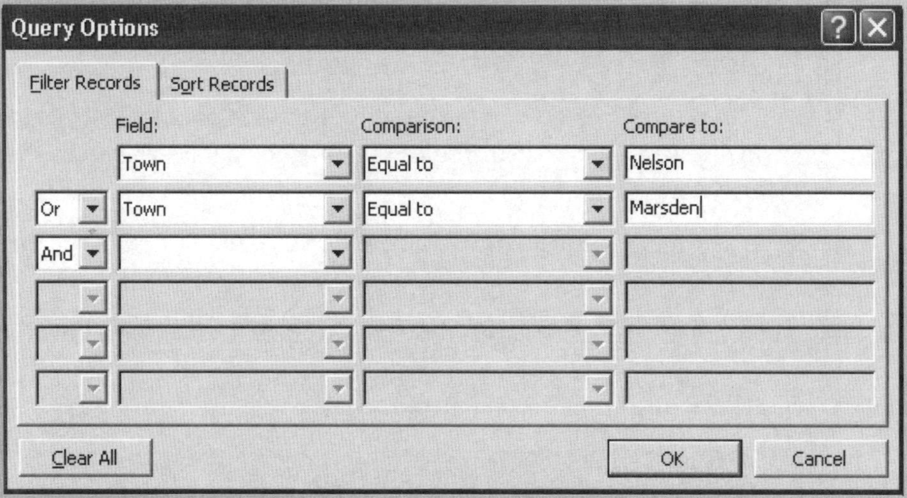

7.6 *Record a basic macro*

Assign a keyboard shortcut to a macro

A macro is a function for saving (recording) a set of several formats that can be used over and over again. It saves time because you don't have to go through the separate (micro) changes each time you start a new document. You can also apply macros to existing documents.

At the beginning of the book, you performed many different formatting functions. These could have been recorded in a macro, ready for you to apply (run).

Method

1 From your folder **Task Files**, open the original file: **Text for Task 1**.

2 Select all the text (**Ctrl + A**).

3 Click on: **Tools**: **Macro**: **Record New Macro**.

Figure 7.11 Click on: Tools: Macro: Record New Macro

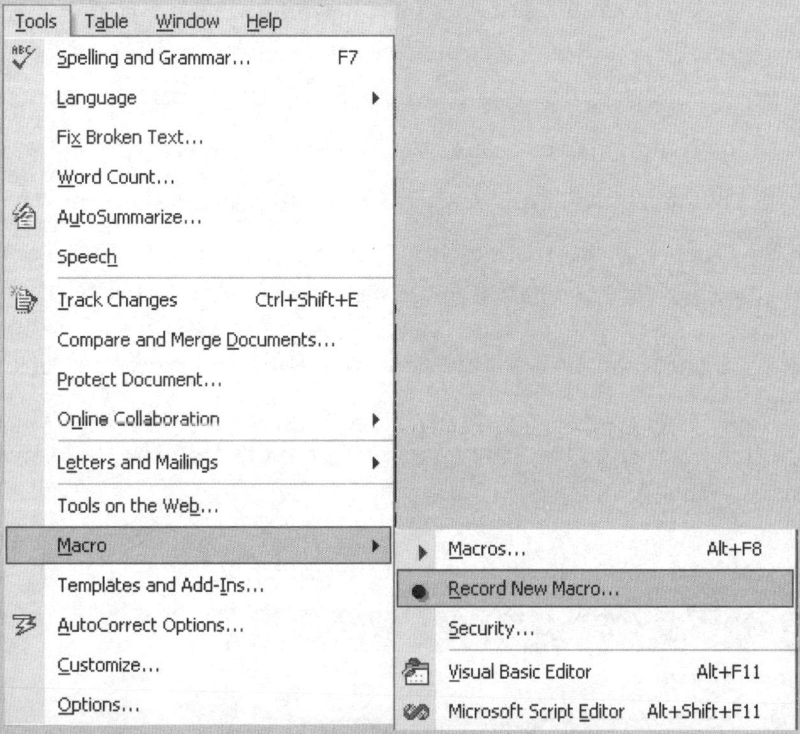

4 A Record Macro dialogue box appears. In the **Macro name** box key in: **LDG_BODY_TEXT**.

Handy Hint

If you want spaces between your words, you need to key in an underscore rather than using the spacebar.

5 In the **Store macro in** box, you will see that Word automatically defaults to saving as: **All Documents (Normal.dot)**.

Figure 7.12 Using the Record Macro dialogue box

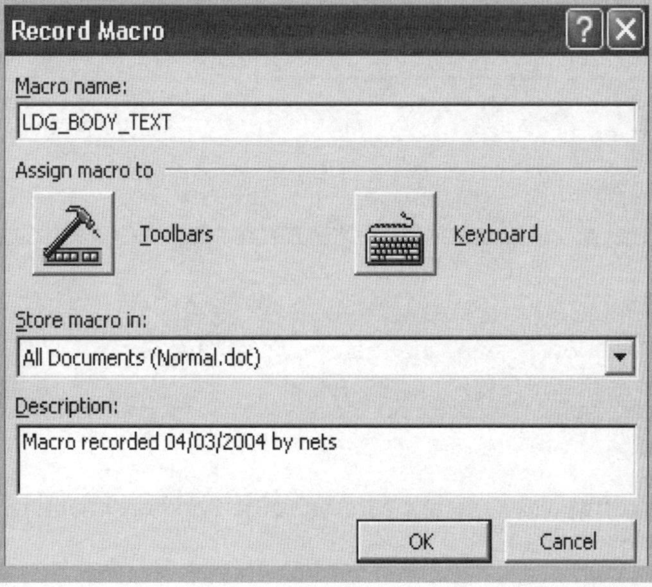

Handy Hint

If you wanted to save the macro in this document only: click on the Store macro in drop-down menu and select the name of the file, i.e. Text for Task 1 (document). The macro will then be unavailable for other documents.

6 In the **Assign macro to** box, click to select: **Keyboard**.

7 A **Customize Keyboard** dialogue box now appears (see Figure 7.13).

In the **Press new shortcut key** box, you have to assign a key. Most of the keys are already assigned: if you use a shortcut that is already assigned it will appear underneath the box. You can use an assigned shortcut if you wish, but it will override the original. Be careful that you don't override a shortcut that you use to format text, e.g. **Ctrl + B** for bold.

Ctrl + . (full-stop key) is not usually assigned, so for this exercise use **Ctrl + .** as the shortcut. Hold down the **Ctrl** key and press the **full-stop** key. Word automatically inserts the + symbol.

Figure 7.13 Creating a shortcut in Customize Keyboard

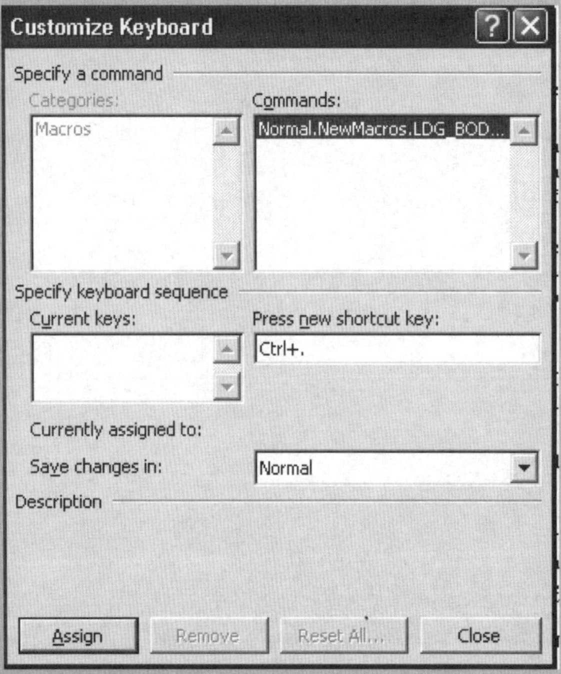

8 Click on: **Assign**.

9 Click on: **Close**.

Handy Hint

If you do not click on Assign, the macro will not work.

The **Stop Recording** box now appears on-screen and an image of a cassette is attached to the pointer tool.

Figure 7.14 The Stop box

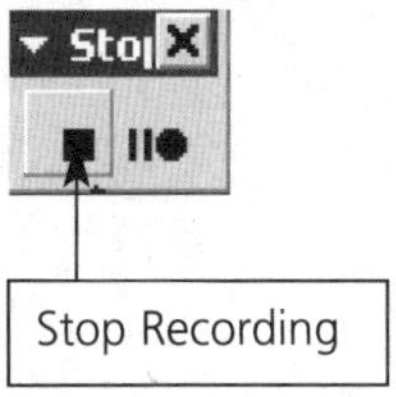

Recording the macro

Don't panic at this stage: the process is not time-bound, i.e. you don't have to rush. You can only work on one section of selected text at a time, then you have to press stop and repeat the process for further sections of the text. For this example, you are going to record two macros.

If you make a mistake just press the stop button and start again. You will be asked if you want to replace the existing macro; click on: **Yes**.

Method

1 Click on: **Format**: **Columns**.

2 In the **Columns** dialogue box, make the following selections:

- Number of columns: **2**
- Click to select: **Line between**
- Width: **7 cm**
- Spacing: **4 cm** (you may need to deselect the Equal column width box).

3 Click on: **OK**.

4 Click on: **Format**: **Borders and Shading**.

5 In the Borders and Shading dialogue box, select the **Page Border** tab.

6 Make the following selections:

- Setting: **Box**
- Color: **Green**

7 Click on: **OK**.

8 On the Formatting Toolbar, click on the **Justify** icon.

9 Click on the **Stop recording** button.

The macro is now recorded and stored for further use.

Assigning a toolbar shortcut to a macro

To set up the next macro:

Method

1 Triple-click to select Paragraph 1.

2 From **Tools** on the main menu toolbar, select: **Macro**: **Record New Macro**.

3 In the **Record Macro** dialogue box, in the **Macro name** box key in: LDG_FIRST_PARA.

This time we are going to use the toolbar rather than a keyboard shortcut.

4 In the **Assign macro to** box, click to select: **Toolbars**.

5 The Customize dialogue box appears. You last used the Customize dialogue box at the start of the book to set the toolbars on a separate row using the Options tab. Now you will use the **Commands** tab.

Figure 7.15 The Customize dialogue box

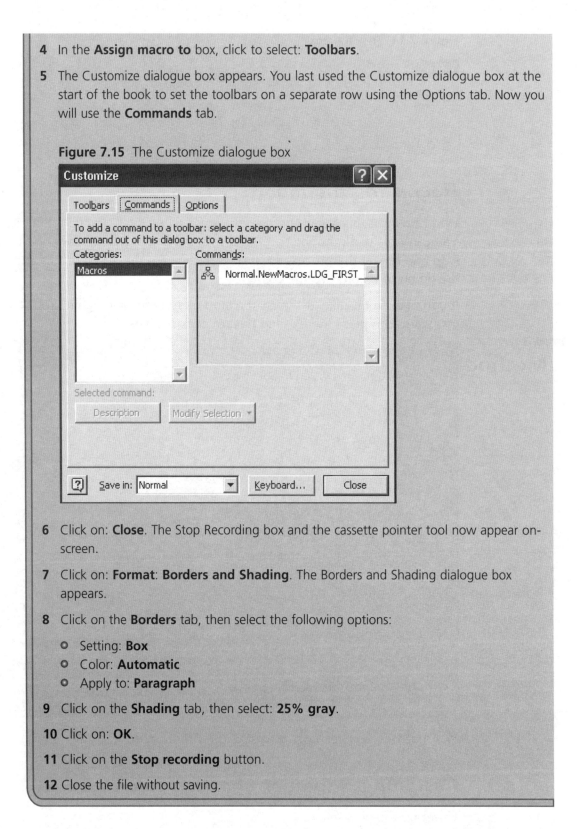

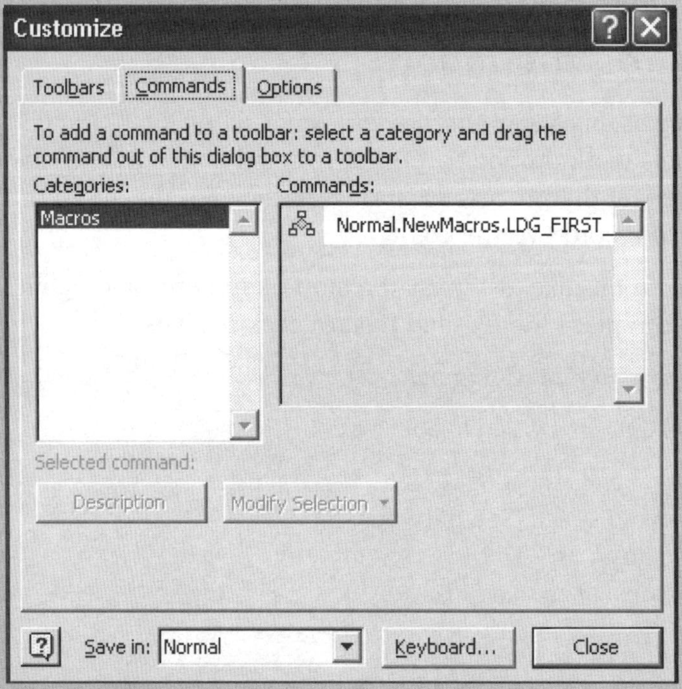

6 Click on: **Close**. The Stop Recording box and the cassette pointer tool now appear on-screen.

7 Click on: **Format**: **Borders and Shading**. The Borders and Shading dialogue box appears.

8 Click on the **Borders** tab, then select the following options:

- Setting: **Box**
- Color: **Automatic**
- Apply to: **Paragraph**

9 Click on the **Shading** tab, then select: **25% gray**.

10 Click on: **OK**.

11 Click on the **Stop recording** button.

12 Close the file without saving.

You have now set up two macros. Close the file without saving. You will not lose the macros as they are saved to Normal.doc and are available to use on any document.

7.7 *Run a macro*

From your **Task Files** folder, open the **Text for Task 1** file. You are now going to run the macros you have recorded.

Run a macro using a keyboard shortcut

You are going to run the macro that was set up with the keyboard shortcut Ctrl + . (full-stop).

Method

Click in the text. Hold down the **Ctrl** key, then press the **full-stop** key.

Handy Hint

If your macro didn't work, you may have assigned it to Text for Task 1 instead of normal.doc.

Run a macro assigned to a toolbar

You will now run the macro that was assigned to a toolbar. One method for doing this is:

Method

1. Click inside the first paragraph.
2. Select **Tools** from the main menu bar, then select: **Macro**: **Macros**. A Macros dialogue box appears, with a list of the macros you have recorded. You can delete any unwanted macros at this point.
3. Select the macro: **LDG_FIRST_PARA**.
4. Click on: **Run**. The formatting should be applied to the text.

One of the most common uses of macros is to record Page Setup details, particularly if the company you work for has a different layout for standard documents than the Word defaults, e.g. wide left-hand margins for hole punching, etc.

7.8 Assign a macro button to a toolbar or create a macro toolbar

You can also assign the macro to a button on the toolbar. You can assign a macro to any toolbar, but where you put it, to remember easily the formatting toolbar is possibly the best option.

Add a macro button to an existing toolbar

Method

1. Right-click on the Formatting Toolbar, select: **Customize**. The Customize dialogue box appears.
2. Click on the **Commands** tab.
3. In **Categories**, select: **Macros**.
4. In the **Commands** box, select the body text macro you want on the toolbar: **LDG_FIRST_PARA**.

Figure 7.16 Using the Customize dialogue box to assign a macro button to a toolbar

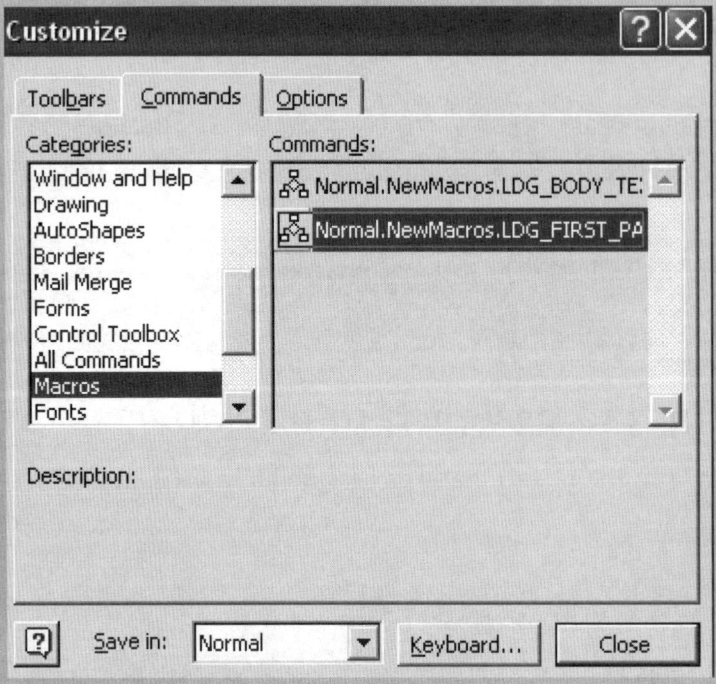

5 Click and drag the selection to the Formatting Toolbar, then release the mouse button. As you move along, the I-beam cursor will show you where the button will end up. The new macro custom button should appear on the toolbar.

6 To exit the Customize dialogue box, click on: **Close**.

7 To test whether the macro button works, from your Task Files folder open the file: **Text for Task 1**. Click on the new macro button.

Be careful not to accidentally click on the macro button when you have a document on-screen that you don't want formatting. Undo does not work with one click! If you have no use for the macro button, it is safer to remove it from the Formatting Toolbar. Click on the drop-down arrow at the end of the toolbar to add or remove buttons. If the macro is not available to remove, click on: **Reset Toolbar**.

Handy Hint

Always save your work just before you run a macro – you may not like the effect! If this is the case, you can revert to the saved version.

Create a macro toolbar

If you would rather have a macro toolbar than assign the macro to an existing toolbar, you can set one up.

Method

1 Right-click on a toolbar to access the pop-up menu, then select: **Customize**.

2 In the **Customize** dialogue box, click on the **Toolbars** tab.

3 Click on: **New**. A **New Toolbar** dialogue box appears.

4 In the Toolbar Name box, type: **Macros**.

Figure 7.17 Create a new toolbar in the New Toolbar dialogue box

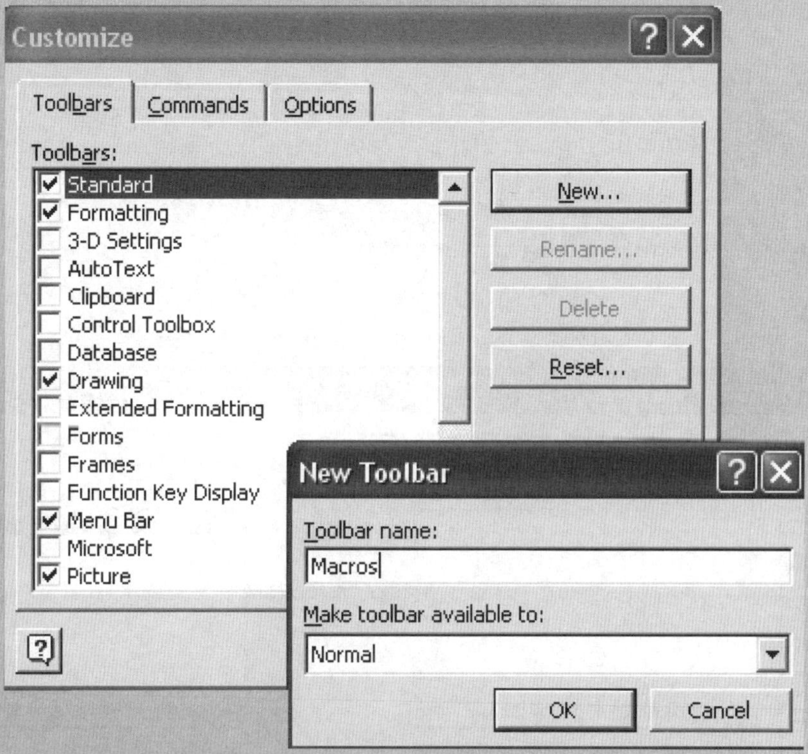

5 Click on: **OK**.

6 Click on: **Close**.

You should now have a small toolbar on your screen that you can assign buttons to as you did when you assigned the macro button to the Formatting Toolbar. If you click on: **View**: **Toolbars**, you will see listed the Macros Toolbar that you have just created.

7 Assign the two macros you have created to your new Macro Toolbar. Use the same method as above, but this time right-click on the Macro Toolbar. As before, click and drag the two macros (the two actions) to the Macro Toolbar.

8 Close the new toolbar by clicking on: **X**.

7.9 *Copy a macro*

There are occasions when you might want to copy a macro from one document to another without it being accessible through the toolbar or keyboard shortcut. To keep the macro within a document, you need to specify where the macro is to be stored when you are setting it up. In other words, you change the saving default from Normal.dot to the name of the document in which the macro is to be stored.

You are going to copy a macro named 'Header' which is stored in the file 'Macro Document' to the file 'Text for Task 1'. This macro is a line of text in a header 'Produced for the Literary Discussion Group'. However, the macro could easily be a standard paragraph, a disclaimer, or other sensitive text that you don't want to have instant access to for all documents.

Method

1 From the Task Files folder, open the file: **Text for Task 1**.

2 Select **Tools** from the main menu bar, then select: **Macro**: **Macros**.

3 In the **Macros** dialogue box, click on the **Organizer** button.

4 Select the **Macro Project Items** tab.

Figure 7.18 The Macro Project Items tab in Organizer

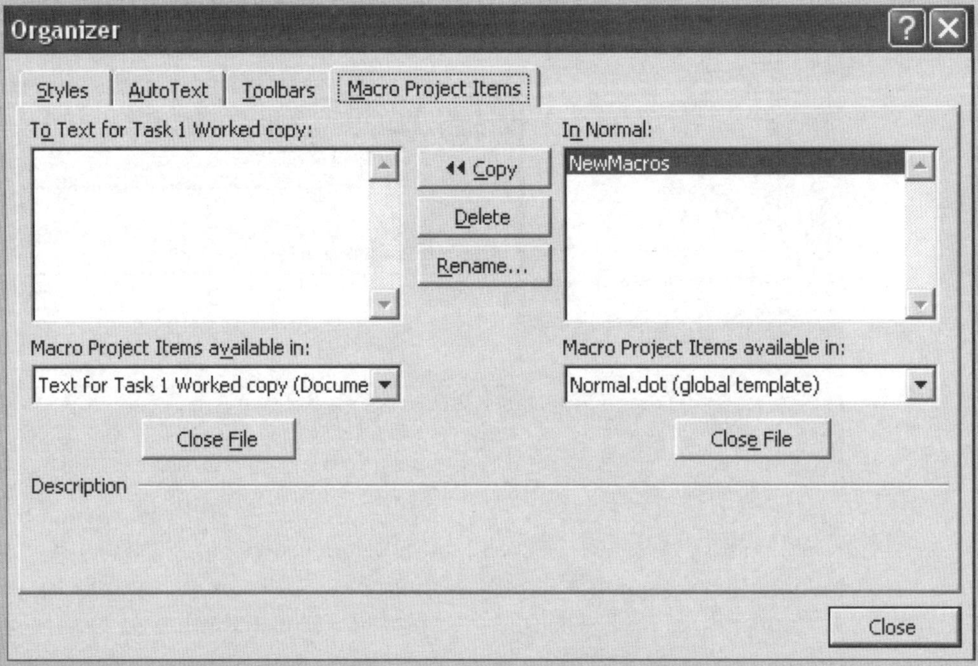

5 Click on both the **Close File** buttons so that you can make your own selections. The buttons change to **Open File**.

6 Click on the right-hand **Open File** button. This is the file that you are going to copy the macro from.

7 From the Task Files folder, select the file: **Macro Document**. To do this you may have to use the **Files of type** drop-down menu to change the selection to: **All Files**.

8 Click on the left-hand **Open File** button, then select the document: **Text for Task 1**.

9 On the **Copy** button, there should be two arrows pointing left. Click on this button and **NewMacros** is copied across to the other document.

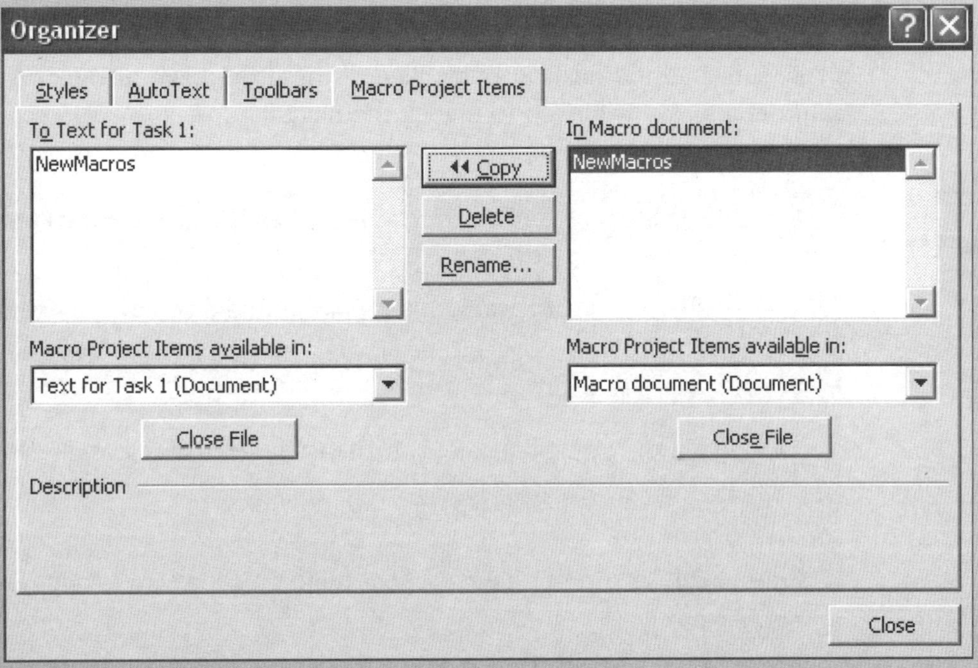

Figure 7.19 Copying a macro from one document to a second document

Note: the macro will not copy if the text 'NewMacros' already appears in the left-hand box. If it does, select the text and then click on the **Delete** button to remove the text. Next, click on the right-hand 'NewMacros' to make it active for copying to the other document. When prompted to delete, click on: **Yes**.

10 Click on: **Close**.

The macro is now within both documents but is not accessible for any other documents, for example, through Tools or Macro, etc.

You still need to go through the procedure of running the macro from the document Text for Task 1.

Method

1. Open the document: **Text for Task 1**, if not already open.
2. Select **Tools** from the main menu bar, then select: **Macro**: **Macros**.
3. In the Macros dialogue box, click to select the macro named 'Header', then click on: **Run**. The Header should appear on-screen.
4. Save your work as: **Text for Task 1**.

Note: if you found that you could not run the macro due to the macros being disabled you will need to change the security setting. To do this click on: **Tools**: **Macro**: **Security** and change the level to medium. It is unlikely that you will be able to change security settings if you are working on a networked PC.

7.10 *Amend or update field code entries*

Some changes need to be made to the staff rota.

Remove Form Field options

Open the file: **Staff Rota**. Before you can make any changes, you will need to make sure that the fields are unlocked. If the drop-down arrow appears next to the staff names, you will need to unlock the fields.

Method

1 On the main menu toolbar, select: **View**, then select: **Toolbars**: **Forms**. The Form Toolbar appears on-screen.

2 Click on the **Protect Form** icon (i.e. unlock). The drop-down boxes disappear.

3 Double-click in the first shaded box: **Week 1, Monday**. The Drop-Down Form Field Options dialogue box appears.

P Wong is not available in Week 1: the name needs deleting.

4 Click on the name: **P Wong**, then click on: **Remove**.

Figure 7.20 Remove Form Field options using the Drop-Down Form Field Options dialogue box

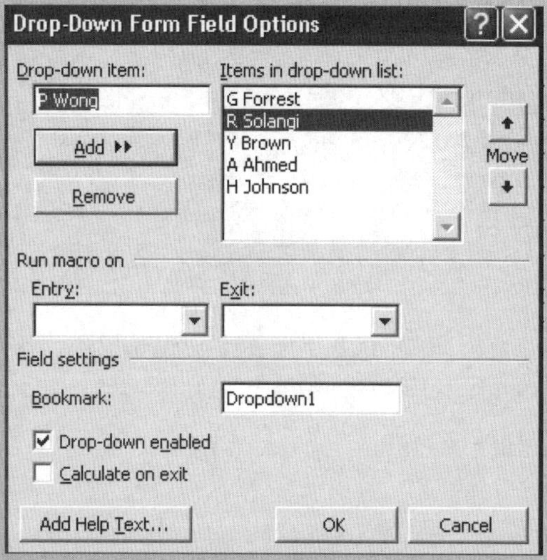

5 Click on: **OK**.

6 Repeat this method for Tuesday to Friday in Week 1.

Update date and time manually

The date and time are set to update automatically, i.e. when you open the file. You can update them manually.

Method

1 Select the **Time** field.

2 Right-click to access the pop-up menu.

3 Select: **Update Field**.

7.11 *Using AutoText*

It would be useful to include a field with the filename so that you don't have to remember where you saved it. You can insert a field as you did for the date and time, but there is another way using AutoText.

Method

To include the filename and path and the date the document was created on:

1. Click at a point underneath the table.
2. From the main menu toolbar, select: **Insert**: **AutoText**: **Header/Footer**: **Filename and path**.

Figure 7.21 Inserting an automatic text entry option

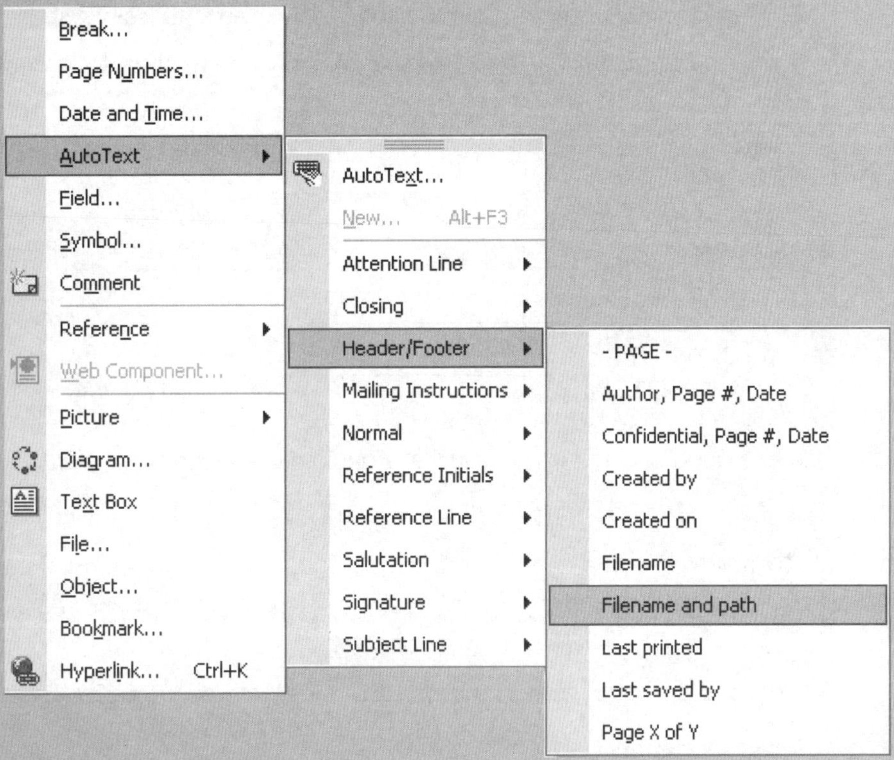

3. If you have already saved your work the name of the file will appear on your document at the insertion point. If you have not saved your work at this point, Word will insert the default filename: **Document?**.

To include an AutoText entry in the header that will show the date the document was created on, you need to select the header first.

Method

1. Click on: **View**: **Header and Footer**.
2. The I-beam cursor appears in the Header. In the **Header and Footer** dialogue box, click on: **Insert AutoText** to access the pop-up menu.
3. Select: **Created on**. The AutoText entry appears in the Header.
4. Click on: **Close**.

7.12 *Using check boxes*

You also need to include a check box for each member of staff on the rota that you can use to indicate when you have contacted them.

Method

1 Key in the names in a list underneath the table, e.g.

G Forrest
P Wong
R Solangi
Y Brown
A Ahmed
H Johnson

2 Click down after the first name and insert 2 spaces (to leave a space after the name).

3 On the Forms Toolbar, click on the **Check Box Form Field** icon.

Figure 7.22 The Check Box Form Field icon on the Forms Toolbar

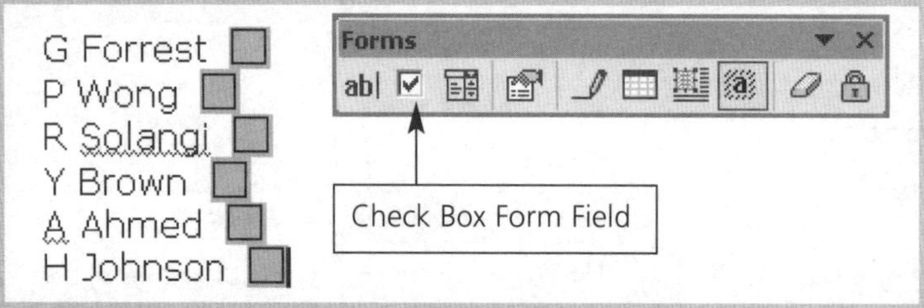

4 At the end of the name field, you should get a shaded square box.

5 Repeat this operation for the rest of the staff.

6 As with the drop-down fields, the check boxes don't work until the form is locked. Lock the form and see the effect that clicking in the boxes has. You should get a black cross when you click on the check boxes.

7.13 *Delete items in a form*

It has been decided that no one is going to work on Friday in Week 4. This field needs deleting.

Method

1 Make sure that the form is not locked.

2 In the table, select the last cell with a field, using the pointer tool.

3 Delete using the **Delete** key or right-click and select: **Cut**.

Figure 7.23 Select to delete a drop-down field in a form

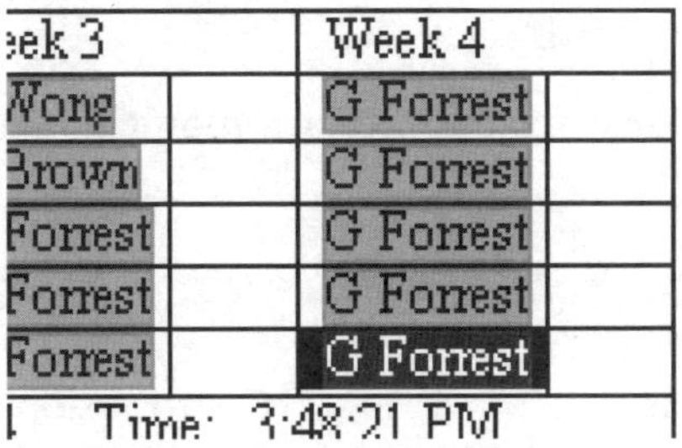

Note: double-clicking will not select the cell: it brings up the Options box. You need to position the pointer towards the bottom left-hand corner of the shaded area in the cell. When a black arrow appears, click to select.

If you are unsure if you have selected the field, to display the field code press: **Alt** + **F9**. Then press **Alt** + **F9** again to restore the text/numbers. The Alt + F9 shortcut is very useful if your fields are not shaded, i.e. if the Form Field Shading icon is not selected.

Try this now.

Method

1. Click on the **Form Field Shading** icon on the Forms toolbar. The shading disappears from the document and it is difficult to see if you have any fields.
2. Press the keys: **Alt** + **F9**. The fields are displayed as code.
3. Press the keys: **Alt** + **F9** again to remove the code.
4. Click on the **Form Field Shading** icon to turn the field shading back on.
5. Lock your form, then: **Save**.

Practice Task — *Task 7*

These exercises are included to help the candidate in his or her training for the Advanced ECDL program. The exercises included in this material are not Advanced ECDL certification tests and should not be construed in any way as Advanced ECDL certification tests. For information about Authorised ECDL Test Centres in different National Territories, please refer to the ECDL Foundation website at **www.ecdl.com**.

Method

You are going to send a memo to all the people in the office that contributed to a local charity.

Handy Hint

The Office Memo template is accessible from File: New: General Templates.

1. Amend the contemporary memo template by:
   - Removing the grey shading (some of which is in the footer).
   - Changing 'Memorandum' to 'Memo'.

- Removing the 'cc' line.
- Removing the 'click here and type' fields.

2 Save your new template in the Templates folder as: **Office memo**.

Handy Hint

Save as Document template.

First name	Surname	Contribution
Julie	Smith	£2.00
James	Guest	£6.50
Richard	Stephens	£0.00
Susan	Bridge	£2.50
Gregory	Cobham	£4.00
Katherine	Duxbury	£0.00
John	Moss	£3.50
Ahmed	Akhtar	£4.50
Bernice	O'Sullivan	£5.20

3 Close the document.

4 Set up the above table of contributions on a new page.

5 Save your work as: **Charity data**.

6 Open up the Office Memo template and mail merge the memo with the data.

The details you need for the memo are set out below:

To: <<First_Name>> <<Surname>>
From: Your name here
Date: Today's date
Re: Local charity
Thank you very much <<First_Name>> for the contribution of <<Contribution>>. It was greatly appreciated.

7 Sort the data in order of surname.

8 Filter out those people that did not contribute.

You should have seven merged memos; the first one should be to Ahmed Akhtar. If your Mail Merge has not worked, you should still have the data and the Form Letter saved, so that you can try again.

9 Save your Mail Merge file as: **Task 7a Answer**.

10 Open a new document and record a simple macro to set up the following formatting:

- a landscape page
- 3 cm margins all around

- 3 columns with a line between
- the AutoText: **Confidential** in the top left-hand corner.

Assign the macro to the toolbar. Name the macro: **A4 Land**.

11 Assign the macro to a Custom button on the Formatting Toolbar.

12 Close without saving.

13 Open the document: **Task 2 Answer**. Unlock it and save as: **Task 7b Answer**. Leave the file open.

14 Open a new blank document. Save the document as: **Disclaimer Text**.

15 Record another macro; name it: **Disclaimer**. Store the macro in: Disclaimer text (document). Record (key in) the following text using Times New Roman 12 pt font.

The restaurant reserves the right to amend or delete any of the set menus at anytime.

16 Go to the document Task 7b Answer. Copy the Disclaimer macro to it.

17 Run the Disclaimer macro in the footer of Task 7b Answer.

18 Update the File Name field in the last row of the table.

19 Remove Set Menu 6 and Set Menu 7 from lunchtime.

20 Split the cells in column 1.

Handy Hint

Highlight rows 2–12. Remove the tick in: Merge cells before split.

21 So that you can indicate which week is the current week, insert a Check Box form field in the new column.

22 Reduce the width of the column so that it just accommodates the check box.

23 In Weeks 1, 4 and 8 there is no lunchtime sitting: remove these fields.

Task 8 Personnel interviews

In this task, you will cover the following skills:

- Use highlighting options to track changes in a document.
  - o Change the formatting of tracked changes.
- Accept or reject changes in a document.
- Add or remove text comments.
- Edit text comments.

Scenario

A new job has come in from personnel for checking. It is a quick simple job. They would like you to check the accuracy of the word processing skills of three interviewees. You already have the master document prepared and the candidates have saved their work to file.

8.1 Track changes in a document

You will track the changes in each of the candidates' files.

Method

1 From the Task Files folder, open the file with the first candidate's work: **Candidate 1**.

2 Click on: **Tools**, then select: **Compare and Merge Documents**. A dialogue box, Compare and Merge Documents, appears.

3 From the Task Files folder, select the file: **Personnel Master**.

Figure 8.1 Selecting a file to compare with current documents

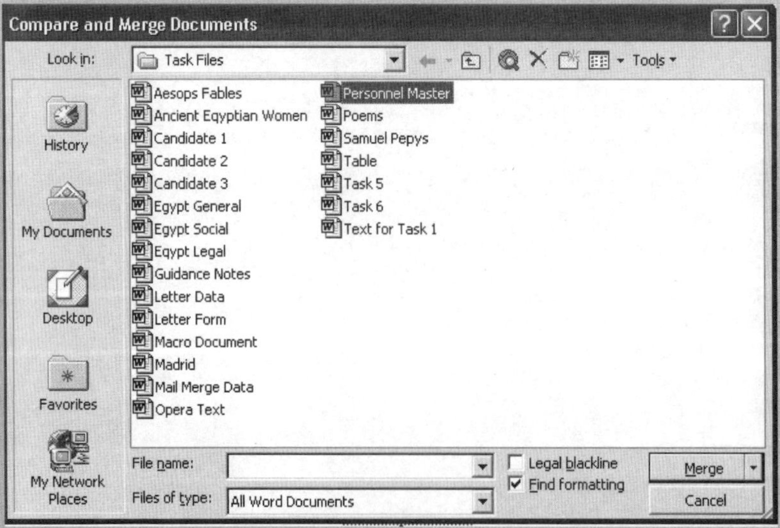

4 Click on: **Merge**.

The file Personnel Master does not open but highlights (compares) the differences between the two documents (Figure 8.2).

Figure 8.2 Comparing the difference between two documents

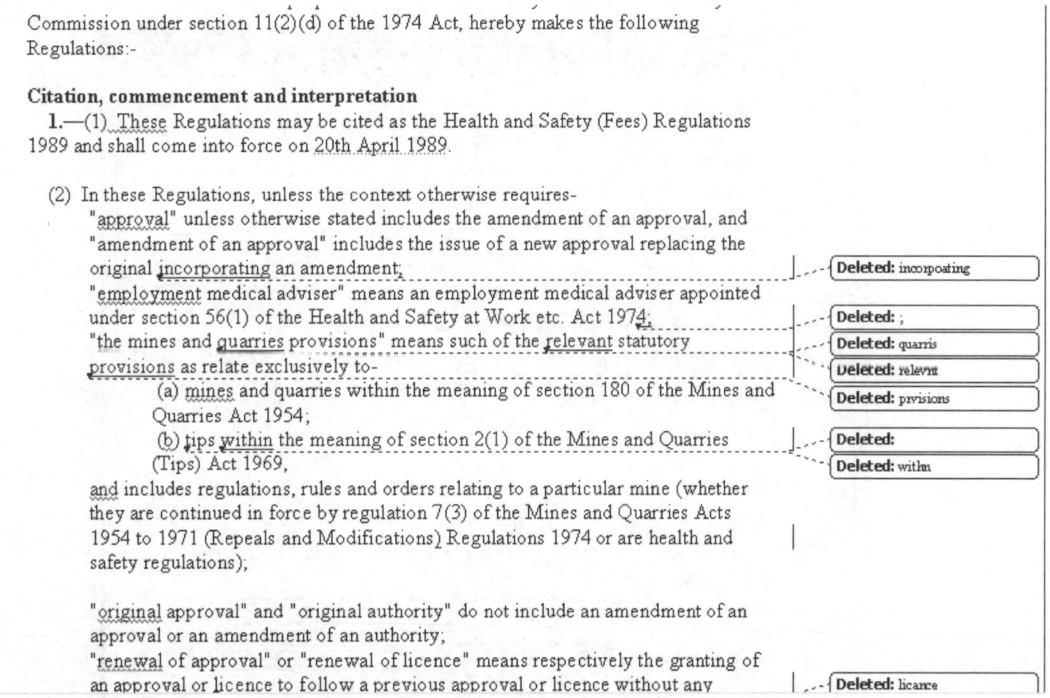
Commission under section 11(2)(d) of the 1974 Act, hereby makes the following Regulations:-

Citation, commencement and interpretation

1.—(1) These Regulations may be cited as the Health and Safety (Fees) Regulations 1989 and shall come into force on 20th April 1989.

(2) In these Regulations, unless the context otherwise requires-

"approval" unless otherwise stated includes the amendment of an approval, and "amendment of an approval" includes the issue of a new approval replacing the original incorporating an amendment;

"employment medical adviser" means an employment medical adviser appointed under section 56(1) of the Health and Safety at Work etc. Act 1974;

"the mines and quarries provisions" means such of the relevant statutory provisions as relate exclusively to-

(a) mines and quarries within the meaning of section 180 of the Mines and Quarries Act 1954;

(b) tips within the meaning of section 2(1) of the Mines and Quarries (Tips) Act 1969,

and includes regulations, rules and orders relating to a particular mine (whether they are continued in force by regulation 7(3) of the Mines and Quarries Acts 1954 to 1971 (Repeals and Modifications) Regulations 1974 or are health and safety regulations);

"original approval" and "original authority" do not include an amendment of an approval or an amendment of an authority;

"renewal of approval" or "renewal of licence" means respectively the granting of an approval or licence to follow a previous approval or licence without any

Deleted: incorpoating
Deleted: ;
Deleted: quarris
Deleted: relevnt
Deleted: prvisions
Deleted:
Deleted: withn
Deleted: licance

Change the formatting of tracked changes

You can change the formatting of the tracked changes, for example, set them in a different colour.

Method

1 Click on: **Show: Options: Track Changes** (Figure 8.3). A Track Changes dialogue box appears (Figure 8.4).

Figure 8.3 Selecting Show: Options Track Changes

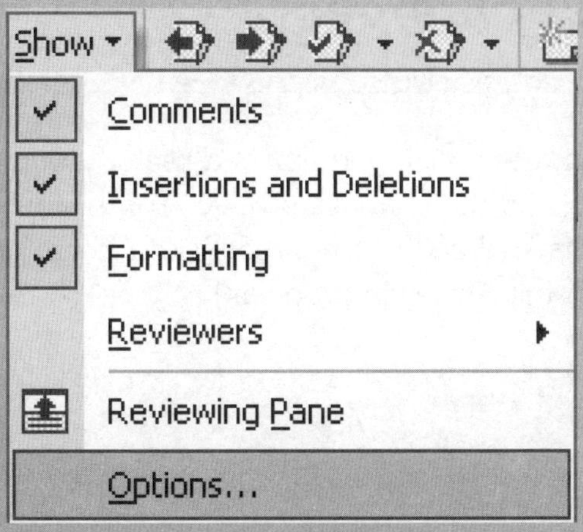

2 Make your changes (Figure 8.4). Click on: **OK**.

3 Make sure that you have **Final Showing Markup** selected from the **Display for Review** drop-down menu.

Figure 8.4 Making the changes

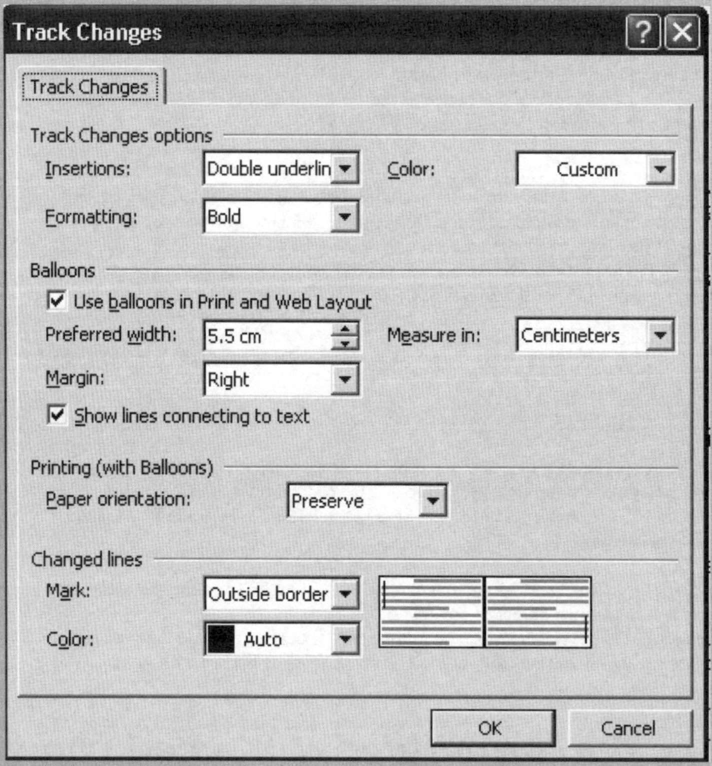

4 The changes should appear.

5 Repeat this method on the other two candidates' work.

6 Compare the documents and change the formatting of the changes. You will need to open candidate 2's work from the Task Files folder.

8.2 *Accept or reject changes*

The **Accept or Reject Changes** dialogue box is a useful tool if you are checking a long document and want to find the changes quickly. Try this on one of the candidate's work that you have already compared. (The Accept or Reject Changes buttons should be visible on the Reviewing toolbar.)

Method

With the candidate's work on screen:

Place the I-beam cursor in one of the changes, then click on either the Accept Change button or the Reject Change button (Figure 8.5).

Close the Personnel Master file.

Figure 8.5 Accepting or rejecting changes

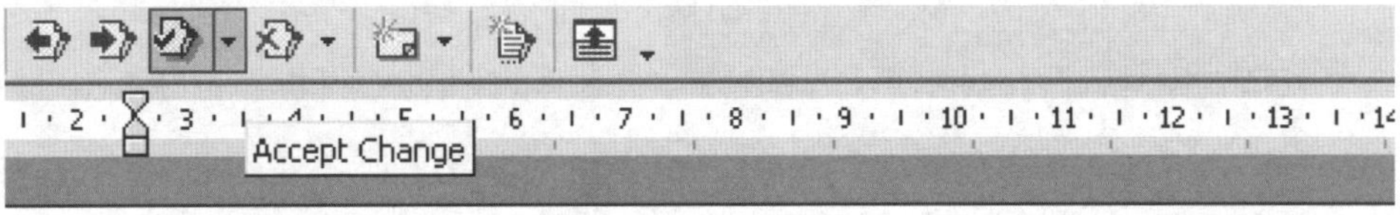

If you click on the **Reject** button you will reject the candidate's amendments and the document will change to match the Personnel Master file. If you click on the **Accept** button you will accept the candidate's work.

Another feature on the Reviewing toolbar is the **Track Changes** button. This is a useful tool when you are editing existing work.

Method

1 Open the file: **Personnel Master**.

2 Click on: the  **Track Changes** button.

You will notice that the **Trk** button is now active on the status bar at the bottom on the screen.

3 Try adding text or deleting text from the document.

Your changes will appear alongside the original text.

4 Turn the tracking off by double-clicking on the **Trk** button or by clicking once on the **Track Changes** button.

5 Close this file without saving.

8.3 Add or remove comments

Now that you have viewed the candidates' work and seen the errors, you can add a comment to the file before you return the files to Personnel.

Method

1 Open the file: **Candidate 1**.

2 At the bottom of the document, you will see the words 'Candidate 1'. Highlight these words.

3 From the main menu toolbar, select: **View**: **Toolbars**: **Reviewing**. You should get a new toolbar underneath the Formatting Toolbar.

Figure 8.6 The Reviewing Toolbar

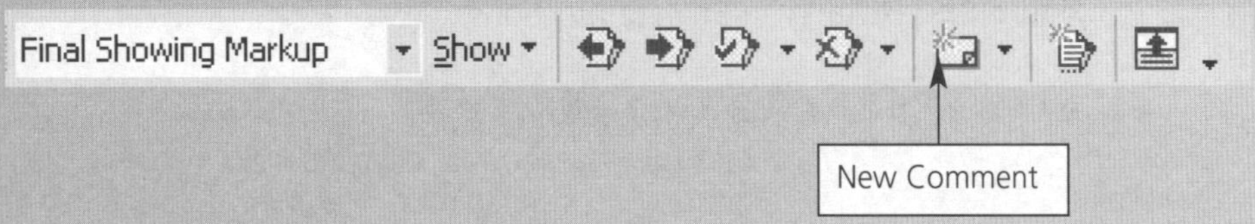

4 Click on the yellow **New Comment** icon. A box is opened at the right-hand side of the screen for you to key in your comments on Candidate 1.

5 Key in: 'This candidate did not complete the work on time and had approximately 9 errors'.

Figure 8.7 Adding a comment to a document using the New Comment icon

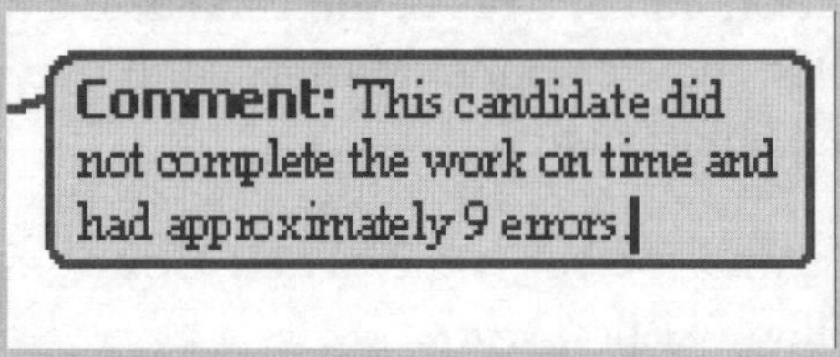

6 To view and print the document without the comments, change the Display for Review selection to Final (Figure 8.8).

Figure 8.8 Viewing and printing without the comments

```
Final Showing Markup        ▼
Final Showing Markup
Final
Original Showing Markup
Original
```

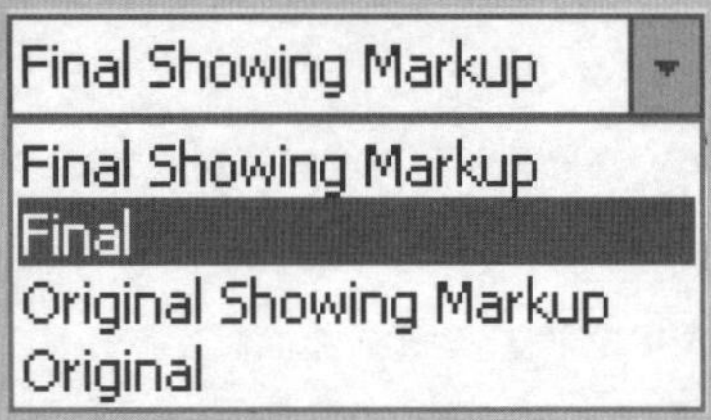

7 Save your work.

8 Repeat this method with the other two candidates' work, putting in your comments. Suitable comments might be:

- **Candidate 2**: Work completed on time – 7 errors.
- **Candidate 3**: This candidate completed the least work and had 8 errors.

The **Cassette icon** in the **New Comment** drop-down menu enables you to add sound to the document. You could, if you had a microphone, record your comments as speech.

8.4 Edit comments

The edit and delete functions are accessed through the **New Comments** drop-down menu.

If you have no comments on your document, these two icons will not be available, i.e. they are shaded out.

Figure 8.9 The edit and delete functions

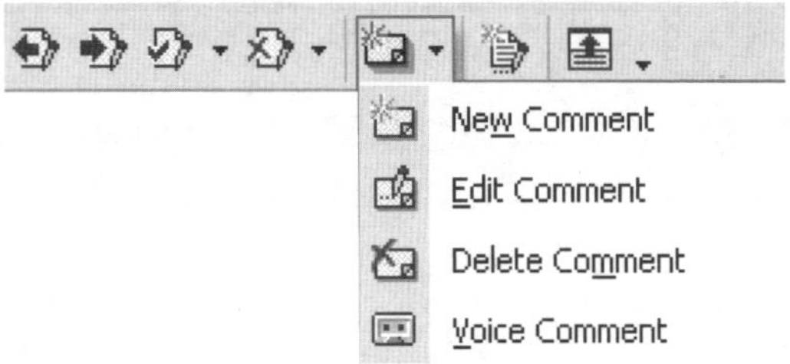

To edit or delete the text comment:

Method

1 Open the file: **Candidate 1**. Make sure that you have **Final Showing Markup** displayed. Click on the **Candidate 1** text in brackets at the end of the document.

2 Select: **Edit Comment** from the **New Comment** menu.

3 The cursor moves to the Comments box. Delete the words 'on time'.

Note: the Delete Comment option deletes the comment but leaves the original text, i.e. Candidate 1.

4 Click on the words 'Candidate 1'. This contains the text comment.

5 Click on the **Delete Comment** icon.

The comment is removed and both the Edit Comment and Delete Comment icons are now not available for use.

Practice Task *Task 8*

These exercises are included to help the candidate in his or her training for the Advanced ECDL program. The exercises included in this material are not Advanced ECDL certification tests and should not be construed in any way as Advanced ECDL certification tests. For information about Authorised ECDL Test Centres in different National Territories, please refer to the ECDL Foundation website at **www.ecdl.com**.

Below is the draft text that is going to form the basis of a document to be sent out to help applicants complete the standard CV form.

1 In the Task Files Folder, open the file stored as: **Guidance notes**.

> Guidance notes
>
> It is essential to tell the truth on a CV as inaccurate or untrue information could lead at the very least to embarrassment or possibly to even more serious consequences. You are not obliged, however, to reveal every small detail of your private and not so private life. For example, if your GCSE grades were low, and you have not been asked to cite grades, simply present the subjects without the grades. It is important to be consistent here – you must not present some grades and not others. In actual fact, few employers will be really concerned about grades you received for exams taken many years ago. Although they will want to know that you have obtained certain qualifications, employers will be far more interested in your recent achievements.

If you are returning to work after a break, it is especially important for you to show that you have been doing interesting and relevant activities during your break from employment. This is because employers see less value in unpaid work than 9–5 paid employment. In your CV, you will need to talk about achievement, paid or unpaid, which you are proud off. Try to avoid emphasising duties that you have had to do and try to show how these activities would benefit the employer.

2 Add the following comment to the heading Guidance Notes:

> This is the first draft and must be revised by Personnel before distribution.

3 Make the following changes and track the changes while editing. Make sure that the options you choose will show the changes when you print in black and white.

- Expand CV to: Curriculum Vitae at the first occurrence.
- Delete the second sentence in the first paragraph.
- Add the following text as a new paragraph to the end of the document:

> REMEMBER: If you are not obliged to mention your weaker aspects, then avoid doing so.

- Change 'few employers will be' in the first paragraph to: 'we are not'.
- Change 'they' in the final sentence in the first paragraph to: 'we'.
- Change 'employers' in the final sentence in the first paragraph to: 'we'.
- Change the final words in the second paragraph, 'the employer', to: 'our company'.

4 Turn off the tracking.

5 Change the text comment to read:

> This is the first draft and must be revised and approved by Personnel before distribution.

6 Save your work as: **Task 8 Answer**.

7 Print your work.

You should be able to see all the changes that you have made to the document.

Task 9 Collaborative document

In this task, you will cover the following skills:

- Create a new Master Document.
- Use outline options.
- Add or remove subdocument within a Master Document.
  - o Add files to a Master Document.
  - o Lock a Master Document.
  - o Display options.
  - o Delete a subdocument from a Master Document.
  - o Amend a subdocument in a Master Document.
  - o Change the order of subdocuments in a Master Document.
- Modify existing character or paragraph styles.
  - o Modify using the Style dialogue box.
  - o Modify using the Outlining Toolbar.
- Create a subdocument based on heading styles within a Master Document.
- Use automatic caption options.
  - o Select caption options.
  - o Insert ClipArt.
- Delete a column break and section breaks in a document.
- Add or delete a bookmark.
  - o Add a bookmark.
  - o Delete a bookmark.
- Create or delete a cross-reference.

Scenario

You have been given a job that is causing problems. Four people are contributing to the final document and thus it is becoming large and unmanageable. To make matters worse, not everyone has finalised their work and some people need to keep updating their sections.

9.1 Create a new Master Document

Master Documents are particularly useful when you are handling a large amount of text, e.g. a book. You can create each chapter or section as separate files and then, when the chapters are complete, bring them all together (as subdocuments) within the book (the Master Document). Working with smaller files (subdocuments) is very efficient: it reduces the time the PC needs to save the file and makes it much easier to move from one chapter to the next.

Alternatively, you could bring together several files from several different people into one master document, e.g. a report. The subdocuments will link back to the contributor's original file(s).

The mechanics of creating a new Master Document are the final stages of 'work in progress'. In the scenario for this task you can create a Master Document that brings together all the sections as subdocuments but which also enables the four contributors to amend their own individual sections. The Master Document updates automatically each time it is opened.

Caution! Master Documents are not to be confused with templates or documents that you may refer to as a 'master'.

Note: before you start on this task you need to have the files you are going to be working with saved either on your PC (standalone PC) or in your home area (networked PC). The files you need to copy from the CD are in the **Task Files Directory**: **Ancient Egyptian Women**, **Egypt General**, **Egypt Social** and **Egypt Legal**. If you do not do this you will have problems saving the Master Document.

9.2 *Use outline options*

You have been given a separate file from each of the four contributors. Together, these will produce one large document on the subject of 'Woman in Ancient Egypt'. To do this, you will be working in Outline View.

Method

1 Open a new blank document.

2 Change the view of the document by clicking on: **View**: **Outline**. The **Outlining Toolbar** appears below the Formatting Toolbar.

Figure 9.1 The Outlining Toolbar

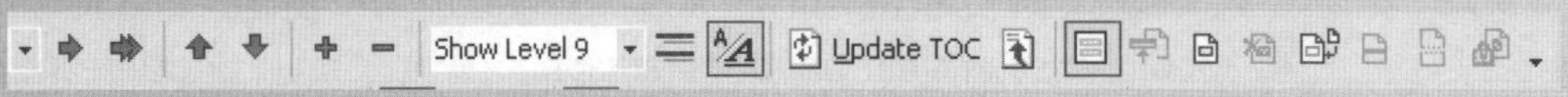

This is the basis of your Master Document.

9.3 *Add or delete subdocuments within a Master Document*

Adding files to a Master Document

The four separate Word files are now going to be combined to create a new Master Document.

Method

1 Click on the **Insert Subdocument** icon .

2 In the Insert Subdocument dialogue box, select the file: **Ancient Egyptian Women**.

3 Click on: **Open**. The subdocument appears in the Master Document.

4 Scroll to the end of this subdocument.

5 Click underneath the text (outside the box) and you should have a flashing I-beam cursor.

6 Repeat the above sequence to add the files **Egypt General**, **Egypt Social** and **Egypt Legal** to the Master Document.

Note: when inserted, the subdocuments will pick up the formatting in the Master Document. This formatting will be changed later in the task.

In Outline View, documents looks very different. The main differences are that images do not appear and there are symbols to the left of the text.

Method

1. Click on: **View**: **Print Layout**: **Print Preview** from the formatting toolbar.
2. Click on the **Multiple Pages** icon (fourth from left). Hold down the **Shift** key and, using the arrow keys, select: 2 × 4 pages. Press: **Enter**. You will see that all four documents are now together in one Master Document.
3. Click on: **Close** to go back to Print Layout View. If you have blank pages in your Master Document and you want to remove them, you can delete the section breaks at this stage by clicking on the **Show/Hide** icon, clicking on the **Section Break/Page Break** markers and pressing the **Delete** key.
4. Change back to Outline View.

Figure 9.2 Using Print Preview to view a Master Document

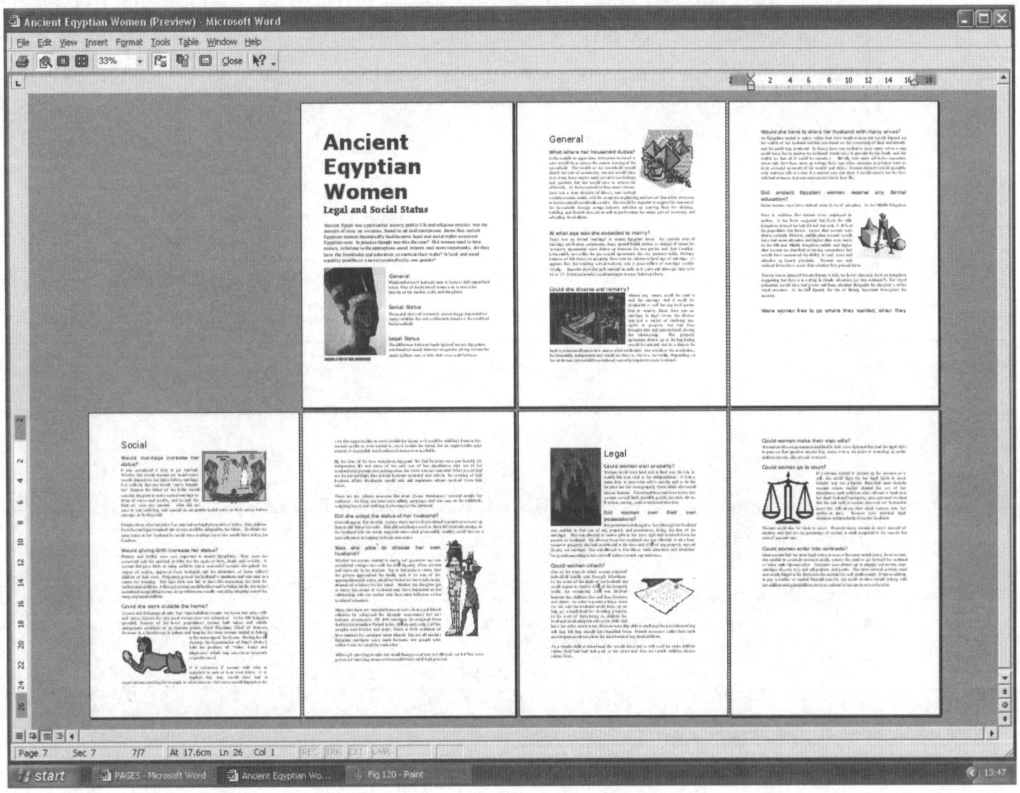

Lock a Master Document

You can lock the Master Document so that no amendments can be made to it.

Method

1. On the Outlining Toolbar, click on the **Lock Document** icon.
2. Save your new Master Document as: **Ancient Egyptian Women Master**.

Caution: you cannot lock the subdocuments within the Master Document if they are already open, for example, if a contributor is making amendments to the file or a subdocument is open on your PC. Word will lock only those subdocuments that are closed and will warn you that not all the subdocuments have been locked.

You should be able to see two small icons at the top left-hand side of each subdocument. The square one indicates the start of the subdocument; the 'lock' underneath shows that the subdocument is locked.

Figure 9.3 Icons to indicate that a subdocument is locked

Display options

One of the distinguishing features of Master Documents is that you can display your document as a list of file names.

Method

1 Click on the **Collapse Subdocuments** icon.

Your document should have changed to show the subdocuments listed as links to where the document is stored.

Figure 9.4 Click on the Collapse Subdocuments icon to display the Master Document subdocument links

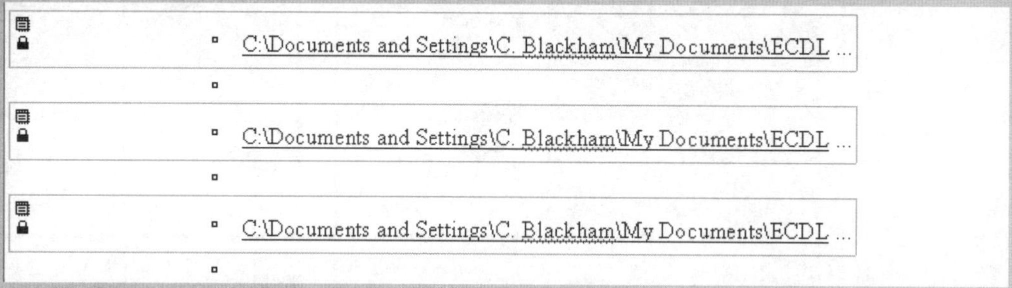

Caution: if this does not work, check that you are working on the file Ancient Egypt Women Master that you have saved to your PC.

Remember, documents inserted as subdocuments have not been moved or amended in any way; they have only been linked together to form the Master Document.

2 Check that the links work by double-clicking on one of the square subdocument icons. The page should now appear in Print Layout view.

3 From the main menu toolbar, select: **Window**. From the drop-down menu, to go back to the Master Document select: **Ancient Egyptian Women Master**.

4 With the four collapsed subdocuments on screen, click on: **Print Preview**. You will be asked if you want to open the documents. Click on: **Yes**. The content of the Master Document appears in Print Preview.

5 Click on: **Close**.

6 The Master Document is now displayed in full in Outline View. To view the Master Document again as links, click on the **Collapse Subdocuments** icon.

You can expand the subdocuments using the same icon that you used to collapse them. Try this now. The name of the icon changes to **Expand Subdocuments**. Click on this icon to view all the subdocuments.

Delete a subdocument from a Master Document

You are going to delete the last subdocument.

Method

In Outline View, with the subdocuments either collapsed or expanded:

1. Click on the square subdocument icon on the left-hand side of the screen alongside the last subdocument. This selects the link (the whole subdocument).
2. To remove, press the **Delete** key.

If you delete the wrong file you can undo, but you will need to unlock the Master Document first.

Handy Hint

This method does not delete the original file, only the subdocument within the Master Document.

Amend a subdocument in a Master Document

You cannot make changes to a Master Document if the original file is open, e.g. if a contributor is making an amendment. When the contributor has saved and closed the file, the Master Document updates automatically the next time it is opened.

Method

1. Show the Master Document links by clicking on the **Collapse Subdocuments** icon.
2. Click on the link to go to the second subdocument.
3. Delete the first subheading: 'What were her …'.
4. Save and close the subdocument.

Note: if you have changed the folder that the subdocument is stored in, you will see the link has changed to show the new pathway to the file.

5. Expand the Master Document and you should see that the subheading is missing from the second subdocument.
6. Save your work.

Caution: if the contributor renames or moves the file from the original location, the subdocument will disappear from the Master Document. You would need to reinsert the subdocument.

Change the order of subdocuments in a Master Document

Before you can change the order of the subdocuments, the Master Document needs to be unlocked. Word will tell you if you forget. The **Unlock** icon is the last button on the Outlining toolbar.

Figure 9.5 Remember to unlock a Master Document before changing the order of the subdocuments

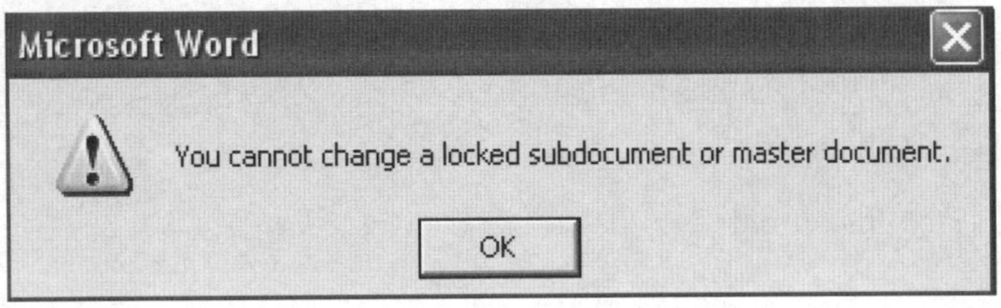

Handy Hint

Reordering the subdocuments is easier to do when the subdocuments are collapsed.

Method

1 On the document icon positioned in the top left-hand corner of the subdocument box, click and hold down the left mouse button.

2 Drag the icon to below the last subdocument.

9.4 Change existing character or paragraph styles

Modify using the Style dialogue box

A request has come to amend the body text on the subdocuments. To do this you are going to amend the existing style that is already applied to the text.

Method

1 Expand all the subdocuments.

2 Click in the first paragraph in the second subdocument.

3 Click into the body text underneath the subheading.

4 Click on: **Format**: **Styles and Formatting**. The Styles and Formatting task pane appears. You can see from the blue borders in the pane that the name of the style you are going to amend is 11pt, justified.

Figure 9.6 Styles and Formatting

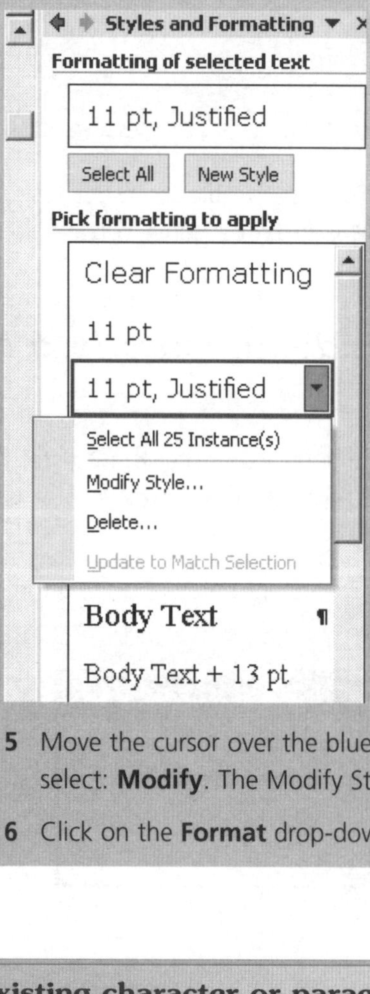

5 Move the cursor over the blue box, click on the drop down menu that appears and select: **Modify**. The Modify Style dialogue box appears.

6 Click on the **Format** drop-down menu. Select: **Font**.

Figure 9.7 Select Format: Font in the Modify Style dialogue box

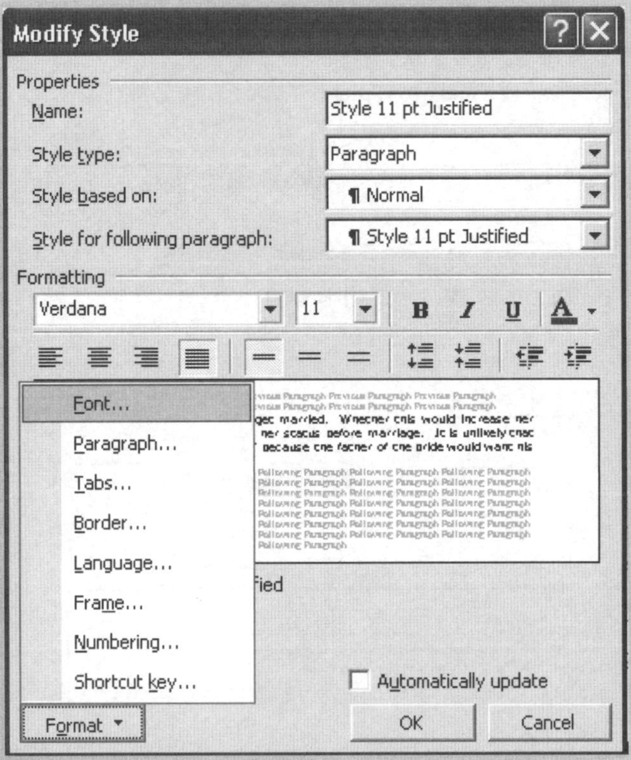

The Font dialogue box appears. Make the following amendments:

- Font: **Arial**
- Font style: **Regular**
- Size: **10 pt**
- Font color: **Dark Green** or a colour of your choice.

Figure 9.8 Selecting font options in the Font dialogue box

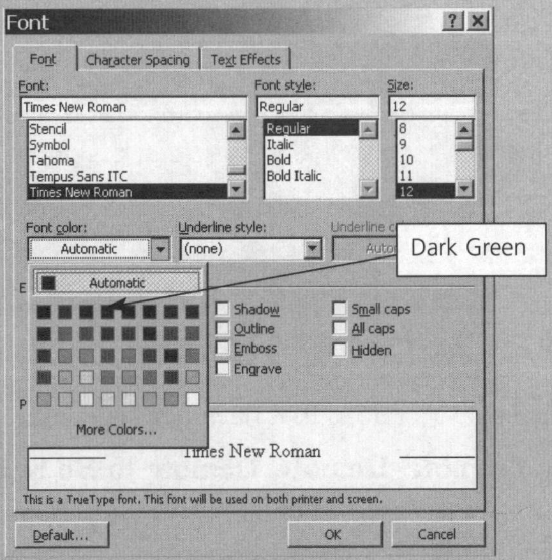

7 Click on: **OK** to return to the Modify Style dialogue box.

8 Click on: **Format**: **Paragraph**. The Paragraph dialogue box appears.

9 Make the following amendments:

- Special: **Hanging**
- Line spacing: **1.5 lines**.

Figure 9.9 Selecting paragraph options in the Paragraph dialogue box

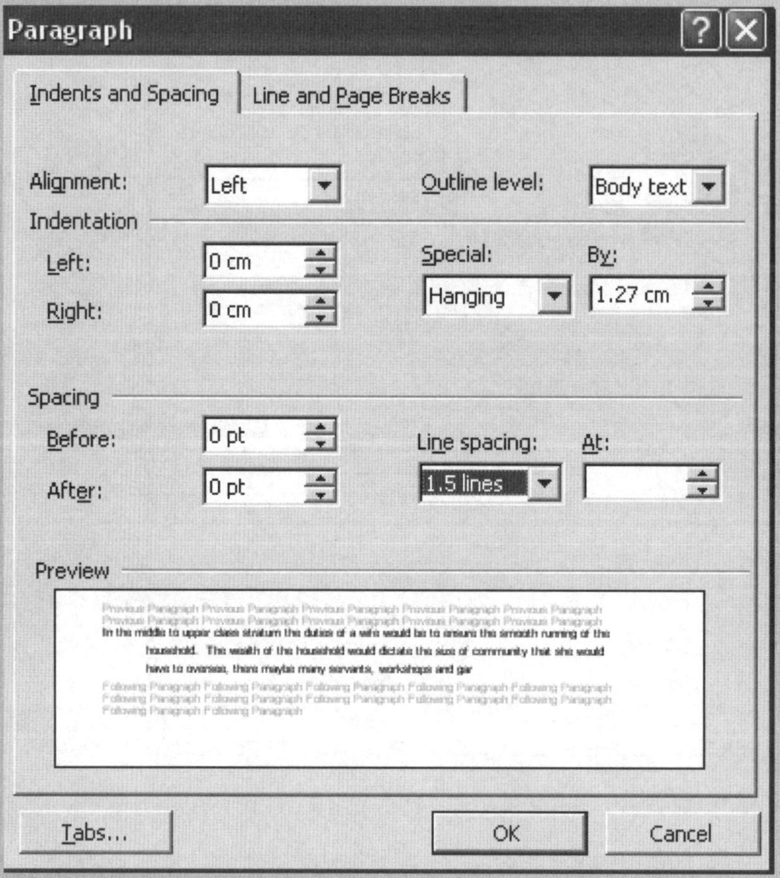

10 To go back to the Modify Style dialogue box, click on: **OK**.

11 Click to select the **Add to template** box. This will make the style available to all new documents, not just this one.

12 Click on: **OK**.

The font should change on-screen.

13 Click on: **Print Preview**. You will see that the formatting has been applied to the whole of the Master Document where the text was formatted to Normal style.

14 Select: **Save**.

Modify using the Outlining Toolbar

There are more Outlining Toolbar buttons that have not been used so far.

The first few buttons are: **Promote**; **Demote**; **Demote to Body Text**; **Move Up**; **Move Down**. These affect the position of the text.

Handy Hint

Unless you unlock the Master Document, not all the Outlining Toolbar buttons are available for use.

Method

Click into the text on the second subdocument. Click on the green arrows on the toolbar.

Figure 9.10 Modify text position icons on the Outlining Toolbar

Experiment by selecting the arrows in turn. To see the effect, click on: **Print Preview**. Undo your selections before you try the next one.

The Show Level drop-down menu will display the headings that have been formatted using the Styles drop-down menu. If you click down on any of the headings you will see in the Style drop-down menu which heading style has been applied to that particular piece of text, e.g. Heading 1 (perhaps your subheading). If you then select Show Level you will get a list of all the text that has the same style of formatting applied, i.e. you will get a list of all your subheadings. This is more evident when you set up a new Master Document with new subdocuments that you have applied styles to. The example you have been working on was a new Master Document using existing files as subdocuments.

Close your work without saving.

9.5 Create a subdocument from heading styles in a Master Document

From the Task Files folder, open the file: **Poems**.

There are 10 poems in the document. Each of the poems needs to be in a separate file. This means that you are going to create 10 new subdocuments.

To create 10 subdocuments in one operation, the headings have to be formatted to a Word heading style.

Method

1 Save the Poems document to your PC. Name the file: **Poems2**.

2 Click in each of the poem titles in turn and, from the **Styles** drop-down menu, select: **Heading 1**.

Figure 9.11 From the Styles drop-down menu, select: Heading 1

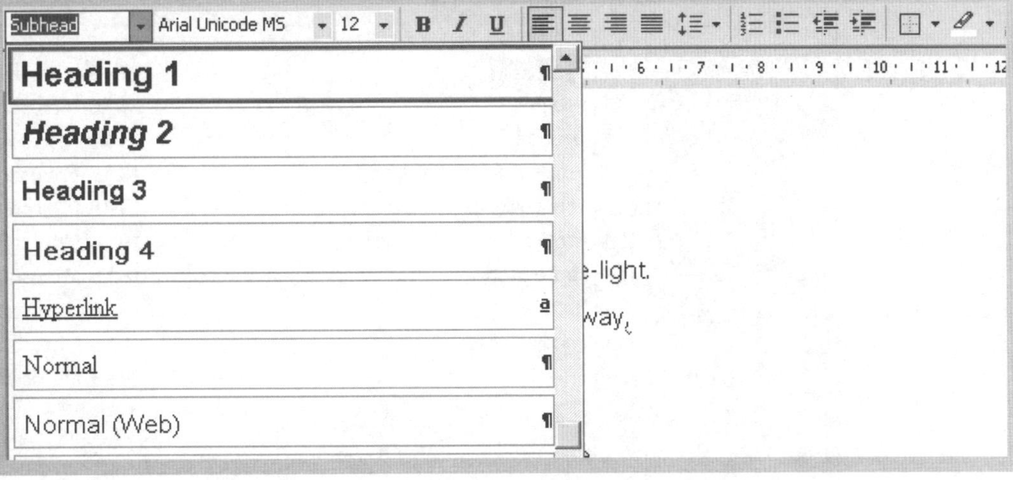

Your Heading 1 may not be the same format as the one in Figure 9.10. The important point is that each of the titles is formatted using the same style. If one of the titles is not formatted, then the poem will not become a subdocument.

Method

3 Click on: **View**: **Outline**.

4 Select all the poems – press: **Ctrl** + **A**.

5 Click on the **Create Subdocument** icon. If the icon is not available, check that you have saved your work to your PC.

The subdocuments should now be created. The poems have boxes around them.

Figure 9.12 Using the Create Subdocument icon to create subdocuments

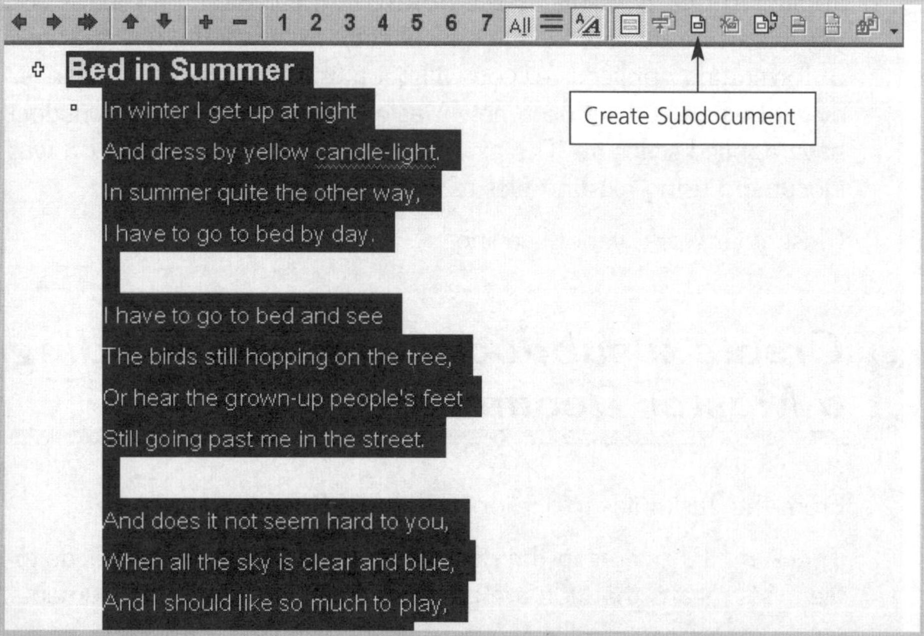

6 Click on the **Collapse Documents** icon (you may be asked to save) and you will see the links to the new subdocuments.

7 Click on one of the links and you will see that each poem is now a separate file.

8 If you click on: **File**: **Open** you should see the new subdocuments listed as separate files.

Figure 9.13 The new subdocuments listed as files in File: Open

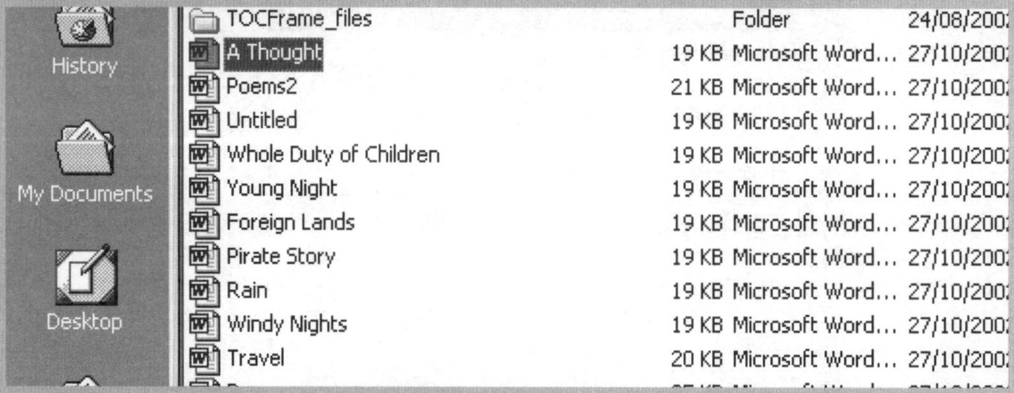

9 Save your work.

9.6 *Insert automatic captions*

The document is not visually attractive and the pages would benefit from pictures being inserted.

Select caption options

Method

Click on: **View**: **Outline**. Make sure that the subdocuments are expanded and unlocked, and that you have the drawing toolbar at the bottom of your screen.

The AutoCaption needs to be made active so that you don't need to set the caption for each individual picture.

Method

1 Click on: **Insert**: **Reference: Caption**.

2 Click on: **Numbering**.

3 In the Caption Numbering dialogue box, from the Format drop-down menu, select: upper case Roman numerals.

Figure 9.14 The Caption and Caption Numbering dialogue boxes

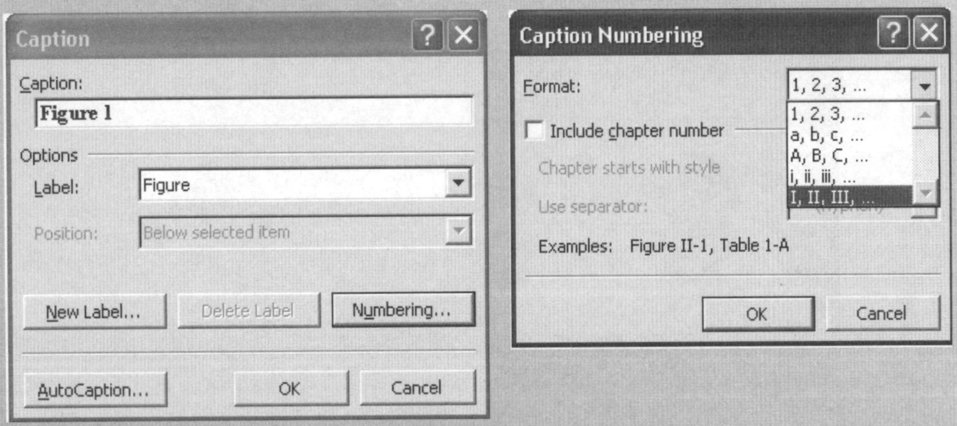

4 To close the Caption Numbering dialogue box, click on: **OK**.

5 Click on: **AutoCaption**.

6 Click on the box at the left-hand side to select: **Microsoft Word Picture**.

7 Click on: **OK**.

Insert ClipArt

The Microsoft Word Picture option was chosen because you are inserting ClipArt. If you were inserting slides from a presentation, the option to choose would be Microsoft PowerPoint Presentation.

8 Position the I-beam cursor at the end of the first poem (within the Subdocument box).

9 On the Drawing toolbar, click on the **Insert ClipArt** icon.

10 In the **Insert ClipArt** pane, search for **weather**.

11 Click on the snowflake image to insert it.

12 Position the I-beam at the end of the second poem.

13 Search for **food** by clicking on the **Modify** button and keying in **food** in the **Search** text box. Select the **Cake** image.

Figure 9.15 Insert ClipArt with selected caption numbering

Figure I
A Thought
It is very nice to think
The world is full of meat and drink,
With little children saying grace
In every Christian kind of place.
Figure II

14 Repeat this process for the remainder of the poems, inserting the following clips from these searches:

- Subdocument 3: search for **baggage**.
- Subdocument 4: search for **tiger**.
- Subdocument 5: search for **animals**.
- Subdocument 6: search for **buildings**.
- Subdocument 7: search for **boats**.
- Subdocument 8: search for **persons**.
- Subdocument 9: search for **dogs**.
- Subdocument 10: search for **air**.

15 Click on: **Collapse Documents**.

16 Save your work.

17 Click on the subdocument links. There should be a captioned ClipArt picture on each page.

18 Close your Master Document and any subdocuments that are open.

9.7 Delete column breaks and section breaks

The Literary Discussion Group have brought back their Daniel Defoe document. They do not like the large gap on the first page and want it removed.

It is the same operation for both column and section breaks.

Method

1 Open your last saved copy of **Task 1**. It should look similar to Figure 9.16.

Figure 9.16 Open the file: Task 1

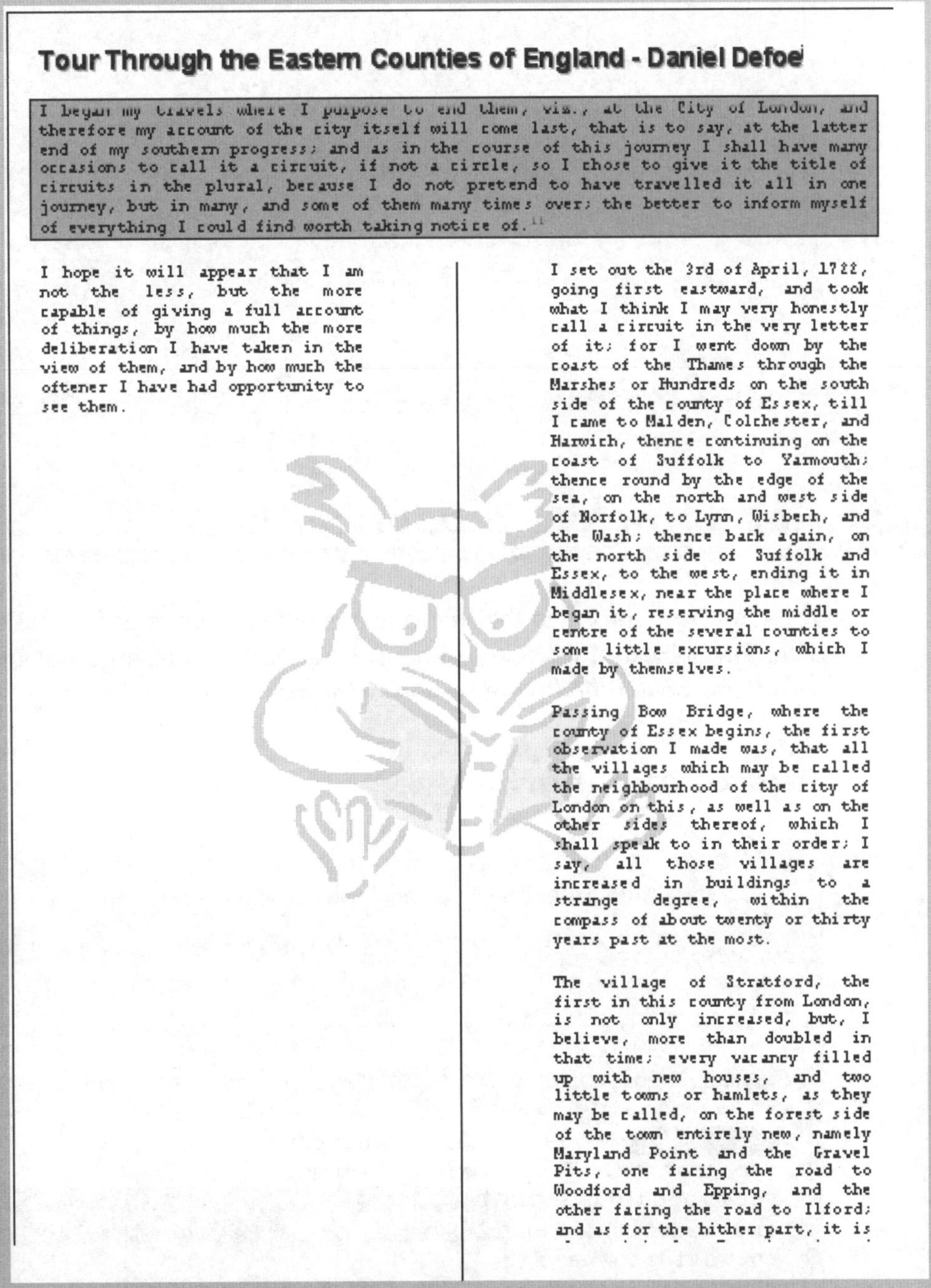

Tour Through the Eastern Counties of England - Daniel Defoe

I began my travels where I purpose to end them, viz., at the City of London, and therefore my account of the city itself will come last, that is to say, at the latter end of my southern progress; and as in the course of this journey I shall have many occasions to call it a circuit, if not a circle, so I chose to give it the title of circuits in the plural, because I do not pretend to have travelled it all in one journey, but in many, and some of them many times over; the better to inform myself of everything I could find worth taking notice of.[11]

I hope it will appear that I am not the less, but the more capable of giving a full account of things, by how much the more deliberation I have taken in the view of them, and by how much the oftener I have had opportunity to see them.

I set out the 3rd of April, 1722, going first eastward, and took what I think I may very honestly call a circuit in the very letter of it; for I went down by the coast of the Thames through the Marshes or Hundreds on the south side of the county of Essex, till I came to Malden, Colchester, and Harwich, thence continuing on the coast of Suffolk to Yarmouth; thence round by the edge of the sea, on the north and west side of Norfolk, to Lynn, Wisbech, and the Wash; thence back again, on the north side of Suffolk and Essex, to the west, ending it in Middlesex, near the place where I began it, reserving the middle or centre of the several counties to some little excursions, which I made by themselves.

Passing Bow Bridge, where the county of Essex begins, the first observation I made was, that all the villages which may be called the neighbourhood of the city of London on this, as well as on the other sides thereof, which I shall speak to in their order; I say, all those villages are increased in buildings to a strange degree, within the compass of about twenty or thirty years past at the most.

The village of Stratford, the first in this county from London, is not only increased, but, I believe, more than doubled in that time; every vacancy filled up with new houses, and two little towns or hamlets, as they may be called, on the forest side of the town entirely new, namely Maryland Point and the Gravel Pits, one facing the road to Woodford and Epping, and the other facing the road to Ilford; and as for the hither part, it is

If you can't find it, there is a copy of the file on your CD in the Suggested Answers folder. It is named: **Task 1 with column break**.

2 Click on the **Show/Hide** icon to reveal the column and section breaks.

3 Select the column break underneath the text in column 1 by clicking in it.

Figure 9.17 Click on the Column Break to select

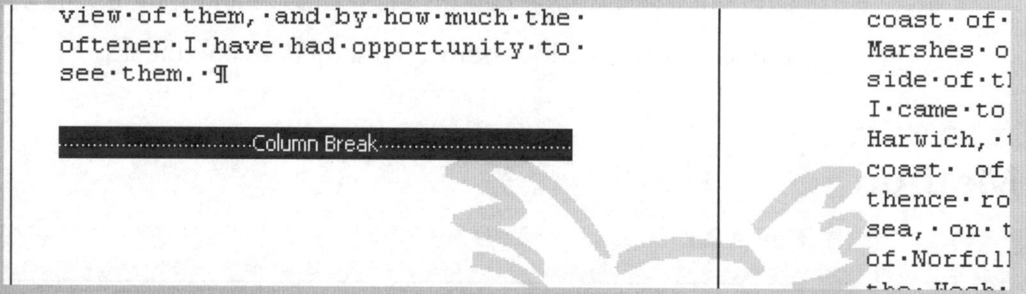

4 Press the **Delete** key.

The text should move from column 2 into column 1.

5 Remove the page break from page 3 using the same method as above.

Handy Hint

Take care that you only delete the page break and not the section break too. You will lose your column formatting if you do.

6 Save your work.

9.8 Add or delete a bookmark

You have been informed that more text is going to be added to Task 1 at a later date. The subject of the text will be Colchester. If you insert a bookmark in the text, you will be able to find the insertion point for the new text quickly.

Add a bookmark

Method

1 Click on: **Edit**: **Find**. The Find and Replace dialogue box appears.

Using the **Find** tab, search for the word: **Colchester**. You will see that there are many instances of the word. You are going to bookmark the instance where 'Colchester' is the first word of the paragraph (see Figure 9.18).

Figure 9.18 Bookmark where 'Colchester' is the first word of the paragraph

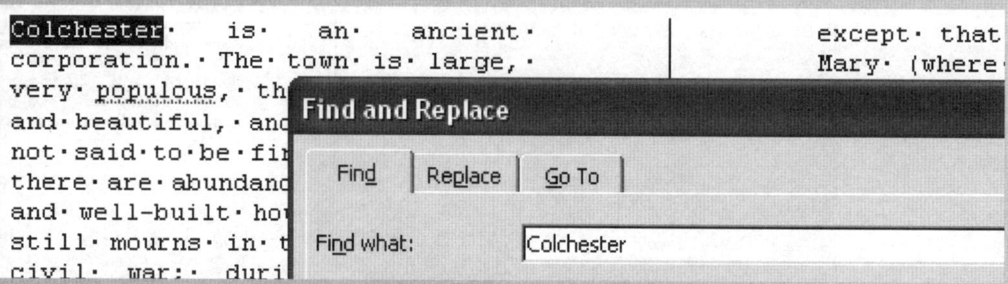

2 Exit Find and Replace by clicking on: **Cancel**.

3 Highlight to select the word Colchester.

4 Click on: **Insert**: **Bookmark**. A Bookmark dialogue box appears.

5 Key in the name of the bookmark, i.e. **Colchester_Insertion_Point**.

Figure 9.19 Key in the name of the bookmark in the Bookmark dialogue box

Handy Hint

You cannot use spaces to separate the words, you must use the underscore key (as you did when you were naming macros).

6 Click on: **Add**.

The bookmark will be inserted. It is not obvious on the document even if you run the cursor over the insertion point.

To test if your bookmark is working:

Method

1 Click on: **Edit**: **Find**. The Find and Replace dialogue box appears.

2 Select the **Go To** tab.

3 In the **Go to what** box, select: **Bookmark**.

4 From the **Enter bookmark name** drop-down menu, select your bookmark: **Colchester_Insertion_Point**.

Figure 9.20 Using the Find and Replace dialogue box to access a bookmark

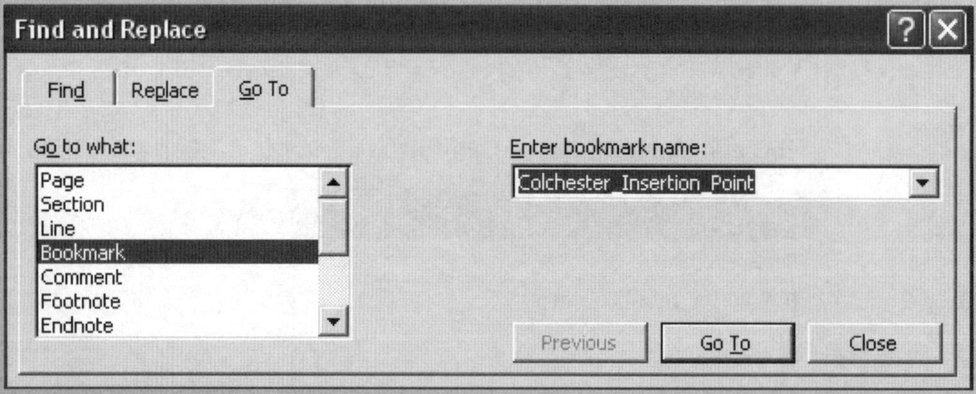

5 Click on the **Go To** button. The word **Colchester** should be highlighted.

6 Click on: **Close**.

Delete a bookmark

Deleting the bookmark is exactly the same procedure as adding a bookmark:

Method

1 Click on: **Insert**: **Bookmark**. A Bookmark dialogue box appears.

2 In the Bookmark dialogue box, select the bookmark you want to delete.

Do <u>not</u> delete the bookmark you have just created for Task 1.

3 Click on: **Delete**.

Figure 9.21 To delete a bookmark, select and click on the Delete button

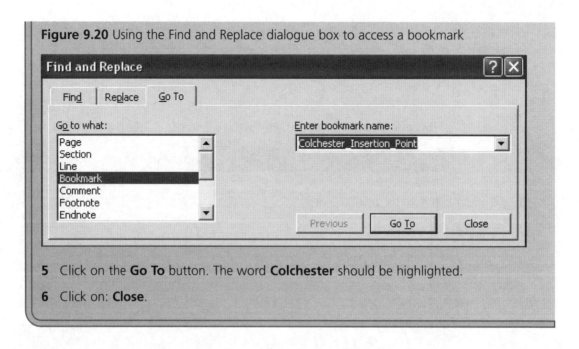

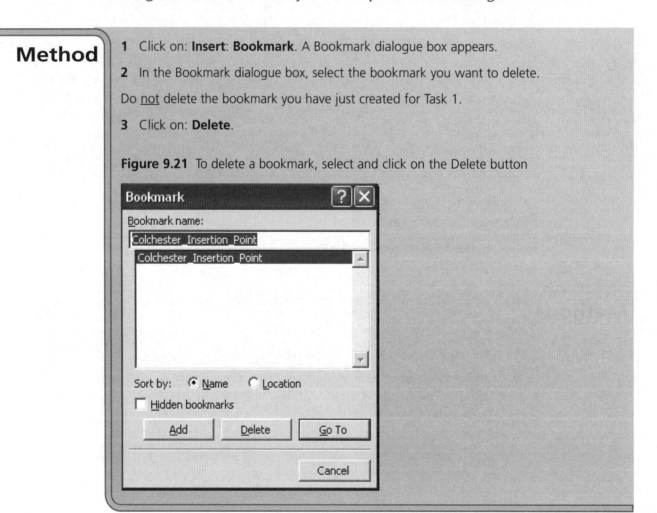

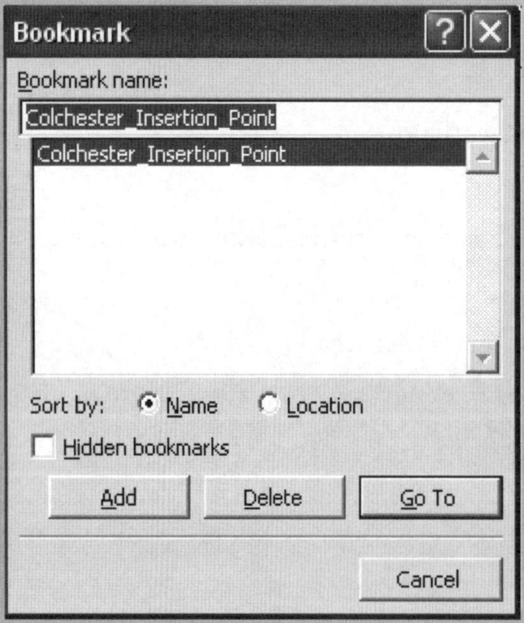

9.9 *Add or delete a cross-reference*

Adding a cross-reference enables you to direct the reader to another piece of relevant information in the same document. You are going to cross-reference (link) a paragraph about the county Essex to the Colchester bookmark.

Method

1 Click at the end of paragraph 4 (that starts 'Passing Bow Bridge').

2 Press the **Enter** key twice to leave a clear line space.

3 In the space that you have just created, key in: **See notes on**:

4 Click on: **Insert**: **Reference: Cross-reference**. A Cross-reference dialogue box appears.

5 From the **Reference type** drop-down menu, select: **Bookmark**.

6 From the **Insert reference to** drop-down menu, select: **Bookmark text**.

7 Click to activate the **Insert as hyperlink** box.

8 Select the bookmark: **Colchester_Insertion_Point**.

9 Click on: **Insert**.

10 Click on: **Close**.

Handy Hint

If you underline the text **See notes on Colchester**, it will be more obvious that the text is a link. Hold down the Control key and click on Colchester and the link will take you straight to the Colchester_Insertion_Point bookmark.

If you want to delete the bookmark and practise again, select the underlined text 'See notes on Colchester' and press the Delete key.

Save your work and close the file.

Practice Task — *Task 9*

These exercises are included to help the candidate in his or her training for the Advanced ECDL program. The exercises included in this material are not Advanced ECDL certification tests and should not be construed in any way as Advanced ECDL certification tests. For information about Authorised ECDL Test Centres in different National Territories, please refer to the ECDL Foundation website at **www.ecdl.com**.

You are going to create a Master Document that contains all your consolidation exercises in one file.

1 Open a new document. Using Outline options, insert all your Practice Task Answer files as subdocuments.

2 When you insert Task 3 Answer, you may be asked if you want to 'Rename the style in the subdocument'; click on: No.

Some of the subdocuments look empty; this is because they contain images that are not visible in Outline view.

3 Lock the Master Document.

4 Save as: **Task 9a Master Document**.

5 Collapse the subdocuments and save your work.

6 Remove the first subdocument.

7 Open the collapsed subdocument 5 and amend the verse title subheading style to:

- Font: Britannic
- Font style: Bold
- Color: Violet

8 Amend the body text style to:

- Indentation: first line, 1 cm

9 Save your work and close the file.

10 Open the file: **Task 6 Answer**.

11 Create subdocuments from each of the fables.

Handy Hint

Select only the fables, i.e. not the front page or the table of contents.

Note: if you get the message 'the selection does not consist of heading levels' you will need to apply a heading level to create the subdocuments. In Print Layout view, click down on one of the fable titles (style Verse Title). Click on: Format (main toolbar): Styles and Formatting: OK. The Styles and Formatting task pane will open with the style outlined. Click on the drop-down menu and select: Modify: Format: Paragraph. Change Outline Level to Level 1. Click on: OK: OK. Change back to Outline view and try again.

12 Print the Outline view of the collapsed Master Document.

13 Using the Automatic Captions, insert a picture from ClipArt into at least four of the fables.

Handy Hint

Insert the images in Outline view with the subdocuments expanded. Make sure that the original document is closed.

14 Save the file as: **Task 9b Answer**.

15 Print: 2 pages, 2 per sheet.

16 Close your file.

17 Open the file: **Task 3 Answer**.

18 Insert a picture from ClipArt. Search for clips relating to the moon, insert your chosen image on your document.

19 Position the ClipArt on page 2 in the gutter between columns 2 and 3.

20 Wrap the text so that it fits tightly around the image.

Handy Hint

You will need to do this in Print Layout view.

21 Increase the size of the image to: Height 7 cm, Width 7 cm.

22 Print the current page.

23 Save as: **Task 9c Answer**. Close the file.

24 Open the file: **Task 6 Answer**.

25 Use Find to locate the word: Hercules.

26 Add a bookmark.

27 Name the bookmark: Hercules Fable.

Handy Hint

Don't forget to use underline to create the space between the words.

28 Test the bookmark to see if it works (Edit: Go To: Bookmark).

29 Using the Hercules Fable bookmark, cross-reference the fable 'The Lion and the Mouse' to the fable 'Hercules and the Wagon'. Insert a hyperlink after the fable title, i.e. after 'The Lion and the Mouse'.

30 Index the following words:

- mouse
- boy
- dog
- bear
- fox
- mole
- lion
- grasshopper
- bat.

There will not be entries for all letters until the remainder of the fables are input.

31 Place the index at the end of the fables, before the table of contents. Mark all the entries.

32 Format page numbers to bold.

33 Apply the format: Classic.

34 Print the last 2 pages, 2 per page.

35 Save as: **Task 9d Answer**.

Answers to practice tasks

Task 1 Answer

MADRID

Panoramic Madrid

The history of the majestic city of Madrid will come to life when you allow your guide to introduce you to its incredible past. Once an Arabian Fortress, this city is now a thriving cultural centre bursting with monuments, galleries and museums. You will even see Santiago Bernabeu Stadium, home of the famous Real Madrid football team.

Artistic Madrid

Introducing one of the world's greatest art galleries. The Prado Museum holds major works from all the great schools of European art, including paintings by Rubens, Rafael, Goya, and El Greco. Let our guides take you there. Then move on to explore the 18th-century Royal Palace.

Toledo, El Escorial, Valley of the Fallen

Journey south of Madrid into a long forgotten world as you discover the ancient city of Toledo, once the medieval capital of Spain. Become familiar with the life of a monk as you tour El Escorial Monastery, and spare some thought for the dead of the Spanish Civil War in the Valley of the Fallen - the history of this country will simply amaze you.

Madrid by Night

At night, Spaniards put on their dancing shoes and step out for an evening of fun, feasting, and friendly flirting. After a panoramic drive to see the city lights, you'll join the locals at the Florida Park nightclub. Enjoy a fabulous tapas meal, a flamenco show, and all-night dancing.♥

♥ See Leaflet 6

Task 2 Answer

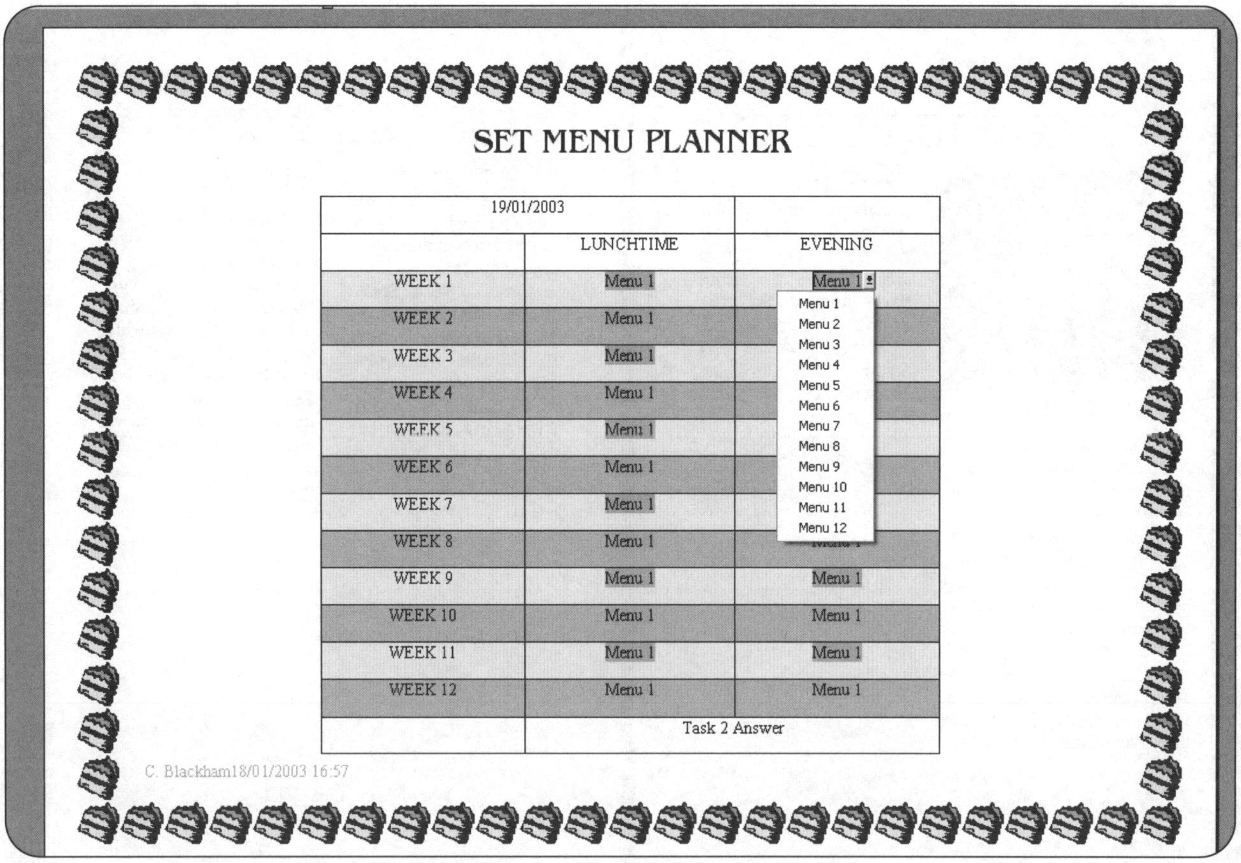

SET MENU PLANNER

19/01/2003		
	LUNCHTIME	EVENING
WEEK 1	Menu 1	Menu 1
WEEK 2	Menu 1	
WEEK 3	Menu 1	
WEEK 4	Menu 1	
WEEK 5	Menu 1	
WEEK 6	Menu 1	
WEEK 7	Menu 1	
WEEK 8	Menu 1	
WEEK 9	Menu 1	Menu 1
WEEK 10	Menu 1	Menu 1
WEEK 11	Menu 1	Menu 1
WEEK 12	Menu 1	Menu 1
	Task 2 Answer	

Menu 1
Menu 2
Menu 3
Menu 4
Menu 5
Menu 6
Menu 7
Menu 8
Menu 9
Menu 10
Menu 11
Menu 12

C. Blackham18/01/2003 16:57

Task 3 Answer

HOLIDAYS BY COACH

MADRID

Panoramic Madrid

The history of the majestic city of Madrid will come to life when you allow your guide to introduce you to its incredible past. Once an Arabian Fortress, this city is now a thriving cultural centre bursting with monuments, galleries and museums. You will even see Santiago Bernabeu Stadium, home of the famous Real Madrid football team.

Artistic Madrid

Introducing one of the world's greatest art galleries. The Prado Museum holds major works from all the great schools of European art, including paintings by Rubens, Rafael, Goya, and El Greco. Let our guides take you there. Then move on to explore the 18th-century Royal Palace.

HOLIDAYS BY COACH

Toledo, El Escorial, Valley of the Fallen

Journey south of Madrid into a long forgotten world as you discover the ancient city of Toledo, once the medieval capital of Spain. Become familiar with the life of a monk as you tour El Escorial Monastery, and spare some thought for the dead of the Spanish Civil War in the Valley of the Fallen - the history of this country will simply amaze you.

Madrid by Night

At night, Spaniards put on their dancing shoes and step out for an evening of fun, feasting, and friendly flirting. After a panoramic drive to see the city lights, you'll join the locals at the Florida Park nightclub. Enjoy a fabulous tapas meal, a flamenco show, and all-night dancing.*

[3] See Leaflet 3

Task 4 Answer

IN WHICH THE AUTHOR OF THIS SINGULAR WORK INFORMS THE READER HOW HE ACQUIRED THE CERTAINTY THAT THE OPERA GHOST REALLY EXISTED

Phantom of the Opera

PROLOGUE

The Opera ghost really existed. He was not, as was long believed, a creature of the imagination of the artists, the superstition of the managers, or a product of the absurd and impressionable brains of the young ladies of the ballet, their mothers, the box-keepers, the cloak-room attendants or the concierge. Yes, he existed in flesh and blood, although he assumed the complete appearance of a real phantom; that is to say, of a spectral shade.

When I began to ransack the archives of the National Academy of Music I was at once struck by the surprising coincidences between the phenomena ascribed to the "ghost" and the most extraordinary and fantastic tragedy that ever excited the Paris upper classes; and I soon conceived the idea that this tragedy might reasonably be explained by the phenomena in question. The events do not date more than thirty years back; and it would not be difficult to find at the present day, in the foyer of the ballet, old men of the highest respectability, men upon whose word one could absolutely rely, who would remember as though they happened yesterday the mysterious and dramatic conditions that attended the kidnapping of Christine Daae, the disappearance of the Vicomte de Chagny and the death of his elder brother, Count Philippe, whose body was found on the bank of the lake that exists in the lower cellars of the Opera on the Rue-Scribe side. But none of those witnesses had until that day thought that there was any reason for connecting the more or less legendary figure of the Opera ghost with that terrible story.

GASTON LEROUX

Task 5 Answer

Holidays in the Sun 1

7-night holidays

Dates	7 nights (£)	Extra night (£)	8 nights
10 May–23 May	210	21	£ 231.00
12 Apr–9 May	340	18	£ 358.00
30 Aug–5 Sep	337	26	£ 363.00
21 Jun–4 Jul	398	39	£ 437.00
24 May–6 Jun	420	28	£ 448.00
5 Jul–18 Jul	440	44	£ 484.00
7 Jun–20 Jun	460	34	£ 494.00
	£ 313.13		£ 340.38

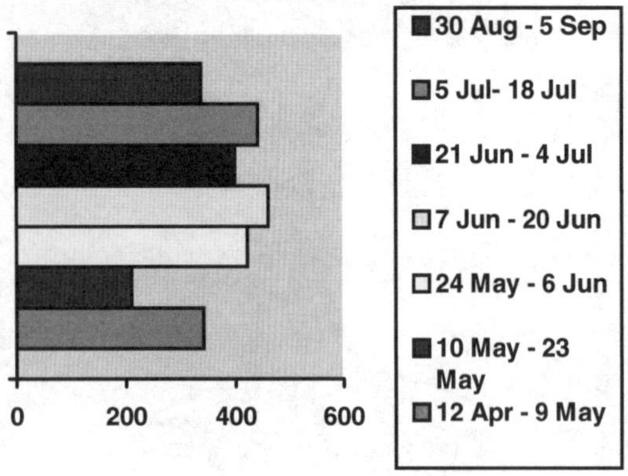

Task 6 Answer

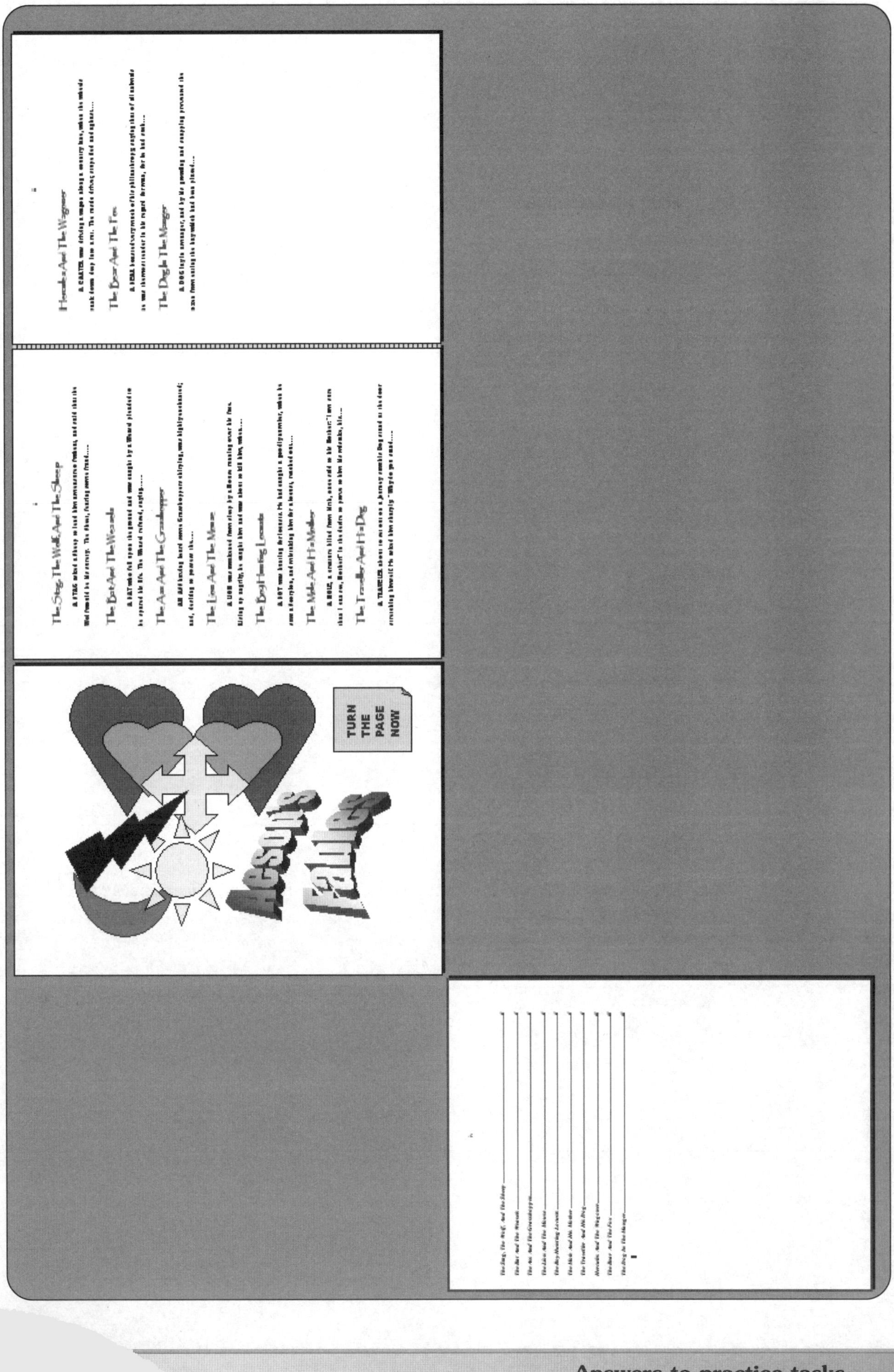

Task 7a Answer

FORM MEMO (LETTER)

Memo

To: «First_Name» «Surname»

From: Your name here

Date: Today's date

Re: Local Charity

Thank you very much «First_Name» for the contribution of «Contribution». It was greatly appreciated.

MERGED MEMO

Memo

To: Julie Smith

From: Christine Blackham

Date:

Re: Local Charity

Thank you very much Julie for the contribution of £2.00. It was greatly appreciated.

(You should have 7 memos)

Task 7b Answer

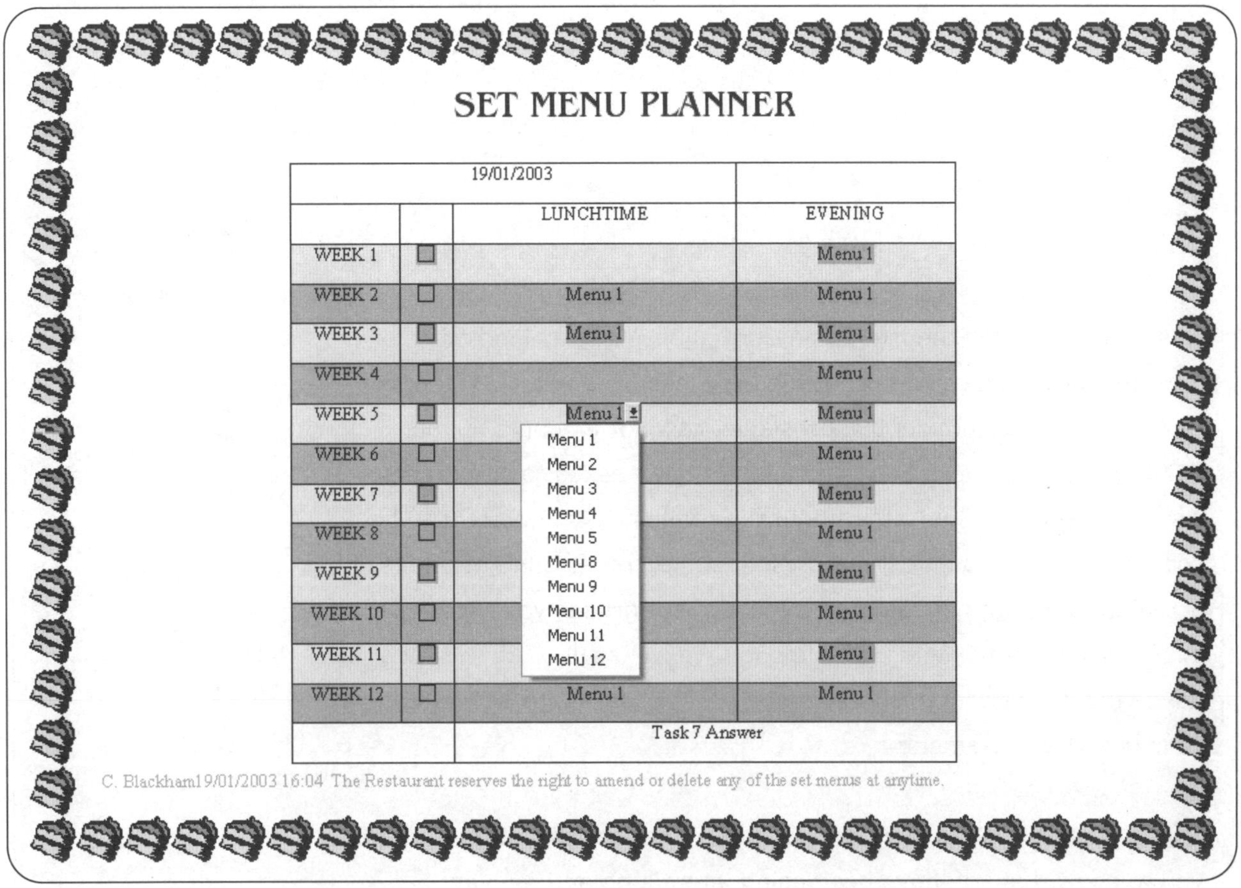

SET MENU PLANNER

19/01/2003			
		LUNCHTIME	EVENING
WEEK 1	☐		Menu 1
WEEK 2	☐	Menu 1	Menu 1
WEEK 3	☐	Menu 1	Menu 1
WEEK 4	☐		Menu 1
WEEK 5	☐	Menu 1	Menu 1
WEEK 6	☐		Menu 1
WEEK 7	☐		Menu 1
WEEK 8	☐		Menu 1
WEEK 9	☐		Menu 1
WEEK 10	☐		Menu 1
WEEK 11	☐		Menu 1
WEEK 12	☐	Menu 1	Menu 1
		Task 7 Answer	

C. Blackham19/01/2003 16:04 The Restaurant reserves the right to amend or delete any of the set menus at anytime.

Task 8 Answer

GUIDANCE NOTES

Comment: This is the first draft and must be revised and approved by Personnel before distribution.

It is essential to tell the truth on a Curriculum Vitae as inaccurate or untrue information could lead at the very least to embarrassment or possibly to even more serious consequences. For example, if your GCSE grades were low, and you have not been asked to cite grades, simply present the subjects without the grades. It is important to be consistent here - you must not present some grades and not others. In actual fact, we are not really concerned about grades you received for exams taken many years ago. Although we will want to know that you have obtained certain qualifications, we will be far more interested in your recent achievements.

Deleted: You are not obliged, however, to reveal every small detail of your private and not so private life.

Deleted: few employers will be

Deleted: they

Deleted: employers

If you are returning to work after a break it is especially important for you to show that you have been doing interesting and relevant activities during your break from employment. This is because employers see less value in unpaid work than 9-5 paid employment. In your C.V. you will need to talk about achievement, paid or unpaid, which you are proud off. Try to avoid emphasising duties that you have had to do and try to show how these activities would benefit our company.

Deleted: the employer.

REMEMBER: If you are not obliged to mention your weaker aspects, then avoid doing do.

Task 9b Answer (Printout 1)

- C:\Documents and Settings\C. Blackham\My Documents\The Stag.doc
- C:\Documents and Settings\C. Blackham\My Documents\The Bat And The Weasels.doc
- C:\Documents and Settings\C. Blackham\My Documents\The Ass And The Grasshopper.doc
- C:\Documents and Settings\C. Blackham\My Documents\The Lion And The Mouse.doc
- C:\Documents and Settings\C. Blackham\My Documents\The Boy Hunting Locusts.doc
- C:\Documents and Settings\C. Blackham\My Documents\The Mole And His Mother.doc
- C:\Documents and Settings\C. Blackham\My Documents\The Traveller And His Dog.doc
- C:\Documents and Settings\C. Blackham\My Documents\Hercules And The Wagoner.doc
- C:\Documents and Settings\C. Blackham\My Documents\The Bear And The Fox.doc
- C:\Documents and Settings\C. Blackham\My Documents\The Dog In The Manger.doc

Task 9b Answer (Printout 2)

ii

The Stag, The Wolf, And The Sheep

A STAG asked a Sheep to lend him a measure of wheat, and said that the Wolf would be his surety. The Sheep, fearing some fraud.....

Figure 1

The Bat And The Weasels

A BAT who fell upon the ground and was caught by a Weasel pleaded to be spared his life. The Weasel refused, saying.......

The Ass And The Grasshopper

AN ASS having heard some Grasshoppers chirping, was highly enchanted; and, desiring to possess the.....

Figure 2

The Lion And The Mouse

A LION was awakened from sleep by a Mouse running over his face. Rising up angrily, he caught him and was about to kill him, when....

iii

Figure 3

The Boy Hunting Locusts

A BOY was hunting for locusts. He had caught a goodly number, when he saw a Scorpion, and mistaking him for a locust, reached out....

The Mole And His Mother

A MOLE, a creature blind from birth, once said to his Mother: "I am sure than I can see, Mother!" In the desire to prove to him his mistake, his....

The Traveller And His Dog

A TRAVELER about to set out on a journey saw his Dog stand at the door stretching himself. He asked him sharply: "Why do you stand....

Figure 4

Task 9c Answer

HOLIDAYS BY COACH

Toledo, El Escorial, Valley of the Fallen

Journey south of Madrid into a long forgotten world as you discover the ancient city of Toledo, once the medieval capital of Spain. Become familiar with the life of a monk as you tour El Escorial Monastery, and spare some thought for the dead of the Spanish Civil War in the Valley of the Fallen - the history of this country will simply amaze you.

Madrid by Night

At night, Spaniards put on their dancing shoes and step out for an evening of fun, feasting, and friendly flirting. After a panoramic drive to see the city lights, you'll join the locals at the Florida Park nightclub. Enjoy a fabulous tapas meal, a flamenco show, and all-night dancing.♥

♥ See Leaflet 3

Task 9d Answer

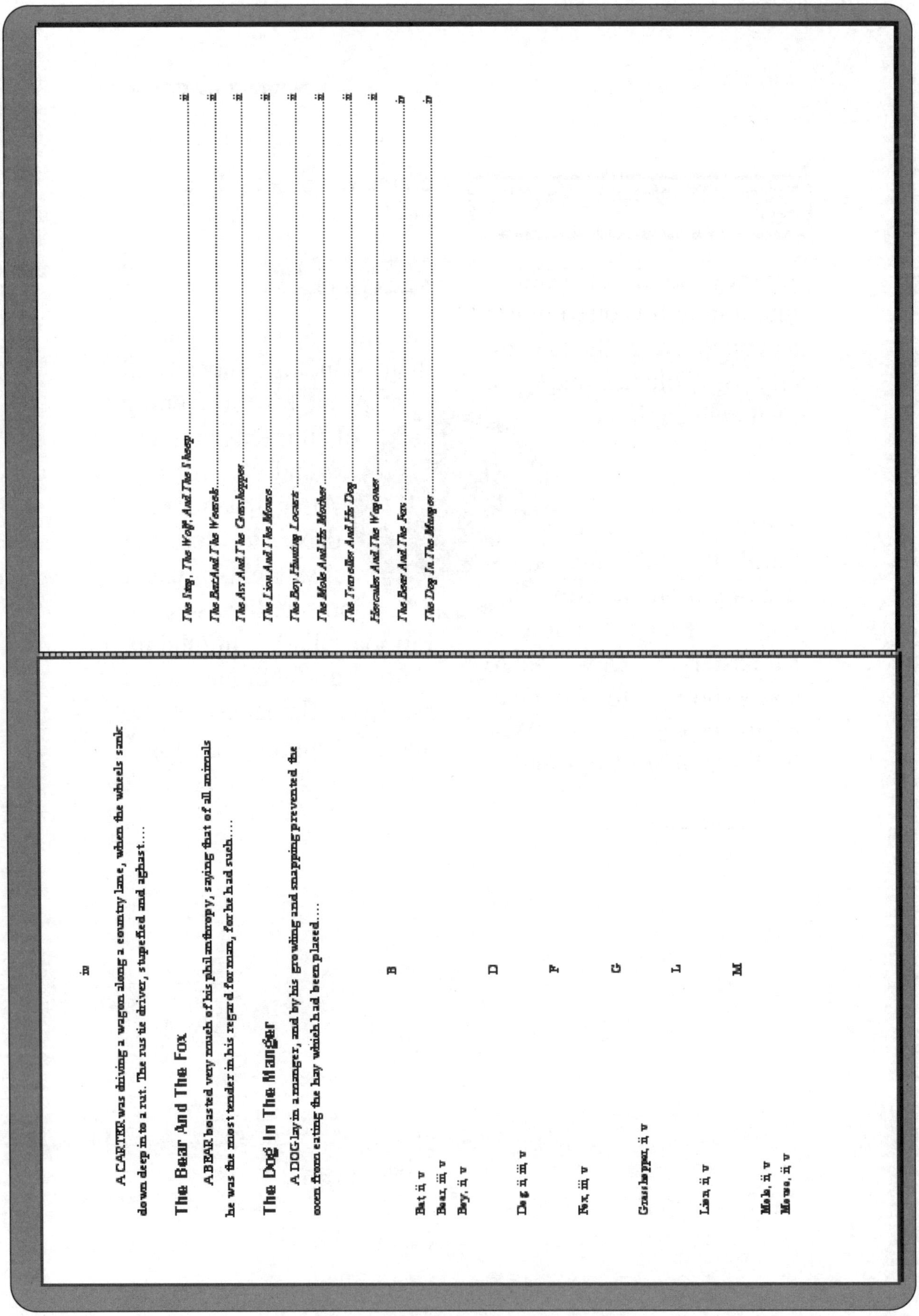
iv

A CARTER was driving a wagon along a country lane, when the wheels sank down deep into a rut. The rustic driver, stupefied and aghast....

The Bear And The Fox

A BEAR boasted very much of his philanthropy, saying that of all animals he was the most tender in his regard for man, for he had such....

The Dog In The Manger

A DOG lay in a manger, and by his growling and snapping prevented the oxen from eating the hay which had been placed....

B

Bat, ii, v
Bear, iii, v
Boy, ii, v

D

Dog, ii, iii, v

F

Fox, iii, v

G

Grasshopper, ii, v

L

Lion, ii, v

M

Mole, ii, v
Mouse, ii, v

Practice assignment

These exercises are included to help the candidate in his or her training for the Advanced ECDL program. The exercises included in this material are not Advanced ECDL certification tests and should not be construed in any way as Advanced ECDL certification tests. For information about Authorised ECDL Test Centres in different National Territories, please refer to the ECDL Foundation website at **www.ecdl.com**.

There is a maximum of 20 marks for each question.

You are to:

- amend a document stored on your CD as: **Samuel Pepys**
- create a chart from data saved on your CD as **Table**
- perform a Mail Merge operation.

1 From the Task Files folder, open the document: **Samuel Pepys**.

2 To the heading 'Samuel Pepys', apply a $4\frac{1}{2}$ point box border.

3 Find the word 'shorthand' in the final paragraph, and position it at the start of the next line. At this point, from the Task Files folder, insert the image: 'shorthand'. Position the image to the right.

4 Below the image, add the caption: Pepys' shorthand.

5 Modify the existing style, Pepys Body Text, to Arial 12 pt. Apply the appropriate formatting so that single lines of text are not left at the top or bottom of the pages.

6 Apply a 2-column format to the paragraphs 'March 1st' and 'March 6th'.

7 Underneath the subheading Contents, create a table of contents based on the style Samuel Pepys Subheading, ensuring that all the diary dates are included. Apply the Fancy format and right-align the page numbers.

8 Apply the Samuel Pepys Subheading style to diary dates February 23rd and May 16th. Update your table of contents.

9 Record a macro to set up the page as landscape with 4 cm inside and outside and 2 cm top and bottom margins. Name the macro: Samuel Pepys. Apply the macro to this document only. Run the Macro.

10 Correct the Old English (Word has underlined the spelling errors) by keying in the more modern spelling to the right of the word. Track the changes while editing. Ensure that the editing can be seen on-screen and will be visible when printed. Turn off the Track Changes tool.

11 To the last word in the last paragraph, add the text comment: This was the last diary entry.

12 On the first line of April 26th, bookmark the word 'Fire'. Name the bookmark: Fire.

13 Underneath the words 'Completed the Exercise?' at the end of the document, insert a Yes/No drop-down selection box.

14 Above the word 'Contents', insert the year '1669' in a text box. Use Arial, 48 pt. Change the direction of the text so that the text runs from bottom to top. Ensure that there is not a box around the text.

15 Include an index as the final page of the document. Apply the Modern format. Mark the following words: God, Lord, wife, Deb, Duke, King, tailor.

16 Apply a WordArt style to the subheading 'Diary extracts'.

17 Add a right-aligned header to include your name and a date field. Insert page numbers at the bottom right-hand side of the page. Number the first page.

18 Print your work and save the document as: **Answer 1**. Apply the password 'Samuel' to protect your file. Close your file.

19 From the Task Files folder, open the file: **Table**. Change the text to Table, and Sort in order of colour.

20 Create a column chart from the table. Format the columns to the appropriate colour to correspond with the data. Right-align the chart.

21 Create a row at the bottom of the table and insert a formula that will calculate the amount of paper used each month. Save your work as: **Answer 2**. Print out the document. Close your file.

22 Mail Merge the file **Letter Form** with the file **Letter Data** to a New Document. Sort the data in order of surname. Produce letters to those living in Accrington. Print pages 3 and 4 on one A4 sheet. Save your work as: **Answer 3**.

Answer 1

Samuel Pepys

1669

diary extracts

Contents

1 JAN
I found my Lord Sandwich, Peterburgh, and Sir Ch. Herberd; and presently after them come my Lord Hinchingbrooke, Mr Sidny, and Sir Wm. Godolphin; and after greeting them, and some time spent in talk, dinner was brought up, one dish after another, but a dish at a time; but all so good, but above all things, the variety of wines, and excellent of their kind, I had for them, and all in so good order, that they were mightily pleased, and myself full of content at it; and indeed it was, of a dinner of about six or eight dishes, as noble as any man ~~mn~~ need to have I think - at least, all was done in the noblest manner that ever I had any, and I have rarely seen in my life better anywhere else - even at the Court.

So to my wife's chamber, and there supped and got her cut my hair and look my shirt, for I have itched mightily these six or seven days; and when all came to all, she finds that I am lousy ~~louzy~~, having found in my head and body above 20 lice, little and great; which I wonder at, being more than I have had, I believe, almost these twenty years.

FEBRUARY 23RD
I now took them *[his wife and girl servants]* to Westminster Abbey and there did show them all the tombs very finely, having one with us alone ... and here we did see, by particular ~~perticular~~ favour, the body of Queen Katherine of Valois, and had her upper part of her body in my hands. And I did kiss her mouth, reflecting upon it that I did kiss a Queen, and that this was my birthday, 36 year old, that I did first kiss a Queen.

MARCH 1ST
But here I do hear first that my Lady Paulina Montagu did die yesterday; at which I went to my Lord's lodgings, but he is shut up with sorrow and so not to be spoken with .... *[Paulina was Sandwich's second daughter an died of "a consumption" in her 20th year]*

MARCH 6TH
This day my wife made it appear to me that my late entertainment this week cost me above 12*l*, an expense which I am almost ashamed of, though it is but once in a great while, and is the end for which in the most part we live, to have such a merry day once or twice in a man's life.

April 8th

Going this afternoon through Smithfield, I did see a coach run over the coachman's neck and stand upon it, and yet the man rose up and was well after it, which I thought a wonder.

April 13th ... as God would have it I spied Deb which made my heart and head to work; ... and I run after her and I observed she endeavoured to avoid me, but I did speak to her and she to me ... and so, with my heart full of surprise and disorder, I away ....

... so home to my wife ... But, God forgive me, I hardly know how to put on confidence enough to speak as innocent, having had this passage today with Deb, though only, God knows, by accident. But my great pain is lest God Almighty shall suffer me to find out this girl, whom indeed~~endeed~~ I love, and with a bad amour; but I will pray to God to give me grace to forbear it.

April 26th

I am told ... of a great fire happened~~happenned~~ in Durham-yard last night, burning the house of one - Hungerford, who was to come to town to it this night; an so the house is burned, new furnished, by carelessness~~carelesness~~ of the girl sent to take off a candle from a bunch of candles, which she did by burning it off, and left the rest, as it is supposed, on fire. The King and Court was here, it seems, and stopped the fire by blowing up of the next house.

April 30th

I did make the workmen drink, and saw my coach cleaned and oiled~~oyled~~; and staying among poor people there in the alley, did hear them call their fat child "punch" which pleased me mightily, that word being become a word of common use for all that is thick and short.

May 1st

Up betimes, called up by my tailor, and there first put on a summer suit this year - but it was not my fine one of flowered tabby vest and coloured camelot~~camelott~~ tunic, because it was too fine with the gold lace at the hands, that I was afeared to be seen in it - but put on the stuff-suit I made the last year, which is now repaired; and so did go to the office in it and sat all the morning, the day looking as if it would be foul~~fowle~~.

At noon home to dinner, and there find my wife extraordinary~~extraorrdinary~~ fine with her flowered tabby gown that she made two years ago, now laced exceeding pretty, and indeed~~endeed~~ was fine all over - and mighty earnest to go, though the day was very lowering, and she would have me put on my fine suit, which I did; and so anon we went alone through the town with our new Liveries of serge, and the horses' manes and tails tied with red ribbon

and the standards thus gilt with varnish and all clean, and green reigns~~raynes~~, that people did mightily look upon us; and the truth is, I did not see any coach more pretty, or more gay, than ours all the day.

May 10th

to my Lord Crewe ... A stranger, a country gentleman, was with him, and he pleased with my discourse accidentally about the decay of gentlemen's families in the country, telling us that the old rule was that a family might remain 50 miles from London 100 year, 100 mile off from London 200 years, and so, farther or nearer London, more or less years. He also told us that he hath heard his father say that in his time it was so rare for a country gentleman to come to London, that when he did come, he used to make his will before he set out.

Thence walked a little with Creed, who tells me he hears how fine my horses and coach are, and advises me to avoid being noted for it; which I was vexed to hear taken notice of, it being what I feared; and Povy told me of my gold-lace sleeves in the park yesterday, which vexed me also, so as to resolve never to appear in Court with it, but presently have it taken off, as it is fit I should.

May 16th

I all the afternoon drawing up a foul draft of my petition to the Duke of York about my eyes, for leave to spend three or four months out of the office, drawing it so as to give occasion to a voyage abroad....

[It was presented on the 19th May, and refers~~referes~~ to the "ill condition whereto the restless exercises of his Eyes requisite to the seasonable dispatching of the Work~~Worke~~ of his Place during the late War~~Warr~~ have unhappily reduced him .. he has fruitlessly made many medicinal attempts ... but is told by his doctors that nothing but a considerable relaxation *from Work~~Worke~~ can be depended upon either for recovery of what Portion of his Sight he~~hee~~ hath lost, or securing the remainder"]*

... And thus ends all that I doubt I shall ever be able to do with my own eyes in the keeping of my journal~~journall~~, I being not able to do it any longer, having done now so long as to undo my eyes almost every time that I take a pen in my hand; and therefore, whatever comes of it, I must forbear; and therefore resolve~~reolve~~ from this time forward to have it kept by my people in long-hand, and must therefore be contented to set down no more than it is fit for them and all the world to know; or if there be anything (which cannot be much, now my amours to Deb are past, and my eyes hindering me in almost all other pleasures), I must endeavour to keep a margin in my book open, to add here and there a note in

PEPYS' SHORTHAND 1

shorthand with my own hand. And so I betake myself to that course which is almost as much as to see myself go into my grave - for which, and all the discomforts that will accompany my being blind, the good God prepare me.

Completed the Exercise? Yes

5

Your name here 02/02/2003

6

Answer 2

|

PAPER USAGE (REAMS)

	JAN	FEB	MAR	APR	MAY	JUN
BLUE	25	21	27	35	21	19
GREEN	23	27	25	22	21	17
WHITE	40	32	20	15	14	35
YELLOW	12	13	9	2	8	9
	100	93	81	74	64	80

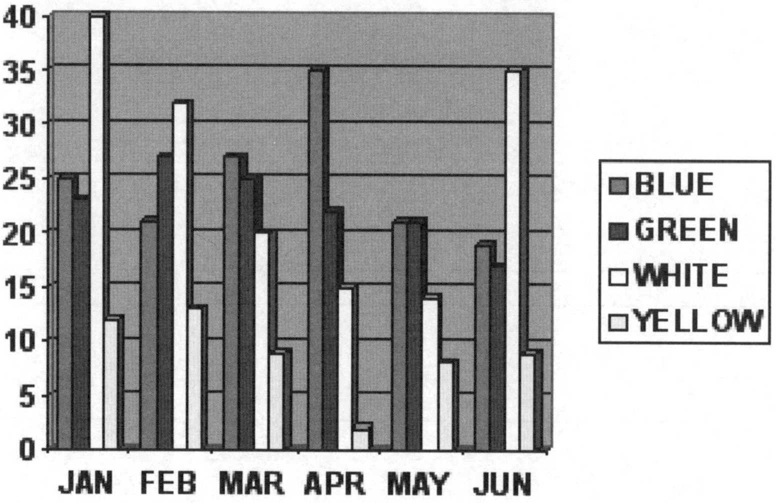

Answer 3

THE WORKS
21 Derby Street
NORTHWICH
Cheshire

Customer Service 01254 123456

02/02/2003

Mrs Heys
6 Quarry Street
ACCRINGTON
Lancs

Dear Mrs Heys

Thank you for your order and your deposit of £325.00. We will forward your receipt with the delivery date details.

In the meantime, if you have any further questions, please contact the Customer Service Centre on the above telephone number.

Yours sincerely

Julie Jones
Sales Advisor

THE WORKS
21 Derby Street
NORTHWICH
Cheshire

Customer Service 01254 123456

02/02/2003

Mr Nicholson
10 North Road
ACCRINGTON
Lancs

Dear Mr Nicholson

Thank you for your order and your deposit of £400.00. We will forward your receipt with the delivery date details.

In the meantime, if you have any further questions, please contact the Customer Service Centre on the above telephone number.

Yours sincerely

Julie Jones
Sales Advisor